The Acadian Diaspora

The Acadian Diaspora

An Eighteenth-Century History

CHRISTOPHER HODSON

OXFORD
UNIVERSITY PRESS

OXFORD

UNIVERSITY PRESS

Oxford University Press, Inc., publishes works that further
Oxford University's objective of excellence
in research, scholarship, and education.

Oxford   New York
Auckland   Cape Town   Dar es Salaam   Hong Kong   Karachi
Kuala Lumpur   Madrid   Melbourne   Mexico City   Nairobi
New Delhi   Shanghai   Taipei   Toronto

With offices in
Argentina   Austria   Brazil   Chile   Czech Republic   France   Greece
Guatemala   Hungary   Italy   Japan   Poland   Portugal   Singapore
South Korea   Switzerland   Thailand   Turkey   Ukraine   Vietnam

Published by Oxford University Press, Inc.
198 Madison Avenue, New York, NY 10016

www.oup.com

Oxford is a registered trademark of Oxford University Press

Library of Congress Cataloging-in-Publication Data
Hodson, Christopher.
The Acadian diaspora : an eighteenth-century history / Christopher Hodson.
p.   cm.—(Oxford studies in international history)
Includes bibliographical references and index.
ISBN 978-0-19-973977-6 (hardcover : alk. paper)
1. Acadians—Migrations—History—18th century.
2. Acadians—Relocation—History—18th century. I. Title.
E184.A2H64   2012
971.5'017—dc23   2011038848

For Sarah

CONTENTS

ACKNOWLEDGMENTS

Embarking on this project a decade ago, I would never have guessed that writing a book about such terrible events could be so terribly enjoyable. I am pleased now to be able to thank everyone who has helped me along the way.

At Utah State University, Len Rosenband taught me the historian's craft. Along with Norm Jones, Mick Nicholls, and Ross Peterson, Len inspired me with his scholarly rigor and creativity while pushing me to refine my own vision of the early modern past. No undergraduate could have asked for better mentors.

Early in my first year at Northwestern University, Tim Breen suggested (in his inimitable way) that a French-speaking historian of early America might do well to look into the Acadian expulsion of 1755. I'm grateful to Tim for this advice, and for his tireless work on my behalf in the years that followed. At Northwestern, Russell Maylone, Sarah Maza, Ed Muir, and Ethan Shagan provided wise counsel as this project developed. Thanks also to Aaron Astor, Justin Behrend, Carole Emberton, Patrick Griffin, Michael Guenther, Guy Ortolano, Karen O'Brien, and Owen Stanwood, all of whom did much to help me clarify my ideas while offering welcome diversions from the daily tasks of teaching, researching, and writing.

After leaving Northwestern, I had the good fortune to spend two years as a fellow at the McNeil Center for Early American Studies in Philadelphia. Dan Richter and Amy Baxter-Bellamy made the center an almost shamefully pleasant place to work. I owe special thanks to my fellow McNeil Center fellows and fellow travelers Wayne Bodle, George Boudreau, Mike Carter, Yvie Fabella, Charlie Foy, April Hatfield, Hunt Howell, Chris Iannini, Cathy Kelly, Daniel Krebs, Justine Murison, Yvette Piggush, Joanne van der Woude, and Mike Zuckerman.

At BYU, I have again been fortunate to fall in among supportive, smart, and overwhelmingly nice colleagues. Kendall Brown, Karen Carter, Kathy Daynes, Eric Dursteler, Craig Harline, Don Harreld, Andy Johns, Paul Kerry, Rich Kimball, Matt Mason, Shawn Miller, Jenny Pulsipher, Jeff Shumway, and Neil York deserve particular recognition for (a) undertaking the thankless task of commenting on many, many drafts of journal articles, book manuscripts, and grant proposals and (b) helping this newcomer to Provo acclimate to the peculiarities and pleasures of BYU. I'm grateful for their efforts on both counts.

Many thanks to the historians of Nova Scotia and the Acadians on whom I have imposed, especially Yves Boyer-Vidal, Régis Brun, John Mack Faragher, Ronnie Gilles-Leblanc, Jean-François Mouhot, Geoff Plank, and John Reid. An equally important group of scholars have listened to or read bits of this book at a variety of conferences and seminars. Bernard Bailyn, Denver Brunsman, Christian Crouch, John Demos, Kate Desbarats, Laurent Dubois, Jack Greene, François Furstenburg, Jennifer Denise Henderson, Eric Hinderaker, Ron Hoffman, Cécile Vidal, and Ashli White all offered crucial advice at crucial moments. Brett Rushforth was repeatedly dragooned into service as an expert reader, crack paleographer, and amateur psychoanalyst, succeeding admirably at every turn.

I am very happy to thank the staffs of the following archives: the Acadian Museum in West Pubnico, Nova Scotia, the American Antiquarian Society, the Archives départementales de l'Ille-et-Villaine, the Archives départementales de la Vienne, the Archives nationales, the Archives nationales d'outre-mer, the Bibliotheque municipale de Bordeaux, the Centre d'études acadiennes at the Université de Moncton, the William L. Clements Library, the Historical Society of Pennsylvania, the Houghton Library, the Library and Archives of Canada, the Library Company of Philadelphia, the Massachusetts State Archives, the McCormick Library of Special Collections at Northwestern University, and the National Archives Mid-Atlantic Region. Without their help, this book could not have been written. No less important were the institutions that supported my research travel, including the American Historical Association, the McNeil Center for Early American Studies, the Society for Colonial Wars, and, at BYU, the College of Family, Home, and Social Sciences and the Kennedy Center.

At Oxford University Press, Susan Ferber guided this book through the various stages of editing with great care, doing her level best to ensure that the silliest of my ideas never made it into the finished product. Alice Thiede produced the wonderful maps that grace its pages. Elements of the book previously appeared in *Early American Studies*, *French Historical Studies*, and the *William and Mary Quarterly*.

From Chicago to Paris, Paul and Sharon Brown, Quinten and Jen Lynn, Adam and Cindy Merrill, Cyrille Minso, and David and Janet Stowell provided juvenile fun, meals, and, on numerous occasions, shelter. My long-suffering in-laws, the Murrays, have been unfailingly supportive. Special thanks are due my parents, Gene and Carol Hodson. They have offered every kindness imaginable over the last decade, buoying me up far more than they realize. My children,

Isaac, Libby, and Luke, have never known a father who wasn't strangely obsessed with centuries-old goings-on in Nova Scotia, the French Caribbean, and the countryside of western France. I thank them for all of the joy, noise, and laughter they have brought into my life. Finally, this book is dedicated to my beautiful wife, Sarah. Life with her really is the best of all possible worlds.

The Acadian Diaspora

The Worlds of the Acadian Diaspora

> The Lord shall cause thee to be smitten before thine enemies: thou shalt go out one way against them, and flee seven ways before them: and shalt be removed into all the kingdoms of the earth. . . . The Lord shall smite thee with madness, and blindness, and astonishment of heart.
>
> —Deuteronomy 28:25, 28

Universal truths are uncommon. But this may well be one: to be torn away from familiar places and people is to know terror. Exiled from first-century Rome to the remote Black Sea port of Tomis, the poet Ovid lamented that his dreams had become "tortures," dark visions of barbarian attacks, enslavement, or, worst of all, "my friends, and my dear wife distorted, disappearing, the wounds of our separation torn open again."[1] For those uprooted en masse and scattered, such horrors crept all too readily into waking hours. "As long as I have lived," exclaimed Shem Tov Ardutiel, a medieval chronicler of Jewish expulsions in western Europe, "I have been in the grasp of unrest, pursued by shame, wandering, isolated, set apart from companions, made strange to brothers."[2] The modern era has produced much, much more of the same. Dispersed by famine, slavery, war, and racial, ethnic, or religious scapegoating, victims know well the panic endured by the Israelites "removed . . . into all the kingdoms of the earth."[3]

The Septuagint, a Greek translation of the Hebrew Bible from the fourth century BCE, uses διασπορά to express this last, most alarming of Jehovah's punishments. It means "diaspora," a word that might be rendered into plainer English as "to sow abroad," and which has come to stand for the dispersal of people belonging to one nation, culture, or place of origin. Although the term once referred exclusively to events in Jewish history, most scholars now recognize that there have been many diasporas, each a reflection of the era in which it unfolded.[4] This book tells the story of one such diaspora, and of the long-forgotten eighteenth-century world it illuminates.

French-speakers call it the *grand dérangement*, a name that captures the terrible richness of the events reconstructed in the pages that follow. *Dérangement* translates to "upheaval," "disorder," or simply "trouble," all of which accurately describe a series of events that began in the fall of 1755 on the shores of the Bay of Fundy. Ringed, then as now, by tide-washed rock arches, green meadows, and endless stands of pine, the bay's natural beauty belied its standing as a bloody friction point between the North American empires of Great Britain and France. To the south and east lay Nova Scotia, a peninsular province ruled by a British government at Halifax on the Atlantic coast. To the north and west, in what is now New Brunswick, was territory claimed by France as a vestige of the dismembered colony of Acadia. Arching across these contested boundaries was a diverse population of Mi'kmaq, Abenaki, and Maliseet natives, along with about fifteen thousand Acadians, descendants of seventeenth-century French migrants, who farmed, fished, and traded in villages hugging the bay's tidal inlets.[5] Wedged between two bristling military powers for generations, the Acadians had taken an idiosyncratic political position: they proclaimed neutrality. The mid-eighteenth century, however, was an unusually bad time for fence-sitting.[6]

Beginning in August 1755, on the brink of what would become the Seven Years' War, a combined force of British regulars and Massachusetts volunteers stormed through the Bay of Fundy's settlements, executing orders to capture and deport every last Acadian they could lay hands on. The campaign succeeded. Within three years, Anglo-American troops had almost emptied the region of Acadian inhabitants, seemingly annihilating a colonial society whose origins predated those of Plymouth and Jamestown. It was an "upheaval" that struck even some of its perpetrators as "sumthing shocking."[7] As for the Acadians, they endured *dérangement* of a different sort as well. The word also refers to mental agitation— the "madness" with which the God of the Old Testament cursed those He dispossessed in the first diaspora. Wrenched from home and separated from neighbors, spouses, and children, Acadians experienced psychological suffering to match their physical hardships. Their lot, declared a shattered exile dumped on Boston's docks late in 1755, "was the hardest . . . since our Saviour was upon the earth."[8]

For many Acadians, though, the hardest was yet to come. In the thirty years after 1755, refugees from the Bay of Fundy turned up in a stunning range of far-flung places. These included port cities of both British North America and the British Isles, France's colonies in the Caribbean and on the South American coast, the Falkland Islands, the uncultivated plains, windswept islands, and urban tenements of western France, the river valleys of eastern Canada, and Spanish Louisiana, where their descendants would eventually be known as Cajuns.[9] Had more radical plans come to fruition, this list of destinations might have included farms in the bone-dry Sierra Morena of Andalusia, the climatically mismatched islands of Corsica and Jersey, a French forest owned by the

Hudson Bay

NEW FRANCE/QUÉBEC

LOUISIANA

NOVA SCOTIA

BRITISH NORTH AMERICA

Gulf of Mexico

SAINT-DOMINGUE

CARIBBEAN SEA

GUIANA

NORTH ATLANTIC OCEAN

GREAT BRITAIN

NORTH SEA

FRANCE

AFRICA

SOUTH AMERICA

SOUTH PACIFIC OCEAN

SOUTH ATLANTIC OCEAN

FALKLAND ISLANDS (Contested territory)

0   1000   2000 Miles
0   1000   2000 Kilometers

The Lands of the Acadian Diaspora 1755 – 1785

French territory

British territory

Territory contested between France and Britain

TERRA AUSTRALIS INCOGNITA

nonagenarian ex-king of Poland, Ile-de-France (now Mauritius in the Indian Ocean), and the "central mass of the Antarctic continent," allegedly discovered by a French seafarer in 1773.[10] Wherever Acadians actually went, poverty and insecurity followed. Writing in the early 1770s, a handful of exiles in the French port of Saint-Malo summed up their pitiful state in a letter to a powerful figure at Versailles. "We are nothing," they told him.[11]

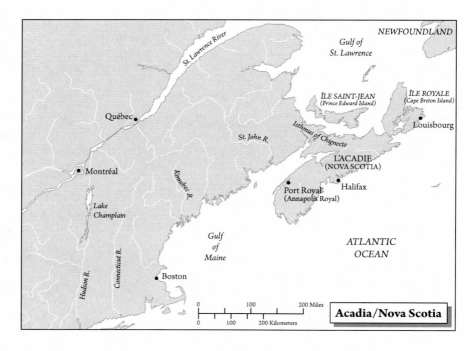

Yet histories of the *grand dérangement* have emphasized continuity, persistence, and a happy ending. For, seen from one angle, the Acadians' stopovers in the odd locations inventoried above are little more than brief, unpleasant interludes. Splintered by the violence of 1755, Acadian society seemed to reconstitute itself by instinct over the next two generations, with each "broken fragment of the former community" moving toward a broader, more lasting reunion.[12] Slowly and tortuously, loved ones found each other again, crossing oceans and continents to gather in villages that resembled, save for a few environmental variations, those they had left behind in Nova Scotia—especially in southwestern Louisiana, where hundreds of Acadians settled beginning in the mid-1760s, and on rivers and streams in present-day New Brunswick, where those who managed to evade the raids of the 1750s established settlements on the ragged margins of British Canada. These areas remain centers of Acadian (or Cajun) life even today.[13] In the face of such tenacity, the Acadians' North American, Caribbean, South Atlantic, and European voyages tend to come off as obstacles that merely reinforced their stubborn particularity and cemented their common desire to lock arms and re-create a lost world.[14]

This book, however, suggests another way of thinking about lost worlds and the Acadian diaspora. The narratives cobbled together here reveal that the dislocations and destinations of the *grand dérangement* mattered a great deal. Indeed, the Acadians' most gut-wrenching decisions in exile—to forge new associations or renew old bonds, to adopt new practices or cling to old ways—were informed by forces beyond the cultural identities they may have shared, or the social cohesion their bayside villages may have fostered in the decades before 1755. The communities they built and abandoned in distant places were not attuned solely to the Acadians' inner desires, but also responded to the harsh imperatives of a vast market for colonial labor. Reaching from Europe toward the New World and into the unknown, this market boiled up out of transformations that shook Atlantic empires in the aftermath of the Seven Years' War.

The story of the Acadian diaspora, then, serves to resurrect not one but two lost worlds, and to show the depth of their entanglement. The first, of course, is the face-to-face world the Acadians made as they shuttled from place to trying place—a world of loss, change, and, frequently, malice among onetime compatriots, all of which confronted exiles as they strained to tailor themselves to suit the demands of the powerful, people-moving states that surrounded them. The second is the wide-ranging world of imperial experimentation that flourished during the 1750s, 1760s, and 1770s—a world that made and remade Acadians even as it was, in part, made and remade by them.

No less than histories of the *grand dérangement*, histories of empire in the mid-eighteenth century have, understandably and often unintentionally, looked to the future. The one-sided outcome of the Seven Years' War encourages as much. For all nations involved, the conflict was a terrible burden. On battlefields from Pennsylvania to Prussia to the Philippines, fighting drained coffers across Europe while killing untold thousands of soldiers, sailors, and civilians. Then, with the 1763 Treaty of Paris, hostilities ended in one of the largest, most abrupt transfers of territory anyone could recall. For their part, the defeated French relinquished all of their North American lands, ceding New France and the disputed Ohio Valley to Great Britain and Louisiana to Spain (via the semisecret Treaty of Fontainebleau); the British also picked up East Florida from the Spanish, as well as French holdings in the Mediterranean, the Caribbean, West Africa, and India. By almost any standard, the peace of 1763 was a severe blow to Louis XV's once menacing empire and a great boon to the British.

The French monarchy, the usual narrative runs, responded to all of this by giving up on overseas expansionism, turning instead toward domestic issues and obsessive plotting against the "new barbarians" across the English Channel.[15] The British, of course, tried to address their war debt and the expense of ruling so many new subjects by imposing new duties and taxes on old colonists, an ill-considered policy that triggered the rupture that would become the American Revolution—or, as the arms-funneling French understood it, sweet revenge on their rivals. These high-stakes, nation-building events have transfixed scholars ever since, and the years immediately after 1763 have all too often been reduced to a prelude, the first set of links in a causal chain leading to the modern era of republican government on both sides of the Atlantic.[16]

Seeing things through the eyes of castoffs such as the Acadians, however, can help uncouple our understanding of this remarkable period from what came next. For example, as the British took to the streets to celebrate the Treaty of Paris, the French refused to abandon their imperial ambitions. In fact, the shock of 1763 triggered an outburst of colonial schemes aimed at shoring up what remained of the French Empire, especially the Caribbean islands of Saint-Domingue, Martinique, and Guadeloupe, along with Cayenne, a hive of hard-scrabble plantations and fortifications on the border of Portuguese Brazil. More expansively, France's numerous "project men" eyed new imperial venues, look-ing at once to the edges of the mapped world and within the kingdom itself for opportunities, lands, and resources that might revive the *patrie*'s fortunes.[17] Across the Channel, postwar officials in London waded through their own del-uge of proposals, all designed to secure, make profitable, and above all populate the newest bits of the crown's overseas dominions. The two enemies, one swollen in victory, the other shrunken in defeat, had something in common after 1763: suddenly both were desperate for work-roughened, loyal, and transportable set-tlers, preferably in bulk.

The realities of postwar imperialism, then, generated a superheated demand for labor that engrossed officials in London and Paris and shaped the way states did business as far afield as Madrid, Berlin, and Saint Petersburg. Crucially, statesmen and entrepreneurs in many of these places had, by the early 1760s, grown suspicious of African slavery's role as the main engine of Europe's impe-rial economy. Not that they endorsed abolition, or really considered forgoing the sugar, coffee, and tax revenue that flowed from plantations into metropolitan mouths and treasuries. Indeed, at midcentury the institution enjoyed broad-based if at times resentful support in both Great Britain and France.[18] But the Seven Years' War had shown just how treacherous both the enslaved and their masters could be in moments of crisis.

Take, for example, Tacky's Revolt. Emboldened by the disorderly comings and goings of British troops and spurred on by wartime food shortages, hundreds of slaves rose up in the northern and western parishes of Jamaica between April 1760 and October 1761. Led by the charismatic, shamanistic Tacky, the rebels killed dozens of whites and brought the Jamaican economy to a standstill before being defeated by two regiments of regulars, the local militia, and, most remark-ably, black guerillas culled from the maroon communities of the island's interior.[19]

The French had wartime predicaments of their own. In 1757 and 1758, a rash of strange deaths swept across the sugar plantations surrounding Cap Français, the largest city in the colony of Saint-Domingue (now Haiti). Estimates and ex-planations varied, but authorities ultimately concluded that dozens of whites, as many as seven thousand slaves, and ten thousand head of livestock had suc-cumbed to poisons administered by François Makandal, an African herbalist turned runaway slave, and his "masses of faithful blacks" who worked unnoticed in kitchens and fields throughout Saint-Domingue.[20] Makandal died at the stake in 1758, but like Tacky's revolt, his "conspiracy" haunted the Caribbean for years. Not accounting for disruptions in trade, contemporaries figured that Jamaica had lost £100,000 in capital and property to the uprising of 1760, while the French king paid former owners 600 livres for each accused poisoner executed in Saint-Domingue.[21] More discouraging still, the actions of black insurgents actually proved *less* costly than those of their masters. In 1759, for example, the planters of Guadeloupe surrendered the island to the British navy after mounting a token resistance; in 1762, the rich inhabitants of Martinique did the same, cheerfully sacrificing the king's property to safeguard their own. "Less attached to their reputations than to their wealth," these tropical subjects provided a bracing illustration of slavery's political limitations in a world of belligerent empires.[22]

All of these characters made Acadians look awfully good. They were, wrote one advocate of a renewed, expanded French Empire in 1763, "the kind of men most proper to found a flourishing colony." [23] And in lieu of disorderly slaves and their spineless masters, French, Spanish, and even British authorities tried to rope Acadians into doing just that.

To be sure, the Acadian diaspora speaks to us of a disturbing injustice, and of the men, women, and children who suffered the "astonishment of heart" that has always gone together with such things. But it also traces the outlines of something at once larger and more particular: an eighteenth-century moment of creativity in which the fashioning of more just, efficient, and muscular empires seemed not just possible but inevitable. But like so many other inevitabilities, this one proved unreachable, and thus forgettable. It is, however, inscribed— painfully and deeply—in the lives of the Acadians whose struggles fill these pages.

This is not, of course, the first book to connect the sensibilities of Acadian exiles to the extent of their journeys.

That genre's best-known example dates back to the fall of 1838, when an Episcopalian clergyman named Horace Conolly told the novelist Nathaniel Hawthorne a story as they took a long walk through Salem, Massachusetts. Hawthorne brooded over its dramatic possibilities but decided to pursue other themes: "It is not in my vein," he concluded. Two years later, however, he goaded Conolly into telling the tale again, this time at the Cambridge home of the poet Henry Wadsworth Longfellow. Overcome by Conolly's fever-soaked conclusion, Wadsworth pounced. Extracting a promise from Hawthorne not to "treat the subject in prose," he announced his intention to attempt an epic poem. After years of delay, eighteen months of writing, and dozens of drafts, Longfellow finished in

February 1847. Published later that year, the final product was called *Evangeline: A Tale of Acadie*.[24]

Although modern readers often balk at Longfellow's saccharine sentimentalism, *Evangeline* remains an affecting portrait of the geographical scope and psychological toll of the *grand dérangement*. The protagonists, Evangeline Bellefontaine and Gabriel Lajeunesse, were virtuous young Acadians raised in what the author called Nova Scotia's "forest primeval." Like their neighbors in the village of Grand Pré, they wanted nothing more than to get married and mind their own business. In 1755, however, as Anglo-American marauders knifed through Acadian country, the pair became separated in the chaos. Tragically, Evangeline and Gabriel ended up aboard different transport ships, which in turn deposited them in different Anglo-American ports on the Atlantic seaboard. Longfellow did not specify destinations but allowed (accurately enough) that Acadians struggled for survival from "the cold lakes of the North to sultry Southern savannahs."[25]

Evangeline started looking for Gabriel immediately, picking up a trail of sightings and rumors that extended for thousands of miles into the American interior. After a near miss on the Atchafalaya River in Louisiana, she tracked him to the presidio town of Los Adayes in present-day Texas, but remained two steps behind as Gabriel headed northeast toward the Ozarks, struck out across the Nebraska plains, and ventured deep into the Wind River Mountains of Wyoming. He doubled back to hunt on the Saginaw River in Michigan, but Evangeline found only his abandoned cabin. Graying, tired, and finally resigned to solitude, she became a "Sister of Mercy" in post-Revolutionary Philadelphia, making nighttime rounds "where disease and sorrow in garrets languished neglected." Then, in 1793, a yellow fever outbreak devastated the city. As Evangeline ministered to the sick and dying in an overcrowded Quaker almshouse, she stumbled, at last, upon a skeletal, sweat-stained Gabriel. He died in her arms. Contented, she died, too, and while Philadelphians shuffled by their unmarked graves unknowingly, the descendants of Acadian exiles preserved their story for generations to come.[26]

Longfellow's narrative packs an emotional punch even today, Romantic-era verbiage notwithstanding. His words proved doubly powerful for American audiences in the mid-nineteenth century. After all, Evangeline's pursuit of her Gabriel took readers on a tour of an American empire in the making. The Acadians tramped through Louisiana, acquired from the French in 1804 but still something of a mystery to northerners; Texas, over which the United States and Mexico waged war even as Longfellow wrote; and the Rocky Mountains, probed in the 1840s by fur trappers, Mormon outcasts, and the land-grabbers and gold-diggers on the Oregon Trail.[27]

In one sense, Longfellow's poetry prefigures the Janus-faced theme of this book—the role of Acadians in building empires, and the role of empires in transforming Acadians. But in ways that echoed the concerns of its day, *Evangeline* turned the *grand dérangement* inside out, repurposing an eastward-leaning, transatlantic diaspora to evoke westward-facing, continental expansionism. And for all the sympathy they won for the Acadians, Longfellow's saintly characters helped perpetuate the notion that exiles coped with *dérangement* in all of its forms by trying to turn back time, restoring all things as they once were.

The Acadian Diaspora, of course, was not written to debunk Longfellow, or to refute the many fine histories informed by his work. Instead, it seeks a reorientation, a new take on those same vivid elements that captivated the poet all those decades ago. Another muse, one not quite so heavenly as Evangeline Bellefontaine, might help chart the way forward—which brings us to Achille Gotrot, the last in a line of Acadian exiles whose experiences best parallel the trajectory of this book.

The very real Gotrot (pronounced *go-tro*, and sometimes spelled Gautreaux or Gautreau) differed from the fictional Evangeline in nearly every way. But his story, and not hers, might easily have become Longfellow's introduction to the *grand dérangement*. For in 1840, the year Horace Conolly told Longfellow the tale that would become *Evangeline*, news of Gotrot's fate buzzed among the ship's captains and sailors who frequented Boston's port. Less than a mile from that port sat Saint Matthew's Episcopal Church, in whose rectory lived Horace Conolly. Had Conolly's ears pricked up around the crews of the Massachusetts whalers *Cavalier* and *Rebecca Sims*, both recently returned from the South Pacific, he could have picked up the whole, sordid account. It was like something out of a novel.

In 1838, Gotrot, captain of the French whaler *Jean Bart*, had docked his ship off the North Island of New Zealand. He then descended belowdecks and shot himself in the temple, despondent over the elusiveness of South Seas spermaceti. His men, apparently unmoved by the suicide ("They still don't know who's boss," Gotrot had grumbled earlier in the voyage), dumped the corpse overboard and then made the five-hundred-mile journey to the Chatham Islands. They were then killed by a group of Moriori warriors who attacked the *Jean Bart* after a round of trading gone wrong. The French ship *L'Héroine* stumbled upon the *Jean Bart*'s charred hulk a while later, finding only "yards broken on the rocks, pulleys, rudder hinges, the ship's bell," and a single letter addressed to Achille Gotrot from Boulogne-sur-Mer in France, where his displaced Acadian ancestors had landed eighty years earlier.[28] The crew of the *Rebecca Sims* heard the entire story while docked off the Chatham Islands; a consular official on the island of Saint Helena told sailors aboard the *Cavalier*. By 1840, Gotrot's tale had reached Horace Conolly's Boston.

Evangeline it wasn't.

Indeed, Longfellow probably would have considered *this* story better suited to his ghoulish literary rival Edgar Allan Poe. But I confess that after a decade spent tracking down eighteenth-century Acadians and meditating on what happened to them, I cannot help but see Achille Gotrot as emblematic of the Acadian diaspora in ways that transcend Evangeline and the timeless constancy she embodies. The impression has grown stronger the more I have come to know his family.

Gotrot's great-grandfather Charles Gautreau *dit* Maringouin (whose nickname translates, in American English, to "Skeeter") was a fourth-generation Acadian. Born in 1711, he lived in Cobequid, a little village at the eastern end of the Bay of Fundy. More than anything else, two related phenomena determined the course of Maringouin's life. The first was the rapid extension of Acadian agriculture, which turned marshlands into productive fields up and down the bay's eastern shores in the first half of the eighteenth century. The second was the sharpening competition between the empires of Great Britain and France for the fruits of those lands, and for the Acadian hands that coaxed crops from what, to outsiders, looked like unforgiving soil. Construed as a kind of zero-sum game by those in power, this contest to secure Acadian labor spiraled into the expulsion of 1755 and anticipated the wider migrations to come. Chapter 1 tells this story.

Plenty of Maringouin's relatives and friends were among the seven thousand Acadians swept up and shipped off in the first weeks of the assault on Nova Scotia. These were offloaded at nine different towns from Boston to Savannah, where they met Anglo-American hosts with no incentive to receive them warmly. Chapter 2 follows these exiles as they struggled to adjust to diminished possibilities, forge new alliances in unfamiliar environments, and understand the imperial transformations that would soon compel many to migrate again.

Maringouin, however, followed another path. With his wife, Marie-Josèphe Hébert, and his two sons, Charles and Gervais, he managed to flee Cobequid before the onslaught of 1755, crossing the Northumberland Strait to reach Ile Saint-Jean (now Prince Edward Island). Once home to a few hundred Acadian farmers drawn from the mainland by French politicking, Ile Saint-Jean's little villages became squalid refugee camps packed with more than two thousand escapees. The British, though, took them as well, seizing a total of three thousand people, including the Gautreau family, after overrunning the island in 1758. Sensitive to protests by the North American colonists forced to receive Acadians a few years earlier, the British shipped these captives to France. And so Maringouin and his boys (Marie-Josèphe's fate is unknown) found themselves in Boulogne-sur-Mer, a minor smuggling and pilgrimage center on the English Channel. He died there in 1760.[29]

Orphaned at sixteen, Gervais Gautreau had no money, few connections, and no idea how to negotiate the new world of old régime France. Four years after his father's death, in 1764, he completed a second Atlantic crossing, this time to the mouth of the Kourou River, twenty-five miles northwest of Cayenne on the South American coast. He arrived with dozens of his fellow Acadians and ten thousand German-speaking peasants, all of whom had been recruited by Louis XV's ministers to power a radical experiment in imperial economics and social engineering: the creation of a Caribbean colony dedicated exclusively to the production of food, and in which African slavery would be prohibited by law. Chapter 3 recounts the origins, development, and terrible end of what the French would come to call the Kourou expedition—as well as the story of Môle Saint-Nicolas, a similar settlement carved by Acadian exiles from the northern coast of slave-rich Saint-Domingue.

Gervais was lucky. He survived the tropics, somehow gaining passage to Boulogne-sur-Mer from Cayenne in 1765. On his way back to France, Gervais may well have crossed wakes with *L'Aigle*, a frigate bearing scores of his former compatriots bound for Port Saint-Louis, an Acadian colony on East Falkland. Chapter 4 unpacks the extraordinary history of this settlement, a product of one Frenchman's obsession with ancient history and his crown's designs on undiscovered lands deep in the Southern Hemisphere.

Even as France's postwar hopes rose and fell with the fortunes of their Caribbean and South Atlantic outposts, Acadians of Gervais's day inspired fresh thinking closer to home. Chapter 5 follows several hundred Acadians to Belle-Ile-en-Mer, an island off the southern coast of Brittany. Taken (embarrassingly enough) by the British during the Seven Years' War, Belle-Ile played host to a bold attempt at making a colony for an age of enlightenment in which rustic, patriotic, and well-instructed settlers would put unused land to the plow while providing an example for the island's benighted natives. For his part, Gervais remained aloof from the Belle-Ile boosters, and from the dozens of French, Spanish, and British schemers proposing new Acadian settlements. But in 1773, he was on the move again. With fifteen hundred other Acadians from France's ports, he descended on the province of Poitou in central France. Divided among six recently built, relentlessly geometrical villages near the town of Châtellerault, the Acadians were to jump-start the region's economy by clearing, farming, and demonstrating proper behavior for local peasants who were, according to one landowner, "mere automatons."[30] It did not work. In 1775, the little colony spiraled into anarchy. Ministerial conspiracies buffeted the Acadians from without, while insubordination, intimidation, and violence overtook them in their villages. In 1776, almost all of the settlers fled to the port of Nantes. Ten years later, most of these Acadians would accept a Spanish offer to migrate to Louisiana. Chapter 6 relates the story of this last, most ambitious attempt to redefine empire, and of the Acadian community it helped forge.

Gervais Gautreau, however, left that community behind. Upon leaving the Poitou colony, he went neither to Nantes nor to Louisiana, but made his way back to Boulogne-sur-Mer. His son Charles became a ship's captain, joining dozens of privateers (including at least one other Acadian, Firmin Aucoin, captain of the much feared *Flying Fish*) who preyed on British shipping for Napoleon's empire.[31] After spending six years imprisoned in Great Britain, Charles, who began rendering his family name Gotrot, became a long-distance merchant, voyaging to Brazil, Martinique, New Orleans, and France's Mediterranean coast.

Born in 1805, his son Achille went along as a cabin boy. Although he sometimes "burst into tears upon leaving Mama at the end of the dock," and once "evacuated all of [his] bile" during a storm in the Atlantic, the sea had his soul.[32] He never quite purged himself of boyhood insecurities, but he passed the exams necessary to become a bona fide whaling captain early in the 1830s—just in time to catch a wave of French enthusiasm over the colonization of New Zealand. Claimed by the British but explored early on by the French mariner Jules-Sébastien-César Dumont d'Urville, New Zealand's North Island played host to an abortive 1837 settlement by Charles-Philippe-Hypolite de Thierry, a con artist who also planned to cut a canal across Panama to ease long travel times. De Thierry's plans failed, but a flood of profit seekers followed him into the Pacific. Among them was Achille Gotrot, the Acadian captain of the *Jean Bart*.[33]

This unhappy ending, I think, marks a good place to start a history of the Acadian diaspora. For the suicide of Achille Gotrot—a troubled young man who, so far as we can tell, rarely identified himself as an Acadian at all—suggests that the *grand dérangement* expanded in multiple directions and led to multiple endings. In one respect, however, the Gotrot family's saga is not so different from *Evangeline*, or from the real-life experiences of Acadians who wound up together in places such as Louisiana and Canada. All of these exiles moved, changed, came together, and pulled apart in dialogue with transformations in the imperial world around them. Its history and theirs are, in effect, one and the same.

The Expulsion

The stranger that is within thee shall get up above thee very high; and thou shalt come down very low. . . . And he shall eat the fruit of thy cattle, and the fruit of thy land, until thou be destroyed.

—Deuteronomy 28:43

A search party found the corpse beneath a clump of bushes. The man had died in agony. Dark blood oozed from his mouth; his fingers remained "clenched full of sand."

His name was André Boudin *dit* Blondain, and along with three fellow soldiers at Fort Beauséjour, an outpost on New France's contested frontier with Nova Scotia, he had made a terrible mistake. A day earlier, on May 15, 1754, they had cooked a pot of soup. Along with some salt pork, they added a "great quantity" of greens and a few carrots. After eating, Guillaume Besse *dit* Languedoc left the fort and returned to his work tending the hospital's garden, but soon collapsed in "violent convulsions." Back inside, Etienne Leroy *dit* Vadeboncoeur and François Visan *dit* Sansoucy suddenly found themselves "racked with vomiting, making the most violent efforts to purge what they had eaten." For his part, Blondain had vanished into a network of grassy trails to the northeast of the fort. He had only moments to live.

Panicked officers sent for the commandant's secretary, Thomas Pichon. Having briefly studied medicine in France before embarking on a checkered military career in Germany and North America, Pichon was the soldiers' best hope. At the hospital, he gave Languedoc an "antidote," but seeing the unmistakable "symptoms of death," Pichon left him and hurried inside Fort Beauséjour to find the others. Frantic, he administered tartar emetic to induce still more vomiting, followed by doses of Venice treacle, a round of cassia-infused enemas, and milk.

Miraculously (if messily), Vadeboncoeur and Sansoucy felt much better the next morning, just in time to see the body of their friend Blondain, who had collapsed several hundred yards down the path to the little French redoubt at

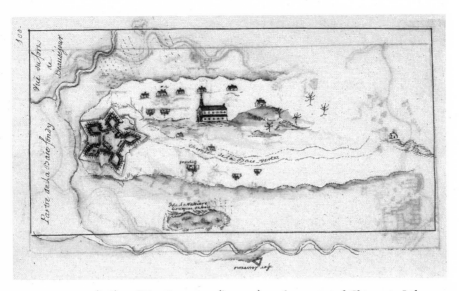

Fort Beauséjour (left) and Fort Lawrence (bottom) on the contested Chignecto Isthmus. *Vue du fort de Beauséjour*, 1750. Courtesy of the McCord Museum, Montreal.

Pont à Buot, carried into the fort. Pichon conducted a "scrupulous" autopsy. He discovered "grayish white" pus in Blondain's bladder, gas in his intestines, and bits of "undigested root" in his stomach. He had no idea what had done the damage. But the omens in Blondain's gut, plus the fact that a few spilled drops of the soup had nearly killed the fort's two dogs, convinced Pichon that he needed to find out fast.

He sought out the surgeon at Fort Lawrence, a British garrison located just two miles to the east across the Missaguash River, a tidal stream that had become the de facto border between New France and Nova Scotia. Although the two forts bristled at each other, trips across the Missaguash were hardly uncommon. In 1753, a French officer had complained that inter-imperial traffic made Fort Lawrence "as frequented as the tomb of Mahomet at Mecca."[1] Pichon and the British surgeon arranged a meeting, compared notes, and came to a reassuring conclusion: Blondain and his friends had mistaken a species of poisonous hemlock for parsley. Convinced that Fort Beauséjour's food supply was in no danger, Pichon went home.[2]

Over the next year, however, he crossed the Missaguash to Fort Lawrence more and more often. Feeling unappreciated at Fort Beauséjour and reasoning that "we are born men before becoming English or French," Pichon began committing treason.[3] He relayed maps, letters, and reports to the British while trying to sow dissatisfaction among the Acadians whose homes and fields lay near Fort Beauséjour, and whose support was essential to its survival. Finally, in May and

June 1755, a force of British regulars and Massachusetts volunteers capitalized on Pichon's information, laying siege to the fort from a rise a few hundred yards to its northeast. Part of a multipronged British attack on French strongholds throughout the North American backcountry, the strike against Fort Beauséjour succeeded. On June 15, after a well-placed bomb destroyed a casemate, killing three French soldiers and one British prisoner inside the fort, the commandant capitulated.

As the Anglo-Americans swept inside, they discovered that a number of Acadians (the "more warlike" of the area's inhabitants, according to Pichon) had borne arms against the British during the siege.[4] In the days that followed, the victors waffled on what to do next. Biding their time, the British set the Acadians to work repairing Fort Beauséjour's ramparts even as they whisked Pichon away to begin his new life as Thomas Tyrrell, a bona fide subject of George II.[5] Within weeks, Nova Scotia's provincial leaders issued a stunning response. In light of the "treachery" at Fort Beauséjour, they launched a plan to deport all fifteen thousand Acadians from the shores of the Bay of Fundy. A year after the death of Andre Boudin *dit* Blondain, the *grand dérangement* had begun.

How had it come to this?

Coerced migration, of course, was nothing new in 1755. Richard Philipps, provincial governor of Nova Scotia during the 1720s, mused about an expulsion in his day but was brought up short by a worrisome prospect: that Acadians might depart like "the jews march'd out of Egypt, not only with their owne effects and what they can borrow, but will first distroy the Country."[6]

Less ancient examples abounded as well. The native Irish, Native Americans, and Highland Scots had been victimized by British or Anglo-American campaigns to uproot, resituate, or just plain get rid of ill-behaved minorities.[7] The British, of course, were not the only aggressors. In the sixteenth century, thousands of indigenous people in Spanish Peru had been thrust into the *reducciones*, vast, mission-centered settlements designed to speed assimilation, Christianization, and the extraction of labor and tribute.[8] Notoriously, Louis XIV engineered the exile of his kingdom's two hundred thousand Huguenots in 1685, scattering French Protestants throughout the Atlantic world.[9] These episodes—and smaller ones, including the repeated "evacuations" of civilians in contested places such as Newfoundland and the Caribbean island of Saint Christopher— were all set against the incessant hum of the slave trade, which moved twelve million captive Africans to the Americas.[10] What happened to the Acadians was no aberration. They had been jerked violently back into the mainstream of lived experience in a harsh New World.

The assault on the Bay of Fundy's villages was hardly predestined; rather, it evolved out of choices made by people such as Thomas Pichon. His betrayal was among the last in a long line of acts that led to those brutal months in 1755. Those responsible for the Acadian expulsion are now reviled: Charles Lawrence, the lieutenant governor whose council issued the order to disperse the Acadians "among His Majesty's colonys"; Charles Morris, a surveyor who in 1753 wrote a plan for the removal; John Winslow of Marshfield, Massachusetts, and Robert Monckton of Yorkshire, England, the army officers who executed Morris's plan; William Shirley, governor of Massachusetts during the 1740s and 1750s, who told anyone within earshot that "the Province of Nova Scotia will never be out of danger, whilst the French Inhabitants are suffer'd to remain."[11]

Perhaps, though, we might step back from the search for scapegoats to take a harder look at the place where the expulsion of 1755 really began. In the 1750s, the Chignecto Isthmus was a true friction point between the French and British empires in North America. There were, of course, others. Pushing south from Montréal past Lake Champlain, a line of French forts ran into a line of British forts running north from Albany to Lake George, while from the Cherokee towns of South Carolina to the Allegheny River in Pennsylvania subjects and allies of the two powers jockeyed for trade, territory, and influence.[12]

Nowhere, however, was imperial rivalry so intimate as Chignecto. Separated by a thin strip of no-man's-land and the muddy Missaguash, men from Fort Beauséjour and Fort Lawrence could see, smell, and hail one another with ease. Brook Watson, a one-legged teenager serving as a secretary at Fort Lawrence, recalled the cold day when seventy head of British cattle made a break for the "greener herbage" on the French side of the river. Watson "stript" and "plunged into the stream," but his wooden leg sank so deep in a mud bank that he got out only by "drawing himself . . . on his belly." After shooing sixty cows toward Fort Lawrence, the half-naked Briton was interrupted by a French officer "whose compassion for a most deplorable object" led him to pilot Watson back across the Missaguash on his own boat.[13] Not all meetings ended so happily, but the unique proximity of empires on the isthmus bred a unique familiarity.[14]

It also bred changes in Chignecto's human and physical geography. Had Thomas Pichon taken the time to look as he raced, antidotes in hand, into Fort Beauséjour in May 1754, he surely would have noticed them. A few years earlier, the outpost had been built on a plateau described by Louis-Thomas Jacau de Fiedmont, a Nova Scotia–born French engineer: "The height . . . falls almost 100 feet in a gentle slope on four sides of the fort: opposite the fifth, the ground rises gradually, almost 2 feet in every 200 yards, until the greatest elevation is reached at a distance of 900 yards from the fort."[15] From the top, Pichon would have seen the village of Beauséjour below. It was unimpressive. Founded at the same time as the fort, it consisted of the unfinished walls of a passable chapel, some livestock "without shelter," and the "wretched hovels" of a few dozen Acadians.[16]

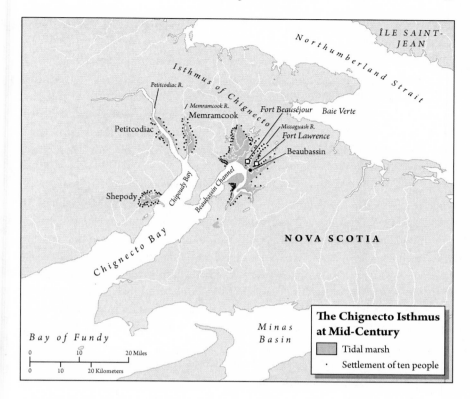

At times there were Indians, too, mostly Mi'kmaq from Shubenacadie, the site of an old Catholic mission in Nova Scotia's interior, but also Abenaki and Maliseet delegations from the Saint John River and beyond. "According to custom," the French gave them presents of guns, powder, and supplies, but "privation" in the village often forced officers to turn the visitors away.[17]

On a clear day, Pichon might have looked west to the *rivières* au Lac, Tantramar, and Memramcook, which emptied into the Bay of Fundy from the north. Here new dikes crisscrossed the waterways, guarding the farms of clannish Acadian settlements such as Pré des Richards and Pré des Bourgs against ruinous saltwater. In the other direction, past Fort Lawrence to the east, sat the village of Beaubassin. Once home to more than two hundred, it was now a charred ruin. Beyond Beaubassin, on the *rivières* Laplanche, Nappan, Macann, and Hébert, dikes were in disrepair, leaving the farms behind them to flood. Had Pichon's vision been unnaturally sharp, he could have turned north, looking beyond the mainland settlement of Gaspereau and across the Cumberland Strait to Ile Saint-Jean (now Prince Edward Island). Hundreds of Acadians lived there in makeshift camps and tumbledown huts, battling field mice and rocky soil to live, as a squatter named Augustin Doucet put it, "like savages in the woods."[18] From on high or up close, the scenery flashing before Pichon's eyes was half formed, raw.

That rawness was the result of a peculiar kind of imperial competition. At stake, simply enough, was food. The lands farmed by Nova Scotia's fifteen thousand Acadians, wrote more than one eighteenth-century observer, had the potential to act as a kind of "granary," enriching and empowering whoever controlled them. For both the French and British empires, securing the fruits of Acadian agriculture, and preventing the enemy from doing so, became the highest priority.

In the early 1750s, the French muscled as many Acadians as they could (Pichon guessed three thousand "refugees" in all) west of the Missaguash or onto Ile Saint-Jean. They were to create replicas of their farming communities in Nova Scotia, strengthening Louis XV's claim to a vital frontier and putting calories in the bellies of men such as André Boudin *dit* Blondain and the native Americans who fought alongside them. The British, however, saw Chignecto as a valve in need of shutting. They cajoled, threatened, and blocked, knowing that an Acadian exodus would augment French power and detract from their own. It was a vicious competition, and in 1755 it would transform all of Nova Scotia, just as it had Chignecto.

For Thomas Pichon, Chignecto was a place of opportunity, reinvention, and self-fashioning. With the British (his "liberators") near, he switched sides on his own, rattling off justifications ranging from his English ancestry to French attempts on his life to a favorable comparison with Shakespeare's Coriolanus (who, after "a light injury" from his Roman countrymen, sacked the city "at the head of an army of enemies, with death and desolation in his heart").[19] But for the Acadians, such freedom of self-definition proved elusive. The logic of imperialism pigeonholed them as laborers suited for agriculture and nothing more. In 1755, that image would prove the Acadians' undoing.

Nova Scotia, of course, had not always been Acadian country. The province's indigenous inhabitants, the Mi'kmaq, had lived there for centuries. They spent summers in coastal villages and winters in smaller groups, hunting protein-rich game (including seals, bears, moose, caribou, and beaver) across the uplands of what would become the Canadian Maritimes.[20]

The first accounts of the Mi'kmaq date to July 1534, when Jacques Cartier came across two "fleets" totaling "forty or fifty canoes" in Chaleur Bay off present-day New Brunswick. Eager for "iron wares," the Mi'kmaq first offered strips of seal meat, but ended up stark naked after trading away their clothes.[21] By the time the Rouen fur trader Etienne Bellenger visited Acadia in 1583, the Mi'kmaq had learned well how to deal with Europeans. As Bellenger told Richard Hakluyt, then a secretary to England's ambassador to France, the Mi'kmaq cut quite a figure. "They weare their hayre hanging downe long before and behynde as long as their Navells," he remembered, revealing that "they go all naked saving for their privates which they cover with an Apron of some Beastes skynn." They were experts in intercultural commerce. In exchange for metal goods, the Mi'kmaq offered Bellenger "hides reddie dressed upon both sides bigger than an Oxe," along with deer, seal, marten, and otter skins, enough beaver pelts to make six hundred hats, and foot-long chunks of venison—any explorer's wish list. But Bellenger also lost two of his men and a small boat in the Bay of Fundy to a group of "cruell and subtill" Mi'kmaq, prompting him to warn others of his "follye in trusting the salvadges to farr."[22]

The Mi'kmaq would remain one of the more stable indigenous societies in North America, experiencing no great collapse like the mound builders of the Southeast and no cyclical wars like those that devastated the Iroquoian and Algonquian peoples of the Saint Lawrence Valley.[23] While they lived and migrated as clans, the Mi'kmaq also retained an overarching political structure called the Sante Mawi'omi, which translates to "Grand Council" or "Holy Gathering." Legendarily founded hundreds of years earlier in response to Iroquois raids from the east, the council brought together the "captains" of seven Mi'kmaq districts for talks on "peace and war, treaties of friendship, and treaties for the common good."[24] Although the Holy Gathering was transformed by the European presence in Acadia, it endured into the eighteenth century. During the winter of 1728, the French governor of Ile Royale fretted over "a considerable gathering of Indians ... for which I have not been able to discover the reason."[25] Numerically strong and politically sophisticated, the Mi'kmaq proved willing participants in colonial economies while remaining blasé about the colonizers. Pierre Biard, a French Jesuit who did his best to minister to the Mi'kmaq in 1611, complained that "they think they are better, more valiant and more ingenious" than any European.[26]

Frenchmen began arriving in numbers in 1604, three years before the foundation of Jamestown and sixteen before the *Mayflower* landed at Plymouth Rock. Henry IV of France granted the first charter for "the country of Acadia, Canada and other lands of New France" to Pierre du Gua, sieur de Monts, a Protestant nobleman who promised to transport sixty colonists across the Atlantic, solidify "the friendship already begun" with the Mi'kmaq, teach the "savages" Christian principles, and quash English claims to the region, all "while taking nothing from the coffers of His Majesty."[27] This was mostly puffery. De Monts wanted to get rich quick through minerals or, more likely, beaver pelts. In the summer of 1605, de Monts and his navigator, Samuel de Champlain, sailed into the Bay of Fundy, through the Digby Gut, and up the *rivière* Dauphin, where de Monts began mapping out a settlement called Port Royal.

Hugging what Champlain called "one of the finest harbors I have seen on all these coasts," Port Royal also sat near a Mi'kmaq village. Ruled by an incongruously bearded sagamore named Membertou (translation: "the game cock who commands many"), the Mi'kmaq sustained the French during those first difficult winters, supplying food in exchange for weapons and tools. For their part, de Monts and Champlain grew enamored of the Saint Lawrence Valley even as independent fishermen, French merchants, and the venerable Hatters' Corporation of Paris began aligning against de Monts's crown-granted monopoly over the fur trade with the Mi'kmaq.[28] Henry IV abruptly revoked the charter in 1607, prompting de Monts to send Champlain to claim the future site of Québec. Guarded against European enemies by several hundred miles of the Saint Lawrence River, which flowed from Québec through the western heartland of the fur trade and, many believed, right on to Asia, *this* would become the focal point of French imperialism in North America for the next century. At three years old, Acadia had become an orphan.

For the next generation, Port Royal was controlled by Jean de Biencourt, sieur de Poutrincourt, and his son, Charles de Biencourt de Saint-Just. Poutrincourt had been one of de Monts's partners on the 1604 voyage, and maintained a dogged determination to turn Port Royal into an agricultural colony. Alongside the naturalist Marc Lescarbot, he thrilled at the "rye . . . as tall as the tallest man" grown in the outpost's gardens (seeking funds at court, he would later present some of that rye, along with four other species of grain and a few geese, to a bemused Henry IV).[29] The Poutrincourt dynasty never realized its goal. Father and son fought with Jesuits and their powerful French patrons, struggled in vain to lure migrants to Port Royal, and suffered a devastating 1613 assault by English freebooters from Jamestown. On a return trip to France in 1615, Poutrincourt was killed while battling an anti-monarchical uprising near his Champagne estates. In Acadia, his son died in 1624, leaving Port Royal's handful of French transients in limbo.

The English crown seized the moment. In 1621, James I had granted a charter for "Nova Scotia" to an idiosyncratic Scots courtier named William Alexander. Eight years later, Alexander's son landed near Port Royal (then abandoned by Acadia's remaining French traders, who had taken up a new post at Port Loméron on the peninsula's western tip), with seventy of his countrymen in tow. Their colony barely survived the winter. In spite of a good reception from the Mi'kmaq and some successful agricultural experiments, a skirmish with the French sealed the fate of "New Scotland." In 1632 the French ship *Saint-Jean* hauled forty-two defeated Scots to England. That same year, the Treaty of Saint-Germain-en-Laye returned Acadia to France—but the English claim would endure in memory.[30]

In 1636, after a failed attempt to establish an outpost for fishermen and fur traders at La Hève on the Atlantic coast, the French turned again toward Port Royal. The prime mover in all of this was Charles de Menou d'Aulnay de Charnizay. D'Aulnay had come to Acadia in 1632 as an agent of his cousin Isaac de Razilly, a naval officer charged with overseeing the "restitution of Port Royal in Acadia . . . which has been usurped by the Scots and English."[31] Both Louis XIII and the Compagnie des Cents-Associés, a royally sanctioned company whose investors claimed control over trade and settlement throughout France's North American possessions, signed off on Razilly's appointment. For reasons that remain unclear, they granted similar powers to Charles de Saint-Étienne de la Tour, a veteran of the Poutrincourt era who maintained a base at the mouth of the Saint John River, across the Bay of Fundy from Port Royal.[32] At first the rival officials got on well. Razilly spent most of his time at La Hève, while de la Tour minded his fur-trading business with the Maliseets. But when Razilly died suddenly in 1635, d'Aulnay asserted himself as the sole authority over all of Acadia, igniting a feud that would last for more than a decade.

The principal episodes border on the tragicomic. After a brief détente in the late 1630s, d'Aulnay blockaded de la Tour's fort on the Saint John in 1642. The latter responded by escaping to Boston. Scraping up capital from Puritans interested in the fur trade, de la Tour recruited three hundred Massachusetts volunteers who routed d'Aulnay, chased his ships back to Port Royal, and sacked the surrounding countryside. While de la Tour visited Boston to court more Protestant backers, d'Aulnay struck back at the Saint John River settlement in 1645. Left behind to hold down the fort, de la Tour's wife, Françoise-Marie Jacquelin, the daughter of a prominent Huguenot merchant, surrendered. D'Aulnay spared her life (although she died a few weeks later, seemingly of natural causes) but forced one of de la Tour's men to execute every last soldier in her husband's garrison. De la Tour skulked between Massachusetts and an awkward exile in Québec.

Five years later, on May 24, 1650, d'Aulnay's canoe capsized in the tidal basin near Port Royal. "Strange currents" pulled on his body with such force that the swim to shore took ninety minutes. D'Aulnay died after dragging himself onto the bank.[33] De la Tour then exacted his final revenge. In 1653, he married d'Aulnay's pragmatic widow, Jeanne Motin de Reux, for "the peace and tranquility of the country."[34] Together they laid plans to bring Acadia, then a collection of rudimentary forts and villages dotting the Bay of Fundy from Port Royal in the east to Pentagouet on Maine's Penobscot River, under one rule.[35]

In political terms, d'Aulnay's life had been a failure. But his attempts to bring de la Tour to heel led directly to the first permanent settlement of French farmers in Acadia. D'Aulnay was a man on the make, and he knew that the fur trade was the fastest route to riches in North America. That meant leaving the fishy isolation of La Hève for Port Royal, where he could stick close to Membertou's Mi'kmaq descendants and compete with de la Tour for trade among the Maliseet, whose hunting parties ranged up the Penobscot all the way to the Saint Lawrence River.

As his long run of names suggests, d'Aulnay was also a member of the French nobility. He looked on Port Royal as a distant annex of his family's estates near Loudun, south of the Loire River in the province of Poitou. The peasants who worked d'Aulnay's land had given the family both riches and prestige. By the 1630s, however, d'Aulnay's holdings, like those of his neighbors, were mired in uncertainty. Religious warfare had decimated the kingdom's economy during the last quarter of the sixteenth century, leaving many nobles "scraping by in their homes" or, as one observer worried, "giving themselves to base commerce . . . buying and selling wheat, wine, salt and other things."[36] Recovery came slow to Poitou as political discontent accelerated. As late as 1622, Louis XIII led an army into the province, putting down armed Protestants accused of instigating "disorders, insolent acts, and rebellions . . . against his authority."[37] Nobles and tenants struggled to remain profitable, while rising taxes often forced those peasants who had owned their own lands to sell on the cheap.[38]

On d'Aulnay's estates, which encompassed La Chaussée, Martaizé, and several other villages south of Loudun, the result seems to have been a glut of dispossessed men and women looking for a fresh start. On his visits home during the late 1630s and early 1640s, d'Aulnay began telling them about Acadia. Along with a few peasants culled from Razilly's estates in Anjou, about twenty families from La Chaussée and Martaizé—with names such as Bourg, Gaudet, Leblanc, and Thibodeau—determined to make new homes in Port Royal.[39]

D'Aulnay's needs and those of his tenants converged nicely. But there was more to the settlement of Port Royal than good fortune. It had to do with tides. From the Gulf of Maine, the Bay of Fundy slices deep into Nova Scotia's igneous bedrock, terminating in twin heads 150 miles to the northeast. Narrowing on the surface and shallowing underwater, the bay acts like a funnel, producing the highest tidal variations on earth. Moving at speeds of up to eight knots, four cubic miles of water rush into and out of the Bay of Fundy during each twelve-hour cycle.[40] The sea rises and falls as much as fifty feet in some spots, spilling saltwater across miles of coastal flatland.

Early on, the tides were notable mainly as a nuisance to navigators. Poutrincourt discovered as much in 1607, when his canoe was prevented from reaching Port Royal by "the tide (which runs swiftly here)" and then wrenched "toward the coast, with its high rocks and cliffs."[41] A similar fate befell Jacques de Meulles. After a shipwreck, the intendant of New France spent the winter of 1685–86 marooned at the northernmost end of the Bay of Fundy, in the tiny Acadian settlement of Beaubassin. When de Meulles finally attempted to sail to Port Royal in April, his twelve-ton sloop eased out of the Missaguash into the bay but was blown onto "a point of clayey land which one could hardly see at that time." The tide, which had been so high that it "overflowed into the meadows," began to ebb. In an hour or two, the ship was "balanced, half of it being in the air," leaving de Meulles and his crew teetering three stories above the water's surface "as if we had been put there on purpose." The water's return saved the high-centered Frenchmen, but the Bay of Fundy would continue to bedevil European sailors for years to come.[42]

The sea's rise and fall did, however, yield some benefits. Tidal waters scour the bay's floor with incredible force twice daily, dumping tons of nutrient-rich red silt onto marshlands along the rivers and streams that empty into the bay. Although gentlemen such as Poutrincourt never knew what to make of these overgrown swamps (he ordered fields tilled on the uplands east of Port Royal, where, as a modern geographer puts it, "the most that can be hoped . . . is a good forest"), others saw creative possibilities.[43] Before decamping for Québec, Champlain laid out a few "gardens" near Port Royal, placing "a little sluice-way towards the shore, in order to draw off the water when I wished."[44] In effect, he was experimenting with land reclamation through diking, using an earthen wall to keep the rising sea out but including within it a mechanism that allowed him to drain fresh water from the field at low tide.

Champlain knew this process well. He came from the French town of Brouage near La Rochelle, site of an enormous dike separating solid ground from the Marais de Brouage, a massive swamp studded with evaporative salt pans.[45] Dikes like this one, some built by Benedictine and Cistercian monasteries as early as the eleventh century, littered the waterways of Poitou, Anjou, Saintonge, Aunis, and Brittany. Many were destroyed during the Hundred Years' War and the religious conflicts of the late sixteenth century, prompting local reconstruction efforts that spread knowledge of diking techniques and technologies among generations of Poitevin workers.[46] In 1599, Henry IV launched a centralized campaign to reclaim the marshes, but political reversals and renewed fighting between Catholics and Protestants stalled new projects until the late 1630s, when a royally chartered company waded into the Marais Poitevin, a vast area of swamps at the mouths of the Lay, Sèvre, and Vendée rivers. More than fifteen thousand hectares would be diked and drained there over the following twenty-five years, a run of activity that revived medieval methods while refining new ones.[47]

D'Aulnay seems to have been steeped in these diking traditions. Nicolas Denys, who arrived in Acadia with Isaac de Razilly in 1632, would later describe Port Royal's hinterland as a "great extent of meadows which the sea used to cover, and which the Sieur d'Aulnay had drained."[48] Three days before d'Aulnay's death, his parish priest watched him return by canoe from the marshes, "soaked with rain and mud-stained up to his belt and elbows" after a difficult day "planting stakes, tracing lines, and marking off with cords another plot of land to be drained."[49] Perhaps more to the point, many of the original settlers of Acadia, natives of villages surrounding the Marais Poitevin, possessed some understanding of the reclamation of tidal marshland—or, at the very least, they did not reject the idea out of hand, as Poutrincourt and many other Frenchmen did. As a modern marine biologist writes, the first Acadians' exposure to western France's engineered marshes became a "source of [their] conviction that equipped only with an ox, a tiny spade, and a pitchfork, they could exclude the world's highest tides" from the Bay of Fundy's shorelines.[50]

Together, d'Aulnay and his recruits spent the 1640s and 1650s launching an audacious adaptation of European technology to an American environment. Along the streams that flowed into the *rivière* Dauphin near Port Royal, colonists worked in teams. They first planted a foundation of rough-hewn timbers, brush, and sod across the stream's mouth, packing in gaps with impermeable clay. Within this waterproof base, Acadians embedded the all-important sluice. In light of the effort and expense of milling lumber, this often consisted of one or more hollowed-out logs—pipes, essentially. In smaller, family-built dikes, these sluices might be less than twenty feet long and ten inches in diameter. Bigger jobs required multiple logs forty-five feet long and three feet across.[51] On the end pointing toward the bay, workers attached a hinged clapper valve sometimes called an *esseau*, or plank, that allowed for freshwater drainage but snapped shut when the salty tide rose.[52]

The dike was then built on top of this foundation. Its walls were made of unusual material. Marc Lescarbot noticed it during the winter of 1606. While making charcoal, an enterprising blacksmith hacked several blocks of sod out of a marsh near Port Royal to cover some smoldering timbers. Examining the empty pit, Lescarbot discovered that the marsh's floor consisted of "two feet of earth which was not earth, but grasses mixed with silt, which have been heaped upon each other annually since the beginning of the world, without ever having been cut."[53] Stretching over hundreds of acres, carpets of this distinctive sod had been formed by the unchecked growth of *Spartina patens* and *Juncus gerardi*, two hardy, salt-tolerant marine grasses.[54] Their wiry root systems penetrated deep into the soil of the tidal marshes, creating an underground matrix that trapped dirt, clay, sediments, and plant matter.

Using sharp diking spades imported from western France, Acadians took to the marshes, harvesting rectangular blocks, or *gazons*, measuring four by ten inches at the surface and a foot in depth. Their durability stunned observers. Isaac Deschamps, a Swiss migrant to eighteenth-century Nova Scotia, marveled at these grasses "whose roots were so sewn as to keep the Sods almost Solid." Even today, when the clay and sediment is blasted out of a sod block with a power hose, the framing roots retain their shape.[55] Arranging the sods like bricks, Acadians built smooth-faced dike walls up to ten feet high, then packed the structure's center with brush, clay, and more "odd" sods. Likely referencing *abotamentum*, the medieval Latin term for dike, and its various iterations in the dialects of western France, the Acadians called their creations *aboiteaux*.[56]

Perfected in the marshes near Port Royal, the Acadians' *aboiteaux* migrated up the Bay of Fundy as the seventeenth century progressed. Guided by Jacques Bourgeois, a would-be fur trader and cattle rancher who had served as d'Aulnay's surgeon, a handful of families headed for Beaubassin on the Chignecto Isthmus in the early 1670s. In 1676, after the governor-general of New France granted a tract of land to a minor Canadian official, Michel Leneuf de la Vallière, the area became a destination for Acadian migrants searching for farms beyond Port Royal. Making ends meet on the isthmus was hardly easy. In the late 1680s, the bishop of Québec reported that the earliest settlers had been "reduced to living on hay" before catching on to fishing—doubtless with the help of the Mi'kmaq—and protecting the marshes with "dikes they constructed with much labor and expense."[57] Working on the *rivières* Missaguash, au Lac, Tantramar, Memramcook, and Petitcodiac, the first Beaubassin colonists drained hundreds of acres within a generation.

The same process transformed the southern shoreline of the Minas Basin, where small rivers emptied into the Bay of Fundy about seventy miles northeast of Port Royal. Several Acadian families including Landrys, Thériots, and Melansons made their way to Minas in the 1680s. Centered on a village called Grand Pré ("Great Meadow"), their settlements extended the Acadians' mastery of the tides. *Aboiteaux* went up fast. To guard Grand Pré against the *rivière* Gaspereau and the bay itself, Acadians eventually built seventeen and a half miles of dikes equipped with more than thirty sluices. Smaller-scale projects littered the area's other waterways, making Minas, in the words of one French visitor, the prime destination for "all of the young people from Port Royal."[58] Although under constant threat from burrowing muskrats, storms, and tidal surges linked to the eighteen-year Saros astronomical cycle, the *aboiteaux* of Minas were built to last.[59] In 1960, when authorities reinforced the modern Wickwire dike on the western shore of Grand Pré, local farmers insisted on retaining a hand-built Acadian *aboiteau* as a two-hundred-year-old insurance policy.[60]

Contemporaries, though, found much to criticize about the Acadians' methods. After conducting a census of Acadia in 1687 and 1688, the sieur de Gargas advised Louis XIV to "force the inhabitants to clear the higher ground." By his lights, the practice of "building levees in the marshes" produced bad grain and needless risks. Better, Gargas thought, to bear the "initial difficulty" of clearing the forested uplands and graze "an enormous number" of cattle in the marshes.[61] Joseph Robineau de Villebon, Louis XIV's commandant in Acadia during the last decade of the seventeenth century, likewise fretted over what dike building meant for the little colony's culture. Drained sixty years earlier, the marshes around Port Royal were, he admitted in 1699, "very productive, yielding each year a quantity of . . . wheat, rye, peas, and oats, not only for the maintenance of families living there but for sale and transportation to other parts of the country." But the ease with which Acadians constructed *aboiteaux*, Villebon wrote, made the settlers lazy. "If the people were as industrious as the Canadians," he complained, "they would in a short space of time be very well off, but the majority work only when it is absolutely necessary." As anyone knew, uplands were "more reliable" than marshes. Villebon speculated that the hard work of clearance might turn easygoing Acadians into profitable colonists—and if not, he advised ceding the high ground to new migrants or discharged soldiers from France.[62]

This, of course, was nonsense. Marshland settlers from Port Royal to Beaubassin knew by experiment and observation what modern science has confirmed: the upland soils of the Acadian peninsula have been losing nutrients since the glaciers began receding ten thousand years ago, while the Bay of Fundy's flats are replenished daily by silt-rich tides.[63] Whatever political leaders thought of them, these reclaimed lands proved fertile enough to fuel extraordinary demographic expansion. From d'Aulnay's original core of families from Martaizé, La Chaussée, and the Angevin countryside, the population of Acadia grew to nearly fifteen hundred by the end of the seventeenth century. Minas was then on the cusp of outstripping Port Royal, with nearly five hundred inhabitants. Beyond these two major hubs, a few dozen Acadians congregated near Beaubassin, along with smaller groups composed of French settlers, Mi'kmaq bands, and their mixed-race children at various places on the Atlantic coast.[64]

Often cast in Edenic terms ("This land could be a land of plenty," wrote one late seventeenth-century tourist, "if it only had a champagne vineyard"), the Acadians' bayside villages, like all similar-sized European settlements in the New World, had good and bad points.[65] Acadians ate well, aged gracefully, and managed to integrate most French, Irish, English, and even Basque migrants into their little societies with admirable equanimity. But the colony's borderland unpredictability produced its share of rough edges. In 1685, a cleric rambling through the "coasts of Acadia" marveled at discovering "eighty-year-old men who remain unconfirmed."[66] In Beaubassin, the hardy few who heard mass did so in a rudimentary shelter with walls of "cob encased in stone," their heads shielded from the elements by "a roof made only of straw." Worse, complained the bishop of Québec in 1688, the village cemetery sat at some distance from the church, forcing grief-stricken villagers to "carry the bodies across a river for burial."[67]

Life lived close to the bone fostered cooperation, especially when it came to the construction of *aboiteaux*. It also made Acadians acquisitive. Indeed, much of the profit from the meadows in Port Royal, Minas, and Beaubassin went toward imported provisions and manufactured goods, especially those on offer from New Englanders. This illicit trade began in earnest in 1654, when an English fleet commanded by Boston militia officer Robert Sedgwick was diverted from New

Amsterdam, its original target, by news of an Anglo-Dutch peace treaty. Not one to let men and matériel go to waste, Sedgwick attacked Acadia for the purpose, he wrote, of extending Boston's "tradinge and fishinge." He waged successful campaigns against de la Tour's garrison on the Saint John River and, across the bay, Port Royal.[68] Until 1670, when Charles II gave Acadia back to France in exchange for a handful of Caribbean islands, England ruled the Bay of Fundy. That rule never amounted to much. Appointed governor of "Acadie, commonly called Nova Scotia," by Oliver Cromwell, Thomas Temple spent most of his time and energy asserting his personal rights to the fur trade.[69]

The English interregnum fostered commercial links between Massachusetts and the Bay of Fundy. Those links made for strange bedfellows. The aging Charles-Etienne de la Tour and his wife, Jeanne Motin, for example, retired in 1656 to Port Royal, living together in the fine house d'Aulnay and Motin had once shared. Over the next few years, the couple imported "6 looking glasses," cutlery, nails, shot, pots, pans, children's shoes, combs, vinegar, oil, wine, and rum from Joshua Scottow, a prominent Boston merchant.[70] Later in life, Scottow would rail against "the *Beads, Crucifixes, Masses and Processions*" of the Bay Colony's "Popish and Pagan Neighbors," casting all French settlers in North America as followers of "IGNE NATE [*sic*] hell-born LOYOLA."[71] Tough talk, but theological harangues did not stop Boston Protestants and Acadian Catholics from engaging in a freewheeling commerce that would persist for decades, surviving wars, régime changes, and mutual religious bigotry.

The flow of goods and produce up and down the Bay of Fundy made new people as well as new fortunes. In the last quarter of the seventeenth century, a little cadre of Bostonians and Acadians laid the groundwork for a transnational, bilingual, cosmopolitan community that would bind the two colonies even as imperial tensions rose. John Nelson and Jacques Bourgeois were among the first to establish such a friendship. Nelson was Thomas Temple's nephew, and after arriving in Boston in 1670 as a precocious sixteen-year-old he dove headlong into his uncle's Acadian trade. Gamely learning French and Algonquian, Nelson struck deals with the gnarled Bourgeois, who built lumber and flour mills in Beaubassin with Nelson's money. Describing this clandestine commerce as "pretty considerable," one observer lamented the near-constant presence of "three or four boats from Boston" in Acadia's waters. Settlers such as Bourgeois, he noted, sold "furs they purchased from the savages" for "little necessities" (an understatement he later amended, tellingly, to "all supplies").[72] Both Bourgeois and Nelson profited from their intercultural experience. Nelson, who grew rich enough to marry into the family of Massachusetts governor William Stoughton, became well known as an expert on Acadian affairs before turning thirty, while Bourgeois served as an interpreter whenever English-speakers showed up in Port Royal, where he still kept valuable property.[73]

By the end of the seventeenth century, then, the settlers of Port Royal, Minas, and Beaubassin had profitably planted themselves on the narrow ribbon of fertile marshland hugging the Bay of Fundy. Although very much a part of the French Empire, Acadia functioned as an offshoot of the Massachusetts economy. During the 1670s, even governor Hector d'Andigné de Grandfontaine sent for "a New England carpenter to build a few little boats." With relatively few goods making their way from France or Canada, ordinary Acadians too dealt with Bostonians as a matter of course.[74] Although Acadian incomes were almost all modest, social divisions and cliquish behavior tempered frontier egalitarianism. In Port Royal, for example, four prominent families—Boudrot, Bourg, Dugas, and Melanson—intermarried with astonishing frequency, preserving their wealth by excluding all but the best-heeled outsiders.[75]

The people of Acadia, Mi'kmaq natives and European colonists alike, enjoyed an enviable security relative to others in the slender, violent "contact zone" on the Atlantic coast. Their position inspired confidence. "This earth that you tread on," one Mi'kmaq "captain" explained to a French official, "is ours, and nothing can ever force us to abandon it."[76] The Acadians probably thought likewise.

Beginning in the late 1680s, things changed in Acadia. It was a great moment of imperial consolidation and conflict, and like Boston, New York, Québec, and Montréal, the Bay of Fundy was caught up in a long run of invasions, treaty making, and power grabbing. In a sense, Acadians were well equipped to ride out the storm. Literally and figuratively, the dikes held. The ground, however, was shifting beneath their foundations—and the Acadians' feet.

Consider, for example, the story of Claude Petitpas and his family. Born in 1663, Claude was a true child of Acadia. As his father toiled unhappily as Port Royal's court clerk, Claude haunted the creeks and footpaths along the *rivière* Dauphin. He grew up in a settlement distinguished by "the debauchery of most of the inhabitants, who have few scruples about living *à la sauvage*," or in the Indian way.[77] Writing in 1686, this critic might have been talking about Claude, for in that year he married a Mi'kmaw woman named Marie-Thérèse and moved with her to Musquodoboit on Acadia's Atlantic coast.

The couple had seven children before Marie-Thérèse died early in the eighteenth century. The rowdy Petitpas clan spoke Mí'kmawísimk and French, and even picked up English from Massachusetts fishermen who stopped to trade. Over time, Claude became attached to the New Englanders. In 1713, a French captain was forced by a notary in Plaisance (Newfoundland) to pay 800 livres for "a boat belonging to the *sieur* Petitpas that I burned in the harbor at Musquodoboit."[78] Whether this incident was a symptom or a cause of Claude's political mood swing is hard to say. In any case, his behavior became more aggressive in its wake. Four years later, he lent his new schooner to the commander of an Anglo-American expedition against French fishermen at Canso on the northeastern tip of the Acadian peninsula.[79] In 1719, Claude went to Boston. Joseph de Monbeton de Brouillan de Saint-Ovide, governor of Ile Royale, claimed that Massachusetts officials "gave [Claude] a payment of 2,000 livres to draw to them the Indians that are attached to us."[80] Saint-Ovide reacted quickly. He visited Mi'kmaq allies who "appeared angry with how little regard the King pays them," and who had received Petitpas a few months earlier. The governor promised presents of powder, lead, and cloth. Although the Mi'kmaq left "happy enough" and showed no signs of heeding the "propositions Petitpas had made," Saint-Ovide recommended sending scouts to capture the Acadian renegade "and his children."[81]

Those children soon drew the lion's share of interest. The youngest, Isidore, had been born in 1703. At seventeen years old, he got an unexpected offer. In recognition of Claude's "tender regard . . . to sundry English captives," the Massachusetts House of Representatives proposed to bring Isidore to Boston, where he would be housed, fed, and trained as a minister at Harvard.[82] The New Englanders hoped that a converted, educated Isidore, who already "spoke Mi'kmaq better than any interpreter," might "win over the Mi'kmaq nation and make them change religion."[83] The teenager took the bait. But after almost three years in Massachusetts, Isidore vanished. Saint-Ovide later claimed to have "found a way to remove the young man from among the English." Whatever happened, it landed Isidore in Québec, where New France's Catholic bishop "told him that he would be placed in the seminary, where he could study and become a priest." The young Acadian would have none of it. He told the bishop that he "wished only to learn to sail." Fearful that Isidore might "become even more dangerous than his father" if allowed to return home to Musquodoboit, the marquis de Vaudreuil and Michel Bégon, New France's governor-general and intendant, came up with a solution. In the fall of 1722, they coaxed Isidore onto the deck of the *Chameau* and shipped him to Rochefort in western France.[84]

Not quite twenty, Isidore received his second scholarship, this time to study with a "master of hydrography" at the great home base of the French navy. Informed of the situation, the duc d'Orléans, Louis XV's hard-drinking regent, ordered the intendant at Rochefort to buy Isidore's books, lodge him gratis, and give him 50 livres per month for food while ensuring "that he does not escape to an English vessel." It was a good arrangement, but Isidore balked. "He is rebellious," observed one official, "and appears displeased to have been sent to France."[85] After Isidore completed stints as an apprentice pilot aboard the *Héros* and the *Français* in 1723, the character traits that had scuttled his church careers resurfaced. Rochefort's intendant, François de le Chaussaye de Beauharnois, did not mince words: "He is a bad subject who will not devote himself to anything . . . women and wine have ruined him . . . he is so enraged when drunk as to be

capable of some dirty trick." Exasperated, Beauharnois sent Isidore to Martinique as a soldier.[86] Either en route or upon arrival, the young Acadian vanished
for the last time.

Isidore's fate, however, haunted his family. In 1728, Saint-Ovide got wind of a
Mi'kmaq faction "corrupted by two young people, sons of a certain Petitpas . . .
who are much more English than French." He captured the pair (almost certainly Isidore's older brothers Paul and Joseph) and deposited them with a ship's
captain "so that he can hand them over to M. de Beauharnois, intendant at
Rochefort." Saint-Ovide petitioned the minister of the Marine to "give orders
that these two young people never again appear in this country." He cited a
helpful precedent. "About ten years ago," he noted, "one of their brothers was
also sent to France, for more or less the same reason."[87]

The fate of the Petitpas family foreshadowed the forces that would pull thousands of Acadians down Isidore's path to exile. Chief among them was jealousy
at the highest levels of imperial government. Bilingual and at ease among the
Mi'kmaq, Isidore was a hot commodity among the British and French in the
1720s. That interest, however, masked a dark truth: that the extraordinary
measures taken to secure Acadian loyalty would be matched by extraordinary
measures designed to keep Acadians from embracing the other side. Isidore's
exiles came about not because he was unwanted but because he was wanted a
little too much. But as the imperatives of empire shifted, go-betweens like Isidore
(especially those with Isidore's habits) came to be seen as passé, inefficient, and
even dangerous. With colonial populations booming and economies integrating
to the south and west, the gaze (alternately flattering and devastating) of men in
power would be fixed on the marshland farms along the Bay of Fundy.

The stage for both Isidore's theatrics and the drama of 1755, of course, was set
by the British takeover of Acadia. That conquest proceeded in fits and starts. In
1690, the first real expedition against Acadia in four decades left Boston for Port
Royal, where the French governor, Louis-Alexandre des Friches de Meneval,
quickly capitulated. Led by Maine frontiersman William Phips, the attackers
harbored two motives. Some aimed to smash Port Royal as revenge for French
involvement in Iroquois and Abenaki raids on the New England backcountry,
while others hoped to cement old trade partnerships with Acadians by bringing
them into the English fold for good. Phips did neither. After dismantling Port
Royal's fort and raiding the surrounding farms, he left. One week later, a new
French governor arrived.[88]

Subsequent New England campaigns against Acadia came about in the same
way and produced similar results. Emboldened by the overt anti-Catholicism of
William and Mary's régime and provoked by French privateers (and, in 1704, an
infamous French-Mohawk raid on Deerfield, Massachusetts), authorities staged
hit-and-run attacks on Chignecto and Minas.[89] Finally, in 1710, the Tory government

in London sponsored an expedition to conquer the colony once and for all. After a brief skirmish, Samuel Vetch, a Scots adventurer who had spent the last decade in New England, took possession of Port Royal in October, renaming the little settlement Annapolis Royal in honor of the British queen. Nearly three years later, the Treaty of Utrecht ended the War of the Spanish Succession, and confirmed Great Britain's right to what ministers called "all *Nova Scotia or l'Acadie*, comprehended within its antient boundaries."[90]

In one sense, the British seizure of Acadia changed very little. The garrison at Annapolis Royal was underfunded from the beginning and represented no real military threat to outlying settlements at Minas, at Chignecto, and on the Atlantic coast. In 1720, the province's governor called his administration a "mock Government" whose "authority never yet extended beyond Cannon reach" of the fort.[91] For their part, the Mi'kmaq rejected the idea that a treaty between the monarchs of Great Britain and France had any relevance to them. "I have my land that I gave to no one and will never give," one sagamore told a delegation from Massachusetts in 1713. "I know the limits and when someone wishes to live there, he will pay."[92]

In Port Royal, too, trouble beset the conquering administration early on. In 1710, for example, the "principal inhabitants" of Port Royal asked Canadian officials to help them flee, complaining that Vetch "looks on us as mere Negroes." [93] A mass migration looked like a possibility. No fewer than 328 heads of family signed declarations of their intent to migrate "to Ile Royale or other lands under

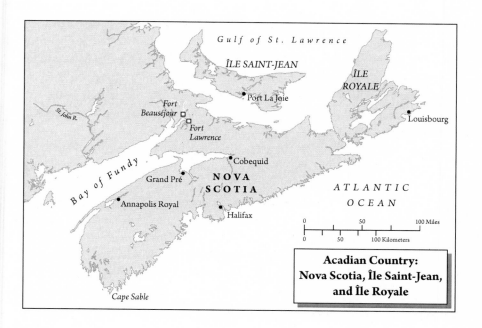

**Acadian Country:
Nova Scotia, Île Saint-Jean,
and Île Royale**

French control" in 1714.[94] In time, affairs under the British settled into a via media between ethnic separatism and political integration. Many Port Royal residents sold their land to British officers or traders and decamped for the countryside, leaving the rest to lament the "Decay and Ruine" of the town's "Empty Uninhabited houses."[95] Marie-Madeleine Maisonnat and Agathe de Saint-Etienne de la Tour, daughters of prominent Port Royal families, stayed home and married Britons, but few followed their example.[96] Although Vetch made no secret of his desire to deport the Acadians, and some Acadians, as "good and true subjects of His Most Christian Majesty," refused to take an oath of allegiance to the British monarch, the colonists' flight from Nova Scotia grew less likely.[97] The Acadians had simply invested too much in their lands on the Bay of Fundy to abandon them. The British in turn valued Acadian subjects as buffers against the still-powerful Mi'kmaq. It was an unsatisfying stalemate, but one that promised a measure of stability.

As New England goods began again to flow up the Bay of Fundy and into the Acadians' villages, Nova Scotia became, as Acadia had been, an economic periphery of Massachusetts at the ragged edge of an expanding empire. Officials at Annapolis Royal dealt gingerly with the Mi'kmaq, blustered at the Acadians' priests, and worked to "gett [the Acadians] over by degrees," subtly adjusting the loyalty oath to absolve them from bearing arms against the French.[98] In the absence of a legislative assembly, the garrison used elected deputies from Minas, Chignecto, and Annapolis Royal to smooth relations with their Acadian subjects. The quality of those relations ebbed and flowed, usually in relation to British dealings with the Mi'kmaq. In 1723, with the British and Mi'kmaq engaged in outright war, Port Royal merchant Prudent Robichaud was accused by two witnesses of visiting some "Enemy Indians" with "a Bagg and Bottle." Robichaud got off with a warning, but in 1725 a similar incident landed him "in Irons and in Prison amongst the Indians . . . in Order to terrify the other Inhabitants from Clandestine Practices."[99] The rough-and-tumble climate was not so different from the French régime, which had its share of problems with natives, clerics, and village ne'er-do-wells.

But as Isidore Petitpas would have testified, the visionary plans spawned by the conquest of Acadia had, in fact, changed everything. Touring the villages of Minas as a crown surveyor in 1720, Paul Mascarene put British aspirations as succinctly as anyone could: "This place," he marveled, "might be made the Granary not only of this Province, but of the neighbouring Governments."[100] Even as the idea of commercial empire swept across the Anglo-American world, smart administrators knew that while the "Galloping Consumption" of British-made goods by colonial subjects turned the system's gears, food supplied the consumers' energy.[101] To Mascarene, a descendant of French Huguenots who made his home in Massachusetts, Nova Scotia's diked fields augured a massive inflow of grain to New England.

Although Mascarene and others might have preferred to import British or German Protestants, new colonists were not forthcoming. The Tory régime in London hoped to manage the conquest of Acadia (and the empire as a whole) on the cheap, and Nova Scotia would have been a tough sell for migrants with land available in better-known places. That meant not just tolerating the Acadian presence but safeguarding it. With "Vast Conveniencys" at stake, Britons knew that "if the French remain in this country, it will tend toward its improvement."[102] As Thomas Pichon later put it, "If the inhabitants left, [the British] could not stay."[103]

Annapolis Royal's officers, then, governed the province via compromises that they hoped would entangle Acadians in a web of British legalities while steering their produce toward a hungry empire. They accepted the Acadians' declarations of political neutrality (after 1730, many even began calling them the "neutral French") and made only half-baked efforts to force the inhabitants of Minas and Chignecto to swear full loyalty to George II on his ascent to the throne in 1727. The British were more aggressive about keeping the Acadians' grain, cattle, and fish from turning up in French markets and mouths instead of British ones. In 1720, Governor Richard Philipps ordered the construction of a storehouse at Annapolis Royal to receive grain "above the supply of each person's family that hath such grain to sell," reserving the surplus for the garrison and "the Indians inhabiting this province who are friends."[104] The funds intended for the storehouse never materialized, while in 1731 a similar project near Grand Pré ended when a group of dagger-wielding Mi'kmaq confronted Acadian René Leblanc and a group of Anglo-American workers, calling them "Dogs and Villains" with "no business There."[105] Subtler British methods of encouraging Acadian productivity proved more effective.

In 1735, for example, the residents of Pisiquid, a hamlet on the southern shores of the Minas Basin, found themselves in a fight with Lawrence Armstrong. A lieutenant governor who would later slash himself to death with his own sword in a fit of despondency, Armstrong had picked up tales of crumbling dikes. He threatened to hold Pisiquid's Acadians responsible for "double the charges of all Dammage & Expense" if British authorities had to repair them, further ordering a crew of "Ancient" inhabitants to inspect the *aboiteaux* annually.[106] The next spring, Armstrong extended both the order and the punishments to all of Nova Scotia.[107] Nor were authorities afraid to nitpick. When, in 1737, Ambroise Breaux complained that brothers Joseph and Alexandre Broussard had neglected some co-owned marshes along the Chipoudy River, Armstrong ordered the shirkers to maintain the dikes or forfeit their property rights.[108] In Annapolis Royal, Philipps harangued Acadians who owned land abutting the garrison in 1724, explaining to "those who . . . would Not Undertake to Repair their Said Marshes" that unless fresh-cut *gazons* found their way into breached dike walls, they belonged to the British crown.[109]

While making decisions aimed at "keeping on the stock of cattle, and the lands tilled," the governor and council also established themselves as arbiters of Acadian land disputes.[110] They did so by charging a pittance for civil litigation. More than 130 suits—most involving two Acadian litigants—came before the council between 1731 and 1736 (his mental state deteriorating, Armstrong feared being drowned in a flood of "frivolous and undigested Complaints").[111] Among them was the case of Alexandre le Borgne, the self-styled "sieur de Bel-ile." Le Borgne had taken an oath of loyalty to the British, in exchange for which the council had given him leave to cut hay and firewood on a plot of "the King's Land" near his Grand Pré home. One day as he exercised the new privilege, his neighbor Charles Richard appeared, spewed insults, and took the hay for himself, "showing the least Regard to the Authority Granted."[112] Summoned to Annapolis Royal to "Show Cause for so much Insolence," Richard arrived with a little girl. Angelique Dugas produced a document signed by her father, who, the pair claimed, had purchased the land in question from Charles de La Tour before the British conquest. The council declared the document void, citing evidence that Richard had "Abandon'd the Province And Retired with his family into the Dominions of France." They ordered him to supply le Borgne with eight loads of hay.[113]

The point of all this, then, was to make Acadians dependent on British insti-tutions while narrowing their economic options to exclude everything but the orderly cultivation and transport of grain along the Bay of Fundy. Thus the smuggling "of Live Cattle & Considerable Quantitys of other provisions" from the pastures of Chignecto to French settlements became a signal offense.[114] So did piracy, which had become something of a tradition among the Mi'kmaq. In 1726, Jean-Baptiste Jedre *dit* Laverdure and four other Mi'kmaq were hanged in Boston for "Piratically and Feloniously" plundering the sloop *Tryal* in the Cum-berland Strait.[115] After that episode, the British tried to ensure that no links per-sisted between Indians like Jedre and their Acadian neighbors. When "Ten or Eleven Indians armed with Guns, Hatchets, & Knives" forced their way aboard Stephen Jones's sloop *Friends' Adventure* near Pisiquid in June 1737, Annapolis Royal seized the opportunity. Jones told the governor that after "threatening to knock his brains out or something to that purpose," the Mi'kmaq made off with £1,500 in goods and beached the ship. The captain walked into the village, where he begged Pisiquid's parish priest, Louis Maufils, and "twenty of the inhabitants" to help him find the culprits. They went along, but "seemed . . . to joke and trifle with the Indians" they met on the way. The Provincial Council ordered Acadian deputies from Minas to explain "why they suffered the foresaid robbery to be committed" and to demand restitution from the guilty Mi'kmaq, "otherwise they will be liable themselves to make good [Jones's] loss."[116] Laying aside the nomadic, militaristic, and illicit ways of the Mi'kmaq (and those of old relics such as the Petitpas family), Nova Scotia's Acadians were best off cultivating their gardens.

The French thought so too. The takeover of Acadia, compounded by the loss of the settlement at Plaisance in Newfoundland in the Treaty of Utrecht, turned France's attention toward Ile Royale and Ile Saint-Jean, the kingdom's two remaining possessions near the mouth of the Saint Lawrence River and the fisheries of the Grand Banks. By 1719, the French began to build the fortress of Louisbourg near Ile Royale's finest Atlantic harbor. But before that project got under way, officials pressured Acadian farmers. Ile Royale's first governor, Philippe de Pastour de Costebelle, told Nova Scotia's remaining "missionaries" to detail for Acadians the "peril" of life among the British, "who will treat [you] as slaves even if [you] change religion."[117] Drawing *aboiteau*-builders to Louisbourg, however, proved a nonstarter. Although Costebelle described Acadians as "absolutely determined to come over," the absence of tidal marshes and abundance of rocky soil turned them off. Only a few fishermen emigrated after 1713.[118] Although disappointed, officials never lost sight of their designs on the Acadians: "The important thing," wrote Jacques L'Hermitte, an engineer on Ile Royale, "is that they should leave Acadia."[119]

For Ile Saint-Jean, perhaps. According to its boosters, the island had every natural advantage. There were "pine trees to make masts . . . boards and beams," a fishery that netted "450 *quintals* per vessel" (a haul "never before seen in Newfoundland or Louisbourg"), "caribou as big as deer" in the forests, and "ground proper to grow all kinds of grain." So said Robert-David Gotteville de Belile, agent of the comte de Saint-Pierre, in 1721. The crown had given Ile Saint-Jean to Saint-Pierre in 1719 on the condition that he plant a colony, and Gotteville reported that migrants arrived "every day from Acadia."[120] He exaggerated. Families came from the Bay of Fundy in an intermittent trickle, gathering at Port-la-Joie, Tracadie, and Trois Rivières. Still, hope endured. "In my opinion," wrote Saint-Ovide in 1725, "this is the only place that will draw the inhabitants of Acadia."[121] "The soil is perfectly good," noted the career navy man, and he hired Félix Pain, once a parish priest in Nova Scotia, to help "attract Acadians to this island."[122] Those who bought Pain's pitch (something like two hundred by 1728) struggled mightily. "I saw with regret the damage done to the wheat of these miserable settlers by some kind of Rat," wrote Saint-Ovide after a visit in 1728. "I do not know how they will survive the winter."[123] And yet the island conjured visions. It could be, wrote a later administrator, unwittingly echoing Paul Mascarene, "the granary of Louisbourg," an Acadian-farmed provisioner for the hub of France's Atlantic empire.[124]

Still, Acadian migration remained a tough sell for the French well into the 1740s. Aside from the superiority of the Bay of Fundy marshes to lands on Ile Saint-Jean or Ile Royale, many Acadians could truthfully describe the British government at Annapolis Royal as "gentle and peaceful."[125] To be sure, there were tense moments, most of which involved confrontations between truculent garrison officers and equally truculent priests from France. But with their status as "neutrals" well established and, after 1740, the pragmatic, French-speaking Mascarene installed as lieutenant governor (no pushover, but a man who could amicably debate "the doctrine of the reformed Churches" with learned French missionaries), Acadians had few compelling reasons to pack up.[126]

The War of the Austrian Succession (King George's War in the British colonies), however, triggered important changes to British policy in Nova Scotia, which in turn pushed the French to press harder on the Acadians. In the summer of 1744, just weeks after authorities in Louisbourg learned of France's declaration of war on Great Britain, they instructed the abbé Jean-Louis le Loutre, then a missionary at Shubenacadie, to organize a Mi'kmaq assault on Annapolis Royal. The fort was, in Mascarene's words, "a patch'd up unfinished place . . . little better than a heap of rubbish," commanded by a dozen officers "not above two or three who ever had seen a gun fir'd in anger." But with timely help from a warship from Boston, Mascarene fended off le Loutre and the Mi'kmaq in June and a much larger force of French troops, Mi'kmaq and Maliseet warriors, and a few Acadian recruits in August.[127]

After celebrating these improbable victories, Mascarene started thinking about the behavior of local Acadians. When the Mi'kmaq departed in June, Acadians had offered up "building materials and fresh provisions with more chearfulness than formerly"—not out of kindness, he now believed, but in the expectation that the British would quickly surrender the now-repaired fort to the French during the next assault. Mascarene also noted that Annapolis Royal's Acadians had "frequented the Enemies Quarters at their Mass, prayers, dancing and all other ordinary occasions" and, after the French forces departed, had gouged the garrison for food and wood.[128] As one of the first to see the value of Acadian farms to the emerging British Empire, Mascarene was stung by the events of 1744. The idea of losing the agricultural bounty he himself had helped foster was almost too much to bear. In 1745, he advised that the Acadians be driven from "the Province of NOVA SCOTIA and replac'd by good Protestant subjects."[129]

That prospect edged closer to reality as King George's War came to Louisbourg. Designed according to the principles of the great military engineer Sébastien le Prestre, marquis de Vauban, the fortress on Ile Royale appeared impregnable. Its inhabitants "did not fear all the World," as one observer put it.[130] But Louisbourg's bravado masked its dependence on goods from Massachusetts and food from the Bay of Fundy. So when, in the spring of 1745, four thousand men and one hundred ships from Boston besieged and blockaded the fortress for seven weeks, the French capitulation was understandable, but still a real feat. As one pamphleteer wrote, the New Englanders "said, *They could take it, and they would take it, and* (to the Surprize and Wonder of all the World) *they did take it!*" [131] In 1748, however, the conquerors' elation turned to exasperation as British negotiators returned Louisbourg, along with the whole of Ile Royale (known to the British as Cape Breton Island) to the French. In modern terms, the concession became a public relations fiasco, and not just in Massachusetts. "France will avail herself more by our restoring Cape Breton," roared one English critic, than if "left in Possession of all the Territories . . . acquired on the continent."[132]

To counteract Louisbourg, the British founded the town and naval base of Halifax in 1749, planting an initial cohort of three thousand colonists on Chebucto Bay, not far from Isidore Petitpas's old home at Musquodoboit. The crown's choice of Edward Cornwallis to head up the Halifax project and become the new governor of Nova Scotia signaled geopolitical seriousness. Cornwallis had earned his military stripes during the bloody repression of rebelling Scots Highlanders a few years earlier and had no qualms about playing similarly rough with the French. He indicated as much upon meeting Mascarene, explaining to the francophone ex-governor that he was "too old and crazy" to be of much use in the new, Halifax-centered province.[133]

Beyond reorienting the geography of empire on the Atlantic coast, Halifax had another, double-edged function: to reduce British dependence on Acadian agriculture while simultaneously diminishing the Acadians' ability to ship their agricultural surplus anywhere *except* outposts of the British Empire. Both were tall orders. Touted by boosters for its "natural Richness," the soil of Halifax turned out to be unforgiving, acidic, and thin. As late as 1762, a visitor reported that there was not "one Family in the town nor in the parts Circumjacent that subsist[ed] by Husbandry."[134] Accounts of rural plenty ("Lobsters . . . as thick as stones in Cheapside" and "Rum at 3s. a gallon," blared the *Boston Gazette*) faded as Halifax's inhabitants ("The worst scoundrels of each nation / Whores, rogues & thieves, the dregs and skum of vice," according to one anonymous poet) settled into the eastward-looking routines of a resource-poor naval station.[135] Measured by the alarm it produced among French authorities, Halifax's new régime was much more successful at limiting the flow of Acadian grain and cattle toward Louisbourg. Already in 1749 Louis XV's ministers were fretting over Cornwallis's "very severe prohibitions against [the Acadians] furnishing . . . livestock or anything else" to Ile Royale.[136]

Gilles Hocquart and Charles de la Boische, marquis de Beauharnois, the intendant and governor-general of New France, had mapped out a response to these sorts of events in Nova Scotia long before Cornwallis's arrival. Acadians, they argued in 1745, wanted to become subjects of France. The proof was in their Bay of Fundy homes: "wretched wooden boxes, without conveniences, and without ornaments." This squalor (fabricated, of course, by Hocquart and Beauharnois, who knew almost nothing about the Acadians' standard of living) was rooted not in poverty but in the Acadians' practice of hoarding the French specie they received in Louisbourg while trading provisions. "What object can they have" in stinting themselves, the two leaders guessed, "except to secure for themselves a resource" for the day when Louis XV's money would be their currency once again? Best to speed the arrival of that day by offering Acadians free land on Ile Saint-Jean, the produce of which might be shipped to Louisbourg without any interference; if they balked, "all difficulties would be overcome by the employment of threats and force."[137]

For "threats and force," the French turned again to the abbé le Loutre. He was in an aggressive mood. After the failed 1744 assault on Annapolis Royal, le Loutre had returned to France. His ship was captured during its return voyage to Louisbourg in 1746, leaving the Spiritan missionary to survive in British prisons, where he took the name Rosanvern to conceal his true identity. Back in Nova Scotia in 1749, le Loutre received orders to head not for his old mission at Shubenacadie in the interior but to Pointe Beauséjour on the Chignecto Isthmus, carrying with him a mandate to "attract as many Acadian families as possible, and profit from the disgust . . . that English operations cannot help but cause among them."[138] According to his enemy Thomas Pichon, le Loutre held a week-long series of interviews at Beauséjour with Acadians from as far off as Annapolis Royal, compiling a detailed list of "fathers of families, children, and even livestock" in each of the Bay of Fundy settlements and sending it, along with a request for "ships to transport all of these inhabitants," to Versailles. That winter, he traveled through Beaubassin, Pisiquid, and Minas, proclaiming to Acadians that if they "stayed on their lands, the English would do to them what they did to the Irish, making them slaves and depriving them of . . . all spiritual succor."[139]

Le Loutre's tactics worked, but not fast enough to suit him. In Annapolis Royal, Mascarene reported that Acadians along the *rivière* Dauphin "are wavering butt dare not separate themselves from the herd," which, for the time being, seemed to be staying in Nova Scotia.[140] During the spring of 1750, le Loutre and his allies flexed their muscles. A group of Mi'kmaq accosted and beat René Leblanc, the pro-British notary from Minas who had butted heads with the Mi'kmaq over the Grand Pré grain magazine back in 1731. For good measure, le Loutre sent René's son Simon to Québec as a "messenger," only to have him jailed upon arrival.[141]

Far from the reach of Halifax's authority, residents of Beaubassin endured even worse. In April, a flotilla of British ships commanded by lieutenant governor Charles Lawrence made its way up the Bay of Fundy to arrest le Loutre as a "public Incendiary." Ironically, given the language of their instructions, they found Beaubassin engulfed in flames. After the British disembarked near the smoldering buildings, "two peasants" scrambled up a dike just to their west and waved a white flag. They did not want a truce. Rather, the Acadians explained, they had been "order'd to plant the Flag on that spot as being the Boundary of the French King's Territories." Surveying the panorama, the British saw that the dike was "lined with Indians from the sea on one end to a thick wood that flanked it on the other," and that le Loutre, a small detachment of Canadian troops, and Beaubassin's entire population were arrayed behind the Mi'kmaq, trudging for Point Beauséjour.[142] Unable to stop them, Lawrence and his men clawed their way to a spot to the east of the Missaguash, where they laid the foundations of Fort Lawrence. To Louis XV, the British ambassador protested that the Acadians "declare openly their abhorrence of these proceedings; but . . . Loutre threaten[s] them with a general massacre of the Indians." The French claimed Acadian complicity, declaring reports of le Loutre's wrongdoing "exaggerated."[143]

The burning of Beaubassin was demographic engineering at its purest. While the rival crowns argued over who owned the mainland west of Chignecto, the French took pains to turn hard-won Acadian labor to their advantage.[144] The exodus across the Missaguash to Pointe Beauséjour seemed to open a floodgate. Of the 2,223 inhabitants of Ile Saint-Jean counted by the sieur de la Roque in 1752, 1,300 had arrived between 1749 and 1751, with 862 in 1750 alone. Scrambling to organize the migrants, military leaders from Port-la-Joie in the south to Trois-Rivières in the east banned fishing, forcing Acadians to clear and farm the land. They meant business, as Marie Boudrot discovered. The "very poor" widow of Pierre Richard and mother of six lived on land granted to her "verbally" in 1750 by Claude-Elisabeth Denys de Bonnaventure, the commandant of Ile Saint-Jean. In time, however, Bonnaventure noted that Boudrot's family had made "no improvements," and so reclaimed the plot in 1752.[145]

At Pointe Beauséjour, Acadian workmen set to re-creating their homeland. They toiled on the ramparts of what would become Fort Beauséjour, framed houses for French officers, and began building *aboiteaux* and drying marshes below. The goal was rustic self-sufficiency: a kind of inland Louisbourg fed by Acadian farmers settled on the tidal inlets west of the Missaguash. French officials worked hard to give the impression of permanence. Le Loutre sent for a collection of "ornaments, sacred vases, . . . candle-sticks, incense burners, lamps, altar decorations, with boxes and bales of books of devotion of every variety." To house his curios, he attracted "a number of people from Minas and Port Royal" to help construct "a magnificent church with aisles, planned like the Cathedral of Quebec, and differing little in grandeur." While that church rose behind Fort Beauséjour, le Loutre organized and supervised the construction of "a remarkable dyke . . . which would provide an area of land more than sufficient for 100 barrels of seed." Versailles gave the priest 50,000 livres to complete the project, which was to have arched across the *rivière* Aulac, drying the massive Tantramar marshes. Although a "terrible tide" broke through the half-built sluices sometime after 1753, the dike—which le Loutre saw as a "necessity . . . in order to be able to settle all the French people who were living near the English forts"—was nearing completion by the summer of 1755.[146]

Le Loutre described these goings-on in biblical terms salted with self-satisfaction. The "esteem, veneration and respect in which he was held" by the Acadian transplants of Chignecto, he claimed, stemmed from his devotion to "the work of Joseph (in Egypt)."[147] After interpreting Pharaoh's dream, that ancient prophet had "gathered corn as the sand of the sea" during seven plentiful years along the Nile, forcing "all countries" to buy grain from Egypt's storehouses when seven years of famine hit—an evocative statement of France's imperial intentions in Nova Scotia's borderlands.[148] No less partial to biblical imagery (he nicknamed le Loutre "Moses" for his role in the exodus from Beaubassin), Thomas Pichon saw firsthand how the French drive for food weighed on Acadians. It was a drive he understood well, even before his arrival at Fort Beauséjour in 1753. Two years earlier, Pichon had helped review a proposal to move Acadians from Ile Saint-Jean to the shores of Lake Bras d'Or in the interior of Ile Royale, where heads of family could expect free land and a ban on "hunting for pelts," a pursuit that threatened to spoil relations with the Mi'kmaq and "distract inhabitants from work that would be more lucrative to them and more advantageous for the colony."[149] The plan never came to fruition, but Pichon, in his way, continued to mull over France's displacement of Acadians.

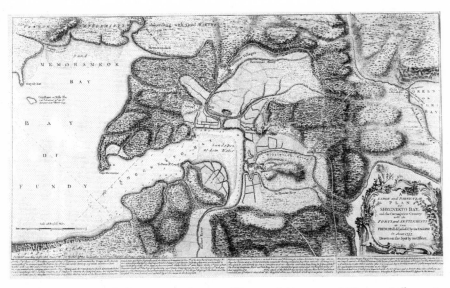

A British depiction of Chignecto on the eve of the *grand dérangement*. Thomas Jeffreys, *A Large and Particular Plan of Shegnekto Bay* (1755). Courtesy of the Museum of New Brunswick, Saint John.

Upon reaching Fort Beauséjour, Pichon began to act as a conduit, communicating France's agrarian designs to the Acadians and relaying Acadian concerns back to French administrators. In February 1754, Pichon wrote to Ange de Menneville, marquis Duquesne, governor-general of New France, attaching four "requests" from local Acadians. In exchange for labor and loyalty, they demanded "provisions for three years," another state-subsidized dike near Fort Beauséjour to allow for the culture of hay, tools with which to "clear the land . . . and build houses," and furniture and clothing. He told Duquesne to grant their wishes, as "the English continue to use any means to try to bring them back to their old homes, where from the first year they would be sure to harvest more than they needed to subsist." Many Acadians had considered such a move until, as Pichon recounted, he assured them that they would "never have Missionaries" and that Louis XV "would abandon them to their sorry lot with no hope of rescue."[150]

Pichon could be stern, but he also gave voice to the Acadians' emerging sense of inhabiting an imperial marketplace for labor. To Antoine-Louis Rouillé, Louis XV's secretary of state for the marine, he painted an afflicting picture. The Acadians' fields near Fort Beauséjour lay fallow, Pichon reported, plowmen and dike builders "having been . . . continually in arms to prevent the English from descending upon them, pillaging them or making other efforts even more dangerous to the interests of the State." Six thousand head of cattle had perished "before their eyes," as service to the government allowed them time to "mow, dry, and profit from only a portion of their hay." Worse, an oppressively small salt ration had prevented them from preserving beef from their dead animals. Impoverishment put Acadians and French administrators in a bind. As Pichon wrote, "The promises made to them by the Crown . . . are today put to a harsh test, especially in light of the flattering offers that the English have made them." Without food, supplies, and money, "it will be impossible to retain them, and . . . equally useless to inspire . . . those still under English domination to leave the interior of Acadia." If the right cards were not played, Pichon warned, France would lose these "11 to 12,000 subjects . . . necessary to establish and people" a key front in the long-simmering conflict with Great Britain.[151]

Pichon's turn of phrase—"11 to 12,000 subjects"—expressed the very notion that would lead to the Acadians' expulsion. By his lights, *all* Acadians were implicated in French efforts to create agricultural communities in Chignecto and Ile Saint-Jean. Like his counterparts in Halifax, Pichon believed that in the end, every last Acadian cultivator would need to live on one side of the Missaguash or the other, their diked marshes either provisioning the French and their Mi'kmaq allies or sustaining the British to the south. No exceptions, no neutrality, no middle ground. For the Acadians, as for André Boudin *dit* Blondain, the food that animated Europe's empires had become poison.

* * *

The endgame was brutally straightforward.

In late 1754, on the heels of a French victory over the young George Washington at Fort Necessity in southwestern Pennsylvania, the British laid plans to strike at forts in the Ohio Valley, northern New York, and the Chignecto Isthmus. Even more aggressive ideas cropped up in the provincial council in Halifax. After the departures of Cornwallis, who left in October 1752, and his successor, Peregrine Hopson, who lasted only a year due to eye disease, Charles Lawrence assumed control of the government in 1753. Immediately he hired Charles Morris, a Massachusetts-born surveyor, to plan the removal of the Acadians.[152] Morris, whose career as a soldier and geographer had made him familiar with the ins and outs of riverine agriculture on the Bay of Fundy, grasped the rationale as well as anyone: so long as Acadians controlled "the chief granary of the country [and] all water communication," Nova Scotia would never be secure. Based on his own experience in Chignecto, Lawrence believed that the French would *always* siphon away Acadian hands, crops, and cattle. Given that reality, he was determined to follow Morris's plan to "destroy all these settlements by burning down all their houses, cutting their dykes, and destroying all the grain growing." Once the devastation was complete, the Acadians would be "transported they know not wither."[153]

As part of the coordinated British campaign against the French, Massachusetts governor William Shirley (who had, back in 1744, fantasized about torching Chignecto, ripping the clapper valves from the Acadians' *aboiteaux*, and ruining the "Granary of those Parts . . . from which the French . . . receiv'd Seasonable Supplies of Fresh Provisions") issued orders in January 1755 to raise a regiment for the attack on Fort Beauséjour.[154] Under the command of John Winslow, an old-stock New Englander with an impressive military pedigree, two thousand young men left the docks and fields of Massachusetts for the Bay of Fundy in May, meeting up with nearly three hundred British regulars led by Robert Monckton. With help from Pichon's intelligence, the Anglo-Americans blasted across the Missaguash on June 4 and began digging trenches opposite the fort. After ten days and a lucky mortar shot, it was over. Busy with the mop-up minutiae of the capitulation, the threat of Mi'kmaq retaliation, and the search for le Loutre (who, after escaping via the fort's back entrance, was caught at sea and spent the next eight years jailed on the island of Jersey), Winslow and Monckton received word from Lawrence in late July. Since Chignecto Acadians had defended Fort Beauséjour, and since the deputies from Minas and Annapolis Royal continued to waffle over taking an oath of allegiance, he wrote, "the whole people . . . shall be removed out of the Country as soon as possible."[155]

It was no half-baked campaign. With Shirley, Lawrence helped plan the attack on Fort Beauséjour, almost certainly viewing it as a chance to put Morris's plan into action across Nova Scotia. Although the process of arresting and deporting civilians seemed a "heavy burthen" to Winslow and his compatriots, they proceeded with vicious efficiency. At Grand Pré, Winslow lured disarmed Acadian men into their parish church under false pretenses. After informing them of his "Melancholly" duty, the New Englander barred the doors and turned the Acadians' holy place into a holding pen, coercing the village's women and children into feeding imprisoned husbands and fathers with the fruits of one last dikeland harvest.

From Annapolis Royal to Pisiquid, similar ruses netted scores of Acadians. When ruses failed, muscle prevailed. Captain Abijah Willard, for example, stormed into tiny Tatamagouche on the northern shore of Chignecto in August of 1755, capturing the men while leaving their terrified families behind. Marching back toward Fort Beauséjour, shackled prisoners in tow, Willard stopped at the home of a nameless Acadian couple. The husband, he reported, treated him "very hansom," while the wife "Toock on very much att [the] Defecultys" of her countrymen.[156] By November, a flotilla of twenty-two repurposed merchant ships had arrived, half from Halifax and half from the Boston firm of Apthorp and Hancock. As winter settled over Nova Scotia, seven thousand Acadians were crammed inside, where they could only imagine their villages and farms, secured by the enduring *aboiteaux*, receding into the distance.

To be sure, there were glitches. On the "Stormy Dark Night" of October 1, 1755, eighty-six Acadians "dugg under ye wall" at Fort Lawrence "& Got Clear undiscovered by ye Centery," while in December two hundred captives from Annapolis Royal subdued the crew of the Maryland-bound *Pembroke*, sailed to the mouth of the St. John River, and escaped to Québec after burning the vessel and handing the sailors over to the startled commander of a French detachment.[157] In all, seven thousand Acadians managed to elude this first Anglo-American sweep through Nova Scotia. Three thousand headed for Ile St. Jean, while the rest fled overland into Canada or hid in the woods.

In the main, however, the expulsion of the Acadians unfolded as one of the smoothest, most successful applications of power in the history of the British Empire. Michel Chartier de Lotbinière, marquis de Lotbinière, admitted as much in 1756. As the engineer toiled to build Fort Carillon near the rapids-laced junction of Lake Champlain and Lake George in present-day upstate New York, he explained to officials at Versailles that the "English have deprived us of a great advantage by removing the French families" of Nova Scotia. Should the king ever contemplate retaking the province, he lamented, "we would have to make new settlements" without Acadian labor and expertise. And that, Lotbinière knew, was impossible.[158]

Acadians, however, experienced the events of 1755 without Lawrence's sense of overarching strategy or Lotbinière's expansive vision of geopolitics. Instead, they saw the *grand dérangement*'s beginning as they had seen forty previous years of settlement, migration, and resettlement—dimly, through a thousand separate pinholes, perceiving only fleeting elements of the whole. To take the measure of what they endured, then, is to be wrenched through disjointed snapshots of confusion, anguish, and weary resolve.

One such snapshot comes courtesy of Josiah Gorham, a British ranger charged in 1758 with "extirpating and destroying the French & their Effects" at Cape Sable, an out-of-the-way Acadian settlement on Nova Scotia's southeastern shore. When he arrived that fall, Gorham found fields "all manur'd and full of potatoes and other Vegetables," but no Acadians. After three weeks of fruitless searching, he stumbled upon "a Village in the Midst of the Woods," the makeshift home of sixty Acadians and their priest, the abbé Jean-Baptiste de Gay Desenclaves. After squeezing what intelligence he could from them, Gorham cast about for other Acadian "safe places," finding one whose residents had left "in a precipitate Manner, leaving a letter on a Pole with a red flag importing their Determination not to surrender" without assurances of safety. Frustrated, Gorham started lighting fires. He burned the Acadians' "dwelling houses" and barns, as well as "sixty thousand head of Cabbages, Potatoes, and other Vegetables" and "innumerable" cattle—enough, he marveled, to feed more than "ten times the Number of People" who lived there.[159]

Far from the Acadians' Bay of Fundy heartland, Gorham's arson conveyed the twisted outcome of the imperial contest for calories in Nova Scotia. Still, the notion of Acadians as imperial agriculturalists died hard. In 1757, even as the Seven Years' War turned sour for the French, the abbé de l'Isle-Dieu confidently declared that Ile Saint-Jean would soon become a "land of wheat" if only the "new Acadians" who had flocked to Louis XV's standards were properly motivated.[160] It was a sensibility born of desperation, and as the Acadians came to understand, it would follow them—*stalk* them—to the ends of the earth.

The Pariahs

Therefore shalt thou serve thine enemies which the Lord shall send against thee, in hunger, and in nakedness, and in want of all things, and he shall put a yoke of iron upon thy neck, until he have destroyed thee.
—Deuteronomy *28:48*

Vermin.

Elisha Stoddard knew them well. As a selectman in Woodbury, a village near the Housatonic River in western Connecticut, he spent more time than he liked with the town poor and their microscopic entourages. Still, Stoddard encountered a case in the winter of 1756 that proved noteworthy. It involved "an old man of 76 years of age and upward" and his seven grandchildren. All were "of the Neutral French [Acadians] sent into this province by Governor Lawrence," and had been hustled to Woodbury by the government in Hartford. They had suffered terribly. Malnourished and "full of vermin," the children, five from one set of parents and two from another, had "by some way and means" been separated from both families early in the 1755 strike against the Acadians. Unwilling to keep the wretched cousins together, Stoddard "put the Children out" to joiners, farmers, and other masters in Woodbury. The youngsters, he reported, took quickly to English "modes," "books," and "business," abandoning French for the language of their schoolmates. As the grandfather wasted away, Woodbury seemed to be on the cusp of subsuming its allotment of Acadians—until January 2, 1757, when four skeletal adults staggered into town and, with "great joy," sought out their seven lost children, clutched them to their ruined bodies, and refused to let go.

"Naked and destitute . . . and withal having the itch, vermin, etc.," the four strangers had completed a remarkable journey. As the Acadian father Paul Landry told Woodbury's leaders, the two couples had arrived in Annapolis, Maryland, from Nova Scotia late in 1755. They spent the next year pestering officials for permission to search for their families, "but [were] denied till at length the Governor sent to them that he had heard their Children was in the

Colony of Connecticut and gave them a pass." The document, Landry explained, had been lost "in the fatigues of their journey," which included ocean voyages to Martha's Vineyard and New London, followed by eighty frigid miles overland to Woodbury.

But Landry's "fatigues" were far from over. Although Stoddard provided a house and a few necessities for the new arrivals, he returned the children to their masters while awaiting orders from Hartford. Landry would not stand for it. He somehow spirited all seven children from their homes in Woodbury to his own shabby lodgings. Confronted there by local authorities, the frantic father "refused to let [the children] return . . . by any argument whatsoever." Citing the parents' "indigent Circumstances" and the crucial "business" of child labor, Woodbury's selectmen separated the families "by force." To Stoddard's eye, this action turned "much to the joy of the children," who soon resumed their "peaceable" routines of work and school.[1] Days later, Stoddard shipped Paul Landry and his wife to nearby New Milford, a town whose leaders had not yet shared "the burden of supporting the French . . . nor tasted the Sweets of having to deal with any of said people." In May of 1757, Landry wrote to Connecticut's General Assembly asking that his children, now seven and five years old, be allowed to join him.[2] The government's response has not survived.

For Elisha Stoddard, Acadians proved doubly offensive. They not only served as hosts for vermin but were themselves parasites, sapping resources from Woodbury in a time of war. Stoddard's actions, however, surely made his soul uneasy. Paul Landry, he later wrote, had undertaken the kidnappings "through zeal to [his] Religion." Concerned for the souls of his own eight children, Stoddard knew the bonds of faith and family well.

His grandfather was Solomon Stoddard, the Puritan divine whose adoption of the liberalizing Half-Way Covenant rocked late seventeenth-century Boston's ecclesiastical establishment. Solomon had been the stepfather-in-law of John Williams, a fellow "Minister of the Gospel" taken captive in the 1704 French and Indian raid on the western Massachusetts town of Deerfield. Williams recounted his wintertime march to Montréal, his sore trials among "so many *Romish Ravenous Wolves*," and his bittersweet homecoming in a best-selling pamphlet entitled *The Redeemed Captive Returning to Zion*.[3] His seven-year-old daughter Eunice, however, remained in Canada, unredeemed despite many missions to bring her home. From the 1740s through the early 1750s, Eunice (now known as Marguerite A'ongote Gannenstenhawi, a combination of her Catholic and Mohawk names) visited New England several times with her Mohawk husband, François-Xavier Arosen. Their presence caused a sensation up and down the Connecticut River Valley, provoking sermons and prayers for Marguerite's soul. Elisha Stoddard could easily have been in the "numerous Audience" that, in the summer of 1741, packed the meetinghouse in Mansfield, Connecticut, to gawk at their lost child Marguerite and her "Indian" children. In 1757, did Elisha think of Eunice's fate and his family's ordeal as Paul Landry scrambled to lay hold on his children in Woodbury?[4]

Apparently not—at least not in any way that made him particularly sympathetic. And there were more memories to brush aside. In the 1730s, Elisha's cousin Jonathan Edwards had transformed their grandfather Solomon's ministry in Northampton into a global concern, using print to spread fear of sin to the ends of the earth.[5] Elisha was likely in attendance when, in 1750, Edwards stood at Solomon's pulpit in Northampton and delivered a sermon entitled *The Justice of God in the Damnation of Sinners*. In it, he compared his self-satisfied generation of New Englanders to "filthy vermin feeding with delight upon rotten carrion."[6]

Harsh words. Had they returned to Elisha's mind as he watched tiny pests feast on Paul Landry's blood or as he plucked Landry himself from Woodbury like a burrowing tick, they might have prompted some uncomfortable reflections about justice, hypocrisy, and who, in truth, was devouring whom.

All across the British Empire, Acadians such as Paul Landry and Britons such as Elisha Stoddard looked on each other through eyes jaundiced by theological suspicion, cultural bigotry, and wartime anxiety. Worse, the refugees and their hosts harbored very different mandates and motivations when it came to the practical side of the *grand dérangement*. Back in Nova Scotia, Charles Lawrence had intended the expulsion of 1755 to shatter the links holding Acadian society together. In a letter to fellow provincial governors, Lawrence rejoiced that the deportees could not "easily collect themselves together again," thus short-circuiting their ability "to do any Mischief."[7] Security likewise mattered to men like Elisha Stoddard. So did money. Uncertain as to who, ultimately, would pay for the Acadians' upkeep, they attempted captivity on the cheap. This sort of penny-pinching took many forms. Often it placed obstacles in the path to what seemed to be the Acadians' only goal: the reunification of families.

Out of malice, carelessness, and the complexity of a massive operation, British troops had separated dozens of Acadians from spouses, children, and other relatives in the fall of 1755. Upon the refugees' arrival in British North America, many worked relentlessly to find their loved ones. Some, such as brothers Pierre and Michel Bastarache, escaped through thousands of miles of American backcountry, reaching their friends and family who had found refuge in Canada.[8] Others used newspapers. The March 1, 1756, edition of the *Boston Gazette*, for example, sought the whereabouts of Alexis Breau, Joseph Vincent, and three other men whose wives had landed in Massachusetts, but who had themselves "been sent to some of His Majesty's Colonies to the Southward."[9] Others made do with the virtual communion of letters. In September of 1757, Joseph Leblanc wrote from Liverpool, England, to his brother Charles in Southampton. Joseph's "dear wife" had "left this world to go to the other" after a long illness. "In tears," he reminded Charles to say hello to his uncle Charles Richard, his aunt Marguerite Comeau, his friend Jean-Jacques Thériot, and "all the Neutral French in general."[10]

Writing in the pained, phonetic French of an eighteenth-century peasant, Joseph Leblanc expressed an idea that now dominates most accounts, popular and scholarly, of the *grand dérangement*: that as they slowly reassembled their families, Acadians rebuilt and strengthened the ethnic community they had known back in Nova Scotia. Exile and absence instilled an even deeper "sense of communal solidarity," prompting refugees everywhere to assert their "cultural integrity" in the face of powerful, corrosive forces arrayed against it.[11] The story of the *grand dérangement*, then, is the story of the parental instinct that drew Paul Landry to Woodbury writ large. As one historian puts it, the Acadians' shared

identity, strengthening as it flexed against resistance applied by the British Empire, "allowed a considerable number of those sent into exile to endure as a community."[12]

Focusing so much on the sameness of Acadian selves, however, risks giving short shrift to the diversity of their destinations. To be sure, the Acadians' reception across the British Empire was shaped by certain commonalities—notably a shared, shrill strain of Anglo-American anti-Catholicism, but also a legal culture that placed a special premium on the humane treatment of war captives. The former was forged in eighteenth-century nation building, the latter in the psychological crucible of colonial warfare fought against (and, at times, with) Native Americans and other non-Europeans. Eager to define barbarism and then distance themselves from it, mid-eighteenth-century writers styled the care of prisoners "one of the *Capital Laws* of *war* among *civiliz'd Nations*," the abandonment of which threatened to unleash "the *scalping Knife*," "Cruelties of *cool Blood*," and "every other *Torture* inflicted by the *Savage*," leading to wars "carried on not by *Men* but by *Monsters*."[13] When it came to French captives during the Seven Years' War, civility often battled xenophobia to a draw. In 1759, for example, Londoners collected 3,131 greatcoats, 2,034 waistcoats, 3,054 pairs of breeches, 6,146 shirts, 3,006 caps, 3,134 pairs of stockings, and 3,185 pairs of shoes for "Frenchmen, Prisoners of War and Naked." Contributors included the "Grand Association of the Laudable Order of Antigallicans" and George Whitefield, a celebrity evangelist who, in 1756, had compared French Catholics to "ravenous Wolves pursuing the harmless and innocent . . . Protestant prey."[14] Colliding all across the British Empire, these two sentiments seemed to promise a similar, if not identical, reception for the first Acadian exiles.

But imperial uniformity was blunted by pervasive localism. For Anglo-Americans from Boston to Savannah, the expulsion triggered a refugee crisis unlike any they had ever seen. In Massachusetts, which would receive nearly two thousand refugees from Nova Scotia, the onset of another war between Great Britain and France spurred Anglo-Americans to revisit "the horrid Butcheries, and cruel Murders committed . . . by the Hands of savage Indians, instigated thereto by more than savage, Popish priests."[15] True, Acadians were neither Indians nor priests. But as "Cincinnatus" argued in the *Boston Evening-Post*, "Priests and Jesuits" had long enjoyed "free Access" to the "Neutral French (a mock Name)," making the Acadians "the chief Instruments . . . of alienating the Indians in all that Quarter."[16] Who could say what such people might do? In the *Boston Gazette*, "Z.P." reasoned that since Catholicism guaranteed its adherents "an high Degree of Happiness, if they were to loose their Lives in the Execution of their Vilanies," the Acadians were as likely as not to "blow up our Powder-House" or "[set] Fire to the Town."[17]

At the same time, the Catholic Marylander Charles Carroll complained that the nine hundred Acadians sent to his province had been unjustly "Sacrificed to the security of Our Settlements" in Nova Scotia. "As Subjects," he noted, "they were intitled to the Benefit of our laws and ought to have been tried and found Guilty before they could be punished." Carroll offered to support fourteen Acadians on his own estate, but provincial leaders balked at the prospect of Catholic fraternizing; he later badgered Louis XV himself into sending 200 livres to Anselme Mangeant, a "poor Acadian" living on charity in Annapolis.[18] For the victims of 1755, then, Anglo-America was less a single, hostile bloc than a patchwork of religious sensibilities, wartime anxieties, tight budgets, and divergent degrees of attachment to a distant metropolis.

In those first years after 1755, Acadian exiles in the British Empire did not retreat mechanically into ethnic solidarity. Instead, they made hard choices. To be sure, some, like Paul Landry, took superhuman steps to find their loved ones. Others, however, reacted to new circumstances the way Paul Landry's children did. One need not accept Stoddard's claim that these young Acadians felt "joy" at returning to their Anglo-American masters to believe that the sight of their parents, gone for eighteen months and disfigured by hunger and disease, would have been unsettling. The comfortable homes, shops, and schools of Woodbury must have seemed awfully secure. With political loyalty and hard labor as their only remaining assets, Acadian adults faced situations no less challenging. Separated from their families, they tried to engage with their captors. In Boston's rural hinterland, Philadelphia's Dock Ward, and below the bluffs of Savannah, arrangements with men like Stoddard were the order of the day. By any measure, such relationships in a British Empire at war yielded mixed results. But as the Acadians burst into the wider world after the Seven Years' War, their capacity to work imaginatively for (and speak imaginatively to) power would serve them well.

In the southernmost provinces of British North America, power lay in the hands of men such as Henry Laurens. As a thousand Acadians surged toward his native South Carolina late in 1755, it seemed dangerously close to slipping from his grasp.

Then a thirty-one-year-old merchant in rice and slaves, the future president of the Continental Congress was suffering from man-made and natural reversals. War fears had reduced Charlestown's thriving Atlantic trade to "a mighty low ebb" that fall, slashing the price of "the produce of this Country near 30 per cent" and turning planters miserly.[19] Worse, a recent seizure of French slaves in the Caribbean had flooded Charlestown's market with "prime Men," sending chattel prices into free fall.[20] And on November 1, 1755, an earthquake struck Lisbon, Portugal, flattening the city, killing ninety thousand people, and triggering a tsunami that hurled docked ships into collapsing neighborhoods and caused tidal disruptions as far away as Barbados.[21] This "General Calamity" eliminated a key market for South Carolina rice, aggravating the "State of Uncertainty" that, as Laurens put it, "perplexes us not a Little in the Mercantile way."[22]

Worst of all, Laurens simply felt alone. As he reported in April 1756, "nothing has reach'd us from England [since] the 1st or 2nd December." He fretted over the equally ominous absence of West Indian or New York ships bearing English news. "We can't forbear thinking," Laurens wrote to a Liverpool associate, "that some thing Extraordinary must have happen'd on your side."[23] Charlestown seemed vulnerable—a vulnerability heightened by the fact that "Our Town swarms with French Newtrals which are a heavy Burthen upon us, & we see no prospect of being reliev'd from them in any reasonable time."[24]

In both South Carolina and neighboring Georgia, the first moments of the *grand dérangement* coincided with events that tore at the fabric of the British Empire. Disbelief was a common reaction. Governor James Glen of South Carolina, for example, groped for an explanation upon learning that four transports packed with six hundred Acadians had arrived in Charlestown harbor on November 15, 1755, apparently destined to stay in his "frontier province." He

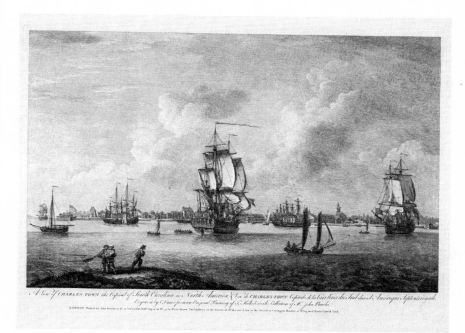

Exiles in a slave society. "A View of Charles Town, the Capital of South Carolina in North America," *Scenographia Americana* (1768). Courtesy of the William L. Clements Library, University of Michigan.

could only guess that Charles Lawrence, fingers cramped from signing documents in Nova Scotia's chill, had left it to "some inferiour Officer to apportion the Quotas to be sent to the respective Governments."[25] Whatever the cause, the number of exiles headed for British North America's deep South appeared to be out of proportion to their hosts' resources.

With a permanent population of about five thousand, Charlestown was the largest Anglo-American town south of Philadelphia. But in the mid-1750s, half that number consisted of slaves who, at the peak of the shipping season, rubbed elbows with hundreds of transient sailors.[26] The "no less than 400 french Papists" who arrived at Savannah in December of 1755 entered a glorified village still confined to the six squares laid out by James Oglethorpe in 1733. It measured 870 yards by 500 yards and housed a few hundred whites and several dozen slaves.[27] Both towns boasted hinterlands, but as the Swiss colonizer John Tobler put it in 1753, "there is still much good land left but few settlers."[28] Seen from the American South, the Acadian expulsion looked much like an invasion of two "weak and defenceless" provinces.[29]

Beyond numbers, these Acadians seemed guilty by association. Most of those who landed in South Carolina and Georgia had been captured in Chignecto, including more than twenty shackled men accused of armed resistance at the siege of Fort Beauséjour.[30] The people of Charlestown already thought they knew much about them. In 1751, during a period of strained relations with the Cherokee, Governor Glen engaged in a common form of censorship, prohibiting the *South Carolina Gazette* from printing reports of disorder and violence in the province's western borderlands.[31] In response, the paper's publisher, an opponent of Glen's policies named Peter Timothy, filled space with stories from Nova Scotia. Some involved Mi'kmaq raids near Halifax. A May 13 report detailed an attack on the nearby settlement of Dartmouth in which a "large party of *Indians*" killed two British soldiers and "murder'd several men and women in their beds," mutilating the corpses "in a surprizing manner." A lone woman who stumbled into Halifax the next morning "with one breast cut off" lived to tell the tale. Within earshot of the Acadian settlement at Minas, a company of British rangers was ambushed by "40 of the enemy" who wounded several, including an officer "whose leg was so shatter'd, that it is since cut off."[32] Other stories came directly from Chignecto. South Carolinians learned in April that French-allied Indians there had "got two more scalps" while capturing a Boston sloop and burning it to the waterline; in June, French regulars and Mi'kmaq warriors struck Fort Lawrence in the dead of night, firing "some hundreds of shot at a sloop" docked in the Bay of Fundy.[33]

Unable to write about supposed Cherokee depredations against Britons, Timothy turned to the Mi'kmaq, but the Acadians were never far offstage. The *Gazette* made clear that the Indians used Acadian dikes as cover while on campaign, and in any case South Carolinians, like most Anglo-Americans, tended to see no difference between "*French* and *Indian* Demoniacks."[34] So, on November 26, 1755, when a delegation from the Commons House held an interview with a few Acadian "seniors" on Sullivan's Island in Charleston Harbor, they had no trouble reaching conclusions.[35] In a report to the governor, the legislators railed against the exiles' "inviolable attachment to the French Interest," their "determined resolution to continue in the public exercise of the Roman Catholic Religion, under the conduct of Priests," and their refusal "to take the Oath of Allegiance, or to fight against His Majesty's Enemies" in Nova Scotia. Fair enough. The Acadians were represented by Alexandre Broussard *dit* Beausoleil, whose family was well known for close relations with the French and Mi'kmaq (South Carolina politicians referred to Alexandre as a "general of the Indians") and who had fought the British tooth and nail at Chignecto.[36]

The Native American connections of men such as Alexandre Broussard *dit* Beausoleil took on an ominous cast in the southern provinces. As everyone knew, the borderlands of South Carolina and Georgia served as an Indian thoroughfare. The Six Nations Iroquois, who dominated diplomacy and warfare in the Ohio Valley from their stronghold in northern New York, had long regarded many southern Indians as natural rivals. Described, with creative license, as "a Sort of People that range several thousands of miles, making all Prey that they lay their Hands on," the Iroquois made frequent forays into South Carolina during the early eighteenth century.[37] A 1742 treaty between the Six Nations and the Cherokee only made for more backcountry traffic. Both groups turned on the Catawba of the South Carolina piedmont, launching raids from "inaccessible" Appalachian staging grounds.[38] By 1751, the Catawba leader Hagler complained that "our Enemies are . . . thick about us," forcing him to travel to New York to contract an embarrassing peace with the Six Nations.[39] In the fall of 1755, even that agreement had collapsed. Iroquois warriors again "infested" the southern wilderness.[40]

This was bad enough. But what if the French managed to turn frontier chaos to their advantage? The prospect was real. In Savannah, fears centered on the town of Coweta (present-day Columbus, Georgia), home of the Lower Creek. Among the most sought-after allies in North America, the Lower Creek were also among the toughest to pin down. Their villages had long attracted Indian refugees and migrants, making them crazy quilts of Yamasee, Natchez, Shawnee, and Seminole subgroups whose agendas and allegiances often conflicted.[41] Although both the Spanish and French had established outposts among them earlier in the eighteenth century, the Lower Creek had maintained strong economic ties with Savannah since the 1730s. But in 1752, the Georgia Trustees, heirs of Oglethorpe's original vision of a refuge for Britain's "worthy poor," had ceded the colony to the crown. George II's ministers lurched into the project of framing a royal government only to find that the Lower Creek wanted a new treaty to match it.

A diplomatic scrum ensued. From Fort Toulouse, a garrison eighty miles from Coweta near present-day Montgomery, Alabama, French agents made their way into Lower Creek territory. Already bound to the Choctaw, whose lands spanned what are now northern Mississippi and Alabama, the French imagined an Indian confederacy stretching from Louisiana to Coweta, the back door to the Anglo-American south. In April 1755, word reached Savannah that "the governor of New Orleans had sent for the [Lower Creek] Head men to meet him at Mobile this Spring, where . . . they would receive large presents."[42] In May, at a brandy-soaked conference at Fort Toulouse, the French made promises of cheap trade goods, prompting the Lower Creek leader Malatchi to threaten war against British settlers.[43] "Dangerous consequences" were clear to Georgians. Losing the Lower Creek meant that "our only Barrier would be removed, and the numerous Nations of Indians in Amity with [the French] would pour in upon us."[44]

South Carolina had it no better. While the Catawba seemed loyal enough ("As to the French," wrote Hagler in October 1755, "they shall never have any of our Land until they have trod us under the Earth we now walk upon"), relations with the all-important Cherokee gave officials fits.[45] Alongside the Lower Creek, the Cherokee were supposed to act as a bulwark against French and Indian invasions from the Ohio Valley. Elements within the two groups, however, were often at each other's throats. In 1752, for example, on the heels of Lower Creek assaults on two Cherokee towns, the Upper Creek warrior Acorn Whistler, a onetime French ally, met twenty-six Cherokees while on a visit to Charlestown. After a friendly greeting on the outskirts of town (the Creek "pulled the Feathers off their own Heads and put them on the Heads of the Cherokees"), Acorn Whistler and his party suddenly opened fire. Four Cherokee men were killed, fumed Governor Glen, "at our very Doors."[46]

Initially, encounters like this one cemented the South Carolina–Cherokee alliance. Officials in Charlestown served as mediators and suppliers, leading headmen such as the "old Man" Skiagunsta to instruct his neighbors to "be well with the English, for they cannot expect any Supply from any where else, nor can they live independent."[47] But by late 1755, Skiagunsta's compatriots vacillated. Some simply favored "Peace with all Kings," while others chafed at the inflow of dozens of British "traders, Pedlars, and Idle fellows" into Cherokee territory.[48] On the one hand, fighting with French-leaning Creeks threatened to distract the Cherokees; on the other, Anglo-American undesirables (and the "Superior address" of French agents) promised to drive them off.[49] Either way, South Carolinians envisioned terrible outcomes. "Thinly inhabited" and "weak by situation," his province was, noted Glen, "the country that has reason to fear the force of France in case of any rupture."[50]

By early 1755, then, all sorts of people were traveling through, settling in, or fighting over western lands in ways that threw off whatever precarious balance South Carolina and Georgia had struggled to establish. The French—who, at Fort Toulouse, Mobile, and elsewhere, "caressed in an extraordinary manner" native leaders who came to call—loomed as instigators and organizers.[51] In October, warriors from Taheo and Chota captured ten French soldiers who claimed to have deserted from Fort Toulouse. The Cherokee "look[ed] on them as slaves," but others portrayed them as "Spies sent by the French to see how the Rivers lye." All of South Carolina grew "very uneasie on that Account."[52]

So when those first one thousand Acadian exiles began arriving in Charlestown and Savannah from the east, they conjured up images of the west. Disorder on the coast portended more disorder in the backcountry. Just weeks after the Acadians' arrival in South Carolina, one legislator cautioned that the exiles would surely "be active in their endeavors to tamper with our . . . Indians, and draw them . . . to the French interest."[53] Slaves posed another problem. Many wondered if "Romish" Acadians "of a turbulent and seditious Disposition," bearing "Principles most pernicious to civil and social Liberty," might find accomplices in African Catholic transplants.[54] If allowed ashore in Charleston, would the exiles not spend their time goading slaves to "run away to Augustine [the town of Saint Augustine in Spanish Florida]," stealing "small Vessels" in anticipation of an invasion by "their Friends the French," and generally "annoying the Province"?[55]

As South Carolinians were unwilling to risk Acadian starvation on Sullivan's Island (or, more to the point, the prospect of hundreds of hungry French families clogging the gateway to Charlestown's harbor), officials began to bring the exiles ashore in December, lodging them in barracks and laying plans to indenture the able-bodied or set them to work on the fortifications.[56] Alexandre Broussard *dit* Beausoleil and his fellow Chignecto veterans quickly confirmed Anglo-American fears. Several parties ran away, seemingly bound for the western frontier. One reached the Santee River plantation of John Williams, "terrified his Wife very much, robbed the House of Fire Arms and Cloaths, and broke open a Box out of which they took some Money." Thirty escaped entirely, but others were captured after being "track'd . . . into the River Swamp."[57] Many spent time in Charlestown's workhouse, while Broussard and some of his friends found themselves in the town's "Black Hole," a dungeon "so small, that they can hardly stand upright in, much less lie down."[58] Although these men were, in the words of Governor Glen, "undoubtedly His Majesty's Liege Subjects, and most of them his natural born Subjects," their behavior revealed that the Acadians as a whole remained "audaciously, as well as unanimously" in the French camp.[59] As a result, by early 1756, South Carolina's Acadians were guarded "narrowly" by a

"Detachment from our Militia, besides a hired Watch, and the Soldiers of the Independent Companies."[60]

Charlestonians expected similar behavior from the nearly 350 Acadians who straggled into the harbor aboard the *Hopson* in January 1756. In the Commons House, legislators declared themselves "utterly averse" to "those distressed yet refractory People," refusing to grant them food and water beyond March. Aboard the *Hopson*, Britons heard familiar rumblings. One hungry exile allegedly muttered that Acadians "would have Provisions by some means or other." An interpreter overheard others anticipating that "by March next [their] own Countrymen would come and relieve [them]."[61] Signs of an even broader conspiracy appeared. In January, several witnesses saw a French man "who pretended to be a deserter from New Orleans" making a detailed map of the city, taking careful account "of all the Houses in it." All this, coupled with the mysterious arrival of "Three Frenchmen from the Colony of Georgia," threw officials into a panic.[62]

As Governor Glen and others looked at the refugees aboard the *Hopson*, however, a different picture emerged. In a letter to the Commons House, Glen himself related his own visit with three who managed to call on him. They came from Annapolis Royal, a town "to which the French could not be so absurd as to pretend the least claim." The ship's passengers, he claimed, had "never abetted [the French] in any shape" and made it a custom to "give notice to the Commanders of our Troops when they discover'd any Party" of Britain's enemies. Glen believed them. The *Hopson*'s commissary, who had done business in Nova Scotia, confirmed the exiles' statements, even describing the case of a "Widow Woman, now on board . . . whose Husband was killed in an Engagement by the French, in the service of the Government." In addition, Glen found that *Hopson*'s interpreter had abused his charges, calling the Acadians "Rascals, Rebels, Traitors [who] . . . deserved to be starv'd and hang'd."[63] Their fidelity to Britain made the Acadians of the *Hopson* "not Objects of . . . resentment, but . . . Objects of great Compassion." Indeed, the governor wished that "we could get rid of most of the others, & receive these in their room."[64]

Thrown into distressed provinces unannounced, Acadians took care to emphasize British subjecthood and, when it made sense, the distinctions that made some exiles dangerous and others harmless. In many cases, cash-strapped Anglo-Americans listened. In Georgia, for example, Governor John Reynolds got word of the Acadians' arrival in Savannah at precisely the wrong moment. In early December 1755 he was at Augusta, nearly 150 hard miles northwest of Savannah, anticipating a meeting with a delegation of Creeks who, in exchange for presents, had promised to help settle "matters of great consequence to the Colony." When a breathless messenger appeared with news of four hundred "French papists" docked at Savannah, Reynolds faced a hard decision. He had already spent ten days waiting for the Creeks, and feared that more time wasted would "give the Indians a very mean opinion" of his government. Reynolds packed up. Hedging his bets, he instructed William Little, a grizzled backcountry trader, to deliver his speeches and convince the Creeks that the "chief arguments" of the French—"that the English wanted nothing but their lands & then to make slaves of them"—were baseless. It was a decision Reynolds would come to regret. The Board of Trade later charged Little with pocketing a share of the presents, exposing Reynolds to accusations of bungling Georgia's key diplomatic relationship. But, as the governor put it, the "extraordinary occurrence" of the Acadians' appearance trumped even the Creeks.[65]

What Reynolds expected to find upon his return to Savannah is unclear, but it was probably not Jacques-Maurice Vigneau. Then in his mid-fifties, Vigneau had grown up and prospered in Beaubassin before le Loutre and the Mi'kmaq burned the town. A pilot and fisherman, he had served two masters with great success, hosting French troops during King George's War and ferrying provisions to British-controlled Louisbourg when the fighting stopped.[66] As Chignecto's once-fluid boundaries hardened, he moved to Pointe Beauséjour with his neighbors, but always resented the heavy-handed French. In 1751, the governor-general of New France complained that some Acadians at Beauséjour, "notably a certain Jacob Maurice [Vigneau], wish to make themselves independent, and have refused to take an oath of allegiance to the King, our master." Although declared "guilty of the utmost ingratitude" and threatened with expulsion if he refused to swear the oath to Louis XV and join the militia, Vigneau equivocated.[67] By 1755, Vigneau picked a side. As far as military fortunes went, he chose well. "Jockey Morris is very good and takes a fatherly care of us," exclaimed Thomas Speakman, a Massachusetts captain; another New Englander, John Thomas, reported that on the morning of July 8, 1755, he and fifty comrades "Refreshed our Selves at one Jacob M[aurice]'s house" on their march north from the conquered Fort Beauséjour.[68] It must have been especially galling, then, when those same soldiers escorted Vigneau and his family aboard the *Prince Frederick* that fall.

Making his way south to Savannah with 280 fellow Acadians, Vigneau surely had some explaining to do. He evidently did it well, for when Reynolds began assessing the Acadians' case in December 1755, the multilingual, Anglophilic Vigneau emerged as a spokesman. He got the governor's attention by proclaiming that he had "always shown great regard for the English, by saving them from frequently being scalped" back in Nova Scotia. Together, the two men came up with a pragmatic if risky solution to their common problem. Eager to be rid of his expensive guests, Reynolds gave Vigneau's "family" (which soon swelled to nearly one hundred Acadians) some old canoes, ten pounds of rice per person, and a pass out of Georgia. "Having no orders to receive or detain them or fund

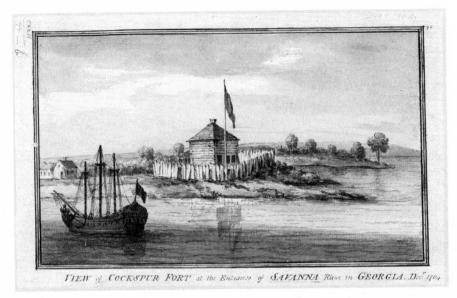

From one borderland colony to another. *View of Cockspur Fort at the Entrance of the Savanna River in Georgia* (1764). Courtesy of the British Library, London.

for their support," Reynolds later wrote, "[I] judged it best to let them go as they were all Papists and consequently enemies to our Religion and Government."[69] Heading up the coast in the spring of 1756, Vigneau sweet-talked officials in both Carolinas and New York before the alert residents of Barnstable, Massachusetts, had the group arrested. This Acadian "family" had paddled a thousand miles but were still at least six hundred miles from their presumed destination. Vigneau spent the Seven Years' War in and around Boston, badgering the provincial government to reimburse him for the canoe it had not let him keep.[70]

The story of Vigneau's journey is spectacularly—and stereotypically—Acadian. Flexible in matters of loyalty, the members of his family were dogged in their attachment to one another, and desperate to get home. But theirs was not the only path. Indeed, even as Vigneau's canoes headed northward, nearly two hundred Acadians found a clearing west of Savannah, built some rudimentary huts, and began to work. It was hardly easy, and the exiles were hardly welcome. In response to their habit of cutting down "Valuable Timber" that did not belong to them, Reynolds assented to a bill authorizing justices of the peace to "bind" Acadians to local landowners as unpaid laborers. The act might have been put into practice if not for the Board of Trade's decision to remove Reynolds from power late in 1756, a decision motivated in part by his mishandling of the Creek conference that coincided with the Acadians' arrival.[71]

His replacement, a gentlemanly scientist named Henry Ellis, exhibited a far more creative turn of mind. A well-connected Irish Protestant, Ellis had completed a voyage to Hudson's Bay in 1747, later penning a best-selling account of Britain's renewed search for the Northwest Passage. In 1750, he journeyed to the African coast aboard a Bristol slaver outfitted with a new ventilation system that reduced the need for sooty candles, kept guns from rusting, and safeguarded both "our cargo and lives."[72] An inveterate tinkerer, Ellis expected big things of small, reform-oriented activities; as he put it, the cumulative effect of "useful Discoveries" would produce "a new and profitable Commerce" for the British Empire while "quickening, improving, and enlarging many old Branches."[73] His drive to foster trade made Ellis more ecumenical than his predecessor, to the point of lamenting the "hard and forlorn Fate" of Savannah's slaves while protecting their masters' right to hire them out as artisans.[74] Although his work in Georgia initially centered on securing the Creeks' goodwill and energizing the province's anemic defenses, the governor clung to a sense that, in the words of his key metropolitan backer and intellectual mentor, "every one should contribute according to his ability, that something may arise from the whole, of use in the improvement of our country."[75]

Upon his arrival early in 1757, Ellis expressed sympathy and admiration for the Acadians. They were, he reported, "very useful to the Colony as they employ themselves in making Oars hand spikes & other implements for sea Craft."[76] In April, he visited the Acadian encampment outside of Savannah in person. "Very much affected to see such a Number of distressed People surrounded with large Families of helpless Infants," Ellis suggested giving the refugees a bit of land. A garden, he claimed, "might enable them to obtain a more comfortable Support."[77] Eager to use the Acadians to further his ambitious vision of experimental agriculture, Ellis offered to supply "all manner of garden seeds," perhaps including some of the exotica (olive and orange trees, rhubarb, Egyptian kale) provincial leaders had recently imported from around the globe.[78] Although Ellis left his post in 1761, his sense of the Acadians' utility stuck. That spring, when private parties bought the commons on which the refugees lived, legislators granted Acadians leave "to build and reside" next to the plot they were forced to vacate.[79]

In Virginia, any such détente between Britons and Acadians was short-circuited almost immediately. Again, the Acadians' troubles started in the backcountry. In July 1755, a force of more than two thousand British regulars under General Edward Braddock had been routed by French and Indian fighters near Fort Duquesne, a French outpost at the site of present-day Pittsburgh. For Virginia's governor, the combustible land speculator Robert Dinwiddie, Braddock's defeat signaled a virtual British abandonment of the Ohio Valley to the French. This, by Dinwiddie's lights, had triggered "really great Destruction among our back Settlers," allowing France's allies to become "Land Pyrates, watching and taking advantage of the . . . innocent People's insecurity, breaking in upon them, robbing some, murdering others, and carrying away the young Women captives."[80] When, on the night of November 16, Dinwiddie received "an Express" from the port at Hampton detailing the sudden appearance of "two Sloops, with four more daily expected, with Neutrals from Nova Scotia," he was enraged. It was, he wrote, "disagreeable . . . to have 1000 French imported, when many of the same Nation are committing the most cruel Barbarities on our Fellow Subjects in the back Country."[81]

Expenses worried Dinwiddie as well. After negotiations, Virginia leaders agreed to support the Acadians out of the governor's own household budget. The "Balance thereof," confessed Dinwiddie, "is so small that I fear it will exhaust the whole." Worse, the expensive guests forced Dinwiddie to make a "handsome Present of at least £500" to the seemingly impatient Catawba by drawing on his personal credit.[82] Unlike Ellis in Georgia, Dinwiddie could see no redeeming value in Acadian labor. The "Neutral French," he reported, "give a general Discontent to the People here, as they are bigotted Papists, lazy and of a contentious Behavior." While settlers around Hampton grew troubled "in regard to [the Acadians'] religious Principles," Dinwiddie himself became "as much alarmed for fear of debauching our Negroes."[83] By the spring of 1756, those fears had been realized. During the winter, the exiles had lived in boats in Hampton's harbor, prevented from landing by order of the government. Dinwiddie claimed that many had spent their infrequent moments ashore "tampering with the Negroe Slaves, which, together with The Invasion of the French and Indians on our Frontiers, made our People extremely uneasy."[84]

For Virginians, one thing was certain: "we can have but a very poor Prospect of their being either good Subjects or useful People."[85] Convinced, Dinwiddie took action. By the summer of 1756, none of the eleven hundred refugees sent to Virginia remained. Nearly a quarter had died of disease and malnutrition. As for the ailing, shipbound rump, the House of Burgesses voted in April to send them to Great Britain.[86] Officials in the mother country expressed much "Displeasure and Disaprobation" as transports appeared in Liverpool, Falmouth, Penryn, Bristol, and Southampton.[87] After smallpox decimated the refugees as they huddled in "warehouses" late in 1756, survivors began to receive a small allowance from the British treasury, slowly recovering after a full year of physical deprivation and mental anguish. Then they began to complain.

Repeatedly and earnestly, Acadians sent from Virginia to Great Britain used their status as subjects of the British Empire to barter for rights, privileges, and connection to the power of the imperial state. Indeed, exiles projected themselves as a community of aggrieved subjects, separated by good political judgment from their rebellious neighbors. Honoré Leblanc, for example, penned a letter to officials in London about his treatment in Liverpool. The father of eight had spent all of his money and sold all of his "linens and goods" to feed his family. Having been "pulled from atop" his possessions by order of His Majesty, Leblanc recounted "the zeal with which he had always carried himself to render service" to British troops during the 1755 campaign in Nova Scotia.[88] Claude Pitré claimed to have "piloted a detachment" of British soldiers to a rendezvous thirty leagues from his home in Cobequid, receiving the promise of a safe return. Instead, the fifty-eight-year-old lived by himself in Liverpool, separated from his wife and children, for twenty-three long months. "The misery is all the more heart-rending," he noted, "as it comes to me from the fidelity I had for His Britannic Majesty, in executing his orders."[89]

England's Acadians felt the limitations of their situation acutely. In Falmouth, brothers Baptiste and Olivier Daigre headed a group who petitioned for freedom of religion, alluding to practices allowed among Britain's other imperial subjects. Sick and poor, they painted a pathetic tableau, lamenting that "young people with neither father nor mother . . . have not received the sacraments or heard the word of God for two years." The Acadians of Falmouth did not demand to be released; rather, they asked to be "led to a place where we may, during our detention in England, practice the Catholic religion as we have in the past; or . . . as do (we believe) many of His Majesty's subjects." The Daigres bowed to Britain's ability to move them. Rather than resist it, they hoped to harness that power for their own modest ends.

For Acadians and their hosts in the Anglo-American South, then, there was more than one way of coping with the *grand dérangement*. Framed by an imperial world at war, local factors—from intercultural politics to the interplay of personalities—determined their fate. While Vigneau's "family" collaborated with the budget-minded Reynolds to escape from Georgia, most of Savannah's Acadians lingered, molding themselves to fit the demands of a coastal economy and the opportunities of Ellis's reformist government. In Maryland, Edward Lloyd surely looked on Virginia's expulsion of its Acadians with envy: after an overseer of the poor deposited sixty exiles on his Wye River estate, he declared himself "liable to a great deal of Danger by their corrupting mine & other Negroe Slaves," of which there were, in his neighborhood alone, "300 that may be call'd Roman Catholics."[90] For Henry Callister of Oxford, Maryland, however, the greater danger lay not in the Acadians' "Papist principles" but in Marylanders' forgetting "the seeds of charity in us" and neglecting the "principle of humanity." With Acadians "now about me in tears," Callister succeeded in finding "good houses" for most of Oxford's Acadians by January 1756.[91] Surveying new landscapes of Indians, slaves, and anxious Britons, the Acadians began, haltingly, to remake themselves in relation to the landscapes around them.

* * *

For five hundred Acadians captured in and around Grand Pré, that process began on Province Island, several miles below Philadelphia in the Delaware River. The sloops *Hannah, Swan,* and *Three Friends* reached the island in November 1755, dumping their passengers into its crowded "pest-house" on orders from Pennsylvania governor Robert Morris.

"At a very great loss to know what to do," Morris wrote to nearly every British official he could think of. The Acadians were not "Neutrals," replied Jonathan Belcher of New Jersey, but "rather Traitors & Rebels to the Crown of Great Britain." Already burdened with "too great a number of Foreigners," Pennsylvania risked "ruin" at their hands.[92] For many in the provincial administration, Belcher triggered visions of the province's "German and Irish Catholicks" making common cause with the exiles and spiriting intelligence to the "Savage Enemys" serving France on the western frontier. "If they were dangerous at Nova Scotia," Morris wondered, "will they not be more so here?"[93]

The Quaker-dominated assembly, however, took a more moderate tack. On the recommendation of the abolitionist Anthony Benezet, who visited the Acadians on Province Island, its members demanded that the exiles be transferred to Philadelphia before the onset of winter, and that some provisions be sent in the interim. Fearful of an embarrassing humanitarian crisis, Morris bowed to their wishes. Although anti-Acadian sentiment still ran high (one pamphlet from the late 1740s had described them as *"French* bigots" liable to "cut our own People's throats whenever the Priest shall consecrate the Knife"), Morris seemed to soften as details of the expulsion came to light.[94] Days after their landing in Philadelphia, he gave Joseph Munier and Simon Leblanc passports to Maryland, allowing the pair to search for their wives. Morris noted that both had been "recommended to me as good and worthy People . . . who have been in the Service of His Majesty."[95]

Seizing on Morris's act and the apparent goodwill of the assembly, the Acadians moved to establish themselves on firmer footing by recasting their history of political flexibility in rigid terms. On February 12, 1756, Jean-Baptiste Galerne, a former deputy from the village of Pisiquid, read a petition to the Pennsylvania Assembly. According to Galerne, the Acadians sent to Pennsylvania had done their utmost to remain subjects of the British king during a difficult period in Nova Scotia's history. In fact, Galerne's own ancestors had made a conscious decision in 1713 not to leave the province. As Richard Philipps took over Port Royal, they "chose rather to remain there, and become Subjects of Great Britain." Their fidelity cost them dearly. During the 1740s, a war party of "500 French and Indians" passed Galerne's home, intent on attacking Annapolis Royal and becoming "Masters of all Nova Scotia." The inhabitants declined to aid and quarter the troops, forcing them to give up and return to Canada. Upon hearing of the foundation of Halifax in 1749, a group of hostile Mi'kmaq stormed through the

The Philadelphia waterfront as the Acadians knew it. *An east prospect of the city of Philadelphia; taken by George Heap from the Jersey shore, under the direction of Nicholas Scull surveyor general of the Province of Pennsylvania* (1765). Courtesy of the Historical Society of Pennsylvania.

author's modest farm, demanding his aid in "Way-laying and destroying the English." Six weeks passed before Galerne recovered from the beating he received upon refusing.

In effect, Galerne split the Acadian population of Nova Scotia into two groups—those who had succumbed to French coercion and those who had not. The root cause of the expulsion, he believed, lay in the "Conduct of some of our People settled at Chignecto, at the bottom of the Bay of Fundi," near Fort

Beauséjour and the village of Beaubassin. Too distant from British settlements at Halifax and Annapolis Royal "to expect sufficient Assistance from the English," these people were "obliged, as we believe, more through Compulsion and Fear than Inclination, to join with and assist the French." The Acadians of Pennsylvania, on the other hand, had always loved Britain. They would, Galerne claimed, "inviolably keep the Oath of Fidelity that we have taken to his gracious Majesty King George," biding time until the moment when, "acquainted with our Faithfulness and Sufferings," their monarch would reward them.[96]

The Acadians did not simply wait on provincial bureaucracy. Later in 1756, an anonymous statement of the Pennsylvania exiles' loyalty arrived in London for George II. The letter echoed many of Galerne's sentiments, placing the blame for the deportation of 1755 even more squarely upon the Acadians of Chignecto. The innocence of those from Minas and Annapolis Royal was, by almost any measure, complete. Had not an "armed force" sacked "the house in which we kept our contracts, records, [and] deeds," the letter claimed, inhabitants of these regions would already have been vindicated. Instead of documents, Acadians offered portraits of loyalty. These included the case of René LeBlanc, a notary captured "while actually traveling in your majesty's service" who spent four years imprisoned by the French. Geography and political culture had long divided the inhabitants of Chignecto from Galerne's blameless lot. In Nova Scotia, the two groups had been "separated from them by sixty miles of uncultivated land," having "no other connexion with them, than what is usual with neighbours at such a distance." Unlike these "neighbours," Acadians in Minas and Annapolis Royal Acadians possessed a "fixed resolution" to Great Britain's interest.[97]

These petitions did not work. Neither Galerne nor the nameless Acadian writing to George II stated a desired outcome. Whether that was a return trip to Nova Scotia or simply better treatment, the exiles did not receive it. Beginning in 1757, a more radical mood swept across Pennsylvania's Acadian community. Although the goal of obtaining access to power remained unchanged, some Acadians pursued it by allying themselves with another group at the margins of Pennsylvania's political culture. Although members of the Philadelphia Meeting had dominated the Provincial Assembly since the colony's foundation, the influence of Quakers waned during the 1750s. Castigated as "inwardly spiritualized fanaticks and enthusiasts," Quakers had become increasingly suspect for their refusal to take oaths, a conciliatory attitude toward Indians, and their opposition to British military action.[98] Galled by the Friends' refusal to "VEX THE MIDIANITES, AND SMITE THEM," Protestant hawks used the popular press to question the Quakers' allegiance.[99] One opponent of Quakerism derided those who "(that like to Lanterns bear Their Light within them) will not swear; Like Mules who if they've not their Will / To keep their own pace, stand stock still."[100] Racked by internal tensions and besieged from without, many within the Society of Friends withdrew from government in 1756, encouraging adherents to concentrate on civic solutions to imperial problems.[101]

A failed merchant turned teacher and agitator, Anthony Benezet took an active interest in the Acadians' plight within the context of an emerging Quaker critique of the British Empire. For Benezet, the Acadians were no abstraction. Beginning early in 1756, many exiles scraped by in cheap lodgings near Benezet's home on Chestnut Street, a stone's throw from Saint Joseph's Chapel, Philadelphia's lone Catholic church and the focal point of Acadian community in the city. From the beginning, he viewed the "neutral French" as ideological kin. For Benezet, the Acadian expulsion, no less than the enslavement of Africans, indicated the corruption of what had been a virtuous political system. He portrayed the imprisonment of innocents as a violation of "natural Justice" and evidence of "the Apostacy of these last Times," noting the "open Wickedness," "superficial Holyness," and "Hardness of Heart" displayed by British officials.[102] At the root of such measures was a thirst for war, profit, and territory. "The lust of dominion; the avarice of wealth; and the infamous ambition of . . . the conquerors and tyrants of mankind," Benezet sermonized in 1759, had begun to dominate British imperial policy. "Heaven preserve Britain," he prayed, "from these 'earthly, sensual, devilish' motives."[103]

In early 1757, as economic conditions grew worse and the relationship between Acadians and Quakers deepened, some among the exiles did something counterintuitive. They began committing treason. "On the Behalf of the whole," Alexis Thibaudeau laid before the Assembly the trials of "an unhappy People, who have never been guilty of any Transgression which might subject us to the Calamity we have been made to endure." As the war took a toll on the rural economy, he explained, overseers of the poor in Philadelphia, and in nearby Bucks, Chester, and Lancaster counties, denied them provisions. Work as day laborers offered no relief. The "greatest Part" lacked physical strength, while others despaired that "the Labour of one . . . is not sufficient to feed and clothe a Wife and five or six Children." They did not, however, want land. Indeed, Acadians had refused items designed to "offer us some Assistance towards procuring . . . a Living, such as Cows, Gardens, &c." Thibaudeau explained why. Confessing that "we shall never fully consent to settle in this Province," the refugees related a promise made to them at the hour of their expulsion. "In the Presence of his Majesty's Council" at Annapolis Royal late in 1755, Governor Lawrence had told Acadian representatives that "he made us Prisoners even like . . . *French* Prisoners." Based on a "solemn Promise" of a leader of the British Empire, Thibaudeau demanded "the same Privileges which *French* Prisoners have enjoyed," namely, "leave to depart . . . to our Nation; or any where, to join our Country People."[104]

Casting themselves as prisoners of war, the Acadians echoed Benezet's stinging critique of Britain's moral failure while creating a legal conundrum. Upon receiving a nearly identical petition a few days later, Governor William

Denny refused it. As for the Acadians' claim that "they were and ought to be treated as Prisoners of War and not as Subjects of the King of England," Denny disagreed, but not until after some reflection. He reread Lawrence's circular informing each province of the deportation, reviewed older documents on "proceedings respecting those Neutrals in Carolina and the other Governments," and even dusted off a copy of the 1713 Treaty of Utrecht, paying close attention to the "Articles of the Cession and Surrender of Novia Scotia."[105] Although the Council declared itself "unanimously of Opinion that [the Acadians] were Subjects of Great Britain, and to be treated on that footing and no other," doubts lingered. As a South Carolina official—one to whom the government of Pennsylvania likely made an appeal during deliberations on the Acadians—had stated some months earlier, "The case is new and difficult; there is no Precedent to lead, nor any Rule to govern us in this Matter."[106]

A second group presented a memorial to the Assembly in February 1757. Bearing traces of Quaker rhetoric, it railed against a plan to apprentice Acadian children to local mechanics and farmers. "Though we read that God has reduced his People under the hardest captivity," they wrote, the Israelites "in *Egypt*, under *Pharaoh*, and in *Babylon*, under *Nebuchadnezzar*," had endured nothing of the sort. The execution of this plan, Acadians held, would violate God's laws, as well as infringe upon their "natural Rights." The petitioners further hoped that a "merciful and good God" might "make Angels" of Pennsylvania's leaders—more specifically, the Acadians had in mind the messenger who had appeared to "*Hagar* and *Ishmael*, when they were both driven out of *Abraham's* House." Showing the exiled mother a well in the desert of Beersheba, the angel "thereby saved the Child's life."[107]

Eager to "join with our Nation in some Place," Philadelphia's Acadians demanded to know "whether we are Subjects, Prisoners, Slaves, or Freemen?" The first category was, to their minds, out of the question. "It appears to us unparalleled," they wrote, "that his *Britannic* Majesty should ever oppress his Subjects in the Manner we have been oppressed." "Neither can we be called Slaves," the Acadians continued, "because Christians have never made a Trade of such as believe in Jesus Christ." In light of their restricted mobility and Britain's attack on their homes in Nova Scotia, their status as "Freemen" was questionable at best. The exiles then "conclude[d] themselves Prisoners, for we must be something, or be reduced to a state of non-existence."[108] For sheer verve, it was a striking passage, just as Benezet, who almost certainly wrote it, hoped it might be.

Although Benezet had declared the Acadians French prisoners of war, rebuked the Assembly for its abandonment of Quaker principles, and taken a jab at slavery to boot, his assistance only hurt the exiles' cause. When John Campbell, Earl of Loudon, George II's commander in chief in North America, learned of the Acadians' maneuvering, he was enraged. In the first place, Loudon believed that colonies such as Pennsylvania, with their parsimonious assemblies and "Eternal Negotiation[s]," could sustain a war against the French only under the guidance of metropolitans such as himself. Even then, their fractious political culture threatened imperial aims at every step.[109] All distractions, especially those fomented by neutral Acadians and Quakers, were to be stamped out. Second, Loudon dismissed complex analyses of the Acadians' subjecthood or legal status and judged them by one simple criterion: language. Late in 1756 or early in 1757, Loudon had received an Acadian petition written in French. He rejected it, declaring his intent to communicate with "the King's subjects" in English only. According to Loudon, Philadelphia's exiles held a "general meeting" in which they agreed to continue writing in French, an act of linguistic treachery that unmasked the Acadians as "entirely French subjects." Suspicious, he "found among those neutrals one who has been a spy," and gleaned the names of "five principal men" who seemed intent on engaging Acadians to join French forces in the backcountry and resisting attempts to put "their children out to work."[110] On March 21, 1757, Loudon confined Jean-Baptiste Galerne and four other Acadian men living in Philadelphia, Chester, Frankfort, and Darby, to the city jail on Walnut Street.[111] Most of them were never heard from again.[112]

As British arms advanced and Quaker moralizing retreated, Pennsylvania's exiles slipped, seemingly forgotten, into impoverished despair. Even as Loudon clamped down on Acadian petitioners, conditions deteriorated. After being pestered for firewood by an Acadian named Pierre Landry, one official lamented the Acadians' "want of many of the Common necessaries of Life." Neglected by local overseers of the poor, they would, he predicted, "perish in a manner that will reflect Disgrace upon any Christian Government" if leaders took no action.[113] And yet Acadians made do. At the corner of Sixth and Pine in Philadelphia, four Acadian women—Nancy Baugis, Genevieve Vincent, Soulier Brasseaux, and Catherine Boudreau—"Kept Batchelors Hall all together." Living in what came to be known as the "French Houses," the women (neighborhood kids called them "nuns") taught Acadian children the Catholic catechism and treated them, as former student Marie Trépagnier remembered, "very kindly."[114] For his part, Benezet engaged in transatlantic philanthropy on the Acadians' behalf for the next dozen years, raising "thousands and thousands of francs" and, as late as 1779, hiring a lawyer to "plead" for Philadelphia's seventy-eight remaining exiles at the court of Louis XVI.[115]

The Seven Years' War energized forces in Pennsylvania society that threatened to tear the province's Acadian exiles limb from limb. Pierre Landry, ostensibly writing for "all the Acadians . . . who are in Pennsylvania" at war's end in 1763, asked the French crown to "withdraw us from slavery, where we have been since [the British] took the few possessions we once enjoyed."[116] But below the province's stark dichotomies—Briton and Frenchman, Protestant and Catholic, good subject and worrisome traitor—the city of Philadelphia, with its bustling market in goods and faiths, played host to a political underworld where victims of empire, whether neutral Quaker or neutral French, could together find a measure of refuge.

No less than in Pennsylvania, the collision of religion and imperial politics shaped the Acadians' reception in Massachusetts, the epicenter of the *grand dérangement* in the first years after 1755. For most of the Bay Colony's inhabitants, responding to the appearance of a thousand Acadians that November was a matter of instinct. However friendly their commercial relations with Nova Scotia might have been, decades of war with the French and their Native American allies had produced a virulent, relentlessly public strain of anti-Catholicism. "Where o'er black deeds, the Crucifix display'd," a widely reprinted poem went, "Fools think heaven purchas'd by the blood they shed."[117] In Massachusetts, religion trumped ethnicity or nationality. Even as Acadians limped off their transports, readers in Boston got word of still more victims "flying hither . . . naked of all worldly substance" after having been "artfully attacked, beset on every side, and ravaged from every quarter" in a distant homeland. These were the harried French Protestants of Languedoc, and Bostonians prepared "a spread of sympathy" for any such co-religionists who made it to their shores.[118] The Acadians were not so lucky.

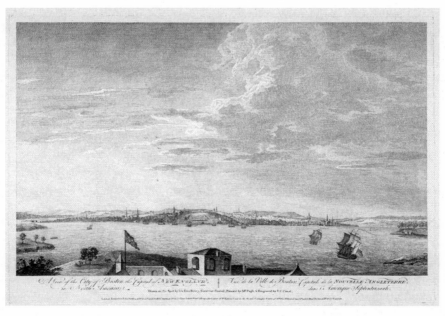

Boston during the Seven Years' War. "A View of the City of Boston, Capital of New England," *Scenographia Americana* (1768). Courtesy of the William L. Clements Library, University of Michigan.

Late in 1755, provincial authorities distributed the exiles among ninety-eight towns, empowering overseers of the poor to "employ, bind out, or support" their charges as if they were simply poor Anglo-American inhabitants.[119] In these provincial villages, the Acadians stared down an uncertain future. They were, in effect, the last link in a great chain of imperial self-exploitation. Local authorities expected to be reimbursed for Acadian expenses by the provincial government, which in turn expected reimbursement from Nova Scotia, which in turn hoped that Great Britain might pay, but whose leaders never pursued the matter with much vigor.[120]

Local anger resulted. In tiny Needham, for example, town counselors protested that "the number of French they had received was out of proportion." Worse, one of the village's thirteen Acadians had spirited himself to Philadelphia, returning with a destitute wife who now demanded support.[121] Thomas Hancock, Boston's most successful smuggler-merchant and a partner in the firm that had supplied the transports for the Acadian expulsion, went so far as to outfit "a vessell for the transportation to North Carolina" of several Acadian families in Boston. Crowded on board and launched toward the Atlantic in May 1756, the exiles overpowered the crew and "came ashore by force." Hancock's efforts to "compel them to go on board" again came to nothing.[122] Isaac Jackson, Moses Craft, and Joseph Ward of Newton submitted a bill to the provincial government for, among other things, 206¾ pounds of pork, 166 quarts of milk, and "Ten Bushels of Indian meal," all supplied to the town's Acadians over a six-month period. Distributing these foodstuffs had been a hardship, to be sure, but doing nothing had not been an option. "There is but two of the thirteen persons that can do much to support themselves," the selectmen explained, "eight of them being Children: and what they have Earnt, has bin laid out for wool and flax to Cloath themselves."[123]

Newton's predicament was a common one. For overseers of the poor, labor was the answer to their financial conundrum. But putting the Acadians to work proved tricky. Although monetized and integrated into the world of Atlantic commerce, the rural economies of Massachusetts retained a strong sense of the personal. Most households kept account books, recording exchanges of money, goods, and work among neighbors and friends. Debits and credits in these account books acted as the community's contract with itself, ensuring that relationships among farmers and laborers weathered the rhythms of agricultural production and the ups and downs of global markets. While wage-earning hands had become more common in the decades before the Seven Years' War, most Massachusetts farmers still lived and worked within a deeply rooted "network of economic interdependence."[124] Households with different resources exchanged them to their mutual benefit. Faced with a diversity of tasks, experienced husbands could, as one practitioner put it, "do this business cheaper by exchanging with each other, than by hiring help."[125]

Simply plugging exiles into such complex systems proved impossible. They were often sickly, always indigent, and, as Catholics, under perpetual suspicion for their most basic behaviors. It was a commonplace in the New England countryside, for example, that the pope himself enjoined his followers to "observe no Faith, or Truth, or common Honesty with those whom they account Heretics," making the "Breach of Oaths . . . no less with [Catholics] than a Vertue, or a necessary Duty."[126] In village worlds built on trust, Acadians looked like liars. Wage labor and piece work were the best alternatives, but these arrangements caused as many problems as they solved. The eighteen- and twenty-five-year-old daughters of Claude Bourgeois, for example, spent their days in Amesbury turning the scraps of wool the family had "managed to save" from their home in Annapolis Royal into clothing they could sell. Doing so apparently offended "ten or twelve" of the town's inhabitants. In April 1756, the group burst into their home, tore the young women from their parents' arms, and hauled them off. When Bourgeois found the girls and brought them home, the town cut off the family's supply of food.[127] After receiving no pay and scant food of "bad quality" for two weeks of work on the Hanover farm of John Bailey, brothers Charles and Nicolas Breau complained to authorities in Boston. A few days later, twenty men "of menacing dispositions" burst into their home, tied them up, placed their geriatric parents in a cart, and wheeled them off to an "unknown place."[128]

Tension over work, wages, and reimbursement made violence a painful fact of life for exiles across Massachusetts. In the fall of 1756, after two months of work in Methuen, Laurence Mius received "three rods of old cloth . . . two pounds of dried cod and one pound of pork fat." When he protested, Mius found himself pursued by an overseer of the poor "armed with a poker" who, although he did not make good on his promise to "kill him like a frog," nevertheless dispensed a beating that caused the Acadian to "spit blood for the rest of the day."[129] Likewise, Augustin Hébert complained that a Watertown resident named Coniglot assaulted him "to the point that he could barely walk for two weeks."[130]

Even when they avoided fights, Acadians could rarely escape the hardships of bad housing. Although he had "lived well" for months in Salem, François Mius despaired of his lot in Tewksbury. Sent there at the provincial government's request in the summer of 1757, he now resided in "the worst house in the world." Rotten timbers strained to support windowless walls, while "stones stacked to a height of about six feet with a hole in the roof" masqueraded as a chimney. Mius wrote to the legislature in Boston asking to return to Salem and promising that "his family . . . will provide for their needs by working, without much cost to the public."[131] In Wilmington, John Labardor's seven children lived in a house "which has neither door nor roof." When he complained of flooding in the home, a town counselor advised him to "build a boat and navigate in it." "For the love of God,"

Labardor pleaded with Governor Thomas Pownall to "stop the injustices" that buffeted his already ruined family.

After all, Labardor explained, he was a friend to the British, and always had been. While living on Ile Royale during the 1750s, he had escorted to safety a British vessel "that the savages had the intention of pillaging." The Indians, doubtless French-allied Mi'kmaw warriors, repaid Labardor with deershot, three balls of which remained lodged in his back. In light of his devotion to British interests, "the thought of seeing oneself exposed to dying of misery . . . broke [Labardor's] heart."[132] Stories like Labardor's, forwarded to officials in the provincial government, seemed like the best defense against local offenses. When Jacques LeBlanc asked permission for his son, exiled to Maryland, to join him in Braintree, he told a similar tale. Years earlier in northern Nova Scotia, he had saved the life of an Englishman named Joseph Lugar. After a band of Mi'kmaq killed Lugar's companions, LeBlanc gave "fifteen dollars for his ransom and completed this sum by giving up his coat."[133]

For their part, Jacques Mireau and Joseph d'Entremont recalled experiences as fishermen on the southern tip of Nova Scotia, "a place far removed and separated from other settlements in Acadia." Deaf to offers made to other Acadians by French officials, Mireau and d'Entremont had behaved as good Britons, "rescuing English fishermen and others of this nation, for which they have always held feelings of friendship." Fearful of being transported to someplace where they might be forced to "cultivate the earth or to give themselves to other work they have never done," they begged to stay near "fishing places" where they could foster ties with the "people they had known."[134] In Marshfield, a fifteen-year-old Acadian named Paul Michelle had the opposite problem. Forced by a cold-hearted town counselor to work on a fishing vessel in spite of persistent seasickness, the young man relied on his father to secure his release. Joseph Michelle recalled living "in good communication with the English" near Annapolis Royal, selling goods to British soldiers and their wives. Blaming the expulsion on "the bad conduct of the French who resided near Mines," he had endured "a large part of their misfortunes without having committed the same faults." His political fidelity, Michelle believed, earned his son the right to work on a farm as the family had always done.[135]

Loyalty made good copy, but Acadian labor ultimately paid the bills. Faced with starvation in Lancaster, a village on the western frontier, Belloni Melançon apprenticed a son to local artisan James Wilder to try to earn extra money. Wilder instead gave the boy "black and blue bruises on the arm," rendering it unusable for a month. Others in town grew weary of the Acadians' perceived freeloading and conspired to remove them. Evicting the Acadians from their house, local toughs tore Melançon's crippled wife from bed and tossed her into a cart, aggravating injuries she had received back in 1755. The family asked to stay in Weymouth, a coastal town where Belloni's skill as a fisherman might be useful.[136] Concerns about such a move abounded. The government had already tried planting thirty-seven Acadians in the fishing village of Marblehead. Locals howled in protest. Near the water, exiles would have "greate opportunity of caballing together & forming designs" to "put themselves aboard a vessel or vesells . . . and make their escape in the night"—and worse, "in the Winter season there will be no imployment for them in this place," leaving them to subsist "at the public charge."[137] Although a committee in Boston found Melançon's accusations "without foundation," the Provincial Council appreciated his efforts to make ends meet on his own. He received permission to fish, some firewood, and a rented house in Weymouth, all paid for by the government of Massachusetts.[138]

Although Acadians looked to British authority for redress, tensions over religion and labor could, on rare occasions, be mediated locally. One such case took place in Westborough, a village thirty miles from Boston, where Ebenezer Parkman spent his days ministering to the members of a tiny Congregationalist church. Harvard-educated, theologically conservative, and perpetually beset by intestinal distress, Parkman did not seem like a man who would take interest in the welfare of French-speaking Catholics consigned to his town. But for some reason, he did so. Perhaps, as one of his sermons suggested, he hoped that by "reproving and warning the Disobedient" while promoting "true Religion," he might appease God and stave off the French onslaught in North America.[139] Where others looked on Acadian exiles and saw the entering wedge of popery and a financial burden, Parkman may well have seen a cosmic opportunity.

Parkman's relationship with the Acadians began on October 19, 1756. To that point, he had followed the unfolding war with trepidation, fearful that Westborough might once again be exposed to attacks by French-allied Indians. But after friends informed him that "a Family of Neutral French, as ye were called," had been commended to the care of a neighbor, Parkman's curiosity overwhelmed his fear. He wasted no time before paying a visit.[140] At the home of a Mr. Bigelow, the minister met Simon Leblanc, once the proprietor of a handsome farm near Annapolis Royal, along with his wife and four children. Describing the patriarch as "about 55" and "Rheumatic," Parkman noted with surprise that Simon was "a Roman Catholic, but is able to read."[141] Two more trips to see the "French Family" followed over the next few weeks, one of which netted Parkman a fine cup of tea.[142] He then invited the family to dine at his home late in November. Simon became ill and declined, but wife Magdalene and daughter Mary came, pleasing the other guests by behaving "with decency."[143]

Parkman then set to the task of dispensing "instruction about Religion." In Simon's cramped quarters that December, he reviewed the Acadian's library. The books contained some disturbing information. In one volume, Parkman noted, the "Ten [Commandments] were very oddly disposed." The second, banning the worship of idols, was gone, while the tenth, which prohibited the coveting of a neighbor's wife and house, was split in two.[144] To Parkman's chagrin, Simon resisted all attempts to correct these abuses. After the minister "injoind" his counterpart "to mind those great matters," Simon retorted that the French "did more about those things than ye English people here did." The Acadian seemed particularly disturbed by the rowdy behavior of the teenagers in Parkman's town. Calling them "wicked," Simon would not "let his sons go much among them." Although Parkman expressed "great Grief" at this "Obstruction in what I would fain do for them," he continued to grope for common cause.[145]

It was hard going. In January 1757, Simon revealed to Parkman that "his sister Mary marryd an Englishman by whom she had a number of daughters." The sister (really his half sister) was Marie-Madeleine Maisonnat, the daughter of a famous Acadian privateer named Pierre Maisonnat and Madeleine Bourg. That marriage had collapsed before Marie-Madeleine turned three in 1698, driving Bourg to marry Pierre Leblanc, a widower who would become Simon's father. Later, Marie-Madeleine married William Winniett, a Londoner of French-Protestant ancestry who had migrated to Nova Scotia in 1710 and became a prominent merchant and member of the governor's council at Annapolis Royal. Three of Marie-Madeleine and Winniett's daughters had married Alexander Cosby, John Handfield, and Edward How, their father's British associates in Nova Scotia's provincial government. In a cruel twist, a reluctant Handfield had spearheaded the operation to deport the Acadians of Annapolis Royal in 1755, a dark bit of family history that Simon chose to keep from the dogged Parkman.[146] With his past in mind, Simon confided in Parkman his nostalgia for the easygoing Annapolis Royal he had once known. There, he recalled, residents "never speak to one another about Religion, but are free . . . ye English to go to their own Church and the French to theirs."

Thinking fast, Parkman said something stunning. "I told him," he recorded, "that I wanted to know His Religion." Simon "was profoundly still." After what seemed to Parkman like a long moment of reflection, he offered the Acadian a copy of the Bible, expressing his hope that the two men might, as equals, learn something from each other. Simon took the book, and Parkman left. Six days later, the Leblanc family was moved from the drafty outbuildings of Bigelow's farm to better lodgings in the town school, a step almost surely taken with Parkman's blessing.[147]

Over the next fifteen months, the friendship between Protestant minister and Acadian exile deepened. The two visited often. Leblanc posed questions about fast days and the Quaker aversion to baptism, pausing to regale the minister with an account of "the fight at Grand Pré" from King George's War in 1746. Parkman gave the exiles a French-language New Testament, a "Catechism & Confession of Faith of ye Reformed Churches in France," and a history of French martyrs.

Making good on his promise to learn about Catholicism, the minister "carry'd a Rosary, or long string of beads, for him to explain."[148] All of this was done, according to Parkman, to "manifest my true and hearty love to him."[149]

The Seven Years' War put that love to a severe test. The British war effort foundered in 1757, leaving Massachusetts grasping for answers. In August, the French captured Fort William Henry in northern New York and, according to the press, participated with Native Americans in a post-capitulation "massacre" that yielded five hundred captives for the Indians while leaving two hundred British soldiers and camp followers dead. In response, officials in Boston instructed sheriffs to "exercise the strictest surveillance" over the Acadians.[150] In Westborough, neighbors recoiled at news of "French cruelty" in the Pennsylvania backcountry, praying hard for the success of British arms. Or most of them did. Parkman later confessed that he had "several times try'd to move my Billy from his purpose of going to war . . . but he remains fervent." "He is also desirous of my gun," the minister lamented. "I yield to please him."[151]

Faced with uncertainty, some turned to God in strange ways. "Muffled in a frock," one such "strange man" showed up at Parkman's church on January 31, 1757, enjoined him to "give solemn warning" to the congregation from the second chapter of Joel, and left without giving his name. "A day of darkness and of gloominess . . . all faces shall gather blackness," the scripture went. But hope emerged from the "great and very terrible" day of the Lord: "I will remove far off from you the northern *army*, and will drive him into a land barren and desolate." Parkman's journal did not mention the prophecy, ending the day on a practical note: "Amon Blanc [Simon's son Armand] at dinner here."[152]

As the Seven Years' War threatened to tear Massachusetts apart, Parkman acted as a magnet, drawing Acadians and New Englanders together. But for all of Parkman's desire to convert Simon Leblanc ("If I had any love to him I must!" the cleric exclaimed in the margin of his journal), labor effectively made the relationship. On April 18, 1757, Parkman reported that Armand Leblanc "worked for me, partly in ye Garden and partly tending the mason[ry]." The next day, Armand and his sister Mary worked alongside two locals named Deacon and Dunlap, while a chatty visit from Simon created "a far greater hindrance" to Parkman's sabbath preparations. Summer saw more of the same. In May, the "French girls" delivered to Parkman "33 yards of cloth, which Magdalene has spun and wove for us," after which Leblanc's daughters stayed for dinner; in June, Parkman noted that Armand "and my two boys Alex and Breck [eleven and ten years old, respectively] hoe my corn." One week later, Armand dug a well "to water the Cattle" at Parkman's house; the next week, Armand arrived with "Stephen Robishow [Robichaud], son of Mr. Joseph Robishow of Uxbridge; he offers hims[elf] to be hir'd to reap today." Parkman paid the exiles to "reap part of ye field behind ye meeting house." But the minister only had so much to offer. In late August, he reported that Armand "comes no more to work for me, having leave from me to work where he can . . . for better wages than I can afford."[153]

After the harvest of 1757, Westborough's experiment in intercultural cooperation regressed toward the Massachusetts mean of standoffishness. For Parkman, there were a last few hopeful moments. In November, Jacques-Maurice Vigneau—he of the canoe journey up from Georgia—dined at his home while on a visit from Leominster. And on December 1, Parkman exulted that his discourse on Psalms 51:11 ("Cast me not away from thy presence; and take not thy holy spirit from me") was attended by Simon and his wife, marking the "first time that he has ever attended upon any of my sermons."[154]

And then the Acadian-Yankee relationship ended. Parkman saw Simon at a funeral in September 1758 and welcomed his children Pierre and Magdalene, with Anne Robichaud and "Modesty Landry" from Acton in tow, to "meeting" on March 1, 1759.[155] But no Acadian ever worked for Parkman again. Perhaps as the British war effort shrugged off early failures, capturing Louisbourg in 1758, Québec in 1759, and Montréal in 1760, the minister's passion for "exhorting and stirring up others" to avoid devastation at the hands of "our merciless and malignant Foes" simply waned.[156] Perhaps Acadians found "better wages" elsewhere. In any case, Parkman—the grandfather of Francis Parkman, whose 1892 masterpiece *A Half Century of Conflict: France and England in North America* painted Acadians as "ignorant of books," an "unambitious peasantry" deficient in "activity and enterprise"—turned away from Simon's soul, away from Armand's toil, and toward his own God.[157]

What happened in Westborough was unusual. And yet the strange friendship of Ebenezer Parkman and Simon Leblanc was emblematic of the experience of those first seven thousand Acadian exiles. Across the British Empire, they were lumped in with French-allied Indians and would-be slave rebels, caught up in a Quaker campaign against British inhumanities, and, in New England, targeted for conversion by some and exploitation by others. Whatever their situation, Acadians wanted redress, and they had few compunctions about blaming other Acadians (those from Chignecto, usually) to get it. They also wanted family. Simon was no exception. He shielded his children from the debauchery of Congregationalist youth and hosted his oldest son, Joseph, and cousin Marien Gourdeau, exiled to Cambridge and Sherborn, as often as he could.[158] Work, however, exerted its own pull. For the summer of 1757 at least, Parkman's property drew Acadian girls with cloth and Acadian boys with muscle enough for ripening grain and half-dug wells. The minister's wages connected Acadians to the people of Westborough, and to each other. Just days after Marie and Magdalene Leblanc sold homespun to Parkman's wife, for example, Marie and her father went "on foot" to Cambridge, using the windfall to see "their friends down below."[159]

The scale differed, but it was much the same elsewhere. The range of possibilities Acadians in exile saw—to stay or leave, gather or disperse—was, in large measure, a function of what sort of labor local and provincial authorities believed them capable of performing. Those authorities were unpredictable. Where John Reynolds ushered Jacques-Maurice Vigneau and his family from Georgia, Henry Ellis encouraged the "useful" exiles to stay, provisioning the coastal trade that drove Savannah's economy. Where Robert Dinwiddie and James Glen saw no place for Acadians among the slaves of the southern lowcountry, Parkman put the Leblanc children on the job in Massachusetts. In Philadelphia, provincial politics pushed Acadians into an underworld populated by patrons and bosses who, like the exiles themselves, chafed at British arrogance. In those first few years of the *grand dérangement*, Acadian lives, like the environments in which they were lived, proved so variable as to defy easy generalization.

But as the Seven Years' War came to a close with the dismemberment of the old French Empire, forces more powerful than frontier ministers or provincial governors trained their sights on the Acadians. At stake was nothing less than the construction of a new imperial world—a vast, baroque project whose need for work-roughened, able hands would, in many cases, bring disconnected exiles together. For the statesmen, economists, and military men in charge, those reunions, like the revolutionary new settlements that were to host them, seemed simple enough to engineer. Yet their execution rarely went according to plan.

3

The Tropics

And among these nations shalt thou find no ease, neither shall the sole
of thy foot have rest: but the Lord shall give thee there a trembling
heart, and failing of eyes, and sorrow of mind. And thy life shall hang in
doubt before thee; and thou shalt fear day and night.
—Deuteronomy 28:65–66

Even the most harried, downtrodden Acadian exile would have admitted it: by
1763, Louis XV had endured several bad years in a row. The king's downward
spiral began in January 1757, when an out-of-work domestic servant named
Robert-François Damiens tried to kill him with a penknife on the steps of the
royal palace at Trianon. Interrogated, tortured, and finally drawn and quartered
in the center of Paris, Damiens haunted his victim. As a British spy reported that
summer, Louis "frequently burst into tears" and even mused about abdicating
the throne.[1]

By then, though, the king had much more to cry about. After a promising start
in North America and Europe, his war had become a disaster. British and Prussian victories over the French and their Austrian allies had spread like a pox:
Rossbach and Leuthen in 1757, Louisbourg and Gorée in 1758, Québec and
Guadeloupe in 1759, Montréal in 1760, Pondicherry and Belle-Ile-en-Mer (a
mere ten miles from the west coast of mainland France) in 1761, Martinique in
1762. Signed on February 10, 1763, the Treaty of Paris ended the Seven Years'
War by humiliating Louis as few monarchs had been humiliated before. Although
France kept the Caribbean colonies of Saint-Domingue, Guadeloupe, and Martinique, losses in Canada, West Africa, India, the Mediterranean, and Louisiana
gave the defeat an air of finality. Worse, territorial downsizing offered limited
financial help for the debt-burdened kingdom, forcing Louis to extend wartime
taxes. For the Parisian diarist Edmond-Jean-François Barbier, it came as no surprise that two weeks after the peace, the spectacle of placing an equestrian statue
of the king on its pedestal in the Place Louis XV (today's Place de la Concorde)

became an occasion for "bad speech" and "indiscreet remarks." Some snickered that the statue was guided into position by four cranes, or *grues*, just as the king himself had become a puppet of his ministers. That *grue* was also slang for "whore" only made the allusion more amusing.[2]

Personally and geopolitically, Louis XV needed a boost. Luckily for him, some-time in 1762, a forty-two-year-old scientist named Jean-Baptiste-Christophe Fusée Aublet had had a great idea.

Its greatness, Aublet knew, sprang from its singularity, and its singularity was rooted in a unique set of personal experiences. While studying botany, chemis-try, and geology at the university in Montpellier, Aublet had cultivated a group of patrons that included the atheist philosophe Paul-Henri Thiry, baron d'Holbach, Guillaume-Chrétien Lamoignon de Malesherbes, the freethinking director of France's book trade, and Bernard de Jussieu, a botanist and sub-dem-onstrator of plants at the King's Gardens in Paris. Spurred on by his backers, the young Aublet took a position with the Compagnie des Indes on Ile de France (now the Indian Ocean island of Mauritius), where he was to found a "labora-tory" to supply the company's outposts with medicines and a garden stocked with "plants that may become useful to the Colony." Aublet had found his dream job. "To train my body and mind for the work that awaited them," he exulted, "I made the journey [from Paris] to Lorient, my place of embarkation, on foot, observing and describing minerals along my route." After three hundred miles of walking, Aublet boarded the *Phelyppeaux* and set sail for a new world.[3]

On Ile de France, Aublet stuck out. He brought no *pacotille*, slang for the trin-kets used in illicit trade, leading some to believe he had come to the island only for a "change of scenery." Their observation was not far off the mark: Aublet changed Ile de France's scenery immediately. He took over an old garden at Pam-plemousse, near Port Louis on the northwest coast, and launched into experi-ments. Sabotaged by unnamed enemies (who "destroyed with as much ardor as I devoted to creation"), Aublet packed up his seedlings and moved inland to Le Réduit, where he "gathered all of the rare, useful, or curious plants I could pro-cure." In time, his duties expanded. After a typhoon ravaged Ile de France in the mid-1750s, Aublet spent weeks cutting a new road across the island, "sleeping in the woods" with a team of "intelligent, energetic, and skillful" Malagasy slaves. With those same "Madagascar Negroes," he built signal stations in the moun-tainous interior, working with his multiracial crew at the edge of a "terrifying precipice" on Corps-de-Garde, a dormant volcano south of Port Louis.[4]

By 1761, however, Aublet had worn out his welcome. Miscalculating badly, he aligned himself against Pierre Poivre, an ambitious botanist in the pay of the Compagnie des Indes, over the cultivation of nutmeg on Ile de France. With his reputation under siege from Poivre's well-connected friends, Aublet arranged his affairs, freed his own slaves, and headed back to Paris.[5] Within weeks of his arrival, the crown offered Aublet work in Cayenne, its colony on the coast of South America.[6] Charged with cataloguing the region's natural resources, the "apothecary-botanist" threw himself into more tropical research.[7] The next summer, as he braved clouds of mosquitoes, impassable barriers of "thorny shrubs," and the threat of "marooned, fugitive, and irritated Negroes" while searching for a much-rumored mercury mine in the unmapped interior, it hit him.[8] He, and perhaps he alone, knew how to make a wronged France right again.

At the heart of Aublet's plan was a trip. Given a canoe and some money, he would "ascend the Amazon, cross Peru to Mexico, there to embark for Manila in the Philippines, stop at Madagascar, and from there sail to Ile de France and return to Cayenne." Along the way, Aublet intended to collect "the most precious plants, such as nutmeg and clove trees." This haul of spices and curatives could first be replanted in the gardens of Cayenne and then transferred to tropical plantations worldwide.[9] Results were sure to follow. Shattering the Dutch monopoly on the spice trade in the East Indies, Aublet's maneuver would turn Cayenne into a hub whose wealth in exotic plants promised to fill Louis XV's coffers at the expense of allies and enemies alike.

Aublet saw his journey as a preemptive strike against British encroachments in the Southern Hemisphere. Even in 1762, months before the Treaty of Paris, everyone suspected that such intrusions were in the works. Henri Pouillard, a panicked merchant from the French port of Le Havre, put it this way:

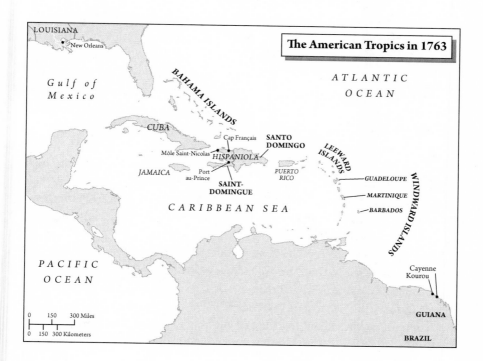

The efforts that the English have made, and will continue to make, to strip us of what remains in Canada, lay before our very eyes their intention to become masters of all of North America. Who can say that in the future they will not push their designs even farther?[10]

To stop the advance of "a restless, petulant nation like England," some hoped to create an equatorial bulwark, pinning Britain in the north by establishing a French stranglehold over cultivation and commerce in the tropics. Michel Adanson, a well-known botanist tapped to work alongside Aublet in Cayenne, had long advocated shipping plants (such as acacia trees, which produced gum arabic) and animals (including, remarkably, elephants and camels) from French Senegal to South America, boosting the economies of both settlements in the process.[11] Given France's position, it all made sense.

Yet Aublet harbored another motive. Put bluntly, he hated slavery. He hated the injustice of it, hated that it drained the "mildness and gaiety" from good Frenchmen, hated that its advocates denigrated Africans as "drunks, libertines, thieves, liars, idlers, and traitors." Cayenne, however, heralded something better. Boosting production to match expanding markets, landowners might be convinced to turn slaves into peasants. Working "in proportion to their needs and desires," African families would pay rent "with the harvest, as in Europe," participate in colonial defense, and in general "do more work than expatriated slaves, who labor for masters they detest."[12] Indeed, Cayenne might provide a haven for Aublet's wife, Armelle, a Senegalese woman whose freedom he had purchased from the Compagnie des Indes on Ile de France, and for their three children.[13]

Combining his familial anxieties and patriotic aspirations, Aublet sent a proposal to Versailles in April 1763, entrusting the document and a box of fruit for Louis XV to the captain of the frigate *Diligente*. Restless, he headed inland "immediately" after the *Diligente*'s departure, penetrating into Guiana's landscape of rivers and creeks with two slaves and Pierre Basson, a "mulatto" guide.[14]

Neither Aublet nor his proposal came through unscathed. As the botanist picked his way through razor-sharp underbrush ("My breeches," he wrote ruefully, "now serve only as rags"), his imperial plan met with criticism no less cutting.[15] Friends and patrons sent endorsements to ministers back in France, but they did little to stave off the attack. While "curious, passionate, enterprising, [and] tireless," reported Cayenne's governor, Aublet was not "easy to handle." Still, the governor explained, "if he loses control sometimes, he is back to his old self soon"—and that old self, he argued, was *the* man to undertake a journey "whose success, no matter what it may cost, will be as profitable for the state as it is glorious for him."[16] Metropolitan leaders lacked even this kernel of faith. Aublet's "courage" notwithstanding, they doubted his health ("He didn't look so good," noted one who had seen him recently) and his ability to conserve samples over long years of travel. The plan was rejected. But ministers made sure to include "some marks of satisfaction" for Aublet himself, hoping to soften the blow and "revive his zeal."[17]

Cold comfort, no doubt. And worse was to come, for Louis XV's ministers had their own South American aspirations. Like Aublet, they had slavery in their crosshairs. Rather than liberate Cayenne's seven thousand Africans, they hoped to lure thousands of white Europeans to a new colony at the site of a Jesuit mission on the Kourou River, thirty miles to the northwest.[18] These migrants would grow food, provisioning sugar islands such as Saint-Domingue as well as the French navy. Remarkably, slavery would not exist among them. The importation of "any Negro, mulatto, or other slave" was to be prohibited by law, creating an all-white preserve at the doorstep of the great plantation societies of the Caribbean. With "soils well suited to all sorts of crops [and] the most beautiful prairies," the Kourou might well have passed for "the promised land" in the eyes of some poor white farmer.[19] But for Aublet, it promised only a prolonged journey in a cursed wilderness.

They would not have known it, but Aublet and the Acadians had a great deal in common. Both were caught up in a cascade of creative, improbable, and ill-fated colonial experiments that promised to remap the Atlantic basin. Almost convulsively, post-1763 European ministers threw reformist ideas, crown funds, and especially settlers at a host of now-forgotten projects.

The results were colorful. Eager to tighten its grip on newly acquired East Florida, the British Board of Trade encouraged the diplomat and physician Andrew Turnbull to plant a settlement of Greeks, Corsicans, and Minorcans at New Smyrna in 1767.[20] Even as Spanish statesmen mulled over plans for populating Louisiana, transferred to them by the French in the semisecret Treaty of Fontainebleau, Catherine the Great recruited entire Moravian congregations from Germany to people Russia's unruly southern frontier. For her part, the empress Maria Theresa of Austria aimed to plant thousands of German- and French-speaking farmers in the Banat region of Habsburg-ruled Hungary, at the doorstep of Ottoman Turkey.[21] As imperial cartography shifted, older assumptions about the nature of empire came under suspicion. With that suspicion came ventures capable of sweeping up tinkering botanists and hardy colonists alike.

In 1763, the Acadians were ripe for the taking. Of the seven thousand captured in 1755 and shipped to British North America, most still lingered near port cities, living on charity and whatever work they could find. Authorities in Virginia, of course, had rejected the nearly one thousand Acadians sent to Hampton, dispatching them to England in the spring of 1756. Eventually these exiles ended up in Bristol, Liverpool, Falmouth, Southampton, and the Welsh port of Penryn. Following a deadly outbreak of smallpox soon after arriving, they settled into the margins of urban society. On orders from local officials, Acadians typically lived near each other (in a run-down neighborhood of Liverpool, or in converted warehouses in Bristol, for example). Some worked odd jobs, but most were "restrained" from doing so "to prevent the Clamor of the laboring People."[22]

As in North America, Acadians in Great Britain were pulled in more than one direction. Many continued to petition for better treatment based on their status as British subjects. Others clung to France as their best hope, a sentiment expressed by Acadians in Liverpool who, during a visit from a staffer from the French embassy on New Year's Eve in 1762, burst into cries of "Vive le Roy!" so loud that neighbors were "scandalized." In Penryn, though, boys apprenticed to British craftsmen had, wrote one observer, "contracted some not-so-French inclinations."[23] In any case, exiles across the British Empire were, at war's end, on the lookout for new opportunities.

These Acadians, however, represented only part of the total number uprooted by the British campaigns in Nova Scotia. Perhaps eight thousand Acadians had evaded capture, taking flight from the Bay of Fundy in all directions. Hundreds hid in the peninsula's forested uplands, hoping to ride out the storm. Others linked up with Charles des Champs de Boishébert, a French commander patrolling the Saint John's River in present-day New Brunswick, to wage a guerilla war against the British. In 1756 and 1757, when the French enjoyed the upper hand in the North American theater, these fighters played a crucial role in the defense of New France. "Independent of charitable motives, which will not permit that we should abandon them," noted one Canadian official, "it is of great importance to conserve [the Acadians] to fortify the borders of Canada, Ile Royale and Ile St. Jean." He even hoped to "make good use of them if circumstances permit us to take action in Acadia."[24] While the insurgents harassed British detachments, stole horses, and took captives, the declining fortunes of the French war effort left them exposed. As the marquis de Vaudreuil lamented in the spring of 1757, many of the Acadians had died in the wilderness, while the sick remained sick due to poor food, "often being forced to eat extremely emaciated horses, sea cows, or cow skins."[25]

A few kept up the struggle. Pierre Doucet, once the proprietor of a farm near Fort Beauséjour, received a commendation for valor at the siege of Québec in 1759 and was picked to command a "company of Acadians" at Montréal in 1760. At Restigouche on the Baie des Chaleurs, a group led by Nicolas Gaultier used a few old schooners to prey on British vessels in the Gulf of Saint Lawrence, marking the exiles' "readiness to attempt anything against the present establishment" of Nova Scotia.[26] But well before the Treaty of Paris, the Acadians who had fled knew, in the words of one of their priests, that "the dice are thrown" and that the enemy had emerged as their "masters."[27] By 1761, even Gaultier and the "pirates of Restigouche" had made peace, gaining assurances from the war-weary British that there would be no repeat of 1755. Although numbers are hard to estimate, by 1763 upward of two thousand Acadians likely lived on the mainland west and north of Nova Scotia, while a handful remained imprisoned in Halifax or elsewhere on the peninsula.

Others had traveled farther. During the winter of 1755–56, Acadians dashed for Ile Saint-Jean in droves. Making the frigid crossing in skiffs and canoes, they crowded into the island's still-new settlements, jostling with the three thousand Acadians who had fled there over the previous six years. They all grew desperate. Jacques Girard, a priest who ministered to Ile Saint-Jean's swollen congregations, later remembered that even though the crown had given pre-1755 Acadian migrants "three years of provisions, tools, [and] clothing, . . . they could not survive" without frequent gifts of food; in the fall of 1755, new arrivals made survival even more tenuous.[28] The island's residents, reported one official in April 1757, "had no means of subsistence, and could not plant their seeds this spring; women and girls dare not go out, being unable to cover their nudity."[29]

Undermined by hunger and increasingly isolated from a harried French military, the Acadians of Ile Saint-Jean put up little resistance when, after the British seizure of Louisbourg in July 1758, Colonel Andrew Rollo sailed into Port-la-Joie with five hundred soldiers in tow. After marveling at the "good land" ("so fine a climate . . . that it must invite settlers, & would soon have been a Granerie for the French Settlements as it abounds in Wheat, Barly, Rye, Oats & some Indian corn"), they launched into a new round of deportations.[30] Although some Acadians fled for Canada from the island's northern coast, Rollo and his men quickly captured nearly three thousand civilians, shuffled them aboard seventeen waiting ships, and sent them off—not, however, to the cash-poor, perpetually complaining British provinces to the south, and certainly not to Britain itself. Instead, these Acadians were shipped to France.[31]

Many never made it. Some succumbed to disease during the Atlantic crossing, but perhaps as many as five hundred Acadians were killed in the shipwrecks of the *Duke William* and the *Violet* off Cornwall, while more than one hundred drowned when the *Ruby* broke up on the rocks near the island of Pico in the Azores.[32] The rest were deposited in French ports including Boulogne-sur-Mer, Le Havre, Cherbourg, Saint-Malo, Morlaix, Nantes, and La Rochelle. Dependent on funds from the crown and the charity of locals, these Acadians endured as much as their old compatriots in North America. During the late 1750s and early 1760s, letters to and from Versailles detailed the exiles' sorry state. Visiting Boulogne-sur-Mer, the British author Tobias Smollett gawked at the Acadians, struggling to imagine how they got by on a "wretched allowance" from Louis XV.[33] Almost immediately after the Treaty of Paris, these exiles were joined in France by the surviving Acadians—just under nine hundred of them—from Great Britain. Gathered by the French ambassador in London, transported to Southampton in convoys of rented "wagons," and spirited across the English Channel on a balmy spring day in 1763, they were first housed in old barracks near Morlaix and later dispersed to towns across northern France.[34] In total, roughly three thousand Acadians had come to inhabit the land of their ancestors.[35]

Dike builders, backwoods traders, and friends to the Mi'kmaq eight years earlier, these Acadians were now disintegrated and marginalized in urban France. Soon after 1763, the Acadian diaspora, already remarkable in its scope and suddenness, would expand again. Pushing the exiles along was a bundle of radical ideas that, taken together, constituted a damning critique of slavery, the coercive institution at the heart of European imperialism. To create new colonies for a

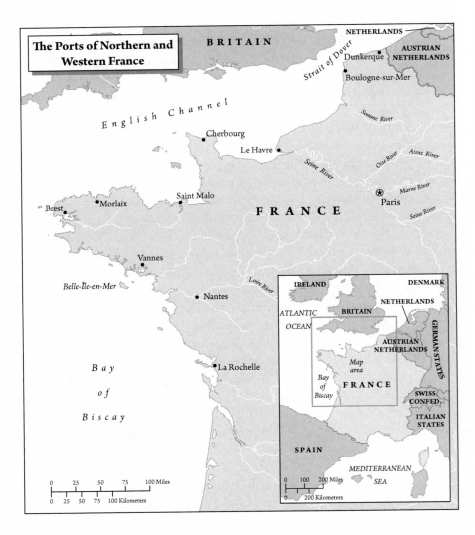

The Ports of Northern and Western France

new world ("nurser[ies] of some good intentions," one reformer called them), powerful Frenchmen contemplated an empire without slaves, in the process transforming scattered Acadians from unwanted pariahs into a "population too priceless not to receive with pleasure."[36] Flanked by men such as Jean-Baptiste-Christophe Fusée Aublet, however, Acadians would learn to be wary of "good intentions" in the American tropics.

Reeling from the losses inflicted by the Treaty of Paris, French ministers believed Cayenne to be a key to imperial revival. Slung across a coastal island near the mouths of the Montsinéry and Mahury rivers, the fortified town was the only bona fide settlement within the larger claim known as Guiana or *la France équinoxiale*. Bordered by Portuguese Brazil, Dutch Surinam, and the Atlantic, Guiana theoretically extended French rule deep into the South American rain forest, but in reality the interior remained something of a mystery. Indeed, while Guiana had attracted French adventurers, religious zealots, and profit seekers throughout the seventeenth century, the colony had long been considered a failure by the crown. Dreams of mineral wealth had been dashed early on, leaving a sweat-stained residue of plantation owners, soldiers, and officials to contend with their own chattel and the region's still-powerful Galibi natives.

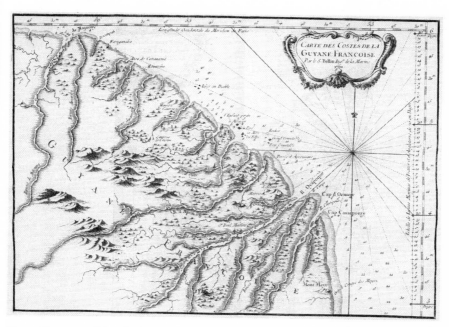

The settlements of French Guiana. Jacques-Nicolas Bellin, *Carte des costes de la Guianne, ou la France équinoxiale* (1763). Courtesy of the Library Company of Philadelphia.

It was a cruel place to live. In 1687, one cleric recited a litany of Cayenne's horrors: churches "menaced with ruin" from negligence, a hospital where the poor and sick were "very badly treated," and whites who refused to feed or clothe their healthy slaves while simply abandoning invalids.[37] Beyond Cayenne, others recoiled at the sheer disorder on Guiana's vast frontier. On the Approuague River to the south, for example, a French official reported on "ghastly acts committed against the Indians," relating his efforts to "remove from one inhabitant an Indian woman that he kept at his home" after the man's white wife "made a complaint."[38] Civilization seemed distant.

From the French perspective, little had improved during the eighteenth century. According to Pierre Barrère, the fortified town of Cayenne was so depopulated in 1743 that one could "kill a person in broad daylight, so to speak, without fear of being seen."[39] At midcentury, the total population consisted of six hundred whites and seven thousand slaves, a "lack of inhabitants" that, argued then-governor Gilbert Guillouet d'Orvilliers, was primarily responsible for the colony's "languishing state."[40] The Seven Years' War only made matters worse. In 1756, when asked by officials in Paris to provide a chart of prices in Cayenne, intendant Antoine-Philippe Lemoyne responded that he could not, as "barter is the only form of trade." Lack of money, he complained, led to demographic weakness. Since 1744, the slave trade in Guiana had existed "only by chance." No ship from "the coast of Guinea" had intentionally docked in Cayenne for more than a decade; the two most recent had limped in after taking on water, with only "infected cargo . . . reduced to less than half by sickness and want of supplies." As sure as "two and two make four," Lemoyne noted, Guiana's survival depended on specie and the slaves it would attract.[41]

For Frenchmen such as Lemoyne, then, slavery looked like the solution to Guiana's problems. "It is only by advancing money, provisions, and reasonably priced slaves to both new and old settlers," wrote one would-be reformer, "that [Guiana] will enjoy the harvest in peace."[42] Seen from a perspective at once more local and more imperial than Lemoyne's, however, slaves hardly equaled stability. First of all, they represented a constant, deadly threat to their masters. In 1726, for example, a company of soldiers on a scouting expedition "four or five leagues" from Cayenne stumbled upon a "dreadful murder." A local farmer had been killed, his wife raped and beaten to death, his "three- or four-year-old child" kidnapped, and his still-breastfeeding baby abandoned "for more than sixty hours . . . among the corpses." According to officials who sent troops toward the Amazon in search of the victim's "Negro and Indian slaves," the murders "concerned all of the colonies in general, and all crowned heads have an interest in them."[43]

To be sure, this was a spectacular case, but the threat of slave violence was ever present. A few years later, a woman named Chateauneuf was tending to her isolated farm while her husband was in Cayenne on business. The woman tried to intervene when a slave attacked his wife with a dagger. Enraged, the husband made a run for the plantation house, found a gun, and shot Chateauneuf in the thigh. "Seeing herself wounded," she dragged herself into a pirogue, or dugout canoe, and paddled for Cayenne. Bloodied and exhausted, she made it; tracked through the swamps by French soldiers and their Indian guides, her assailant did not.[44]

Seemingly savage and capricious, slaves—although necessary for agriculture in the Caribbean vein—made Guiana's planters uneasy. Ensuring African submissiveness was, of course, always a primary goal, as one Frenchman with designs on Guiana made clear in 1761:

> The American way demands that we keep the blacks in the most strict subordination and the harshest submission to make ourselves feared, and to impress upon them that we are as much above them as they themselves are above the animals. They are so ingrained and convinced of this that they say, in their language, to the horses: *Me slave of the white man, and you slave of the Negro.*[45]

But slaves so persuaded of their own inferiority were, as the evidence suggests, a figment of the French imagination.

Unlike small Caribbean islands such as Martinique or Guadeloupe, Guiana offered slaves endless chances to cause havoc by escaping to the colony's ungoverned interior. "Louis, a Negro, slave of Sieur Gourgues," did just that in 1747, only to be captured by a French patrol. Clapped in irons and questioned, the fifteen-year-old told a worrisome story. After being whipped by his master, Louis's father gathered some supplies, stole a canoe, and took the boy up the Mahury River, spending "several weeks" hiding in the woods. One day, as if by magic, a former slave named André emerged from the brush and led the pair toward the "headquarters of the maroons." Although the path was shrouded and tough to follow, the wilderness soon yielded to sown fields and a bustling camp, where dozens of ex-slaves enjoyed "provisions from the common store," cowered under the whip of "Captain André" when they shirked their duties, and carried "hatchets and billhooks" on raids to the nearby plantations of Tonnegrande.[46] Officials sent expeditions against the maroons in 1749 and 1750 but succeeded only in forcing André's villages to "abandon their old settlements." In 1753, troops reconnoitering the Kourou River basin crept up on the maroons' new villages. Surrounded by fields of corn and manioc, the Africans were singing within a central grouping of huts. After a soldier's footsteps alerted the maroons to the detachment's presence, the village erupted. Most of the ex-slaves took flight as the French opened fire, but one woman was killed and "five or six" children, who watched in silence as the soldiers burned the village, were taken "to serve as guides."[47] Even in 1756, as war with Britain began, Cayenne's militia fought to neutralize "these wretches . . . who only shoot from behind trees." In an engagement early that year, frightened soldiers fired wildly into the forest upon meeting some maroons in a clearing, but as their leader explained, "they do not know whether they killed any."[48]

Slavery in Guiana, then, generated a persistent, ever-growing threat in the west. It did much the same on the Atlantic coast. In 1759, with South America on the lookout for the British navy, Cayenne's governor, d'Orvilliers, took the unusual step of manning the town's fortifications with slaves. Since the king would pay for any slave "killed or mutilated," d'Orvilliers demanded "the elite" from nearby estates. Planters protested on financial grounds, while others questioned the plan's military wisdom. "Exposing our slaves to . . . a capitulation," wrote an unimpressed Lemoyne, would create "an object too attractive to hope for any mercy from the enemy."[49] Given slavery's negative effect on white migration (a 1762 inquiry found 125 whites in Cayenne capable of bearing arms), colonists had little choice but to defend royal property with their own.[50] For his part, Lemoyne thought so little of d'Orvilliers's tactics that in the event of an attack, he recommended burning Cayenne to the ground, assembling "all of our forces capable of rendering an occupation useless" in Guiana's interior, and launching guerilla raids on the British. Ironically, these raids would include slaves: "harassed during the day by whites, during the night by Negroes capable . . . of undertaking things impossible to even the most determined white," the British (or anyone else) would simply give up.[51] The plan exposed the contradictions and dangers of Guianese slavery in a world of belligerent empires.

Slavery made the French Caribbean profitable. But given Guiana's lack of strong institutions, maroon-friendly geography, and susceptibility to invasion, it remained unclear that the establishment of a slave society along the lines of, say, Saint-Domingue's would be either possible or desirable. In fact, a rising chorus of French thinkers during the Seven Years' War had constructed a compelling argument against slavery in general, but especially in half-formed places such as Guiana. The most influential such thinkers went by the name *les economistes*, or, to their enemies, *la secte*. We know them as the physiocrats.

Headed by the royal physician François Quesnay and his protégé Victor Riqueti, marquis de Mirabeau, this "first modern school of economics" used dizzying calculations and baroque diagrams to reach a simple conclusion: that the laws of society should agree with the laws of nature.[52] Agriculture, then, deserved more emphasis than any other economic activity, for it alone created surplus wealth and state revenue, while commerce and industry merely moved money around. "Let the Sovereign and the Nation never lose sight that the soil is the only true source of riches," wrote Pierre-Samuel Dupont de Nemours in 1768, "and that it is agriculture that multiplies them."[53] During the 1750s and 1760s, physiocracy made numerous converts. French aristocrats saw in

Quesnay's doctrine a way to revitalize the traditional, agrarian values of their order. For others, physiocracy promised universal applicability in an age of relativism. "There is one natural, essential, and general order that contains the . . . fundamental laws of all societies," claimed Nemours, while Pierre Poivre cast agriculture as the "thermometer" by which to measure any society's adherence to that order.[54] Certain that the laws of economics were as clear as Newton's laws of physics, the physiocrats built up a robust, demanding worldview—and slavery had no place in it.

Put simply, physiocrats believed that slavery infringed on "the first fundamental law of society," that of property over one's person.[55] "The laws of nature and of the *true interest* of all men . . . *obviously* forbid slavery," explained a contributor to the physiocratic journal *Ephémérides du Citoyen*.[56] Slavery threatened the rise of free markets for goods and labor. Fostered by enlightened rule, such markets would steer Frenchmen away from the sterile pleasures of urban life toward farms, families, and fecundity, they argued. Slavery, however, promoted artificial inequality, linking agriculture with what Mirabeau called the "lowest rank" in society and spurring the advance of luxury and depopulation.[57] On this last point physiocrats became especially animated. Thinkers in Europe had long lamented the demographic effects of the slave trade on Africa.[58] Mirabeau brought such concerns home. If slavery went unchecked, a disastrous trend would spread from the New World. "Little by little," he predicted in 1756, "the population of slaves will rise, and that of the masters will diminish." Slaves would constitute a global underclass, their increase squeezing whites, for whom farming was by now a marker of low status, into colonial cities where no mates could be found, hampering the "spirit of population" that promised to reanimate Louis XV's empire.[59]

After 1763, many Frenchmen rejected colonialism altogether, declaring Europe's overseas ventures morally repugnant or concluding, like the abbé Gabriel Bonnot de Mably, that "this kingdom can be . . . very powerful without colonies."[60] In general, the physiocrats were not among them. Most saw the colonies Louis XV had left as crucial to France's economic independence, as "new province[s], capable of producing commodities that have become necessary, which cannot be produced on . . . old lands."[61] The key idea was agricultural integration between colony and metropolis. "Colonies are simply newly cleared lands," Mirabeau noted in 1764 (in a book whose title promised that the ideas within its covers would "ensure the prosperity of empires"), linking France's colonies with freshly drained swamps near Bordeaux and felled forests on the German frontier.[62] If properly planned and executed, physiocrats argued, the rebirth of Louis XV's empire could herald a new era in European imperialism.

Not that the physiocrats were abolitionists. "I would not undertake to ban the use of Negroes," wrote Mirabeau in 1756, doubtless aware of the importance of

Saint-Domingue, Martinique, and Guadeloupe to the French economy. "But do you want to limit [slavery], and soon enough make it unnecessary? Encourage cultivation of the land in the colonies." As new, enlightened settlers led the way by "presiding over their own crops" and never "disdaining to put their own hand" to the plow, the progress of a more diversified French agriculture in the Americas would, in time, promote the demise of slavery and the growth of empire. Here Mirabeau could not resist an agrarian metaphor. The "gold of Peru," he wrote in 1756, had been "lime at the foot of the tree" for Spain; Britain's commerce had spawned an "aquatic, swamp-dwelling plant" with "floating, unsupported leaves" soon to fall from the plant altogether. France, by contrast, would nourish the agrarian "root of state."[63] If the monarch followed the natural order, Mirabeau predicted, not only would the French Empire overcome its adversaries, but land-owners in places such as Guiana would also come to "prefer workers, and even farmers earning a wage to slaves for which one must pay dearly, and who are almost always burdensome and disloyal."[64]

Two strands of French anti-slavery—one rooted in the raw, brutal experience of the Guianese frontier, the other in the physiocrats' high-minded theorizing— collided in July 1762, when a man arrived in Paris from South America. Jean-Antoine Bruletout de Préfontaine had spent the previous twenty years running his own plantation near Cayenne and leading French soldiers and Indian path-finders into the backcountry in search of maroons.[65] Like Aublet, Préfontaine's life at the edge of the French Empire had, he believed, given him some insights. Upon reaching Paris, the visitor made contact with his friend Joseph de Jussieu, a prominent botanist who had spent time in Guiana. At Jussieu's invitation, Pré-fontaine presented his ideas to a group of agriculturalists who met at Jussieu's home. They included Jean-Baptiste Thibault de Chanvalon, a former member of the *conseil supérieur* of Martinique and author of a natural history of that island; Etienne-François Turgot, a nobleman who had served for fifteen years on the island of Malta; and his younger brother Anne-Robert Turgot, a royal intendant in the backwater province of Limousin who would later become Louis XVI's first finance minister. To one degree or another, all were followers of physiocracy, and Préfontaine sparked their imaginations.

In some ways, Préfontaine's plan was traditional. It involved a new settlement on the Maroni River, a hundred miles northeast of Cayenne near the border of Dutch Surinam. He proposed a town composed of fifty new plantations to be populated by three hundred French whites and six hundred slaves transported directly from West Africa. Préfontaine, however, had taken to heart at least some of the concerns over slavery generated by Guiana's past. Migrants to his Maroni River settlement would, he hoped, shun cash crops in favor of growing food (at least in the beginning), and he hoped to keep the African population small and well regulated.[66] But with the future of the empire and valuable patronage up for grabs, the men gathered in Jussieu's drawing room thought bigger. Seizing on Préfontaine's ideas, the salon physiocrats used their political connections to make the project their own. Bewildered, Préfontaine found himself whisked to meetings at Versailles, culminating in a November audience with Etienne-François de Stainville, duc de Choiseul, Louis XV's foreign minister. Choiseul was receptive, having long believed in Guiana's strategic importance.[67] By February 1763, he had named the elder Turgot governor and Chanvalon intendant of what they had all come to call "La Nouvelle Colonie." He had also recruited several investors ready to purchase land, and had reserved a choice plot of Guianese soil for himself.[68]

Little of Préfontaine's original vision remained. Instead of a thousand masters and slaves, the colony would be populated by ten thousand white peasants and a handful of great proprietors. Capital-rich entrepreneurs bound for Guiana, declared Choiseul, would be granted land and laborers "in proportion to the money [each] contributes." The colony's "peasants" would be given small plots, but they would not be allowed to exploit these holdings for five years after their arrival. Instead, they would clear and till for the great landowners, receiving wages from their employers along with an allowance from the king.[69] One element of Préfontaine's plan did survive: his injunction that planters grow food "to eliminate the fear of famine" during the first few years.[70] Even this point was amplified. Not only would the *first* settlers grow food *initially*, but *all* settlers would grow food *indefinitely*, creating a breastwork of farms that could, by Choiseul's lights, produce "livestock and provisions" with which to "supply the *Isles du Vent*, and create a regular trade with them."[71] To help landowners resist the allure of sugar, coffee, and indigo, Choiseul took a radical step. Citing Louis XV's desire to "multiply and increase the population and strength of this part of his possessions in America," he barred the importation of "any Negro, mulatto, or other slave."[72]

None of this had anything to do with African humanity. Broadly speaking, Choiseul and physiocratic fellow travelers such as the Turgot brothers had one important principle in common: they championed the cause of "rich farmers." Men of means, talent, and agrarian savoir faire, these rural aristocrats were to enclose massive tracts of land within France itself, transforming subsistence plots into profitable farms and backward peasants into wage-earning laborers.[73] "La Nouvelle Colonie," in a sense, represented a colonial trial run for the metropolitan future. For Choiseul, it also made geopolitical sense. Arguing that "the English made their conquests in the late war by means of their northern colonies, which are solely populated by whites," he advocated emulation. Anne-Robert Turgot agreed. "I see only one way to make a solid settlement," he wrote to Chanvalon, "and that is to cultivate and populate with whites." A quick influx of free settlers alone, Turgot offered, could raise the colony to the "degree of population" capable of resisting a British attack.[74] What Préfontaine thought of

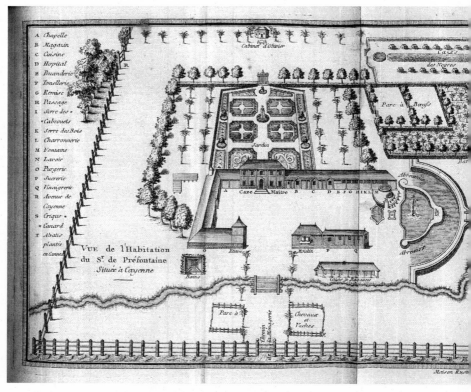

A traditional vision of colonial prosperity through African slavery: the Guiana plantation of the chevalier de Préfontaine, portrayed in his *Maison rustique, à l'usage des habitans de Cayenne* (1763). Courtesy of the Charles Deering McCormick Library of Special Collections, Northwestern University.

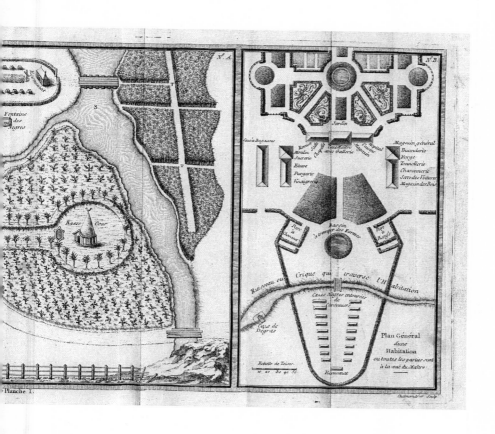

Planche I.

Fontaine des Negres

Basse Cour

N. A.

N. B.

Jardin

Case à Bagasses

Magasin général
Buanderie
Forge
Tonnelerie
Charonnerie
Serre des Voitures
Magasin des Bois

Bassin à tremper des Rames

Parc à Bestiaux

Parc à Bestiaux

Ruisseau ou Crique qui traverse l'Habitation

Case de Dégras

Cazes Negres entourées de Cocotiers

Plan Général
d'une
Habitation
ou toutes les parties sont
à la vüe du Maître

Echelle de Toises.
10 20 30 40 50

all this is unclear. He did, however, agree to accompany the first migrants back to Guiana, but only after receiving the Cross of St. Louis, France's highest military honor, and 18,000 livres.[75]

Leaders set to the task of finding settlers. Acadians intrigued Choiseul most of all. In the spring of 1763, as nearly eight hundred refugees crossed the English Channel to France, Choiseul received a memoir describing their character from Louis-Jules Barbon Mancini Mazarani, duc de Nivernais, France's ambassador in London. Good Catholics with a "tenacious attachment for France," the Acadians were also good workers, he testified. As "yeomen" in Nova Scotia, they had toiled "constantly" to build dikes, sow crops, and reap the harvest. Unlike the besotted peasants and artisans of the metropolis, idle moments found the Acadians weaving cloth or fishing.[76] While Nivernais may have admired the refugees, he had a clear motive for presenting them as "all given to hard work" on soils that "demanded diligent farming."[77] He owned Ile de Bouin, an uninhabited, sandy island at the mouth of the Loire River, and hoped to make it "a particular settlement for the Acadian prisoners in England." Envisioning them as just the tenants to make a wasteland profitable, Nivernais began the process that would eventually land Acadians in Guiana, transforming them from an unknown quantity into a cohesive community of ideal agricultural workers.[78]

Choiseul had little trouble seeing the Acadians' value. Indeed, competition for the refugees' services had become lively. A British agent had contacted Acadians living in the Norman port of Cherbourg in 1763. Feigning interest in wooden sabots carved by the refugees, the man took them aside and promised them "a happy lot in Acadia" and "Irish Priests for the exercise of the Catholic Religion."[79] Rumors also swirled of settlement offers on the island of Jersey, where farmers expelled from Nova Scotia might fortify another frontier of the British Empire. The prospect of Britain retaking the Acadians gnawed at Choiseul. "It is important for the State not to lose this people," he told the controller general of finances, Henri Bertin, "which would augment . . . the English; you feel the consequences of this as well as I do."[80] Choiseul rejected the Ile de Bouin scheme, telling Nivernais that the king "has for a long time had designs on [the Acadians] for a new colony." Although at times "indolent," Acadians were "laborious, good farmers, in general proper for anything as they were obliged to do everything in their country . . . building their own houses, chopping down trees, milling them, [and] constructing fishing boats."[81] In short, they were perfect.

Choiseul also had a darker motivation for favoring the Acadians for Guiana: they were bleeding his treasury dry. Upon arriving in France, the refugees were given a royal allowance, or *solde*, of six sols per day, or slightly more than a laborer's daily wage. Compassion was not at the measure's root. Louis XV was simply trying to match the British, who had given the Acadians "sixpence per day for their Subsistence, and . . . what may be reasonable for Lodging" in their metropolitan ports.[82] By 1763, Acadians across France had grown dependent on government assistance. The corporate nature of the old régime, in which guilds and *compagnonnages* regulated labor, made work hard to come by. All Acadians, even men such as François Arbourg, a freebooter noted for "tavern debts," and Aimable Henry, who left the Norman port of Cherbourg in 1758 for the "Guinea coast . . . aboard a slave ship," used the *solde* to get by.[83]

Like much of France's financial apparatus, the amount paid to Acadians remains shrouded in a mist of venality and grift, but costs likely rose to nearly 200,000 livres per year, paid directly from Choiseul's budget.[84] He sought to ease the strain. In 1761, Cherbourg officials began employing their Acadians on public works, withholding the allowance as they worked.[85] Choiseul legitimated the move, declaring that "persons unmarried and in condition to work, those that while married . . . can procure a living, and finally artisans" should be removed from the list of those receiving aid.[86] In response, Acadians begged. Once sympathetic, the *cherbourgeoisie* turned sour. "Inhabitants of this town who . . . have given them food, clothing, and other needs," a functionary named de Francy worried, "have begun to refuse them." With locals unable to cope with Acadian destitution, the burden once again fell to the crown. Guiana, then, offered Choiseul financial relief at home.

For refugees on the dole, recruitment proved to be an unpleasant process. Using incentives that had worked in the past—a payment of 50 livres for each family, plus 10 livres per child and the promise of arable land in Guiana—de Francy pitched the plan to an assembly of Acadians late in 1763. Seventy-five out of two hundred accepted, then changed their minds over the next few days, apparently thinking better of a move to the tropics.[87] Although he exempted self-proclaimed nobles (unaccustomed as they were, he assumed, to the "painful work of their hands"), Choiseul declared that those Acadians who refused to migrate would lose the *solde* and were, from that point on, "free to become what they wished," having misused the king's "support and kindnesses."[88]

Acadian resistance to these measures rarely ended well. Nastazie Doré Gaudet and Marie Henry, for example, accepted the crown's offer early in 1764, then reneged and gave the 50 livres back. De Francy "threatened to make them leave by force." Henry vanished into Cherbourg's alleyways, while Gaudet endured more frustration. Convinced that her fiancé had signed on for Guiana, she approached de Francy and once again asked to leave, only to discover that the young man had no intention of departing for South America or of marrying her. She "kept herself hidden" for weeks thereafter.[89] Others languished on the town's docks, or tried to demonstrate nobility by showing De Francy "excerpts of [noble] titles."[90] In June, nine Acadians struck from Cherbourg's welfare rolls gave in, bringing the number destined for South America to one hundred. By summer, the would-be migrants had trekked from Cherbourg to Le Havre, where they waited aboard ships destined for Guiana. Still more prepared to sail from Saint-Malo, Morlaix, and Boulogne. For Choiseul, the affair was a success. Acadians were deployable, dependent, dependable, and, at only 50 livres per family, compared to 2,000 livres for a healthy African slave, cheap.

As these Acadians (probably two hundred in all, although precise figures are hard to come by) assumed their too-familiar positions belowdecks, Préfontaine had reached Guiana. He had more than one hundred French, Canadian, Savoyard, and Irish pioneers in tow, along with Marie-Madeleine Boudrot and Madeleine Lapierre of Beaubassin, two Acadian women who had married a baker from Auvergne and an artillery officer from Normandy, respectively.[91]

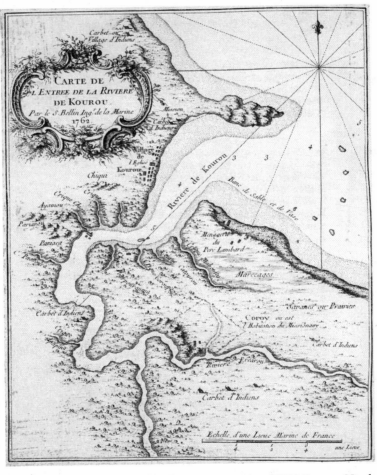

The Kourou River as it appeared before the great migration of 1764. Jacques-Nicolas Bellin, *Carte de l'entrée de la riviere de Kourou* (1763). Courtesy of the Library Company of Philadelphia.

Reconsidering the Maroni River site, he chose instead the Kourou, likely hoping to use the remaining buildings of an abandoned Jesuit mission. The group soon built a fort, drained marshes, and planted gardens. Counting on a "gradual peopling," Préfontaine surveyed the river, portioning out farmland for the two thousand additional colonists he expected within a year. Joined by a regiment of soldiers and a few *concessionnaires*, the wealthy landowners recruited by Choiseul, the original colonists thrived. The death rate was only 5 percent.

Arriving on Christmas Day 1763, the intendant Chanvalon waxed messianic about the Kourou colony. It was "singular," he wrote, to reach Préfontaine's settlement on the day on which "the church sings, *Today the Child is born, Today the Savior appears.*" After a chilly reception at Cayenne, Chanvalon had traveled overland to his destination, where "the entire colony was at arms on the shore." Breaking decorum, the colonists embraced their leader with great "tenderness" inspired by the "impulses of the heart."[92]

Failure was the furthest thing from Chanvalon's mind. "Never, since the discovery of America," he wrote, "has there been an enterprise so grand, so well supported . . . executed with more zeal, toil, and fidelity!"[93] Others, however, were less sanguine. Jacques-François Artur, a physician at Cayenne, found it odd that Chanvalon had not consulted anyone in the old settlement on the prospects of an "entirely white colony."[94] Some of Cayenne's longtime inhabitants, Artur reported, feared a repeat of 1717, when French passengers aboard *Le Roy Guillaume* had infected hundreds with smallpox. Late in the summer of 1763, word from the Kourou colony of stricken soldiers on the *Prothée* and the *Corismande* triggered old fears.[95]

Those fears would soon be realized. In February 1763, even as Choiseul began to train his eye on the Acadians, he also dispatched agents across France's eastern border in search of good colonists. The inhabitants of German-speaking regions such as Alsace and Bavaria had endured a great deal during the Seven Years' War. Exchange ground to a halt, marauding armies decimated crops, and news of peace brought little relief. French representatives, however, carried word (on custom-made German broadsheets) of a good deal for all willing migrants. After giving proof of "good conduct and manners," German colonists bound for Guiana would receive money to transport themselves and "a certain quantity of goods or effects" to an Atlantic departure point—usually Rochefort in western France. Louis XV promised to take care of them. The crown would provide "food, clothing . . . household implements, hammocks, beds, sheets, medicines . . . treatment from doctors and surgeons, tools for farming and crafts, [and] seeds for planting" upon arrival in Guiana.[96] These gifts would continue for three years, after which migrants would support themselves on their own lands. At the outset, though, the colony's "little people" would grow food— emphatically not "the country's principal commodities, which have made the most necessary provisions expensive and even scarce"—on the estates of Guiana's big landowners.[97] It was, Choiseul knew, a formula for success. Properly supplied and supervised, the Germans would thrive. And when the Acadians who remained in France "receiv[ed] news from their compatriots" in Guiana, Choiseul predicted, "they will little by little lose the dangerous ideas that they have fabricated" about the tropics.[98]

In June 1763, Choiseul picked Baron Louis de Bodelschwingh, a Prussian aristocrat who had served as a battalion commander in the German theater, to spearhead and consolidate recruitment efforts in the Palatinate. Bodelschwingh started out in Landau, where he produced a new "invitational placard" complete with maps, a poetic description of Guiana (a "beautiful country" that yielded "two harvests per year"), and a statement explicitly welcoming Jews.[99] He emphasized the pleasures of the transatlantic crossing itself, including shipboard musicians such as Jacques-Blaise Ruisson, a smallpox-scarred, snub-nosed nineteen-year-old from Marseille who, for 50 livres, signed on to "play the tambourine for the amusement" of migrants headed west.[100]

Something then went horribly wrong. The first signs of trouble appeared that fall on France's eastern border. "Men and women are coming in droves," warned one of Choiseul's aides in Strasbourg, reporting two hundred to three hundred arrivals per day in October.[101] Concerned, Choiseul ordered Bodelschwingh to

Wishful thinking: an artist's depiction of the disembarkation of migrants to the "new colony" on the Kourou River. *Le Débarquement des François pour l'établissement de la nouvelle colonie dans le port de la nouvelle Cayenne ou la France équinoxiale* (1763). Courtesy of the John Carter Brown Library at Brown University.

"suspend, for three months at least," all new departures.[102] The Prussian either did not get the message or ignored it. Making final preparations for his own departure from his estate in Normandy, Étienne-François Turgot received a letter from Bodelschwingh at the end of October. Five thousand migrants were on the way, Bodelschwingh reported triumphantly, with more soon to follow. Turgot begged Choiseul not to reject "men so precious." "If this opportunity is lost," he warned the minister, "all will return to the English, and will aid them in establishing new colonies."[103]

Soon, however, events escaped Choiseul's control altogether. Flush with money (or, more often, IOUs from Bodelschwingh), nearly seventeen thousand German-speakers began marching across France to the sea.[104] Coalescing into town-sized bands, the would-be colonists begged, got drunk, and slept in churches along the way. In an effort to stagger their arrival, Choiseul tried to create six "staging points" at 150-mile intervals between the eastern frontier and Rochefort, but by late November they had been swamped.[105] That administrative paralysis set in should come as no shock: the number of prospective migrants to Guiana doubled the annual outflow from Great Britain to its North American colonies during the boom years between 1760 and 1775, and outdistanced any single colonial migration in French history by at least a factor of ten.[106] About eleven thousand of those Germans ultimately reached Rochefort, doubling the mud-splattered port's population upon their arrival. Fearing a disease outbreak, officials petitioned Choiseul for advice. He responded with orders to rush the migrants' departure at all costs.

As Rochefort's Germans were herded onto a hastily assembled fleet of transports, the roughly two hundred Acadian recruits assembled at Le Havre, Saint-Malo, Morlaix, and Boulogne sailed for Guiana. They left no journals, no firsthand accounts of what they experienced as they left Normandy for South America during the first months of 1764. But from his perch at the helm of one of the Germans' transports, the *Duc de Praslin*, Captain Etienne Garcin saw it all and recorded his observations.

On April 23, Garcin sailed from Marseille with 350 Germans crammed belowdecks, avoiding the diseased chaos of the Rochefort embarkation. His six-week crossing was mostly uneventful. On the second night in the Mediterranean, a "little child" died of smallpox, after which the crew "threw her into the sea." Seven more deaths followed: two children, four and eight years old, of smallpox; a five-year-old child, two teenage boys, and a fifty-year-old man, of "putrid fevers"; and Marguerite, one month and twenty days old, because "her mother had no milk."[107] Leaving their bodies in his wake, Garcin sped for Cayenne's harbor, where he dropped anchor on June 10.

Officials in Cayenne shooed the *Duc de Praslin* away. They informed Garcin that the disembarkation of new settlers would take place on the Iles du Salut, three rocky islands a few miles off the Kourou's mouth. Guided by a local pilot, Garcin left Cayenne early on June 13. At eleven that morning, as the islands' jagged silhouettes emerged from the haze beyond the *Duc de Praslin*'s bow, the passengers noticed something in the water—a pirogue in which sat an exhausted, frightened African man. Garcin launched his own canoe and "went out and got him." Adrift for three days after a "shipwreck," the man belonged to a Cayenne merchant named Romain. The Germans gathered and gawked as the dehydrated slave was plucked from the *pirogue* and hauled onto Garcin's deck, an uncomfortable meeting between Guiana's bright future and its grim past.[108]

More unexpected encounters followed. As the *Duc de Praslin* neared the Iles du Salut, a flotilla of ships came into view. Garcin listed the *Zélé*, the *Bénédiction de Dieu*, the *Balance*, the *Amphitron*, the *Roland* from Le Havre (with a complement of Acadians on board), and "seven other ships whose names I have forgotten." Together, they held over three thousand migrants. After a brief visit with Préfontaine and Chanvalon on the mainland, Garcin returned to the anchored *Duc de Praslin* and waited. A week later, he offloaded his 343 passengers onto small boats from Kourou, watched as the Germans scrambled onto Ile du Diable's rocky beaches, and ordered his crew to "sweep, scrape, and wash" the *Duc de Praslin*'s decks. Garcin then haggled with Chanvalon over flour (the captain wanted to sell what remained in the ship's hold, but the intendant claimed to have "more than I need") and a few financial details before making preparations to depart for Cap Français in Saint-Domingue. On July 7, after a few days of bad weather, the *Duc de Praslin*'s "canoe" was commandeered to help "disembark Captain Pinates's Germans." Garcin told his crew to be ready to sail the moment the canoe returned, so that "no ship can prevent us from casting off." He had good reason to hurry—"fevers" were on the rise around the Iles du Salut.[109]

Garcin's instincts were more right than he knew. What he perceived as a disaster in the making was in fact a disaster in full bloom. In late February 1764, Chanvalon had received word that the frigate *La Ferme* would soon arrive with four hundred German passengers. Unable, he thought, to receive them on the mainland, he set up makeshift camps on the Iles du Salut. When *La Ferme* arrived, however, the ship's captain passed on bad news. Two thousand more Germans, he reported, followed hard on his heels, with an unknown number of vessels lined up behind them. By April, the tone of Chanvalon's dispatches to Choiseul had changed: "I cannot hesitate to say it: all is lost without hope, if you do not give the most prompt and precise orders to stop these prodigious deliveries of men." On the Iles du Salut, the migrants either expressed "confusion" or hinted at "sedition"; most, however, were too weak to be much of a threat.[110] "We have three kinds of disease that predominate here," wrote a physician on Iles du Salut, "namely fevers, scurvy, and dysentery." His remedies "had, after a certain time, absolutely no effect," leaving patients to "certain death."[111] Even with the occasional killing of a giant tortoise, the doctor lamented the absence of "fresh meats, the only means by which to recover the sick." Piled atop smallpox, typhoid, and diarrhea was an "epidemic" of ophthalmitis (a painful eye inflammation common aboard slave ships), a growing number of "illnesses of inaction," and, thanks to sailors from the *Fortune*, an outbreak of venereal disease.[112] By July, Chanvalon had all but given up. "The new colony is full of grief and desolation," he told Choiseul. "We are surrounded by the dead and dying."[113]

No one really knows how many people perished. Thomas Knowler, a British naval officer who passed by Iles du Salut in March 1765, understood that of "fourteen thousand people that came out to settle the colonies . . . ten thousand of them died." Turgot, who only reached Guiana in January 1765, found himself "surrounded by a multitude of emaciated and pale widows and orphans of both sexes . . . who clasped their hands and raised their eyes toward heaven." He guessed nine thousand deaths in all. After twelve of his own family members and servants died of "contagious illness," he turned on Chanvalon, accusing the intendant of hoarding food and cruelly rationing water from the lone spring on Ile du Diable.[114] By that winter, Chanvalon was moldering in prison on Mont Saint-Michel, where, in 1767, he would hear of the seizure of his fortune to fund

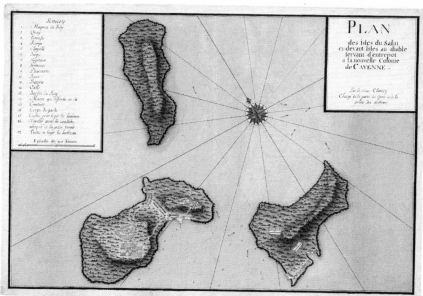

Original in the John Carter Brown Library at Brown University

The Iles du Salut, formerly the Iles du Diable, where Acadian, German, and French migrants to the Kourou colony succumbed to starvation and disease in 1764. *Plan des Isles du Salut, cy-devant les Isles au Diable, servant d'entrepot a la nouvelle colonie de Cayenne* (1763). Courtesy of the John Carter Brown Library at Brown University.

a hospital in Cayenne and "a perpetual mass for the souls of the inhabitants who perished."[115] Set against the devastation of Native Americans by Old World diseases and warfare, or the staggering human toll of the slave trade, the Kourou colony's collapse seems small in scale. But for white settlers, it remains the deadliest single episode in the long history of European colonization in the Americas.

Although the Acadians sent from northern France clearly suffered, they emerged better off than most. Indeed, nearly one hundred managed to avoid the overwhelming mortality on the Iles du Salut, making their way to a tiny settlement at Sinnamary, far to the north and east of the Kourou River. In 1765, even as a despondent Turgot threatened to suppress government aid to Sinnamary unless its inhabitants left the colony for France, the Acadians—including brothers Joseph and Pierre Saulnier, Augustin Trahan, Jean Boudreau, and Joseph Lejeune—dug in their heels alongside a few Canadian and French neighbors. Some, such as Anne Thériot, whose husband had died in Guiana, did flee, but others remained to enjoy some success as poor, non-slaveholding farmers.[116]

Acting as governor at Cayenne beginning in 1766, Louis-Thomas Jacau de Fiedmont held the Acadians in high esteem. Born on Ile Royale to an Acadian mother and a French father, Fiedmont had served as an engineer at Fort Beauséjour during the 1750s. Perhaps wistfully, he saw Sinnamary as an analog to the Bay of Fundy. Like "our settlements in Acadia," he wrote, the exiles' farms were "washed over" by runoff from nearby hillsides, thus "trapping compost [*engrais*] in the soil's depths."[117] In 1768, Fiedmont tried to coax "a number of Acadians, working as sailors aboard English vessels" into staying in Sinnamary.[118] None came, but Guiana's original Acadian core endured. François de Barbé-Marbois reached Sinnamary after his deportation from France in the left-wing coup d'état of 18 Fructidor 1797. "Welcome," an Acadian widow told him, "our fathers were banished like you . . . [and] we feel pleasure in offering you consolation and an asylum in our cabins."[119]

No doubt, theirs is an intensely human story of coercion and pain, resilience and adaptation, but the Acadians sent to Guiana also lived and died within a larger context. Although 1763 is often considered to be the terminus of the early modern French Empire, the Kourou affair reveals the persistence of imperial ambition in Louis XV's kingdom. It also hints at the massive scale of a postwar movement to revolutionize the very nature of the European presence in the New World. This eruption of new thinking consumed many of France's best minds (from brash physiocrats to the philosophe Denis Diderot, who got his lover's nephew a job in Guiana) and most influential statesmen (notably Choiseul, who hoped to build a "European system" of social and political life in the American tropics).[120] The Acadians were caught up in these events, but they also had a hand in causing them. The presence of three thousand colonists—a "population too priceless not to receive," as Choiseul put it in 1763 or, as another official styled them, "vassals to be desired"—helped make anti-slavery ventures like the Kourou colony thinkable.[121]

Thinkable, and also stupid. Or so Jacques-François Artur, Cayenne's contrarian physician, told anyone who would listen after 1764. By his lights, Acadian and German settlers had labored under "cruel servitude" and "harsh slavery." Condemned to work for rich *concessionnaires*, they "and their posterity" would have "perpetually" lacked the "power to change or better their condition." Given the choice, Artur would rather have been a slave, for "even a Negro can better his lot, become free, and acquire all the rights of a citizen." As he saw it, France's new imperial vision for the Caribbean had not so much replaced slavery as redirected the institution's coercive energy.[122]

Had Artur known that in a "deserted corner" of Saint-Domingue a smaller version of the Kourou experiment was under way, he would have been stunned.

Before 1763, Môle Saint-Nicolas had never attracted much attention. Perched at the western tip of Saint-Domingue's northern peninsula, it had long consisted of a few unimproved land claims strung along the Saint-Nicolas River. It was far removed, both geographically and culturally, from the colony's centers of power, the bustling metropolis of Cap Français and the slave-rich sugar plantations of the Northern Plain, and Port-au-Prince, the province's fledgling administrative center. Not that Môle had no good points. Royal hydrographer Jacques-Nicolas Bellin described it as ideal for the cultivation of "vegetables and cotton" and raising livestock, cataloguing a host of "wild bulls, pigs . . . pigeons, turtledoves, and a few guinea-fowl" to supplement the diet of any settler.[123] Still, the region's rugged terrain and lack of roads seemed likely to keep it a backwater.

The Seven Years' War, however, thrust Môle Saint-Nicolas into the spotlight. As the most lucrative of France's remaining colonial possessions, Saint-Domingue garnered plenty of attention from Versailles after the Treaty of Paris. At issue was loyalty. Stung by the seemingly easy capitulations of Guadeloupe and Martinique, and by the planters' clear preference for the British slave trade over its less consistent French counterpart, the monarchy embarked on the delicate task of reining in Saint-Domingue's creole elite, a group notoriously suspicious of metropolitan rule and, as the abbé Raynal wrote, "less attached to their reputations [as good French subjects] than to their wealth."[124] The quest to cement Saint-Dominguan allegiance led to two shifts in policy. First, in the spring of 1763, France dismantled the colony's system of military government, ending the much-hated practice of mandatory militia service and instituting parish elections for civilian officers to replace once-powerful militia commanders. Concerned over the new régime's perceived inability to maintain order, Versailles reversed course in 1764, reinstituting the militia and placing

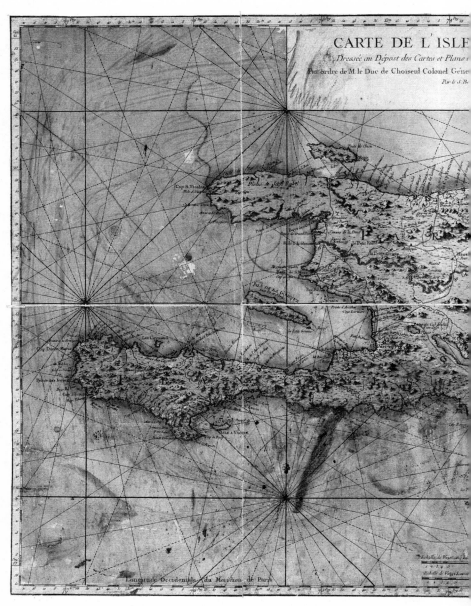

Saint-Domingue, the slave-rich core of France's Caribbean empire. Jacques-Nicolas Bellin, *Carte de l'Isle de Saint-Domingue* (1764). Courtesy of the Library of Congress.

SAINT DOMINGUE,

e. Pour le Service des Vaisseaux du Roy.

ses et Crisons Ministre de la Guerre et de la Marine .

la Marine .

Charles-Henri-Hector, comte d'Estaing, a career navy man, at the head of a rein-vigorated military government.[125]

Whipsawing between civilian-driven economic liberalism and military-minded authoritarianism, reform in postwar Saint-Domingue produced violent debates over means but left little doubt as to France's desired ends: keeping the colony securely in Louis XV's fold while using it to extend the king's power in the Caribbean. In light of these concerns, Môle Saint-Nicolas became, as one high-ranking official wrote in early 1764, "essential to settle."[126] Jutting out past Tortuga toward the southern coast of Cuba, Môle overlooked a prime shipping channel to and from Jamaica and the western Caribbean. Properly colonized, the entire peninsula might become a base of operations for a resurgent French navy. Alternatively, if Môle were somehow seized by the British, it would provide great advantages to the enemy. As d'Estaing proclaimed, "Môle St. Nicolas . . . seems placed by nature to belong to the dominant naval power in the seas of America."[127]

Remarkably, even in the Caribbean's most self-consciously pro-slavery so-ciety, the Seven Years' War had made both Saint-Dominguans and royal officials skittish about using African labor in places such as Môle Saint-Nicolas. As in Guiana, some worried that the isolated northern peninsula might become a haven for maroons. After all, hundreds (possibly thousands) of escaped slaves had, over the previous half century, established long-standing communities on the outskirts of frontier towns such as Jacmel and Les Cayes in Saint-Domingue's sparsely populated, similarly mountainous southern peninsula.[128]

In addition, recent experience had made Saint-Dominguans fearful of slaves who remained on their plantations. Mostly it had to do with poison. This was hardly a new problem. In 1712, one resident of Cap Français complained that "for a long time" he and his neighbors had endured "considerable losses in live-stock and slaves from causes unknown, leading them to suspect some of their Negroes of poisoning them." The death of a "handsome enough" horse belonging to a local militia captain gave planters "the opportunity to look into these mat-ters." A slave named François, "who seemed to understand the use of poisons," quickly fingered the militia captain's slave Thomas, who in turn had purchased the poison from Claude Roy's slave Colin—or so they all said after "having been put to the flames." The existence of this little network of poisoners posed a "del-icate" problem, the planters admitted.[129] In most cases, solutions were anything but delicate. In 1723, a maroon named Colas Jambes Coupées was broken on the wheel in Cap Français for poisoning several slaves, his mangled body put out to cure as a warning to anyone contemplating the same crime.[130]

After years of sporadic local flare-ups, poisoning became an epidemic during the Seven Years' War. In the spring of 1757, a slave named Médor made an apparently uncoerced statement implicating himself in an old poisoning case. He also accused the slaves Madeleine, Margot, and Angelique in the more recent death of their mistress, one Dame Delarue. Imprisoned and shackled, Médor kept talking until, "seeing that he would be delivered to justice, he stabbed himself to death" in his cell.[131] From his testimony, authorities began to see the outlines of a vast conspiracy involving dozens of slaves, free blacks, and maroons. Meanwhile, cattle, slaves, and masters died at a frightening pace around Cap Français. A nine-month-long search netted one hundred arrests and thirty executions, culminating in the capture of François Makandal, a maroon identified by many slaves as the source of their poisons, and of the occult "secrets" needed to make proper use of them. After confessing to his part in the conspiracy, Makandal was burned at the stake in Cap's central square. Famously, he somehow broke his bonds and leapt from the flames, but French soldiers (spooked, no doubt, at the sight of the African conjurer defying death) threw him back in.[132]

This execution notwithstanding, the poisoning phenomenon seemed unstoppable. "The truths of the Christian religion," wrote one planter, "which should have destroyed [the slaves'] superstitious practices, seem instead to have fortified them; and Slavery, far from putting a brake on their vices, appears only to have added to them."[133] The body count slowed in 1758, but rumors only circulated faster.[134] Twisted sabbath ceremonies, with talismans of wax, holy water, old Hosts, nails, and "bones, especially those of baptized children"; white families "who could only eat and drink with secret worries, not knowing who to suspect among the Negroes serving them"—this was the frenzied mind of wartime Saint-Domingue.[135]

As the fighting ended, there were no reassuring conclusions. Asked why they had done it, condemned slaves mouthed that "the Devil had tempted them," but investigators found a jumble of motives: "hopes of future liberty, love affairs, envy, revenge, harsh punishments, exaggerated weakness, games of chance." Whatever the particular causes, suggested a 1762 summary of the poisonings, "these epidemic crimes have so corrupted the hearts of the slaves that . . . in vain do we tell ourselves that they will die out on their own."[136] A postwar influx of poor white Frenchmen made matters worse. "Where the colony has so few women, it is not surprising that men of all ranks enter into relations with Negro women, slave and free," explained one Saint-Dominguan observer. Both "criminal" and "against good mores," these unions produced the sorts of "jealousies, animosities, and disorders" that had triggered the "scourge" of poisonings in 1757.[137] Falling prey to slave women and "mulatto mistresses," this "mass of people" flooding into Saint-Domingue "has polluted the country," complained Claude-François Borthon, an attorney with a plantation near Limbé.[138] These demographic realities only heightened Saint-Dominguan paranoia about poisoning at the hands of "these monstrous assassins." "Fire and scaffolds have not destroyed the contagion," a memorialist wrote to Louis XV in 1764, for "this plague, almost always hidden, will be forever lethal to this Colony; may it not cause its ruin!"[139]

Getting rid of slavery, of course, was not an option. It was "the political essence of agriculture in the colonies."[140] But after 1763, colonists and royal officials seemed more willing than usual to work with something other than the blunt instrument of African labor. D'Estaing, for instance, lobbied to bring free "lascars" from the Indian Ocean to Saint-Domingue, hopeful that these "Moorish sailors" might instruct "many blacks" in the science of extracting and processing coconut oil.[141] As a key element in France's broader imperial plans for the Caribbean, the colonization of Môle Saint-Nicolas was more important than coconuts—and having just endured "an unhappy war with the English . . . while keeping up an internal conflict against even more dangerous Negroes," slaves looked like a risky, expensive bet.[142] For his part, d'Estaing flirted with the idea of using crown funds to purchase three hundred slaves at "one thousand livres per head" to work on fortifications and "even grow food," but worried over the "onerous" cost and inevitable "abuses" sure to follow.[143] Run-of-the-mill white migrants would never do, and not just because of their boorish behavior. Early in 1764, intendant Jean-Bernard de Clugny reported that of sixty "workers" recently arrived in Port-au-Prince from northern France, forty-five had died within a few months and ten had gone home "because of their health," leaving only five.[144] That left Acadians.

Those destined for Môle Saint-Nicolas took a tortuous path to Saint-Domingue. After hearing of France's redemption of Acadians in England early in 1763, exiles across British North America sent notes to Choiseul's offices, each brimming with the "meager, poorly dictated thanks of your poor servants, the neutral French of Acadia."[145] They asked for a place under Louis XV's "standards," but, hedging their bets, Acadians also wrote to Port-au-Prince. A group in South Carolina tried to send representatives to Saint Domingue in 1763 to ask the governor-general's "assistance . . . to draw us nearer to him." That voyage failed due to "bad winds," but others succeeded.[146] Later that year, with plans for the Môle Saint-Nicolas colony under way, Clugny and his associates hatched a scheme to transport Acadians from northern seaports. They hired a New York captain named John Hanson and passed secret instructions to Acadians to find him on the city's docks. In a second circular spirited to Acadians that summer, Saint-Domingue officials promised that they would "be maintained by the King during the first months of their stay, that they may be able to earn a living themselves."[147] The pitch worked.

A sense of precisely what would be built at Môle Saint-Nicolas developed even as hundreds of Acadians made their way from British North America. The final plan was drawn up by intendant Clugny and Pierre-André de Gohin, comte de Montreuil, a veteran of the Canadian theater of the Seven Years' War who had surely known Acadian refugees at the defenses of Québec and Montréal. The settlement at Môle would function both as military base and as rural breadbasket. Acadians would do the farming, French regulars the fighting. As soon as the Acadians had disembarked, leaders were to set up camp using "tents, covers, and hammocks such as those given to Negroes." When these materials had been offloaded, the Acadians would erect "barracks, a blockhouse, a hospital, and the officers' quarters." In addition, they would cut a road leading from the source of the Saint-Nicolas River to the sea, in order "to transport by coach . . . the supplies and tools necessary for the Settlement." A surveyor would mark out plots of "ten *carreaux* of land" along the river, each belonging to an Acadian family as "certain and incontestable property." It came at a price. Those who "refused to give themselves to the operations of the settlement" risked confinement in a prison constructed by their own hands.[148]

The Acadians arrived at Môle Saint-Nicolas by sea from Cap Français on February 2, 1764. Among them were Marain Leblanc, a master carpenter initially exiled to South Carolina with his family, a young mason named Jean-Baptiste Doucet, and Joseph Poirier, a cartwright.[149] Most of the others were farmers, or had been before 1755. What is known of their first months in Saint-Domingue comes not from their own testimonies but from the letters of Bertrand de Saltoris, a grasping, career-minded naval scribe charged with overseeing the settlement. Desperate to make a good impression, he penned his first report to Clugny "on a knee," unwilling to wait for his desk to be unloaded from the ship.[150] His Acadians were "the best people in the world," especially when given some wine

Môle Saint-Nicolas in the eighteenth century. *Le Môle Saint-Nicolas dans l'Isle de Saint-Domingue*. Courtesy of the Library of Congress.

to "refresh their blood, [which had been] corrupted by too much salted meat."
Saltoris's decision to ban hunting, fishing, and washing in the river caused some
murmurs, but no real upset.[151] "The Acadians love me and fear me," he exulted,
promising to continue "to inspire in them these two feelings at once."[152] Aside
from a few cases of diarrhea, the first week at Môle Saint-Nicolas passed quietly.

Hardships soon began. A storm left the settlers "flooded in our tents" and
broke one of Saltoris's boats on the rocks. The water also ruined several sacks of
hardtack, much to the relief of Acadians disgusted with military rations.[153]
Through these initial difficulties, Saltoris wrote, the Acadians proved themselves
to be "angels . . . who lacked the bad qualities of other men while surpassing
them in goodness." Instead of shrinking from Môle's challenges, settlers worked
hard and celebrated harder. A few weeks into the project, the entire community
gathered on Fat Tuesday for what turned into a two-day-long feast in honor of
twenty-three marriages to be "renewed or contracted." Packing more than four
hundred people under a makeshift arbor, the Acadians displayed the kind of
rustic sociability Saltoris knew only from Rousseau. "There we were," he
exclaimed to Clugny, "men, women, children, all mixed together . . . until 11
o'clock at night, when we all embraced and went to bed." Plenty of dancing
("young, old, whoever could jump the highest"), drinking ("two and a half
casks of wine"), and eating ("one calf, twelve pigs, two barrels of flour, and one
great cheese"), but no "bad speech" or "indecencies." Throw a similarly raucous
party for fifty Frenchmen, Saltoris imagined, and at least one of them would
surely emerge "with one eye missing." The Acadians were, he concluded, "not
ordinary men."[154]

Nor were they simpletons. After surveying the Saint-Nicolas River, ten Acadians returned to Môle "saddened" by the quality of the soil.[155] Officials did their
best to reassure them but could barely hide their own worries. Puzzled by the
river's weak current, Saltoris trekked upstream by himself, "walking not on the
banks but in the middle, in boots." He discovered that dozens of fallen trees
blocked the flow, creating pools that liquefied the soil along its banks. Fatefully,
Saltoris advised that the Acadians be employed in dredging the river and divert-
ing its course. The project would slow Môle's progress but would benefit Saint-
Domingue in the long run. More worrisome to Saltoris, work along the river
threatened to damage his ability to impress patrons. "I am mortified," he wrote to
Clugny in mid-February, "to be obliged to use the wrong hand [to write], but I
wounded my thumb yesterday in the forest."[156]

Although the scribe remained "content with the Acadians," colonists
raised tough questions about their relationship to the French empire, which
now claimed them as subjects. For Saltoris, altering the river's course was in-
separable from cultivation, the Acadians' role in the new Saint-Domingue. It
was in everyone's best interest, then, that the refugees do the work. Once

rumored to be en route toward Môle, slaves from a nearby town had not arrived. Healthy white workers demanded high wages. In Port-au-Prince, officials lamented that "the *journée* of a white . . . has risen to ten sols per day."[157] Indeed, Saltoris would claim that a local contractor had estimated the cost of dredging at 300,000 livres. The Acadians, he boasted, could do the same job for 1,800 livres. He put the point to the new intendant in Port-au-Prince, René Magon: "You can hardly send us more hands; we must make do with those we have."[158]

In a bold move, the Acadians demanded money. "Our Acadians are murmuring," Saltoris reported, "and I do not believe it will be possible to make them work in the riverbed without paying them." When Montreuil suggested that Acadian laborers be given goods instead of a wage, Saltoris disabused him. "These people are absolutely persuaded that the King should feed and clothe them," he wrote, making clear that for unexpected work, the Acadians wanted pay above and beyond what had already been promised.[159] No pay came from Cap Français. Dredging moved forward slowly. Saltoris grew embittered. Although the Acadians "were still the same," he admitted in April to "swearing a bit too much these last few days."[160] He chased a young couple, Nicolas Vaudois and Marie-Louise Dubois, from the settlement for fighting with each other, describing the woman as a "real demon" who had been "marked and whipped at Louisbourg."[161] Mostly he complained about the other French officials who, when not "getting drunk, smoking, or sleeping," passed their time circulating rumors about him among the Acadians.[162] To d'Estaing, who finally reached Saint-Domingue in late April, Saltoris promised to reveal the colony's "progress and growth" during the new governor-general's visit to Môle, after which the scribe would happily accept a promotion.[163]

D'Estaing made that visit in July. He took a brief tour through what Saltoris had described as a bustling town of "several hundred hardworking, happy Acadian farmers who cherished those who administered to them." What he saw pierced him to the core:

> I found a few scattered men without shelter, dying beneath the Bushes, supplied in abundance with *biscuit* and salted meats that they could not eat, as well as tools they were in no state to use; they cursed an existence that, out of discouragement, they did not care to preserve. . . . . . . The greatest criminal would have preferred the galleys to a torture session in this plague-stricken place.[164]

Magon described the scene in equally shocking terms. "We found the settlement in the worst condition," he confided to his journal. "Of the 556 Acadians sent here, 104 had already died," with the rest well on their way to the grave.

"Solely concerned with his own interests," Saltoris had lied about everything, or so Magon concluded. The scribe had treated the Acadians "like slaves," barring them from hunting while he, in the style of a proper French nobleman, enjoyed free rein over Môle's beasts. Even children were not safe. Saltoris had, Magon claimed, "pushed his inhumanity to the point of refusing milk to children who died without this resource."[165] Justice came swiftly. After enduring threats that "four soldiers would lead him away if [he] did not leave in two hours," Saltoris was "thrown in a boat" in Môle's harbor. He stayed there for five days with only peas and salt to eat. Taken to Cap Français, he sold the possessions he had managed to carry off, while the rest of his effects rotted at Môle Saint-Nicolas. Saltoris continued to dash off rambling protests, but the recipients paid him no mind.[166]

What had been a unique experiment in labor organization quickly reverted to the status quo. "Men in a condition to work should have been sent first," Magon seethed, castigating Môle's planners for not sending at least "a few blacks" at the very start. To replace Saltoris, d'Estaing and Magon tapped a former ship's captain named Salomon, "a man accustomed to risking his life for little, and used to the kind of harshness needed to inspire today the man who will seemingly die tomorrow."[167] Under his command would be a familiar kind of laborer. "We will make a purchase of blacks," Magon promised Salomon, "for the work which the Acadians, burdened by sickness, are no longer capable of performing."[168] To mark the slaves as the king's, the intendant burned a fleur-de-lys into their cheeks.[169]

Imagining an empire without slaves proved much easier than building one. But, as Acadians discovered along the Kourou and Saint-Nicolas rivers, imagination had real consequences when paired with political desperation. Just as Africans had for decades been captured, categorized, and used up in the service of colonial production and metropolitan consumption, these refugees became instruments of empire.

A coda to all of these strange events shows their transformative power. Salomon, who replaced the hapless Saltoris at Môle, turned out to be anything but an improvement. Except for beginning "some nonsensical building projects" and attempting "grand theft" from the outpost's coffers, he did nothing. D'Estaing replaced him in the late summer of 1764.[170] None too soon, for ships loaded with nearly one thousand Germans from the Kourou River had recently arrived in Cap Français. Concerned about disease outbreaks and other disorders, d'Estaing intended to shift the migrants to Môle. He sent for an experienced hand to guide them. The new director—a "poor, uncouth devil, but honest and clever," a man "unique in his species . . . fanatical about anything that concerns his work, as singular as he is learned"—sailed into Port-au-Prince in September. He picked up his instructions and a few farm implements and headed for Môle.

Having escaped from Guiana "half dead," Jean-Baptiste-Christophe Fusée Aublet "knew better than anyone what we can expect" from Saint-Domingue's all-white settlement.[171] With his African wife and mixed-race children still a world away on Ile-de-France, the botanist went to work again. Suspicious of Môle's arability, he left the remaining Acadians there, moving the German settlers several miles south to a new settlement called Bombardopolis after the sieur de la Bombarde, one of Aublet's metropolitan patrons. While Bombardopolis made steady progress, Môle floundered. For his part, d'Estaing believed that the Acadians' old village "will soon find itself depopulated . . . [and] all of these houses, built at such expense, will be left without occupants."[172] The task of settling and fortifying Môle Saint-Nicolas, he wrote, "will succeed only if the King has many Negroes" to clear, till, and haul in ways that people like the Acadians, "perpetually stalled by illnesses and lethargy," could not.[173]

For Aublet, the physical, political, and emotional hardships of Môle became too much. His temper resurfaced. "He treated me very cruelly yesterday," wrote one of his subordinates in March 1765, "and I do not know why."[174] That summer,

BOMBARDOPOLIS ou BOMBARDE DANS L'ISLE DE S.t DOMINGUE.

1. Église   *2. Place d'Armes.*

Bombardopolis ou Bombarde dans l'Isle de Saint-Domingue (1765). Courtesy of the John Carter Brown Library at Brown University.

after working with the Acadians on terraced gardens near their houses, Aublet informed d'Estaing of his decision to retire. Sickly and disheartened from exposure to France's postwar struggle over anti-slavery and imperial reform, he left for France in September.

Despite Aublet's departure, d'Estaing's suspicions, and the Acadians' precarious health, Môle Saint-Nicolas and many of its inhabitants endured. To be sure, some fled. Dozens—hundreds, perhaps—crossed the Gulf of Mexico to Spanish Louisiana. They followed a route traced by the renegade Joseph Broussard *dit* Beausoleil. After being liberated from captivity in Halifax at war's end, Broussard gathered up two hundred of his compatriots and headed for the Caribbean, stopping at Cap Français in January 1765 on their way to new lands just west of New Orleans at Attakapas.[175]

Others took a different path. They clung to footholds in Môle and in spin-off settlements at Plateforme, Jean-Rabel, and Mirebalais. "Almost everyone who is *not* Acadian has deserted," wrote one Môle official in September 1765, grateful for the refugees' persistence. In February 1766, Marain Leblanc was busy leading a team of carpenters including Charles Cormier, Firmin Comeau, and Anselme Poirier. At Môle's barracks, they worked alongside nine young Acadian apprentices (who constituted "the nursery that will shortly yield our best people," according to their French commander) and eleven Acadian children ("who work fairly well, but who are not yet men"). Alain Daigre, by contrast, toiled in the woods, "driving the Negroes" who felled trees and cut planks. Daigre's crew of slaves included Mabiala, Goma, and L'Espérance, or Hope. Scores of African women—Bouinga, Venus, Big Jeanne, Babel—hauled the Acadians' water, while an enslaved child, Henry, played the tambourine.[176]

By June, all these Acadians and the king's slaves remained in or around Môle, along with four hundred white farmers and laborers "not employed on the works."[177] Most of this last group consisted of Acadians as well. Over time, these men and women integrated into Saint-Domingue's rapidly changing society. A few married other Acadians, but others did not, instead forming families with French, German, and Genoese migrants. Some later became slaveholding planters, but most scattered across Saint-Domingue's northern peninsula, pursuing livelihoods on the margins of the colony's booming sugar economy.[178]

Although plans for white colonies to defend and provision France's sugar islands failed, they speak to the continued resonance of imperial thinking even after the stinging defeat of 1763. As outlandish as France's plans for the Caribbean may now seem, they transformed the displaced Acadians' sense of place and the quality of their most intimate social relationships. And almost unbelievably, the Kourou colony and Môle Saint-Nicolas were hardly the strangest or most far-flung imperial projects pressed upon Nova Scotia's refugees.

4

The Unknown

Before the specter of enslaved poisoners on Saint-Domingue, before disease and hunger turned Guiana and Môle Saint-Nicolas into charnel houses, a few French thinkers held that the Caribbean was beyond redemption. It was a hard case to make. "Intelligent people," wrote the pro-colonial economist François Veron de Forbonnais, "acquire lands in climates proper for staples they lack."[1] Voltaire, whose 1757 *Candide, or Optimism* fired off smirking critiques of imperialism and slavery, drank two gallons of coffee (often laced with sugar and chocolate) per day—a combination of colonial addictions shared by millions of French subjects no longer willing to settle for milk and honey.

The human cost of their consumption, however, was evident on both sides of the Atlantic. The harshness of Caribbean slavery was well known. The philosophe Denis Diderot could only conclude that transporting an ordinary European "beyond the equator" was the equivalent of returning a domesticated tiger to the jungle: "The thirst of blood takes hold of him once more."[2] While some attributed the seeming anarchy on the West African coast to inhabitants with "souls as black as their bodies," others disagreed: "You yourselves," one critic told a French audience complicit in the slave trade, "[are the] instigators of their tyranny, which causes so much devastation in those sad countries."[3] In France itself, the rise of an economy of luxury rooted in colonial goods "ceaselessly turn[ed] thousands of cultivators into artisans and valets," swelling the ranks of city dwellers and sapping the kingdom's rural heartland.[4] Early French imperialism had, it seemed, become a living machine whose gears now ensnared and ground up anyone who approached. "The harm was not done in creating settlements in America," explained Charles de Brosses in 1756," but to have done so without rules, without policy, without forethought."[5]

Besides being the president of the *parlement* of Dijon, de Brosses was one of the old régime's great polymaths, an expert on the archaeology of Herculaneum, fetishism in African religion, the origins of languages, and the history of the Roman Empire. His breadth of learning made him the most articulate midcentury proponent of a risky but remarkably popular approach to French colonialism: starting over. By de Brosses's lights, the conflict between Great Britain and France had reached a familiar crossroads as the Seven Years' War began. Like Rome during the Punic Wars, Britain was "aspiring to universal monarchy," forcing France into a fight from which only one power would emerge.[6] De Brosses had a solution. France, he wrote, should imitate the Phoenicians of Tyre, the merchant-mariners who had founded Carthage two millennia earlier. "The solid base of their immortal glory," he argued, was "to have planted their colonies . . . from the *British Isles* to the *Cape of Good Hope*, perhaps; but at least as far as Senegal."[7] Louis XV, however, would go one step further, undertaking nothing less than "the discovery of *Terres australes*."[8] In an end run around British commercial might, France would dispatch a fleet to the long-predicted southern continent, there to exploit the last untapped market—a land whose peoples, kept in "useful dependence," would snap up boatloads of "our colored glass beads, our little textiles, our paper, our *eaux de vie*, our iron tools, our hardware, our little mirrors at 7 f. per dozen."[9]

The British Empire had made the consumer king, but finding a new population at the bottom of the world would allow the French to begin their own cycle of metropolitan manufacturing and colonial consumption on a massive scale, beating the British at their own economic game. Doing the finding, though, presented some thorny problems. But for scientists, explorers, and philosophers across eighteenth-century Europe, the reality of *terra australis incognita*, or the unknown southern land, was in the air. Back in 1686, Bernard le Bovier de Fontenelle had jabbed at readers for their lack of curiosity toward "that part of the earth called Terra Australis" and its inhabitants, "for we and they are aboard the same ship; they possess the prow, and we the poop, and yet there is no manner of communication between us."[10] By midcentury, the idea of an imperial presence in the southern seas, complete with the mercantilist exchange of French products for colonial staples, had seeped into the most unlikely corners of popular culture. The protagonist of Charles-François Tiphaigne de la Roche's 1761 novel *Giphantie* reveled in the discovery "very lately made in Terra Australis" of transparent cotton, a textile which "will defend from the weather, and at the same time give us a sight of that admirable bosom, those charming arms, that divine leg."[11]

Less prurient French thinkers believed that colonial ventures in the highest latitudes of the Southern Hemisphere, shaped by lessons learned over the past two centuries of harsh experience, would resolve a host of moral and practical concerns about empire in an age of enlightenment. With de Brosses at their head, some advocated a sea change in thinking about antiquity, empire, and society. By the 1750s, Frenchmen had come to see their country as "a new Rome," identifying not with the vast *imperium* but with the virtuous republic whose "heroic prototypes" became "the stock in trade of a wide spectrum of reformers and enthusiasts."[12] Developing alongside French reverence for Rome was "laconomania," whose lone symptom was admiration for the republic of Sparta.[13] Roman "zeal for the common good," coupled with the strict patriotism and "spirit of community" fostered by Spartan rulers such as Lycurgus, proved inviting models for those weary of arbitrary rule, divisive privilege, and foppish apathy.[14] This political analogy allowed no room for the trappings of colonialism. "We cannot flatter ourselves to see Sparta reborn in the midst of commerce and the love of gain," wrote Jean-Jacques Rousseau in 1751.[15] As the abbé Mably explained in that same year, was not the fall of Rome rooted in the turn from self-government and material modesty to "an insatiable drive toward pillage and conquest"? And had not the Spartans' distaste for "booty and tribute" made expansion a nonstarter until thoughtless reforms ushered in the contagions of "avarice" and empire?[16]

Perhaps, but a rising chorus in France touted the virtues of classical colonizers—commercial savvy, maritime skill, geographic curiosity, and the intent to "create" allied nations rather than conquer hapless natives. Again, the Phoenicians set the example, having "formed the Greeks, & given rise to the other savages of Europe that the Greeks and Romans succeeded in shaping later on." "The Europeans of these early centuries," de Brosses reminded the French, "were hardly more brutish" than the inhabitants of *terra australis*.[17] Casting out toward the teeming land mass to the south (one post–Seven Years' War booster estimated its population as "probably more than 50 millions"), the French would position themselves to "give law" to other nations while triggering an economic boom attuned to both competition with the British and the demands of the Enlightenment.[18]

Above all, proponents of these projects hoped to avoid the "exploitation of mines, the thirst for gold, and the false allure of a quick fortune" that had led to the original sins of European settlers in the New World. That meant starting small, with a self-sustaining agricultural colony whose incremental growth would set in motion the exchanges that would ultimately "employ on land and sea an infinite number of [French] men in all that concerns trade and navigation."[19] Much depended on a good group of pioneers. Ideally, this would be a "hardworking and intelligent set of people" accustomed to long winters and dealing with native peoples.[20] Like the builders of the Kourou colony and Môle Saint-Nicolas, the proponents of *la France australe* turned to families such as the Cyrs.

Jean-Jacques Cyr, his wife, Marie-Josèphe Hébert, and their eight children were not typical Acadians. They sometimes worked on farms for wages, but mostly they ran a tavern near Pont à Buot on the Missaguash River, serving up hospitality at the friction point between the British and French empires. Robert Hale of Beverly, Massachusetts, washed up at the Cyr place in 1731. After a meal of bonnyclabber (a curdled milk dish akin to yogurt), fish, soup, and bread, he witnessed "some of the Family on their Knees paying their Devotions to the Almighty." The tavern suddenly became a jumble of religiosity and sociability. Some of the Acadians prayed, but others remained in the room "talking, and Smoaking, etc." Unlike fair New England women, Hale noted, the Cyr girls' complexions had been darkened "by living in the Smoak in the summer to defend against Muskettoes, and in the winter against the Cold."[21] It was a habit that would serve them well.

After their expulsion from Ile Saint-Jean in 1758, Jean-Jacques, Marie-Josèphe, and their children ended up in Saint-Malo, on the northern coast of Brittany. Six years later, they found themselves in Port Saint-Louis, France's outpost on the eastern shore of the Falkland Islands. Intended as a way station for French ships headed for bigger, better lands, Port Saint-Louis was, in its day, the southernmost European settlement on earth. Although the South Atlantic landscape was unlike anything they had known ("a vast silence," wrote one eighteenth-century visitor, "broken only by the occasional cry of a sea-monster, everywhere a weird and melancholy uniformity"), the Cyrs made lives for themselves there.[22] Daughter Marie gave birth to twins in 1767, while twenty-one-year-old Françoise married Frenchman Julien Brard in the settlement's makeshift chapel in 1769.[23]

Their presence on East Falkland testifies to the allure of *terra australis incognita* for French imperialists eager to sap British might. In that sense, the impulse to populate the icy corners of the South Atlantic and the hot, sticky banks of the Kourou River came from the same source: a desire to marry economic efficiency and moral sensibility to the power of empire. Far from fading away in the diplomatic aftermath of the Seven Years' War, the old régime's dying empire evolved at breakneck speed into dozens of variants, each of which drew on different strands of political economy, historical interpretation, and previous colonial experience.

For ministers such as Choiseul, it was a fleeting moment of hope. Acadians too had reason to look to the future. Although Port Saint-Louis and the Kourou treated their inhabitants very differently, both colonies taught the refugees the same stinging lesson: whether via the tropics or the poles, all roads led toward the bottom of the labor market undergirding the eighteenth-century Atlantic world.

Snaking in an irregular path between 49 and 55 degrees south latitude, the Antarctic Convergence is one of the most important climatic barriers on the planet. For oceanographers, it marks the frontier where cold polar waters flowing north from Antarctica dive below the warmer, southbound currents of the Atlantic, Pacific, and Indian Oceans. Just north of the convergence, climates are unpleasant and vegetation minimal. "As to the aboriginal productions," wrote an early visitor to the Falkland Islands, "it will easily be seen that nature has not been very liberal in bestowing her favors."[24] Lands below the convergence, by contrast, are hostile to all but the hardiest forms of life. In the seventeenth and eighteenth centuries, the transition was mysterious. Since 1675, when the French Huguenot mariner Antoine de la Roche was blown over the line and lived to tell the tale, even the most rugged sailors grew reflective at the sight of the great fog banks marking the convergence, beyond which the temperature dropped fast and low.[25]

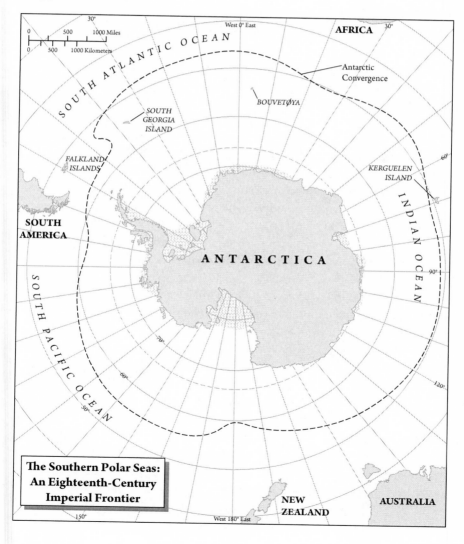

The Southern Polar Seas:
An Eighteenth-Century
Imperial Frontier

Yet by the eighteenth century, this sudden atmospheric change had become more enticing than discouraging for Europeans. As men such as Charles de Brosses knew, the idea of *terra australis incognita* had captivated the best minds and wildest imaginations of Western civilization for well over two thousand years. Their fascination was rooted in a long-standing series of philosophical speculations and geographical misunderstandings. In the fourth century BCE, Aristotle knew the earth to be spherical, and in the interest of symmetry suggested the existence of antipodes, or landmasses diametrically opposed to the Greeks' known world. Two centuries later, Ptolemy played on Aristotle's ideas to come up with what he believed to be the first accurate map of the globe. A bad estimate of the earth's circumference, however, led him to make the world too small. As a result, Ptolemy pushed Africa toward China, shrank the Pacific, and enclosed the Indian Ocean with a vast southern continent.[26]

For centuries, no one corrected him. Many early Christians did not care about such matters. Saint Basil, the fourth-century bishop of Caesarea, summed up their position: "Of what importance is it to know whether the earth is a sphere, a cylinder, a disc, or a concave surface? What is important is to know how I should conduct myself towards myself, towards my fellow man, and towards God."[27] Others, however, saw *terra australis* as a serious threat. Separated from Adam's posterity by the impassable torrid zone, inhabitants of the antipodes could not have known original sin, the Messiah's redemption, or the teachings of the original apostles, making their existence a theological impossibility. Still, the idea of mysterious lands and peoples in the Southern Hemisphere continued to bubble up across medieval Europe.[28] Painted onto the ceiling of a cathedral in Burgo de Osma, Spain, one eleventh-century world map features a slice of southern land populated by a lone skiapod, a human endowed with a single, table-sized foot used for shade against a blazing sun.[29] Such images remain striking in their absurdity, but even sober men such as Albertus Magnus, mentor to the even more sober Thomas Aquinas, somehow believed the southern continent to be very real.[30]

Early modern exploration only sharpened European expectations for the discovery of *terra australis*. The French adventurers Jean and Raoul Parmentier sailed from the English Channel port of Dieppe to Sumatra in 1529. The brothers died there, but their navigator returned to confirm the existence of "Java la Grande," a land "which extends down near to the Antarctic pole," and whose northern promontories extended nearly to the equator. Java la Grande appeared on French maps throughout the sixteenth century, influencing the German cartographer Gerard Mercator, whose "Magellanica" became the standard depiction of *terra australis* for decades.[31] For its part, Spain sent ships toward the South Pacific in 1537, 1567, and 1595, reaching the Solomon Islands, the Marquesas, and the Santa Cruz Islands.[32] In 1605, Pedro de Quirós led another Spanish voyage that stumbled upon the New Hebrides and declared them outliers of the southern continent. Seeking money from the Council of the Indies to plant a settlement there, a breathless Quirós described *terra australis* as "twice greater in Kingdoms and Seignories, than all that which at this Day doth acknowledge Subjection and Obedience" to the Spanish king, reveling in the "incredible Multitude of Inhabitants" whose lands and bodies might now serve the crown.[33]

Frenchmen likewise pled for the establishment of colonies in the deepest south. During a fleeting break in the wars of religion that bloodied the kingdom at the close of the sixteenth century, a Protestant soldier turned scholar named Lancelot Voisin de la Popelinière proposed a new division of the earth's lands. The "First World," he wrote in 1582, consisted of lands known to the ancients and occupied by their descendants; the "Second World" encompassed the Americas, where the Spanish, Portuguese, and English had no intention of making room for French interlopers. The "Third World," however, was "a southern land . . . thirty degrees from the equator, of a much greater extent than all of America." Doubtless intended to spur settlement attempts by his fellow Protestants, Popelinière's well-received book commanded attention from Catholics as well. In 1586, the Jesuits at the Collège de Lyon (among Popelinière's worst theological enemies) made their students debate "the necessity of undertaking an expedition to the third Magellanic world."[34]

In ways that would have distressed Popelinière, French interest in *terra australis* was, during the seventeenth century, yoked to the forces of Counter-Reformation Catholicism. The prime mover in this process was an unremarkable monk named Jean Paulmier. In 1654, Paulmier, a canon of the cathedral of Lisieux in Normandy, wrote a short treatise advocating the establishment of Catholic missions in "the Third World, otherwise called Terra Australis." It was never published. Sometime after finishing the text, however, Paulmier appears to have made a stunning discovery in his family's papers—a manuscript penned by Binot de Gonneville, a long-dead Norman merchant, relating the explosive details of a failed 1503 voyage to the East Indies.[35]

Inspired by "great riches in spices and other rarities" offloaded from Portuguese ships in French ports, Gonneville intended to round the Cape of Good Hope and cruise the coasts of India, Southeast Asia, and Sumatra, accumulating profits as he went. He and his companions reached the cape in high spirits, but soon the ship's pilot died of a seizure and a storm kicked up. Driven by the winds for three weeks, the crew found shelter in a handsome bay on what they believed to be the coast of *terra australis*. Welcomed by a local "king" named Arosca, the Frenchmen were treated like "angels from heaven." Promising to teach Arosca's son Essoméricq about firearms (the equivalent, remarked Gonneville, of promising "gold, silver, jewels, or the secrets of the philosopher's stone to a Christian") and return him in twenty months, the Frenchmen took the boy with them upon leaving.[36] They limped back to France in 1505. Unable to fund a return voyage, Gonneville adopted Essoméricq, who converted to Catholicism, took the name Binot, and lived out his days in Normandy, marrying and having children of his own. Jean Paulmier was shocked to realize that he was one of Essoméricq's great-grandsons. Energized by this revelation and, as he put it, "urged by my blood," the monk began telling his family's story.[37]

Too loudly, as it happened. In 1658 royal officials informed Paulmier and his siblings that they were subject to the *droit d'aubane*, a heavy tax on foreigners and their descendants living within the kingdom. Scrambling to avoid the penalty, he lodged a successful protest on the grounds that Essoméricq had been taken to France against his will. Paulmier hurriedly began work on a book designed to "awaken in France a holy ambition . . . to seize the glory of the apostleship of this Third World."[38] Beating Islamic Arabs and Protestant heretics to *terra australis* would, by his lights, conquer "for Jesus Christ not a city, a State, or an Empire, but . . . a great Continent, a part of the Universe."[39] After rehearsing the standard descriptions of *terra australis*'s size and wealth, Paulmier pled, as one of Essoméricq's "posterity," for the goodwill of the "most Christian Gauls" toward his "southern" kin.[40]

Published in 1663, Paulmier's book was no best seller. But plenty of important people read it, including Louis XIV's chief minister, Jean-Baptiste Colbert, and Vincent de Paul, François Pallu, and Pierre Lambert de la Motte, three clerics who in different ways proved instrumental in founding Paris's Seminary of Foreign Missions in 1663. For these men, Paulmier's clear demonstration that *terra australis* did indeed exist, and that France alone held its right of discovery, set an important precedent. As de Brosses put it in 1756, Gonneville's feat "easily assures the French nation of the honor of the first discovery of southern lands, 16 years before Magellan's departure."[41]

France's push to the south proceeded in fits and starts. In 1714, the Compagnie des Indes floated the idea of a "trading settlement" on what is now South Georgia Island, touting its "good climate" and location near the Straits of Magellan, which opened onto the markets of Peru and China.[42] Nothing came of the plan, partially because Jean-Baptiste-Charles Bouvet de Lozier, a rising star within the company, worked to turn French attention away from Cape Horn and back toward the Cape of Good Hope, where Gonneville's adventure had begun. After poring over Paulmier's *mémoire* and the transcriptions of Gonneville's own account, Bouvet sailed from France in the summer of 1738, diving into the cartographic blind spot midway between the southern coasts of South America and Africa. He aimed to sail east in long zigzags until he hit land. Expecting to find a continent on which to "plant the cross of Our Lord Jesus Christ," Bouvet instead entered the soupy fog of the Antarctic Convergence in November and remained there for several weeks, dodging cathedral-sized icebergs and reassuring his

unraveling crew. Finally, on January 1, 1739, he discovered a glacial, moun-
tainous spot of land he christened "Circumcision Cape" before it receded into a
dangerous mix of mist and grinding sea ice.[43] In the wake of Bouvet's discovery
(not a cape at all, but the island of Bouvetøya), doubts emerged. Helpfully, one
official offered up the theory that in 1503 Gonneville had landed not on *terra
australis* but in "the province of Maryland, north of Virginia."[44]

Although Bouvet's voyage had proven disheartening, and although Dutch
ships in the Indian and Pacific Oceans continued to pare down the dimensions
of *terra australis* during the eighteenth century, French hopes proved particularly
resilient. Even the fog that so vexed Bouvet, and which we now know to be generated by the unseen collision of powerful north- and south-going currents,
became good news. The thick "vapors . . . that hampered Bouvet's navigation,"
explained de Brosses, could only have been produced by the rapid melting of
vast amounts of ice at the onset of the southern summer. And since seawater
could not freeze (or so scientists then believed), the ice had necessarily emerged
from "lands rising from the sea up to lofty mountains, from which flow great
rivers that freeze during the long winters of this climate." The quantity of fog and
mass of Antarctic icebergs admitted only one conclusion: what Bouvet had seen
was no "little country."[45]

Advances in geodesy suggested the same. Since the time of Aristotle, the
concept of balance had guided geographical theorizing about *terra australis*. It
made sense that there should be an area of land in the Southern Hemisphere
equal to that in the Northern. The British circumnavigator Woodes Rogers
believed it "agreeable to Reason, that there must be a Body of Land about the
South Pole, to counterpoise those vast Countries about the North Pole."[46]
Revelations about the earth's shape confirmed this suspicion. Since 1718,
when the astronomer Jacques Cassini presented the results of research conducted in the Parisian basin and Brittany, most European scientists held that
the earth was in fact an elongated sphere, stretching at the poles and flattening
out at the equator. To answer the question once and for all, the Academy of
Sciences in Paris sent out two expeditions to measure the length on the ground
of one degree of arc. Louis Godin and Charles-Marie de la Condamine headed
for the interior of Peru in 1735, while Pierre-Louis-Moreau de Maupertuis
trekked through Lapland in 1736. Maupertuis's arctic arcs measured half a
mile longer than an arc measured in France, and longer still than Godin and
Condamine's near the equator. The earth flattened out at the poles and bulged
in the middle.[47]

Plugged into the Newtonian physics of rotating bodies, these new data produced a compelling case for *terra australis*. Alexander Dalrymple, royal hydrographer of Great Britain during the 1760s and 1770s, explained the theory in
layman's terms:

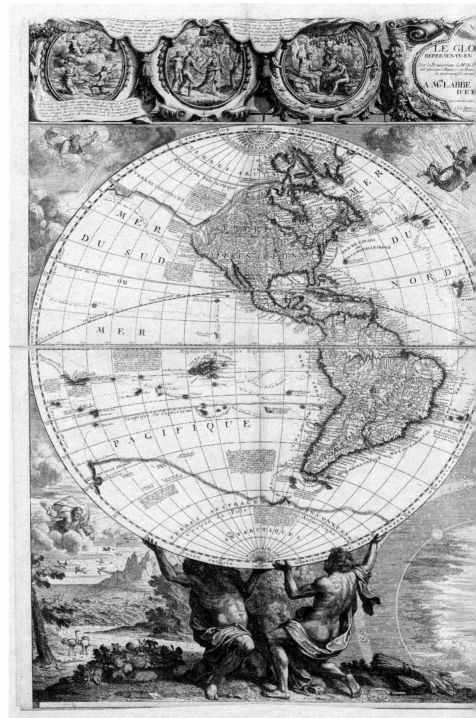

A vivid depiction of France's hopes for a vast, exploitable *terra australis incognita*. Jean-Baptiste Nol
Le globe terrestre (1714). Courtesy of the Library of Congress.

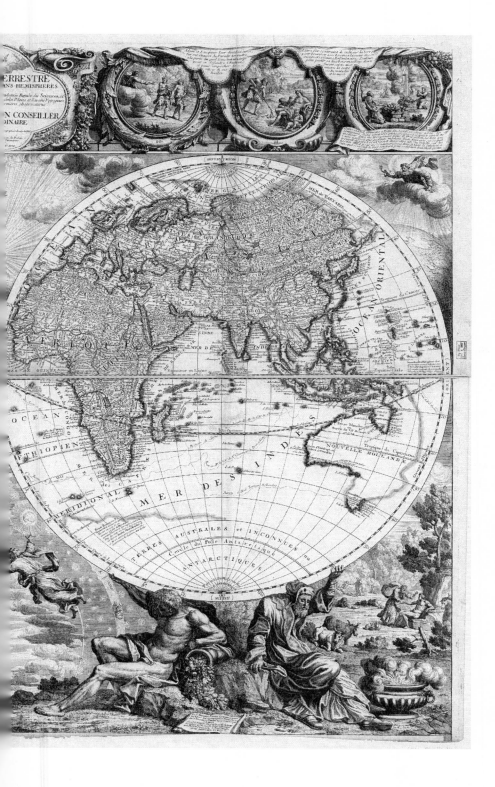

To demonstrate the inhabitability of the southern continent, Nolin locates the antipodes of Madrid, Paris, Vienna, Rome, and Constantinople. Detail of Jean-Baptiste Nolin, *Le globe terrestre* (1714).

> If we then suppose the earth, in its original state, to be a ball covered every where with water, when it was first set in motion, the violent concussion it endured before it attained the spheroidal figure natural to that degree of motion, would throw up the land in irregular bars, and carry the water towards the equatorial parts. This hypothesis, so natural, is entirely warranted by what is known of the globe; for we find within the tropicks the proportion of water to land is as two to one, as far as hitherto discovered, the land increases in a certain ratio towards the pole. . . . From thence arises a very strong argument for a continent on the S.[48]

De Brosses found Condamine and Maupertuis's evidence compelling. The nature of the earth itself virtually guaranteed "some immense continent of solid earth to the south of Asia, capable of holding the globe in equilibrium in its rotation and serving as a counterweight to the mass of northern Asia."[49]

At midcentury, the case for *terra australis* appeared rock solid. Combining the knowledge of ancient philosophers with the observations of modern scientists, de Brosses and Dalrymple had built up methodical, sensible arguments for the continent's existence. Less rational but equally exciting were European conjectures about native Australians. Expressing a common opinion, Dalrymple declared that the fifty million inhabitants of *terra australis* were doubtless "*white people*, of our stature . . . and cloathed with very fine cloths."[50] Such numerous

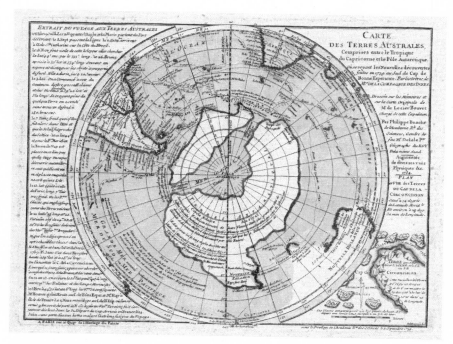

Terra australis at midcentury. Philippe Buache, *Carte des terres australes* (1757). Courtesy of the Princeton University Library.

and "highly polished" peoples were not to be trifled with, lest they enrich another European kingdom.[51]

During the darkest days of the 1760s, France's wartime collapse, coupled with the disloyalty of Louis XV's Caribbean subjects and their slaves, made the mysteries and possibilities of *terra australis* look promising. Rather than leave imperialism far behind, many post–Seven Years' War Frenchmen laid plans for its extension into the unknown. Among them were two brothers, Jean-Pierre and Louis-Antoine de Bougainville, former students of the renowned mathematician Jean le Ronde d'Alembert and the king's own cartographers. Their academic training had taught them everything about the scientific basis for the reality of *terra australis*. But as they saw it, what mattered most was not finding the place but determining how to organize its intercultural relationships. To that question, history provided an answer. Indeed, lessons from the depths of the European past guided the Bougainville brothers toward a truly new imperial age in which France's benevolent power would wash across the globe. In every age, however, ends demanded human means—a truth that drove these French reformers to seek out the Acadians.

Even when consigned to Guiana and Saint-Domingue, Acadians were hardly slaves. But they were not free either. To be sure, uncaring, uncontrollable, and impersonal forces structured the lives of early modern people everywhere. Markets rose and fell, wars began and ended, and faraway subjects felt the consequences. Unmoored from safeguards such as land, long-standing commercial relationships, and family, Acadians suffered from an acute version of this phenomenon. Obscure, seemingly unrelated factors—the economics of physiocracy and the threat of slave revolt in the tropics, for example—proved more than capable of uprooting the exiles from whatever landing places they managed to find. Although it displaced fewer people than France's attempts to settle white laborers in the Caribbean, there is no more revealing illustration of this process than the quest, spearheaded by the Bougainville brothers, to reach *terra australis incognita*. The origins of their obsession with the southern continent, then, make for a story worth telling. For the Bougainvilles' road to *terra australis* demonstrates not only the frantic creativity of French imperialism but also the deep powerlessness that would, in time, inspire equally frantic creativity among the Acadians.

Although the southern seas were on the old régime's mind in a general sense, the events that led the Acadians to the Falkland Islands began, bizarrely enough, with a two-man row over theology. Sometime in the 1690s, the cardinal de Polignac, a thinker, statesman, and cleric attached to the court of Louis XIV, made his way to Rotterdam. Once there, he sought out Pierre Bayle, the famous Protestant skeptic. Upon finding him, Polignac asked a simple question: "To which of the sects . . . in Holland was he particularly attached?" Bayle responded by reciting "some verses of Lucretius," the ancient Roman champion of Epicureanism. Pressed again, Bayle barked out a second passage of Lucretius, this one "longer and more energetic than the first." Polignac left unsatisfied. Upon his return to France, he read more of Lucretius's writings and felt nauseated. "The refutation of his system," Polignac concluded, "would be of use to religion."[52] He thus devoted the next fifty years of his life to a poem, a twelve-thousand-line war engine of words composed in Latin hexameter, whose purpose was to grind Lucretius, Bayle, and their philosophy into dust.

L'Anti-Lucrèce attacked on two fronts. First, Polignac laid out the "fundamental principles of religion" in contrast to what he deemed Bayle's "atheism." More subtly, the poem defended the Cartesian distinction between the worlds of mind and matter against Epicurean atomism, which admitted "no distinction, as to the essence, between the soul and the body."[53] Polignac wrote during carriage rides and lulls in conversation, slipping bits of the swelling manuscript to Newton, Pope Clement II, and Voltaire. The author delayed publication for years, struggling to keep up with new philosophies.[54] In 1741, time ran out. On his deathbed, Polignac gave *L'Anti-Lucrèce* to Charles d'Orléans-Rothelin, abbé de Cormeilles, a fellow member of the Académie des Inscriptions et Belles-Lettres, the old régime's great literary think tank. Eager to find a translator to render

Polignac's flowery Latin into French, Rothelin squired the manuscript through-out Paris, finally settling on Jean-Pierre de Bougainville, a young man possessing classical erudition and a debilitating case of asthma.

Born in 1722, Jean-Pierre had been raised by his father, a notary, and, after the death of his mother in 1734, his aunt. The family enjoyed connections at Versailles thanks to Jean-Pierre's maternal uncle, Jean Potentien d'Arboulin (the royal mistress Madame de Pompadour referred to d'Arboulin, whose position as postmaster allowed him to intercept her rivals' mail, as "Bou-bou").[55] As Jean-Pierre began to plow through Polignac's poem in 1742, he did so with d'Arboulin's blessing and the help of Rothelin's circle of friends. Like intellectuals across Europe, these men bounced from topic to topic, holding forth on everything from politics to biology. The recent Maupertuis and Godin-Condamine expeditions, however, had triggered a craze for geography and geodesy among the *savants*. Particularly taken was Rothelin's colleague Nicolas Fréret. An obsessive student of cartography (at his death, friends would find 1,357 hand-drawn maps among his effects) and ancient history, Fréret took a keen interest in Jean-Pierre's translation of Polignac's poem.

In their research, the two men were fascinated by one section of Lucretius's *De rerum natura* that Polignac, in his zeal to defend the faith, had never addressed. Directed at Lucretius's patron, Memmius, it had to do with *terra australis*:

> In this connection, Memmius, give a wide berth to the belief of those who . . . suppose that all heavy objects in the antipodes press upward and rest on the earth in a reversed position, like the reflections of things we observe in the water. Similarly they argue that animals roam upside down and cannot drop off the earth into the regions of the sky any more than our bodies can of their own accord shoot up into the celestial precincts; that inhabitants of the antipodes see the sun when we are looking at the stars of the night; that they share the seasons with us alternately, and that their nights correspond to our days.[56]

Polignac had surely read the passage but likely dismissed it as one of the Roman's lesser mistakes. For Jean-Pierre, however, Lucretius's wrongheaded approach to the antipodes became an obsession.

L'Anti-Lucrèce was published in 1749, by which time Jean-Pierre and Fréret had turned from poetry to the practical side of French intervention in the deep south. In 1745, Jean-Pierre submitted a prize-winning dissertation lauding ancient Greek colonization in the Mediterranean. "Sometimes," he reminded readers, "curiosity alone removed them from their native land," where they founded provinces with "natural alliances" to older city-states.[57] The next year, he turned to the most curious Greek he knew, reading before the Académie his

"Explanations of the Life and Voyages of Pytheas of Marseille." An inhabitant of the Greek colony of Massalia (present-day Marseille, France), Pytheas had written an account in 320 BC of a voyage beyond the known world. *On the Ocean*, which survived only as fragments in the works of other authors, detailed a journey to the coasts of France, Britain, the Orkneys, and a frigid island the author called Ultima Thule. Critics including the Roman geographer Strabo and the loathsome Pierre Bayle himself derided Pytheas as a liar. Jean-Pierre, however, believed, as most modern scholars do, that the Greek seafarer had in fact discovered the British Isles, perhaps traveling as far north as the Shetlands.[58]

More important than Pytheas's route, however, were the lessons he could teach the old régime and its adventurers. Where others cast Pytheas as a rogue, Jean-Pierre styled him a commercial envoy of the Massalian republic, a forward-looking polity eager to "found a number of colonies . . . less in view of pushing its borders outward than extending and protecting its trade." These goals could best be accomplished by "the discovery of lands whose goods commanded the markets of one's trading partners."[59] Pytheas, Jean-Pierre insisted, had done just that. Bouncing from estuary to estuary and eventually into the open ocean, the Massalian located rich sources of tin, an important component of bronze, and amber, valued across the Mediterranean as jewelry.[60] "Love of country," Jean-Pierre concluded, had spurred Pytheas on far enough to come tantalizingly close to what would have been the greatest discovery in ancient history. Tacking to the northwest, he was stopped short of Iceland, Greenland, and the Americas by what he mysteriously described as "marine lung," a Dantean elemental union in which sea ice and freezing fog met at the horizon and enveloped the ship in one undulating, suffocating mass.[61] As all of Paris would have known, Pytheas's about-face was a perfect analog to the frigid endgame of Bouvet's southern voyage only years before. Breaking through such climatic barriers, Jean-Pierre argued, would have done both Massalia and France a world of good.

Who was up to the challenge? Although Bouvet would go on to the governorship of Ile-de-France in the Indian Ocean during the 1750s and 1760s, he concluded that the coasts of *terra australis* were too close to the pole to serve any useful function. Neither he nor anyone else from the Compagnie des Indes sailed into the southern seas again.[62] For his part, the Lapland explorer Maupertuis had long expressed enthusiasm for a frigid *terra australis*. "Savage, furry men with tails, a species midway between monkeys and us," would live there, he predicted in 1752, exclaiming that he "would prefer one hour of conversation with them than with the greatest mind of Europe." But he had helped found the Berlin Academy of Sciences and Belles-Lettres in the 1740s and was now consumed by obscure disputes in theoretical mathematics; he was also getting old, and age had not improved his bad seamanship.[63] Jean-Pierre surely wanted to go. His asthma, however, prevented him from attending lectures at the Parisian academies, much less voyaging to the Southern Hemisphere. Still, with Britain's trade expanding and its arms dominating the War of the Austrian Succession, time was short. Seeing no Frenchmen with the right stuff for so crucial a mission, Jean-Pierre resolved to create one himself.

In search of a model, he pushed deeper into the classical past to a figure whose exploits had inspired Pytheas himself. As Jean-Pierre would report to a September 7, 1754, session at the Académie des Inscriptions, an "admiral" named Hanno had sailed from the North African city of Carthage around 570 BC with "sixty ships, which carried a multitude of passengers."[64] Armed with maritime knowledge (including, Jean-Pierre believed, descriptions of the Cape of Good Hope) passed down from his Phoenician ancestors, Hanno intended to "pass beyond the straits [of Gibraltar], and seize the west coast of Africa, by scattering a series of colonies to serve as trading posts."[65] He did so, planting settlements while bartering with nomads in present-day Morocco, gawking at a volcanic eruption along the Ivory Coast, and hunting down the strange creatures his men called "gorillas."[66] After thirty-eight days of sailing, Hanno's fleet turned back toward Carthage, where they were received as heroes; the admiral placed the skins of the female "gorillas" his men had killed in the temple of Juno and his own account of the expedition, known as a *periplus*, in the temple of Saturn.[67]

Hanno's colonies helped fuel an economic boom. In 340 BCE, the Greek historian Pseudo-Scylax reported a vibrant trade between "Ethiopians" and Carthaginians on the African coast. Hanno's descendants "brought earthen vases, tiles, Egyptian perfumes, and some jewels of little value for the women," receiving in return ivory, lion and panther skins, and leather "for armor and shields."[68] Wealth flooded the metropolis, yielding "fields thick with plowmen, prairies covered with flocks, . . . superb houses surrounded by avenues," and an "infinite number of workshops."[69] Unfortunately, the Roman destruction of Hanno's Carthage had, Jean-Pierre believed, deprived the world of "an infinite number of facts."[70] While their enemies focused on war or philosophical gamesmanship, the Carthaginians had discovered the proper balance of agricultural development, trade, and politics. "Rich but frugal, they were cultivators *because* they were statesmen and merchants," Jean-Pierre wrote, pushing back against the farming-obsessed physiocrats.[71] This Gordian knot had been retied long ago; academics and prime ministers had worked their hands and minds sore in the interim, but none had cut quite so well as Hanno.

Could Carthaginian history be repeated in eighteenth-century France? Jean-Pierre thought so, but only if the French reached for lands as new as the African coast, with its nomads, "gorillas," and "Ethiopians," had been to Hanno.[72] While such activities were best undertaken by "sovereigns, or companies formed under their auspices," men had to execute them. That challenge, wrote Jean Pierre, demanded a man who was at once pilot, merchant, soldier, general and legislator; a wise adventurer . . . with a sure eye to distinguish between the difficult and the impossible, he must have a mind clear enough to prefer the solid to the dazzling, remembering, while loving glory, that glory was neither the sole, nor even the principal object of his enterprise.[73]

To the relief of a man whose lungs seemed in perpetual revolt, Jean-Pierre's search for a French equivalent began and ended close to home.

Like other boys of his social rank, Louis-Antoine de Bougainville learned Latin, Greek, and ancient history at the Collège de Beauvais in Paris during the 1740s. Seven years older than Louis-Antoine and far more accomplished than their father, Jean-Pierre started using his growing list of connections to shape his younger brother's upbringing. He convinced the mathematician Alexis Clairaut, a veteran of Maupertuis's 1736 Lapland expedition, to tutor Louis-Antoine in calculus; the philosophe d'Alembert, a few years removed from fame as an editor of the *Encyclo-pédie*, pitched in as well, helping shape the boy into a mathematical prodigy. In the mid-1740s, when Louis-Antoine was still a teenager, the two brothers used breaks in study to pore over the papers and maps of the deceased Nicolas Fréret, including material from Bouvet's abortive 1739 voyage to *terra australis*.[74] Calculus had awakened Louis-Antoine's faculties; geography focused them, as he would later write, on sailing the "French flag . . . to the extremities of a new world."[75]

For all his mind's ambition, Jean-Pierre's steadily weakening body could not lead Louis-Antoine everywhere. So, at twenty-one, Louis-Antoine joined the *mousquetaires noirs*, the personal army of the French king and a launching pad for ambitious men of the minor gentry. Even after his departure for France's north-eastern frontier, he continued to study mathematics, publishing his *Traité de cal-cul intégrale*, which would later earn him membership in the British Royal Society, in 1753. After a stint in London negotiating over French and British claims to the Ohio Valley, twenty-five-year-old Louis-Antoine was appointed aide-de-camp to Louis-Joseph, marquis de Montcalm, commander of Louis XV's armies in North America. He sailed for the Canadian theater on the *Licorne* in March 1756. In a letter that doubtless pleased Jean-Pierre, he wrote that the ship's captain, "an officer of the highest distinction" named the chevalier de la Rigaudière, had "promised to teach me as much of sailing as possible during the crossing."[76] To be sure, Jean-Pierre had not orchestrated every aspect of his younger brother's early life. Still, one can scarcely imagine a set of experiences (many of which Jean-Pierre *had* arranged) more conducive to molding Hanno's heir than those of Louis-Antoine de Bougainville.[77]

As Louis-Antoine tracked across Canada with Montcalm, hunting the British and marveling at the French-Canadian-Indian infighting that crippled the French war effort, Jean-Pierre's classical world was never far from his mind. He loathed the marquis de Vaudreuil, New France's American-born governor-general, complaining that he treated Frenchmen "the way the Lacedaemonians treated the Helots." François Bigot, intendant of New France, resembled Verres, the corrupt governor of the ancient Roman colony on Sicily. Only Virgil ("Ah! Flee the cruel lands, flee the cruel shore!") had the words to express Louis-Antoine's shock after France's Algonquian allies killed dozens of British prisoners at Fort William Henry in 1757.[78] Less metaphorically, Louis-Antoine's 1758 proposal to evacuate thousands of French troops from Canada to Louisiana before capitulation was culled from Xenophon. The Athenian philosopher's account, detailing the 401 BC retreat of ten thousand Greek mercenaries from Persia through hostile Armenian and Kurdish territory, seemed to suggest how France might hold on to some part of North America: "The French are worthy to do what the Greeks did," he wrote, "and the retreat of the ten thousand is one of the strokes that has most immortalized Greece."[79] Never so openly pro-Carthage as Jean-Pierre, Louis-Antoine scoured all of antiquity to make sense of his imperial present.

In 1760, a year after Montcalm's defeat on the Plains of Abraham, Louis-Antoine surrendered to the British outside of Montreal. Shipped to France as a prisoner of war, he received a warm welcome at the Department of the Marine. Louis-Antoine read for the first time Charles de Brosses's work on *terra australis*, published during his years in North America. De Brosses confirmed what Jean-Pierre had taught—that the southern continent did indeed exist, and that its colonization would constitute "the greatest, most noble, and perhaps most useful enterprise that a sovereign can undertake." Such an expedition demanded "an intrepid, faithful leader, with brains to match his courage." As if speaking directly to Louis-Antoine, de Brosses compared this leader's impact on the natives of *terra australis* to that of Romulus, Sisyphus, and Cadmus on the "savages" of the ancient Mediterranean.[80]

Even before the French Empire was pulled apart in 1763, Louis-Antoine's course was set. Choiseul offered him the governorship of Cayenne, but he refused, keeping his eyes on weightier matters. "Seeing that the North was closed to us, I thought of giving to my country in the Southern Hemisphere what she no longer possesses in the Northern," he later recalled. "I searched and found the Malouine Islands," the French name for the Falklands, given in reference to intrepid sailors from Saint-Malo, on whose ventures Louis XV's claim rested.[81] That city in Brittany was also home to more than a thousand Acadian refugees.

Louis-Antoine proposed a settlement on the Falkland Islands in November 1762. Although *terra australis* had always generated outsized enthusiasm, the Falklands had a bad reputation. They were a "morsel of rock . . . somewhere at the bottom of America," a frigid outpost "almost at the last confines of this hemisphere," and as useful as the "Dog Star and the Great Bear."[82] Encompassing two large islands and hundreds of smaller ones, the archipelago attracted the attention of an English captain named John Davis in 1592. In search of a passage to Cathay, Davis took shelter on the islands during a storm, but he was too scared to name them. The Englishman Sir Richard Hawkins, the Dutchman Sebald de Weert, John Strong (an opportunist who named the islands for William of Orange's treasurer of the navy), and various French whalers followed. These probes were contested by Spain, which claimed all of South America, save Portuguese Brazil, through the 1494 Treaty of Tordesillas.[83] Louis-Antoine, though, ignored this legal tangle, relying on the principle that settlement alone conferred sovereignty.[84] Instead of changing the color of the Falklands on some European map, he intended to change the islands themselves—by introducing their first permanent human inhabitants.

Initial plans called for Bougainville to sail east after establishing France's claim to the Falklands, "seeking to discover lands in this location and to reach . . . Circumcision Cape, reconnoitered in 1739 by M. Bouvet." If he succeeded, Louis-Antoine would plant a colony "equally advantageous to [France's] navy, her commerce, and her glory." If he failed, he intended to return to the Falklands for supplies, swing around Cape Horn, and "make a settlement to the north of California." Unable to resist, Bougainville quoted Virgil again: "And another shall replace Typhis [navigator for the Greek hero Jason], and there will be another *Argo* to carry the chosen heroes."[85]

As negotiators finalized the Treaty of Paris late in 1762, Louis-Antoine knew that time was of the essence. The British had their sights set on the Falkland Islands as well. Their interest had been common knowledge for well over a decade—since 1748, when the clumsily titled *A Voyage Round the World in the Years MDCCXL, I, II, III, IV* had become an international best seller. The book related the adventures of George Anson and his crew as they circumnavigated the globe. There were plenty of adventures to write about, including shipwrecks, encounters with exotic Pacific islanders, and, most of all, the capture of the *Nuestra Señora de Covadonga* as it sailed between Acapulco and Guam. In all, the Spanish galley contained 1,313,843 pieces of eight and thirty thousand ounces of silver.[86] Along with the quarter of his men who had survived the journey, Anson hauled his treasure on a triumphal parade through London in 1744. Medals were struck, celebratory poems were composed, and Anson became a very rich national hero. The numerous editions and translations of *Voyage Round the World* also gained Anson fame across Europe.

Britain's designs on the Falklands were right there in the book's pages. Anson had passed the islands by without stopping in 1741. The rest of his journey, however, showed him their "great consequence to this Nation." From "Falkland's Isles," ships could reach the western coast of Chile in just over a month, opening "facilities of passing into the Pacifick Ocean." Such ease of movement off the heart of Spain's Empire could "in time of war . . . make us masters of those seas." Better still, the Falklands offered the key to New Spain itself. When conquistadors first began hauling gold out of the Aztec and Inca empires, Anson reasoned, Indians in Chile had caught on and concealed the best mines. If the British, from an outpost on the Falklands, made contact with the native Chileans, they would trade for arms, "for then their gold, instead of proving the means of enslaving them, would procure them weapons to assert their liberty." Britain would then receive "that wealth, which . . . has been most mischievously lavished in the pursuit of universal Monarchy."[87] Anson's readers, then, knew precisely what the British were likely to do, once they got the chance. As early as 1750, Louis XV's colonial minister remarked to France's ambassador to Spain that British plans had been "well known for a long time; but especially since the publication of Anson's voyage."[88]

Louis-Antoine, then, was in a race. He proposed a flotilla reminiscent of Hanno's expedition down the African coast. He hoped for 450 sailors and 250 soldiers, 60 "workers of diverse professions," and 20 or 30 women who might "unite, by marriage, with some men in these budding colonies," both on the Falklands and on *terra australis*. The crown was willing, but its funds were lacking. Weighed down with postwar debt (and with so much dedicated to the new colony on the Kourou River), Choiseul could supply only two ships and some artillery. He did, however, hint that the crown would support a private company's efforts in the South Atlantic. Scrambling, Louis-Antoine and Jean-Pierre (whose asthma had worsened dramatically) started building one early in 1763. Louis-Antoine contacted his rich uncle d'Arboulin and his equally rich cousin Michel-François Nerville de Bougainville. Together, they cobbled together 200,000 livres to create the Compagnie des Malouïnes, dedicating the money to provisions and improvements to the ships. Reluctantly, Louis-Antoine determined that the search for *terra australis* would have to wait until a second voyage. But as always, he retained the drive to "seek out southern lands, which [we] hope to discover about 3 or 400 miles from the Falkland Islands."[89]

In the spring of 1763, Louis-Antoine went to Saint-Malo to oversee the outfitting of his ships, named *Aigle* and, in a nod to the mission's secretive nature, *Sphinx*. He focused on picking skilled sailors for the voyage and tight-lipped carpenters (lest British spies catch on) for the docks. He also reacquainted himself with the Acadians. From his days in New France, Louis-Antoine knew of their endurance. In 1757, after hearing rumors of starvation and disease among Acadian refugees in the wilderness west of Nova Scotia and on Ile Saint-Jean, he saw it firsthand. Two groups totaling three hundred arrived in Québec, one by boat from Miramichi, the other driven "out of the woods" west of Nova Scotia by hunger.[90] If, as de Brosses suggested, colonies in the South Atlantic were to "cultivate the natural productions of the land," who better to deal with tricky soils

and uncertain harvests than those who had already proved their physical resilience and their "strong and faithful attachment" to France?[91] In any case, Louis-
Antoine believed that the raw weather of the Falklands might actually be a draw
for the Acadians. Unlike recruiters for the Kourou colony (who were, at that very
moment, twisting Acadian arms in Saint-Malo), he could tout a climate "more or
less the same as that of Acadia, their old home."[92]

That white lie notwithstanding, Louis-Antoine gathered up some recruits.
Among them were Augustin Benoit, a twenty-three-year-old Acadian baker, his
wife, Françoise Thériot, and their two-year-old son, Nicolas-Jean-Sébastien.
Françoise's unmarried sister Geneviève, then fifteen, also signed on, as did eigh-
teen-year-old Joseph Taillebot, a sailor from Ile Saint-Jean. Guillaume Mervin
and his wife, Anne Bourneuf, onetime French inhabitants of Louisbourg,
brought along their two little children and Anne's two sisters, twenty-year-old
Jeanne and sixteen-year-old Sophie. In addition to another family consisting of a
man known only as Boucher, his wife, brother, two sisters-in-law, and two children, there were likely a few unnamed Acadians who signed on as well.[93] A mot-
ley crew, to be sure, but one that Louis-Antoine expected to build on, convinced
as he was that Acadians "who had made the journey [would] convince their
compatriots to settle in the South."[94]

In September 1763, they all boarded the *Aigle* and the *Sphinx*. Louis-Antoine
did so grieving, for Jean-Pierre's lungs had finally given out in June, only weeks
before the beginning of an adventure shaped, in the most profound way, by the
elder Bougainville's lifelong wrestling match with antiquity. At one minute past
midnight on the ninth, the two ships weighed anchor in Saint-Malo's harbor.
Contrary winds and rough seas delayed their departure for several days—long
enough for Louis-Antoine to deposit one Acadian colonist, along with his
"ill-tempered wife" and luckless father, on shore at nearby Saint-Cast, punish-
ment for the young man's refusal to help as the crew struggled to haul down the
Aigle's topmasts during a squall.[95]

For the remaining settlers, the next months passed in a blur of shipboard routine broken only by the crew's antics and dramatic shifts in the weather. In October, Louis-Antoine ran across a British merchant vessel off the coast of North
Africa. In a breach of maritime etiquette made grave by the threat of Barbary
pirates, the British captain failed to hoist his kingdom's flag promptly. Pulling
close enough to see his face, a bilingual French mariner aboard the *Aigle* barked
out his hope, "seasoned . . . with the energetic terms of sailors," that the ship
might soon "sink to the bottom."[96] By November, hard rains (strong enough to
force the *Aigle*'s pilot to cover his hammock "four or five times a day") alternated
with "stifling heat" that made sleep impossible belowdecks.[97]

Crossing the equator, Louis-Antoine and the Acadians endured an initiation
by "Bonnehomme de la Ligne," a sailor turned gaudily dressed demigod who

welcomed newcomers to the South Seas with a mock baptism. After a riotous round of hazing directed at the ship's officers, Bonnehomme turned to two of the unmarried Acadian girls. He asked if they were virgins; over the shrieks of Augustin Benoit's terrified little son, they said yes. Bonnehomme then marked their faces with mysterious black powder and poured water on their heads, eliciting promises not to "break the bonds of conjugal faith, if you marry a sailor."[98] By December, the convoy reached the island of Santa Catarina, off southern Brazil. Portuguese officials welcomed Louis-Antoine with "much politeness" and a gift of ten sides of beef. While the Acadian women did the officers' laundry on shore, three men deserted.[99] A free African healer cured Augustin Benoit of stomach pains and his sister-in-law Geneviève of swollen ankles using little more than herbs and guava seeds.[100] As the group moved south into the antipodal autumn, low skies and high seas came but rarely went.

The journey ended on February 17, 1764. Louis-Antoine and his crew offloaded passengers, supplies, and animals at Port Saint-Louis on East Falkland, not far from present-day Stanley. The colonists set to work at the base of a moss-covered hill, building a barracks, some huts for the families, and the rudiments of an earthen fort capable of holding fourteen cannon. Between jobs, they took the measure of their home. Privately, Louis-Antoine had no illusions. East Falkland was, he wrote, "a country lifeless for want of inhabitants; neither pasture-lands nor forests for the encouragement of those who are destined to become the first colonists."[101] There were no "traces of any inhabitants," and there was no wood.[102] The ground, as a visiting priest put it a few years later, was "so low and boggy, that after a shower of rain it is impossible to stir out, without sinking up to the knees in mire."[103] In search of something to burn, sailors hacked several blocks of peat out of the earth—otherworldly versions of the marsh grass *gazons* the Acadians had used to construct their *aboiteaux* back in Nova Scotia. After getting used to their monstrous appearance, some of the Acadian girls took a liking to sea lions, tossing rocks into their mouths "which they swallowed as we would a strawberry."[104] More pragmatically, one Acadian killed and skinned three of the giants, leaving the blubbery carcasses facedown in the mire after checking for meat and oil. Port Saint-Louis was certainly alien. But in some ways it was familiar enough.

On April 5, Louis-Antoine dedicated an obelisk in the heart of Port Saint-Louis, burying at its base a medallion featuring two inscriptions, both in Latin. On one side, it read *Conamur tenues grandia*: "Small though we are, we undertake great things." On the other, from the *Georgics* of Virgil, it read *Tibi serviat ultima Thule*: "May distant Thule be subject unto you."[105] And then, promising to return in a few months, Louis-Antoine went home.

Versed in the Antarctic horrors of the Shackleford expedition and by now acquainted with the Acadians' luck, modern readers might reasonably expect a

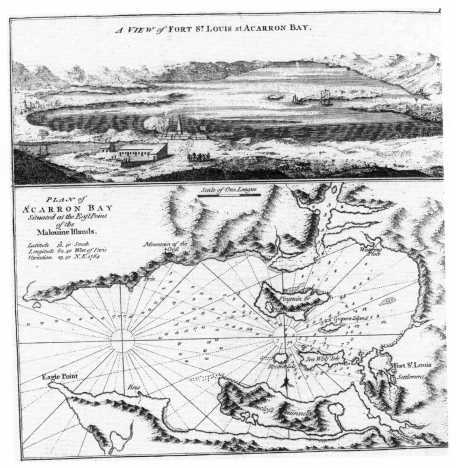

A VIEW of FORT St LOUIS at ACARRON BAY.

PLAN of
ACARRON BAY
Situated at the EastPoint
of the
Malouine Islands.

Latitude 51.40 South
Longitude 60.40 West of Paris
Variation 25.30 N.E.1764

Scale of One League

Acadians in the southernmost European settlement on earth. *A View of Fort Saint Louis at Accaron Bay* (1766). Courtesy of the John Carter Brown Library at Brown University.

story of failure, if not cannibalism. But when Louis-Antoine sailed back into Port Saint-Louis on January 5, 1765, he found Nerville, the soldiers, and the Acadian colonists in fine shape. Only one of the original thirty inhabitants, a nameless Frenchman who fell in a hole while hunting, had died over the winter. Nerville guessed that the others had killed, eaten, or salted more than fifteen hundred bustards, a turkey-like, protein-rich bird. "You would have found us big and plump," Nerville wrote to a friend in France.[106] The Benoit family had welcomed another son (the first of their three children born in Port Saint-Louis), while three other women had turned up pregnant, forcing an amused Louis-Antoine to perform some hasty marriages. "The country is good for reproduction," he concluded.[107]

Even farming had gone surprisingly well. "Our agriculture gives every hope of success," noted Nerville, understandably proud of the little patches of grain and peas that adorned the settlement's outskirts.[108] Louis-Antoine's satisfaction was shared by the Acadians who came with him in 1765, a group that included Jean-Jacques Cyr and Marie-Josèphe Hébert, eight of their children (two of whom were themselves married), and four grandchildren, along with single Acadian men such as Paul Babin, François Henry, and Félix Breau.[109]

These Acadians had allowed Louis-Antoine to put forward ambitious plans for the Falklands while in France between voyages. He counted 333 Acadian families in Saint-Malo, totaling more than thirteen hundred people. Although neither he nor the crown could cobble together the funds to ship them all off, he remained convinced that a "considerable part" of the port's refugees would eventually make the Falklands "the key to the South Seas."[110] In fact, their presence was downright necessary. Far removed from any other French possession, with only the Spanish at Montevideo and the natives of Tierra del Fuego within hailing distance, Port Saint-Louis had to be self-sustaining. Moreover, Louis-Antoine's vision of the Falklands as a whaling, fishing, and sea-lion-hunting hub (and, of course, as a launching pad for missions to *terra australis*) required a source of provisions. For that reason, Louis-Antoine "consecrated" his return trip to Port Saint-Louis to "different experiments on agriculture and the natural produce of the new colony."[111]

The Acadians succeeded admirably. "Everyone was happy," explained a naval commissioner in Saint-Malo. "The work had been considerable, but with [the colonists] well paid, well clothed, well housed, received with kindness and humanity when sick, treated mildly but firmly, everything went perfectly well."[112] Administrative exuberance, perhaps, but arrival of Acadian children in quick succession suggests that the settlers may have shared it. Three were born to Geneviève Thériot and Frenchman Guillaume Guichard, three to Anne Cyr and Georges Charpentier from Ile Saint-Jean, and three to Marie Cyr and Joseph Granger, all within a few years. Compared to what some of their former neighbors were enduring on the Kourou River, these Acadians had found a good, safe place.

But on January 12, 1765, just days after Bougainville's second landfall at Port Saint-Louis, Captain John Byron, the grandfather of the romantic poet of the same name, guided the *Dolphin* and the *Tamar* into a harbor on West Falkland, seventy miles from the French settlement. A few months later, an officer stationed at the British settlement of Port Egmont found a discarded bottle indicating that "some other Frenchmen had lately been here."[113]

Word of the dueling colonies reached Europe in 1766. By then Louis-Antoine had returned to France, but soon Nerville welcomed Captain John MacBride to Port Saint-Louis. Straightforwardly enough, MacBride stated the British intention to "sustain their rights . . . to the Falkland Islands, discovered by that nation during the reign of Elizabeth."[114] Just as Anson had suggested, they hoped to use the islands to speed British ships toward the Pacific, dominating "the Ports & Trade of Chile, Peru, Panama, Acapulco, and in a word all the Spanish Territory upon that sea."[115] Louis-Antoine pressed Choiseul's ministry to push back. Port Saint-Louis, he explained, was an economic and military boon in the making. More important, the colony would spur "our search into the rest of the unknown Universe; the lands of the Antarctic pole ... an immense continent which reaches above the equator between the [East] Indies and Peru."[116]

Politics, however, won out. Unwilling to risk a diplomatic rupture but loath to lose to the British once again, Choiseul surrendered France's right to the islands to the Spanish, who had claimed them all along. Bearing a letter to that effect from Louis XV himself, Louis-Antoine sailed for the islands aboard the *Boudeuse*, reaching Port Saint-Louis in March 1767, but only after making a stop in Buenos Aires to pick up two Spanish ships, one of which carried the settlement's new governor. Clutching the royal edict, Louis-Antoine and Nerville assembled the soldiers and Acadian families outside the governor's house. The cousins said that in the interest of maintaining "friendship" with the Spanish (and, it needed no saying, harming British interests), the king had given up the Falkland Islands. Everyone now had a choice. Louis XV gave his "royal word" that those who wished to stay in Spanish territory could, at any time, return to France and enjoy "the rights and privileges of my other subjects."[117] Alternatively, they could leave as soon as ships arrived to carry them off.

Most began packing. In September 1767, Nerville sailed for France with "the greater part of the French families."[118] Augustin Benoit, Françoise Thériot, and their children made the return voyage alongside Françoise's sister Geneviève, Geneviève's husband, Guillaume Guichard (now going by his strapping carpenter's nickname, "Thousand Men"), and Geneviève and Guillaume's daughter and son. Madeleine Henry, the Beaubassin-born wife of Frenchman Michel Beaumont, abandoned the Falklands as well.[119]

The Spanish were not impressed with Port Saint-Louis. "The state of the houses we now possess *in this Versailles*," sneered one officer, "leaves us cut off and damned in every way, for this island has nothing and produces nothing."[120] To believe one of the Franciscan friars sent to Port Saint-Louis in 1767, the Spanish governor grew misty-eyed watching ships leave the harbor, declaring himself willing to give up his office to return to Buenos Aires "though in no higher station than a cabin boy."[121] The few colonists who remained (38, compared to 125 who departed) had done so, one Spaniard declared, because "they had no reason to go anywhere else."[122] In any case, with the growing Cyr clan as their anchors, these veterans of Louis-Antoine's colony hung on until 1772, when they seem to have returned to France.

After leaving Port Saint-Louis and the Acadians behind, Louis-Antoine completed one of the most celebrated circumnavigations of the eighteenth century. Aboard the *Boudeuse* and trailed by the *Étoile*, he rounded Cape Horn and sped into the Pacific in 1766. Each morning, on Louis-Antoine's orders, the *Étoile* veered south until its pilot could barely keep the *Boudeuse* in sight; and each night, the two ships converged again, having failed to discover the shores of *terra australis incognita*.

The expedition did, of course, make landfall on Tahiti, the New Hebrides, and the Solomon Islands. Louis-Antoine's account of these places and their inhabitants reflected his classical instruction at Jean-Pierre's feet. Positioned on the *Boudeuse*'s quarterdeck, the Tahitian who "carelessly" dropped her covering cloth in full view of the sailors "appeared to the eyes of all beholders, such as Venus shewed herself to the Phrygian shepherd." The Polynesian tattoos that so baffled the crew made perfect sense to Louis-Antoine, as "when Caesar made his first descent upon England, he found this fashion established there," marking the practice as common among cultures that "bordered upon a state of nature." Louis-Antoine was sheepish about his comparisons, considering them ungainly: "I have lost a brother, whose productions were admired by the public, and who might have assisted me in that respect."[123]

Returning home by way of New Guinea, the Dutch East Indies, and Ile-de-France, Louis-Antoine reached Saint-Malo in March 1769, throwing the harbor into a commotion before rushing off to Versailles. What Augustin Benoit, Geneviève Thériot, Madeleine Henry, and the other Acadian veterans of Port Saint-Louis living near the Breton port thought of all this is unknown. They might have felt a measure of pride. After all, in 1764 their combination of industriousness and homelessness had helped make Port Saint-Louis a reality, and their strange settlement had laid the groundwork for Louis-Antoine's glorious, if not fully successful, voyage of discovery.

But as Louis-Antoine eased into the life of a celebrity of the old régime, publishing his *Voyage autour du monde* in 1772 and making plans for an ambitious polar expedition, the Acadians came to painful conclusions about their place in the order of things. Much of their disappointment had practical roots. Surviving the streets of Saint-Malo turned out to be more difficult than hunting bustards on East Falkland. In July 1769, only months after Louis-Antoine's homecoming, Madeleine Henry and her three children lived in "the greatest indigence." They begged officials to "procure our subsistence."[124] Augustin Benoit and several others claimed that Nerville owed them money, but reported in 1772 that he had stopped responding to their letters. As they proclaimed to ministers at Versailles, the Acadians had known much "toil and misery" in the Falklands, and would "forever remember Montevideo, Encenada de Baragon [a minor Argentine port], and Buenos Aires," stopovers on the voyage to and from the South Seas. Benoit and company pressed their case against Nerville but understood the odds against them. "We are poor and he is rich," they confessed. "He is powerful and we are nothing."[125]

They only knew the half of it. For Nerville, Louis-Antoine, Jean-Pierre, Charles de Brosses, and the other boosters of Port Saint-Louis were not simply powerful. They were the fruition of an imperial vision whose gnarled intellectual roots stretched far back into history: past the eighteenth-century physics of the bulging equator and hemispheric balance; past early modern explorers barreling toward the Antarctic convergence; past the southern monsters of medieval map-makers; past the *terra australis*–denying Epicureanism of Lucretius, recovered and attacked by the cardinal de Polignac; past the African voyage of Hanno of Carthage and the northern advance of Pytheas the Massalian; all the way to Aristotle, who first opened the European mind to the world below. After 1763, *terra australis incognita* enjoyed its greatest burst of notoriety, and not just from the desperate French. In 1770, Alexander Dalrymple advocated the discovery of southern lands as a means of heading off the imperial crisis in British North America. With "new markets" of fifty million consumers to "take off our manu-factures," the American colonies "would be unable to compel this country to a precipitate concession."[126]

But as Louis-Antoine had begun to suspect, everyone had been wrong about *terra australis*. In hindsight, it was easy to see the folly of becoming, as Samuel Johnson put it, "encroachers on the waste of nature."[127] Yet even this most out-landish of empire-building schemes had at once ensnared Acadians and been energized by their potential. As faithful, hardy tillers of what seemed to be unco-operative soils, they were, as Louis-Antoine had exclaimed, "the kind of men most proper to found a flourishing colony."[128] And that, ironically, made them "nothing."

Still, Acadians helped inspire big ideas until the very end. In 1772, a Breton nobleman returned to France to report on an exciting voyage. Bearing south from Ile de France, Yves-Joseph de Kerguelen-Trémarec claimed to have sighted "the central mass of the Antarctic continent." He thought it was a promising place. The soil there yielded "all the vegetable productions of the metropolis." Whales, sea lions, and fish swarmed thick in its coastal waters, and one could even find dyes, copper, lead, crystals, diamonds, rubies, sapphires, and other treasures in mountainside mines. "New men," Kerguelen speculated, might live there. "All that our eyes have seen is crisscrossed by woods and greenery," Kerguelen lied about his island, "which seems to announce a peopled land, cul-tivated with forethought."[129]

He envisioned the new settlement as a breadbasket for Ile de France and other French outposts in the Indian Ocean, supplying grain to a colony where none grew. The produce of *terra australis*, he predicted, would "give new life to Ile de France and Ile de Bourbon, tripling their annual commerce by sea." With patience, bigger things might follow. From a perch "overlook[ing] India, the Moluccas, and China," southern lands might allow the Bourbons to "command

Cook's Voyage Octavo.

A View of CHRISTMAS HARBOUR *in* KERGUELEN'S LAND.

The Acadian colony that wasn't: Ile Kerguelen, two thousand miles southeast of the Cape of Good Hope. George Cooke, *A View of Christmas Harbour in Kerguelen's Land* (1811). Courtesy of the Library of Congress.

Asia and America," shaking off the yoke of British oppression. To populate the islands, Kerguelen hoped to recruit "a few families chosen from among the poor Acadians, who today live in several parts of France in the most frightful poverty."[130]

Kerguelen had discovered not Antarctica but Ile Kerguelen, a cold, Corsica-sized rock well over three thousand miles southeast of the southern tip of Africa. The island's continuing status as a *territoire d'outre-mer*, or overseas territory, marks it as the only remnant of France's eighteenth-century assault on *terra australis incognita*. No Acadian ever settled there, and with the completion of James Cook's 1775 circumnavigation, the unknown southern continent finally retreated south of the Antarctic convergence. The notion of using Acadian labor to create an agrarian paradise on remote islands, however, died hard. The French simply shifted their ambitions, and the Acadians' destinations, closer to home.

5

The Homeland

Thou shalt carry much seed out into the field, and shalt gather but little
in; for the locust shall consume it. Thou shalt plant vineyards, and dress
them, but shalt neither drink of the wine, nor gather the grapes, for the
worms shall eat them. Thou shalt have olive trees throughout all thy
coasts, but thou shalt not anoint thyself with the oil; for thine olive
shall cast his fruit.

—Deuteronomy *28:38–40*

Told in reverse chronological order, the story of Joseph Leblanc *dit* le Maigre is
a heartening tale of hard work and just desserts. It begins on a farm in western
France. There the protagonist suffers, living on charity while barred from the
opportunity he craves. So le Maigre ("the Thin," a tongue-in-cheek nickname for
heavyset men) takes bold action, migrating to the island of Miquelon off the
southern coast of Newfoundland. The move backfires. The island is barren of
vegetation but overcrowded with seekers just like him. Dispirited, le Maigre sails
for home, where he gets a fortunate break. During the 1740s, he seizes a chance
to fight the British, displaying heroism that earns praise from Louis XV's ministers. After receiving compensation from Versailles, he moves again, this time to a
handsome ranch on the Bay of Fundy. Financial and paternal increase ensues.
Surrounded by a growing family, herds of handsome livestock, and well-tended
fields, le Maigre settles into a life of good harvests and better company.

But it did not happen this way. Indeed, le Maigre's real story reflected some of
the harsher realities of living as an uprooted refugee in the post–Seven Years'
War French Empire. Born in Acadia in 1697, Joseph Leblanc married Anne
Bourg in the early 1720s. For him, it was a good match. Anne's father, Alexandre
Bourg *dit* Belle-Humeur, was descended from one of Acadia's most prominent
families and served as a deputy to the British government at Annapolis Royal.
The couple farmed, raised cattle, and dabbled in trade near Grand Pré, trans-
forming Anne's dowry into a burgeoning estate. As King George's War consumed

Nova Scotia in 1744, le Maigre sensed an opening. He helped French troops as they marched toward Annapolis Royal, billeting François du Pont Duvivier's soldiers and furnishing them with "all that was necessary."[1] When the French siege failed to dislodge the British, le Maigre paid a heavy price for transgressing the bounds of neutrality. Neighbors informed, and the British gave chase. They caught up with le Maigre in the Strait of Canso between Ile Royale and Nova Scotia, where he was paddling a "bark canoe" dressed as a "simple hunter."[2] Thinking fast, he threw the documents he was smuggling from Louisbourg into the water, then played the fool. "If I broke the law, it was purely by ignorance," he told British authorities, and while he promised to find out "what was doing" with France's Mi'kmaq allies, no leads emerged from his interrogation.[3]

The British let le Maigre off easy, but they were less forgiving when, in September 1746, he participated in a scheme to provision a massive French fleet commanded by the duc d'Anville and destined to attack Annapolis Royal, Boston, and the British West Indies. Le Maigre drove fifty head of cattle and two hundred sheep across Nova Scotia to Chebucto Bay (now Halifax) to feed nearly eleven thousand French soldiers and sailors. Disease and accidents, however, hamstrung the expedition in the Atlantic, and d'Anville's sudden death just days after his arrival in Nova Scotia left le Maigre and his livestock high and dry. In 1747, Governor William Shirley ordered his extradition to Massachusetts along with other "notoriously guilty" Acadians.[4] Arrested and spirited to Boston, le Maigre freed himself (or so he later claimed) by sawing through the iron bars of his jail cell and making a "stealthy" escape across New England. Informed of his return to Grand Pré, the government at Annapolis Royal banished him, sending soldiers to "pillage, raze, and burn all [his] buildings."[5] With his family, he fled to Port Toulouse on Ile Royale, where in 1750 one official took pity on the run-down rancher, a "good Frenchman . . . reduced to begging."[6]

The British campaign against the Acadians in 1755 worsened his already bad lot. Fleeing Acadians swarmed onto Ile Royale, triggering panic and food shortages. When the British took Louisbourg in 1758, le Maigre departed for "the coasts of Miramichi" on the mainland, where over the next three years he became a pirate, seizing several British "prizes" in the Gulf of Saint Lawrence. By 1761, however, the French had failed to retake Québec and British warships were cruising the gulf with little resistance, leading the Acadian insurgents to sign what they believed to be a "treaty of peace and neutrality." For le Maigre, it turned out to be an excuse for more "vengeance, cruelty, and inhumanity." Contravening the terms of the treaty, the British confiscated his meager possessions and imprisoned him in Halifax. After two years there, he joined his wife on a hand-built skiff bound for Miquelon in the spring of 1763. A storm dashed the vessel to bits as they neared the island, ruining the few "little effects" the couple had managed to acquire. Exhausted, Anne Bourg died three years later. Le Maigre stared down his last choices alone.[7]

Then nearly seventy years old, the patriarch petitioned Louis XV to rejoin his son Joseph on Belle-Ile-en-Mer, an island off the southern coast of Brittany where the crown had founded a colony for "repatriated" Acadians. There, on the morning of February 5, 1767, in the town of Le Palais, le Maigre endured another affront. To gain access to the 6 sols per day earmarked for Acadian refugees, he was forced to appear before a panel composed of his old friend the abbé le Loutre; the "venerable and discreet" Jacques-Marie Choblet, a local rector; and Jacques Fronteaux de Lacloir, representing Louis XV himself. As many of the parish registers of Nova Scotia had been lost, the men were charged with determining the "filiations" of Acadian families at Belle-Ile, thwarting impostors with pretensions to the king's lucrative graces.[8]

To prove himself a "true Acadian," le Maigre literally gave the performance of his life. From memory, he ranged across time and geography to reconstitute the world he had lost. There was Marguerite, his eldest daughter, dead on Ile Royale in 1752 at twenty-eight; his sons Simon and Olivier, both shipped to Maryland in 1755, one of whom he had not seen since then; his son Joseph's second wife, dead at Southampton, England, in 1756; dozens of grandchildren he had never known.[9] He passed the test and got the money, but it was never enough. In 1771, le Loutre begged the king to grant le Maigre a pension, of which "this poor old man has great need."[10] The request went unheeded. Poor and forgotten, le Maigre died sometime after 1773.[11]

Among the many personal tragedies of the Acadian diaspora, le Maigre's was one of the more tragic. The greater import of his sad story, however, may lie in the setting of its final act. In its way, Belle-Ile-en-Mer was as unlikely a backdrop for French imperialism as the Falkland Islands. Less than ten miles south of Brittany's Quiberon Peninsula, the island had been known to the ancient Roman settlers of Gaul, who called it Vindilis. By the eighteenth century, farmers and fishermen had been living on Belle-Ile for hundreds of years. Where the remote Falklands had drifted in and out of European cartography so often that by the 1760s "even their existence has been called into question," Belle-Ile was scarcely more mysterious than the streets of Paris.[12] Yet le Maigre was pulled to its shores by the same forces that landed the Cyr family in Port Saint-Louis: France's quest for imperial innovation, filtered through the lessons of the classical past.

At issue was less ancient geography than ancient demography. For early modern kings and queens, the science of population was a touchy subject. The health or decay of a state was measured in multiple ways, but birthrates and population figures functioned as one of the most reliable indicators. By all appearances, the Bourbon monarchs and their contemporaries had failed. Charles-Louis Secondat, baron de Montesquieu, devoted a large chunk of his 1721 book *Persian Letters* to the problem of depopulation. After some quick figuring, Montesquieu's

An Island Outpost of the French Empire: Belle-Île-en-Mer

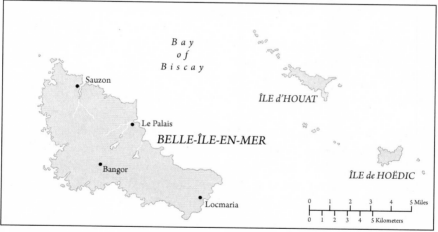

Rhedi offered a sobering assessment: "I have come to the conclusion that there is scarcely a tenth of the men on the earth that there was in former times."[13] The reasons, Rhedi's correspondent Usbek explained, flowed from the imposition of Islam and Christianity over older, less artificial religious and political systems. Where Muslim polygamy made men too exhausted to father many children, Christian prohibitions on divorce simply "took the pleasure out of marriage." The celibacy of the Catholic clergy hurt matters, as did European wars and the twin evils of colonialism and African slavery. Dramatic alterations in "customs" had sapped the "prodigious fertility" of classical Europe while speeding the exportation of depopulation to the rest of the world.[14]

Although not everyone agreed on the particulars, evidence of the ancient world's demographic superiority accumulated as the eighteenth century progressed. "If one believes Herodotus," wrote Étienne-Noël d'Amilaville in Diderot and d'Alembert's midcentury *Encyclopédie*, certain pharaohs of Egypt had commanded some "410,000 soldiers, all born Egyptians," protecting some thirty million inhabitants.[15] D'Amilaville had still more proof. Homer reported that the Greeks had transported more than a hundred thousand soldiers to the siege of Troy; in the third century AD, Athenaeus estimated the population of Greece at fourteen million; Diodorus of Sicily claimed that the ancient Assyrian king Ninus had put nearly two million men in the field against four hundred thousand Bactrians; Julius Caesar counted thirty-two million inhabitants in Gaul, far more than the *Encyclopédie*-era population of the kingdom of France. Even artificial additions failed to slow the kingdom's decline. "Since the beginning of the last century," d'Amilaville noted, "this monarchy has taken several large, well-peopled provinces; yet its inhabitants are less numerous by one-fifth than before these acquisitions."[16] Intellectuals and political figures obsessed with the reproductive gap between the ancients and moderns, wrote one observer in 1751, "talk of nothing but propagating the species."[17]

War only heightened anxieties over birthrates, and not just in France. Imperial dominance was at stake, for, as one Anglo-American writer declared in 1747, "it is the PEOPLE which are the true Riches, Beauty, and Strength of every Kingdom, Nation and Province; and when *the People are taken away*, and the Country thereby thin'd and made bare of Labourers and Inhabitants; *then also*, almost *every Blessing is taken away with them*."[18] In 1753, a proposed census to "ascertain the collective strength of the nation . . . [and] what number of men might upon a sudden exigency be levied for the army" failed in the British Parliament. Opponents thought the idea "subversive of the last remains of *English* liberty," fearful that measuring their population would lead Englishmen to be "pressed into the fleet" and "transplanted like felons to the plantations abroad . . . driven from place to place as graziers do their cattle." A contributor to *Gentleman's Magazine* held that a census would harm the war effort by inspiring needless worry. When threats arose, he argued, the British would "raise a force proportioned to the exigency, let the number . . . be what it will."[19] Others had less faith in raw bravery. In 1755, the Reverend William Brakenridge published research alleging that the population of London had declined since 1700. With war in the offing, his findings caused a stir. Thinkers such as David Hume debated the problem anxiously, as did ordinary subjects.[20]

In 1755, 1756, and 1757, as British arms suffered loss after agonizing loss in the American theater, the writer and politician Joseph Massie blamed rural expropriation for what he deemed the "national weakness" of depopulation:

> Some hundred thousands of farmers and cottagers, who were most to be depended on for the Defence of the Nation, and the Increase of

People, have been bereaved of Property or Interest in Land, the only certain means to maintain wives and children . . . and have been driven to seek for maintenance, by uncertain means arising from trade; wherein luxurious living or poverty of circumstances, and the want of manly exercise, or being much confined, have impaired their health and bodily strength: from whence have followed, decreases in the number, stature, and vigour of their posterities, from Generation to Generation, which have ended in their total extinction.

Massie's solution involved tough love for prostitutes and other members of the "lawless population" whose dissipation had caused "A RAPID DECREASE in the Number of People" and the ascent, however short-lived it would prove to be, of French power.[21]

Battlefield victories, however, managed to cure what ailed the British, reducing fears over depopulation to mere background noise in national politics by the early 1760s. Not so for the French. With their military fortunes plummeting in North America, the Caribbean, Europe, and the Indian subcontinent, Louis XV's ministers cast about for immediate sources of blame. Even before the war ended, they hauled luckless officers such as Charles des Champs de Boishébert (accused of war profiteering in Canada and dereliction of duty while commanding Acadians in the Nova Scotia borderlands) and Thomas Arthur, comte de Lally (who surrendered the Indian outpost of Pondicherry to the British in 1761), before tribunals. Generally, these trials reflected the sense that France's nobility—once deemed men of "sword and wrath," the cutting edge of a strong French society—had abandoned the virtues that had animated their martial courage.[22]

But in a moment of surging nationalism, the French concluded that aristocratic failures were symptoms of a deeper illness. The cancer of depopulation seemed to have taken root in the most fundamental institutions of the absolute monarchy. From the Catholic Church to the French army, everything seemed to conspire against reproduction. While priestly strictures made legitimate fatherhood an impossibility, the soldier's very equipment worked against his proper sexual performance. Horseback riding on campaign, some claimed, had emasculated the ancient Scythians, and probably had done the same to the French cavalry.[23] When the soldier was out of the saddle, the *encyclopédist* Nicolas-Luton Durival recognized, he had a pressing need "to safeguard the loins against humidity." Durival proposed that the monarchy issue special leather breeches to "conserve men of such a precious kind . . . in the decline, unhappily all too noticeable, of our population."[24]

A fanciful solution, but the problem had penetrated beyond the army to the very heart of the French nation. A midcentury observer in the village of Frontenay in eastern France, for example, noted that a recent militia draft had netted twenty-three young men. They were not much for conjugal duties. During the preceding eighteen months, only one marriage and one baptism had taken place in Frontenay, and the latter involved "the child of the Lord's new gamekeeper, who arrived with his wife pregnant."[25] Confronted by an enemy whose "luxury and population . . . have risen in the same proportion" even as it populated "vast colonies," Frenchmen from Louis XV down had ample reason to worry.[26]

Since, as the military engineer Sébastien le Prestre de Vauban had written early in the eighteenth century, "princes without subjects are nothing more than inconvenienced private individuals," both Louis XV's officials and concerned patriots alike embarked on a program of demographic revitalization in the wake of the Seven Years' War.[27] Ideas proliferated fast. Some mused about awarding lucrative privileges to "fathers of twelve living children," while airier notions—Durival's sperm-conserving uniforms, the legalization of polygamy and divorce, the abolition of warfare and clerical celibacy, and the marquis de Mirabeau's campaign to turn woods and flowerbeds into wheat fields for the nourishment of more and more Frenchmen—made appearances at the margins of the argument.[28] Whatever their specific recommendations, though, French populationists all groped for a moral catalyst that might spark in their countrymen a revival of the traditions of male virility and female nurturing that had so effectively peopled the ancient world. The key, it appeared, was to excite in ordinary people the desire for "emulation," presenting vivid examples of virtues (modeled, naturally, by the social and intellectual elite) to be copied in the interest of the public good. During the early 1760s, emulation became something of a cure-all, a remedy for everything from inefficient farming to bad painting to economic self-interestedness.[29] Why not depopulation?

Acadians, as it happened, provided a perfect example. Their fecundity had long been the stuff of legend. Back in 1708, an aspiring poet named the sieur de Diéreville published an account of a voyage to Port Royal he had made ten years earlier. While marveling at the simplicity of Acadian sociability and the sublime beauty of the Bay of Fundy, Diéreville was interrupted by a remarkable, joyful "swarming of Brats." He traced the gang of children to two families, Acadian neighbors "united by love and the bonds of marriage," with eighteen living children apiece. Another couple, locals told the stunned Frenchman, "had made it to twenty-two, and promised still more."

Marriage among the Acadians, Diéreville later revealed in verse, began when two young people fell in love. After that,

> All that remains is to people the world;
> Which is, in any case, what they do best,
> Never dividing their tenderness,
> From the first transports of callow youth,
> They have many children well into old age.

Even enemies admitted that when it came to procreation, the Acadians had, as Diéreville put it, a "capacity in the business."[30] Like "Noah's progeny," declared Richard Philipps in 1730, the Acadians of Nova Scotia were rapidly "spreading themselves over the face of the Province." In Massachusetts, William Shirley likewise marveled that six thousand "fighting men" lived along the Bay of Fundy in 1746.[31] The French were even more impressed when the refugees began arriving in 1758. The Acadians were, exulted one metropolitan observer, "big, robust, hardworking, and very fecund." Scores of pregnant women, evidently game for childbirth even under the hardships of exile, highlighted the point.[32]

By 1763, then, Acadians looked like the right sort of people to serve as models for the seemingly impotent inhabitants of the French countryside. Although powerful men from the duc de Choiseul to Louis-Antoine de Bougainville would, in the immediate aftermath of the Seven Years' War, think of France's nearly four thousand refugees as potential settlers for overseas colonies, an equally powerful bundle of ideas promised to replant them in the metropolis. The abbé Gabriel-François Coyer laid out the rudiments of the argument in 1756. France's troubles, he wrote, began not with widespread moral failings or monarchical despotism but with unused farmland. The kingdom's "25 million acres of pure loss," most of which was owned by impoverished or backward noblemen, had hampered economic growth for decades. He proposed a two-step remedy. First, landowners who could not afford to put their lands to the plow were to abandon the fields entirely, instead participating in commerce. This, of course, meant that noblemen who followed Coyer's advice would shatter one of the old régime's most durable cultural and legal taboos, a controversial sullying of aristocratic honor that prevented many readers from considering step two. Once they had made a little money, Coyer wrote, the "trading nobility" would reinvest in land. Moving peasant-tenants onto fallow soil and directing the work of clearing, planting, and harvesting, such men would ensure their own fortunes while creating the conditions for a baby boom. "If we wish to favor population," Coyer explained, the French must "clear new lands" in the kingdom's interior— the equivalent of "conquer[ing] new countries without making any victims."[33]

In effect, Coyer was describing the colonization of France itself, the most radical of all the revisions of empire to emerge from the disappointments of the Seven Years' War. During the late 1750s and early 1760s, a growing, diverse cadre of thinkers and writers played with the idea, linking internal imperialism and a revival of agriculture in a potent remedy for the kingdom's ills. Among them was Philippe-Auguste de Sainte-Foix, chevalier d'Arcq, an illegitimate son of an illegitimate son of Louis XIV, and Coyer's main opponent in the controversy over the role of the French nobility. Although d'Arcq focused on noblemen as warriors, he practically equated rural development with combat. "Gentlemen who exploit their lands," he argued, merited military-style "marks of distinction," especially those who "recover an abandoned field," thus increasing the kingdom's yield of crops and men.[34]

Ange Goudar, a philosophe and European traveler, was more explicit. Decades of aping British "designs of commerce," he complained, had induced France to empty its "towns of vagabonds . . . to bolster our colonies in America." By contrast, he advocated "peopl[ing] the countryside of France" by sending "colonies to our husbandmen."[35] An influx of new migrants would provide a valuable kick start in both international politics and economics. "Agriculture is the engine of battle, the soul of victories," Goudar wrote, for it alone gave "empire of the land and the sea to the nation that establishes it as the first principle of its administration."[36] After the Treaty of Paris, the benefits of self-colonization seemed self-evident. Many bought into the conclusions of the marquis de Mirabeau in his 1764 physiocratic manifesto, *La philosophie rurale*: that France would be best off settling "colonial lands . . . in the fallow soil of the kingdom's interior."[37]

Theorists such as Coyer, Goudar, and Mirabeau were soon joined by ministers with concrete plans. Initially these centered on the eight hundred or so Acadians redeemed from Great Britain in 1763. The duc de Nivernais commissioned an estimate of costs for settling those refugees somewhere in France. For "120 habitable houses, each with an oven and a chimney," he estimated 16,000 livres. For "instruments of farming and gardening" including "pickaxes, hoes, hatchets, saws, [and] hammers," as well as household items like "a kneading bin, a cauldron, and a pot," 10,000 livres would do. In addition, the colonial booster suggested "two fishing boats . . . common to the colony, as the Acadians had in their land." All of this added up to 120,000 livres—a hefty sum, especially for a king saddled with war debt. But given the twin problems of depopulation and agricultural decline, the benefits would outstrip expenses. "The acquisition of 120 families which over the course of 20 years will produce 240 families of faithful, hardworking subjects" seemed a wise investment. These Acadians, Nivernais continued, "will produce for the state, by the augmentation of their work and consumption, [a dividend of] more than 10 percent after the second year."[38] Nivernais's hope, of course, was to lay hold of funds from Versailles to settle the Acadians on Ile de Bouin, his island domain on the Atlantic coast. Choiseul killed that project, ostensibly because the Acadians had been reserved for the Kourou colony. But the minister had his own attachments to internal colonization. Behind Nivernais's back, he ordered the managers of his estate near Amboise in central France to find parcels of land for "a part" of the Acadian community.[39]

Soon after the Treaty of Paris, like-minded proposals flooded Versailles, floating through the ministry alongside plans for Guiana, Saint-Domingue, and the Falkland Islands. Although the controller-general of finances, Henri Bertin, mused about Acadians as miners (a suggestion that even the unsentimental Choiseul found "cruel"), most of these initial settlement schemes focused on farms where Acadians might, as one booster later put it, "perform the miracle" of demonstrating proper work habits to slovenly peasants.[40] Some argued that Acadians could clear the "king's woods" or dry ancient marshes near Blaye, just north of Bordeaux on the Gironde River, while others touted a hemp-growing project in Brittany aimed at supplying the French navy with rope.[41]

Louis-Elizabeth de la Vergne, comte de Tressan, an old-régime polymath known for his translations of medieval poetry, crafted a proposal that illuminates the ambitions of internal colonizers and the pitfalls facing their would-be colonists. Centered on the town of Bitche, a woodland village on France's border with the Holy Roman Empire, Tressan's lands had a complex history. During the Thirty Years' War, Gustavus Adolphus had "devastated" the area, scattering its peasants and consuming their crops and livestock. Late in the seventeenth century, the duc de Lorraine tried to revive Bitche, hiring Vauban himself to rebuild his château and paying for a new parish church in the village square. The area "began to repopulate, but slowly." In 1736, Bitche was inherited by Stanislas Leszczyński, the former king of Poland and son-in-law of Louis XV. Progress continued. An overgrown basin outside the village was cleared, and by 1763 even the gullies that sliced through the plains surrounding Bitche held crops. But with the area to revert to the French monarchy after Leszczyński's death (born in 1677, the ex-king seemed perpetually at the grave's edge), much work remained. Bitche and its neighboring villages "contained only twenty thousand inhabitants," Tressan reported. By his lights, the population should have been double that. The region, he wrote, remained "seven-tenths covered by forests" whose trees would, once Leszczyński died and passed the territory to Louis XV, "yield nothing for the king."

The main impediment to Bitche's development was dirt. "The base of the soil is sand that appears thin and sterile, which it in fact is," Tressan confessed. He had already attempted to implant outsiders onto the land, only to have soil stop him. Years earlier, Tressan had participated in a venture that would have settled wounded German soldiers and their families in the forest. Given free land and tools with which to clear it, the invalids were destined not just to grow food but also to raise children to serve in "our German regiments." It became clear, however, that the soldiers had no talent for demanding farm work, and the plan fell apart. Not so, wrote Tressan, for refugees from North America. "Leaving a cold and sterile country," both Acadians and Canadians were accustomed to the backbreaking toil needed to extract potatoes and grain from Bitche's soil. Given six hundred colonists, one hundred dairy cows, two hundred goats, thirty-six oxen, five hundred sheep, 25 livres' worth of salt per year, and timbers for construction, Tressan promised great things. While the cost of the new settlement would rise to 200,000 livres after the sixth year, in year seven the colonists, by then certainly under Louis XV's direct rule, would begin to pay taxes and perform corvée duties for twenty days each year. Second sons could be sent to the army.

If supported, the enterprise would pay for itself within twenty years. For all these benefits, Tressan demanded only that the king give him 40,000 livres and 120 tenants for his own lands.[42] The plan died later in 1763 when Choiseul "changed his opinion."[43]

Rejecting Tressan and others like him, Choiseul confirmed his administration's postwar turn away from the eastern frontier and toward the Atlantic. South America, the Caribbean, the South Atlantic, and a renewed confrontation with the British dominated his agenda—and the last of these demanded that attention be paid to Belle-Ile-en-Mer. The strategic island had shown signs of succumbing to the scourge of the mainland. In 1755, officials fretted that sluggish trade and a declining sardine fishery "tend to depopulate this island."[44] Then, in 1761, Belle-Ile played host to one of France's most embarrassing moments of the Seven Years' War, succumbing (after a long, valiant defense) to a British invasion. Having taken the island by force, the enemy then used Belle-Ile as a staging ground for assaults on the mainland and as leverage in negotiations. Traded to France in exchange for the Mediterranean island of Minorca via the Treaty of Paris, Belle-Ile, along with several other vulnerable islands on the Atlantic seaboard, suddenly became a priority for Louis XV.

Geopolitical imperatives seemed destined to push at least some Acadians toward Belle-Ile even as others made sail for the Kourou River and Port Saint-Louis. Occurring even as the Kourou colony imploded and Bougainville's settlement on East Falkland succumbed to diplomatic pressures, the movement to Belle-Ile also produced the profound realization that the Acadians had become commodities. From the monarchy's perspective, the refugees were simply demographic and economic spackle—a means of filling gaps. As so many Acadians would discover during the mid-1760s, that status could lead to some horrific outcomes. But others came to see the value of living, acting, and thinking like commodities, playing off monarchical desperation in order to obtain rights and redress.

Louis Courtin benefited from that desperation one night in September 1764. Courtin had spent several weeks moldering in the prison of Landivisiau, a landlocked town in northern Brittany. He had been convicted of murder, and an unexplained delay in handing down a sentence was taking a psychological toll. Suddenly a courier arrived from Versailles bearing "expedited and sealed" letters from Choiseul himself to the local judge. The minister demanded that the judge release Courtin from prison without so much as a fine. "The poverty of this individual" and his "long detention, which has caused him to lose the few possessions he had left," factored into the king's decision to spare the man. Ultimately, Choiseul explained to the judge, "I flatter myself that you will obey [the king's orders] all the more willingly because . . . His Majesty accords a special protection to all the Acadians."[45]

Assured of that "special protection," Courtin eventually reached Belle-Ile, taking up residence in the parish of Sauzon on the island's northern coast. Ironically enough, Courtin had reaped lifesaving benefits from the king under somewhat false pretenses. Born in Fréteval in central France, he was not an Acadian at all—but in 1760, he had married Annapolis Royal native Marie-Josèphe Martin in Cork County, Ireland. How Courtin and Martin ended up in Ireland together remains a mystery, but after the Treaty of Paris the couple and their infant daughter headed for Morlaix, taking up residence near the other Acadians redeemed from Great Britain. A year later, Courtin turned up in, and then was turned out of, the prison of Landivisiau.[46]

To be sure, few Acadians would get away with murder. But Courtin's close call speaks to a side effect of internal colonization that would reshape the refugees' lives in two hemispheres. Suddenly, unexpectedly, but officially, it paid to be an Acadian.

As a destination, it was hardly exotic. But Belle-Ile-en-Mer had at least one thing in common with Guiana and Saint-Domingue: it had once been inhabited by slaves. Or so said the island's royal governor, the marquis de Saint-Sernin, in 1741. During a dinner meeting at his residence in Le Palais with the island's four parish priests and a variety of local officials, Saint-Sernin made an aggressive proclamation of his own authority. He was, he declared, "a viceroy on your island, and here you shall have neither intendant nor *parlement*." As for Belle-Ile's commoners, he deemed them "serfs and slaves" whose sole function consisted of paying the taxes he chose to levy. With a "respectful but lively liberty," a subdelegate of the intendant of Brittany reminded Saint-Sernin that "slavery was unknown in France, and the slave acquired his freedom by merely setting foot in France, and that the residents of the island were under the authority of laws." Surprised, the governor started mumbling. Finally he managed to state that whatever anyone else thought, "he was the master . . . and no other authority, however respectable it may be, would prevent him from following his path."[47]

This uncomfortable argument illustrates what the reformers of the 1760s saw as the key problems in Belle-Ile's history. The island had long suffered from confusion over who ruled. Through the medieval period and into the eighteenth century, Belle-Ile had been private property, passing from religious orders to noble families with remarkable frequency. In 1658 the island was purchased by Nicolas Foucquet, Louis XIV's minister of finance. When, three years later, the king arrested Foucquet, tried him on charges of treason and gross peculation, and banished him from the kingdom, Belle-Ile remained in the disgraced minister's family. The monarchy, however, whittled away at the family's authority, constructing royal fortifications at Le Palais during the 1680s. Finally, in 1718, Foucquet's grandson deeded Belle-Ile back to Versailles. Retaining the right to appoint a royal governor,

Louis XV's regent gave control of the island to the Compagnie des Indes; a few years later, Belle-Ile's government passed to the farmers general, a syndicate of financiers who contracted with the crown to collect taxes. In 1759, the crown shuffled the deck again, placing the Estates of Brittany in charge. The result was a multilayered jumble of offices and claims that made governing Belle-Ile a tall order even in good times. The sort of inefficiency encouraged by this state of affairs became evident during bad times—as in 1674, when Dutch ships attacked the island, or in 1703, 1746, and 1761, when British vessels did so.[48]

For Belle-Ile's inhabitants, the geopolitical importance attached to the island must have seemed all out of proportion to its resources. With under 85 square miles of surface area, Belle-Ile hosted a dispersed population of perhaps five thousand prior to the British assault. It was no economic powerhouse. Much of the correspondence to and from the island during the eighteenth century dealt with decay and corruption. In 1742, for example, the rector of the parish of Bangor complained to mainland officials that François Bescond de Kermarquer, Belle-Ile's *receveur du domaine* (a sort of royal treasurer), was committing "a species of highway robbery." Kermarquer gave wheat to needy farmers only if they promised to make declarations to a notary that he was "an honest man, and they had no cause to complain of him." He also went door-to-door with his own "certificates of good conduct," extorting signatures from illiterate peasants by claiming that the document was in fact a marriage contract requiring witnesses.[49] The rector's other letters whipsawed between condemning the "injustices, vexations, and frauds" of profit-minded officials and describing the "epidemic diseases," including contagions and food poisoning from moldy grain, that struck down his parishioners.[50]

Disease was but one aspect of Belle-Ile's harsh environment. Although visitors praised the soil, good farmland was hard to come by. In October 1749, tenants near Le Palais reported a near-total crop failure, the consequence of a wet summer and "sea-water, which flowed over all their lands." Earlier that year, villagers near Bangor watched as a "hurricane" ripped their houses apart and tore up fields, threatening ruin if the government did not intervene. By 1750, more than three thousand of Belle-Ile's inhabitants (perhaps 60 percent of the total population) appeared on parish poor relief rolls, receiving a grand total of 220 bushels of grain. With nowhere to turn and their own agriculture flagging, island officials contracted with merchants in the mainland town of Vannes, who supplied and transported wheat to Belle-Ile for a tidy profit.[51] In a way, the marquis de Saint-Sernin had been on to something. The inhabitants of Belle-Ile may not have been slaves, but their island did resemble someplace in the French Caribbean. Although potentially profitable, the island could neither defend itself nor grow its own food, leaving its poor laborers vulnerable and uncertain about the future.

The 1761 siege of Belle-Ile by the British only made matters worse. Launched in April, the attack, along with the nearly simultaneous invasion of Martinique, formed part of William Pitt's grand plan to make off with a maximum of French territory before pressing Louis XV for a debasing peace. The siege pitted a fleet of 115 British ships bearing nine thousand ground troops against fewer than four thousand French regulars, most of whom were holed up in the fortifications at Le Palais. It lasted just over a month.

The siege turned Belle-Ile upside down. After an amphibious landing, hungry British troops planted themselves in Belle-Ile's villages while their artillery blasted away at Le Palais. After the French surrendered and departed, they left the British with a viable base overlooking the key naval ports of Brest and Roche-fort, as well as the Compagnie des Indes's home base at Lorient. The French also left behind five thousand confused islanders (the *bellilois*), who had no inkling what might happen to them under the new régime. Most of their oxen, cows, and sheep, reported one observer, had been requisitioned by the French in the weeks before the siege of Le Palais. After their victory, the British snapped up the rest at low prices. Deprived of seed and supplies from the mainland and unable to plow, the *bellilois* got by on British wages. Some worked on the docks or helped patch up the walls of Le Palais. Others, though, crossed the Gulf of Morbihan looking for jobs or charity in Brittany.[52]

Holding the island for its military and diplomatic value and unconcerned with its economy, the British allowed Belle-Ile to revert to what eighteenth-century philosophes would have identified as a state of nature. Upon retaking control in 1763, one French official described the island as "more or less as it was when it emerged from the hands of the Creator."[53] Pierre d'Isambert, an envoy from the Estates of Brittany sent to assess the damage, despaired at what he saw: "One sees villages totally destroyed, and their number is considerable. All that remains in some are gables, walls, and stones, and in others few houses are left standing, . . . the British having taken the beams and planks for firewood."[54] Others recoiled at the "extreme misery to which nearly all of the inhabitants are reduced . . . the greater part of their lands having been burned." Without help, the Estates warned the crown, Belle-Ile risked a "general desertion" of its prewar population.[55] French officials gamely made up a list of damages owed by the British, but those debts were swallowed up in the payments France owed Britain to redeem prisoners of war. Versailles could only promise limited aid to the *bellilois*, "however urgent their needs."[56]

No less than the wild Kourou River or the uninhabited Falkland Islands, Belle-Ile became a canvas for reformers. The new governor, the baron de Warren, an Irish émigré who had participated in the failed Jacobite invasion of England during the 1740s, took over in the summer of 1763. Pieced together with the help of royal and local officials, his vision for the revival and repopulation of the island was steeped in the principles and aims of internal colonization. Everyone agreed that Belle-Ile needed a catalyst to remedy its "shortage of cultivators, of which we have complained for so long and with such reason."[57] "To inspire the love of work among the other settlers [the old *bellilois*]," wrote Isambert, "we would do well to place more industrious people in the different villages." Warren seconded him, demanding colonists who "would provide an object of emulation for the natives of this country, who are very lazy and who possess no industry."[58] On Belle-Ile, the audacity of postwar imperialism could be expressed as it could be nowhere else. Guiana was too insalubrious, Saint-Domingue too scarred by generations of slavery, the Falklands too remote. Belle-Ile, however, offered the chance to remake French society in miniature, washing away the accumulated errors of the ages and creating not just a new place but new people.

The stakes were high. It would be in the state's best interest, wrote one colonial booster, "to make Belle-Ile better cultivated, more abundant, and better peopled. . . . Being by its location one of the most important places in the kingdom, anything that may add to its security, fertility, and growth is worthy of the king's attention."[59] Well suited to agriculture (which was, reported one Breton observer in 1763, the Acadians' "preference, and their principal talent") and legendarily fecund ("the populationist spirit of the day certainly clamors in their favor," as an Acadian admirer in Morlaix wrote), refugees from Nova Scotia were ideal candidates to resettle the island.[60] Perhaps just as important as rustic skill or reproductive capacity was the Acadians' history of patriotic sacrifice. Showing a praiseworthy "attachment to our religion," wrote the curés of Saint-Malo, the Acadians had "abandoned their settlements, regardless of how well cultivated they were, rather than subject themselves to another monarch."[61]

These were the same images of Acadians used by proponents of migration to Guiana or the Falkland Islands, but with a twist. In the case of Belle-Ile and France's first, halting attempts at self-colonization, the Acadians helped to produce those images themselves. "Some deputies of this respectable colony of ours (I mean to say the Acadians) came to find me," recalled one resident of Morlaix who sent a letter to the Estates of Brittany in the summer of 1763. "They begged me to solicit you in their favor," he wrote, and after rattling off a list of Acadian virtues, he declared himself "united with them in beseeching you to do all that you can. . . . [And] I cannot imagine that you would ever regret having done too much, for they are honest people."[62] With deep traditions of political petitioning in Nova Scotia in their heads, eight years of exile under their belt, and a bewildering hodgepodge of colonial schemes in the air, the Acadians had no choice but to become savvy managers of their reputation.

Soon enough, some of the refugees tried to use what leverage they had acquired. In July 1763, three Acadians from Morlaix visited Belle-Ile. They declared that nearly eighty Acadian families might settle on the island, leaving room for the original *bellilois* inhabitants. After the group returned to Morlaix, however, the process of recruitment stalled. Transported from Great Britain only a few months earlier, most of the town's Acadians balked at plans drawn up by the Estates of Brittany. Joseph-Simon Granger, Honoré Daigre, and Jean Hébert made a first attempt at bargaining. In a memorial dated October 30, 1763, they laid out some demands. The first had to do with the allowance, or *solde*, granted them by Louis XV. "As it relates to the *solde* of six sols per day," they told the Estates, "it is impossible for us to survive and establish ourselves unless it lasts at least six years." This struck them as natural, considering that even the hated British had given them an allowance during the seven years of their captivity and had "very much wanted to continue doing so, had we become their subjects." The memorial further stipulated that masons be hired to help them build houses, that sheep be provided gratis, and that a single all-Acadian parish be established, ensuring that the refugees would receive "the good land with the bad," rather than being shuffled onto the worst parts of the island's four parishes. The Acadians also worried about history repeating itself. "As Belle-Ile is evidently more exposed to the enemy," an expulsion was hardly out of the question. All in all, they preferred to go someplace within the kingdom besides the island.[63]

The Estates of Brittany called on the duc de Choiseul to break this impasse, and he in turn called on someone the Acadians knew well: the abbé le Loutre. Now sixty years old, the aging priest had not only a "knack for leading" but also a desire for a new challenge.[64] Captured by the British in February 1756, le Loutre had spent more than seven years imprisoned at Elizabeth Castle on the Island of Jersey. He had endured painful economies. While his jailers had hoped to receive six shillings eight pence per day for his upkeep, officials at Whitehall only sent one shilling for the man they called "the Otter."[65] Released in August 1763, le Loutre headed for Morlaix that winter, armed with a mandate from Choiseul to push the Acadians toward Belle-Ile. "It is high time that they settle somewhere," the minister snarled.[66]

Le Loutre played the role of broker well—too well, perhaps, for Choiseul's taste. Instead of browbeating the Acadians he became their advocate, drawing up on behalf of seventy-seven interested families a counteroffer that reached Versailles in February 1764. While they gave up on the idea of a single Acadian community on Belle-Ile, the Acadians demanded to be settled in three parishes instead of four. This arrangement would allow them to "live like they had always lived, always neighbors, always in close proximity to one another," sheltering them from the Breton-speaking *bellilois*, whose "language was unknown and foreign to them" and who might cheat them in matters of trade and justice.

Le Loutre had his own reasons for touting a concentrated settlement. "I cannot dissimulate," he would later write to Warren, "that I would like better to see the Acadians in three parishes because I could then be among them, to encourage them to work." His age made the prospect of far-flung parochial visits on horse-back seem unpalatable.[67] The Acadian families also demanded a twenty-year exemption from "all sorts of taxation," including tithes and the dreaded *vingtième*, a royal tax that swallowed up 5 percent per of all net income. They reiterated their need for experienced masons (Acadians were, le Loutre explained, "not used to building . . . in the French style") while claiming an assortment of special privileges: the right to plant pine trees on their land to hold the soil in place, exclusive use of several ovens and mills lest the *bellilois* lock them out, and so on.[68]

An uncomfortable period of negotiation followed. Belle-Ile languished, Choiseul and the Estates of Brittany stewed, and the Acadians weighed a surprising number of options throughout the summer of 1764. Self-proclaimed "enemies of idleness," they nevertheless had no intention of working in any but the best conditions they could procure.[69] That meant thinking hard about an offer from the mysterious comte de Laz, who offered land near Pontivy in central Brittany.[70] Floated by both private individuals and crown officials, other options included uncultivated lands in Carhaix, Poullaouen, Douarnenez, or Aoulanhiry, all underdeveloped Breton hamlets.[71] With word of the Kourou disaster electrifying French ports that fall, the Acadians and le Loutre pressed their advantages even more forcefully.

They got much of what they wanted. Drafted under Choiseul's guidance and with the help of the Estates of Brittany, final plans for Belle-Ile included plenty of tax exemptions, a continuation of the *solde* until the Acadians' first harvest (and perhaps after), free farm implements, and guarantees of help with the construction of homes. Emulation, however, carried the day when it came to living arrangements. The prospect of displacing *bellilois* families to create a single Acadian parish struck officials as cruel and impractical, not least because it would deprive these "old islanders . . . of the example of [the Acadians'] activity and love of work."[72] Internal colonization aimed at radical social and cultural transformations, not just economic and military gains. "I find it to the advantage of the king, and in the interest of the province," wrote the comte de Warren, "to distribute [the Acadians] in the four parishes of the island . . . that all the inhabitants may have one spirit and become one people."[73]

Although less invasive than they might have been, these plans still necessitated fundamental changes on the island. Using new surveys, planners divided Belle-Ile into 551 separate plots of roughly twenty *journaux* (plural of *journée*, a variable old-régime unit that referred to the area one man could plow or harvest in a day) each. Three hundred and seventy-five of the plots went to farmers among the *bellilois*, while 108 belonged, more controversially, to *gourdiecs*. This Breton-language slur referred to agricultural workers, fishermen, and artisans imported from the mainland to speed the rebuilding of the island. Finally, seventy-eight plots, a number derived from le Loutre's recruiting spree in Morlaix and Saint-Malo, were earmarked for Acadians. The plots, some of which were preexisting farms while others had been pieced together from multiple sources, had been carved from dozens of villages in all four parishes, displacing some old residents toward the coast.[74] Some *bellilois* were slated to "decamp," in the euphemistic official language, to make way for the Acadians; others, such as Guillaume Thomas of Le Cosquet and Albin Legallin of Pouldon, were to be "expelled" for "laziness."[75]

As in Guiana and Saint-Domingue, the postwar reconstruction of Belle-Ile yoked imperial designs, enlightened ambitions, and coercive practices in a volatile embrace. Le Loutre's seventy-eight families finally agreed to come to Belle-Ile, although haggling over details in the ports and material preparations on the island took so long as to delay their departure until the late summer of 1765. In some quarters, hopes ran high. Isambert predicted that once the Acadians and Belle-Ile's old settlers had been mingled together, "they will soon get along, and will even marry one another."[76] Elsewhere, old alarms sounded. How, wondered one Belle-Ile planner, could the French satisfy "the interests of these different inhabitants" without creating "grounds for animosity"?[77]

Still pockmarked and charred by British guns, the walls of the citadel at Le Palais rose directly from the sea to loom over the Acadians' port of entry, looking for all the world like the burned-out shell of Louisbourg, another symbol of French power and insecurity. The Acadian families passed beneath the walls in late September or early October 1765, only to discover that the island was not yet ready to receive them. Surveyors were hurriedly triangulating and measuring in the interior, while the arrival of hundreds of hungry *gourdiecs* made for unneeded chaos. Welcomed ashore by le Loutre, Warren, and Isambert, the Acadians were shuffled off to temporary lodgings in an oat warehouse, an abandoned mill, and the home of "Dame Kermarquer," which had once been a barracks.[78]

The promoters presented the Acadians their contracts. The documents confirmed the agreement hammered out by le Loutre and offered a host of incentives for hard work and good behavior. Each Acadian family was promised a house composed of two rooms and a loft, totaling about twenty-seven square meters. In addition, each family was to receive two oxen, a cow, and a horse, along with carts, spare axles, hoes, spades, and sickles. Like peasants across the kingdom, Belle-Ile's settlers owed corvée labor for the repair of roads, mills, bridges, and other structures, facing fines if they did not comply. For the first four years on the island, they would pay no taxes. After 1769, two small dues, both paid in grain, were to be given to royal officials in Le Palais each year, while a minuscule tithe would support the island's clergy. If the new colonists managed to clear, till, and farm the land successfully, it became their private, inheritable, incontestable property. But Belle-Ile's settlers could not sell their land until January 1, 1776, nor could they leave it uncultivated.

The penalty for both offenses was expulsion from the island.[79] Perks notwith-standing, the Acadians had signed up for a decade-long hitch as glorified serfs.

Trouble cropped up early. Le Loutre dispatched the seventy-eight Acadian families toward their lands as soon as land transportation became available, di-viding the migrants into mutual-assistance "brigades" of thirteen families each. But since none of their houses had yet been built, the new arrivals were lodged with old inhabitants and *gourdiecs*.[80] Relations soured quickly. In Bernantec, a hot dispute landed one Acadian in a *bellilois* barn, while in Kerzo another lived in an abandoned smithy. In Kergoyet, not far from Le Palais, the *gourdiec* widow of Henry Loreal put up a fight over a single room destined for an Acadian family, claiming that her brother-in-law, the house's original owner, had left it to her before abandoning Belle-Ile for the mainland. Her actions, wrote representatives of the Estates of Brittany, "cannot be punished too soon or too severely, because this woman, who lives only by charity, might draw many *gourdiecs* toward her, inspiring among them the same resistance."[81]

Officials tried to silence them, but women such as Loreal had long acted as agitators for a nascent *bellilois/gourdiec* insurgency. On Monday, March 25, 1765, several months before the Acadians' arrival, the abbé Pierre-Jacques-Philippe le Sergent had crisscrossed his Bangor parish, informing heads of *bellilois* families of their impending displacement. They seemed "happy enough" about the new arrangements. The next day, however, a group of men interrupted le Sergent at

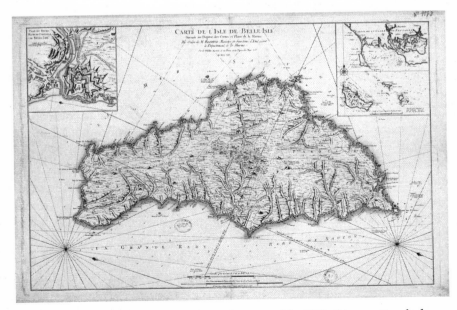

Belle-Ile-en-Mer in the eighteenth century. Courtesy of the Bibliothèque nationale de France, Paris.

the rectory in Bangor, telling him that upon hearing the news their wives and children had "cried aloud, and refused to cede their places to the Acadians." If they were to be moved, French officials "may as well come to bury them."[82] It stood to reason, the *bellilois* families complained, that they "should receive the same treatment as the new colonists, the same event having stripped *us* of *our* possessions."[83]

Le Loutre, who had taken pains to identify himself with the Mi'kmaq in Nova Scotia, had no sympathy for these natives. "The old settlers think everything belongs to them," he complained, accusing the *bellilois* and their *gourdiec* allies of "not permitting the Acadians to labor."[84] On a visit to Kerbellec in the late spring of 1766, le Loutre and Isambert informed villagers of their determination to take from them "eight *journaux* of arable land, of which they have too much." Unsurprisingly, the *bellilois* protested, but in le Loutre's ears their words registered only as "invectives and nonsense."[85] The old missionary's ham-fisted style of advocating for the newcomers (when Charles Granger came to him "upset and chagrined" in June 1766, he fired off pointed letters on behalf of "*my* Acadian") triggered an ecclesiastical war that contributed much to the growing unrest on the island.

In their priestly way, the participants were vicious. Jacques-Marie Choblet, the parish priest of Sauzon, helped the illiterate *gourdiec* Marc Querel of Chubiguier write an angry complaint against le Loutre and Isambert for unjustly dispossessing him of a house.[86] Scarcely hiding his contempt, le Sergent went on the attack against le Loutre and Isambert in the summer of 1766. Seeds and tools provided by the Estates of Brittany had, he claimed, been distributed "by predilection and fantasy," with Acadians taking the lion's share and the *bellilois* the leftovers.[87] Dozens of *bellilois*, "strong and robust" young people capable of laboring, had been deprived of land by le Loutre and Isambert, leading all four of the island's curés to condemn them for favoritism.[88] The old colonial dream of intercultural unity proved no easier to realize in a new setting.

As Belle-Ile's settlers struggled to build, clear, and plant, the prospect of violence became real. In the village of Antoureau near Le Palais, the *bellilois* François Thomas's house burned down one frigid night in January 1766. Isambert reported that Thomas and his family had saved only a few effects from their ground-level room and nothing from the barn, but that the man deserved "no charity, . . . being very lazy and always begging." The Estates of Brittany agreed, noting Thomas's unwillingness to "give himself to work" and his refusal to help provision the French military during the 1761 siege. Indeed, the Estates went so far as to order Isambert to drive Thomas from Antoureau and give his land to an Acadian. Once it was done, Isambert drily reported that "this Acadian bothers the old tenant."[89] Weeks later, Thomas "armed himself with a pitchfork and made various threats" against the Acadian, le Loutre, and Isambert.[90] He eventually left, but Thomas's outburst signaled things to come. That April in Parlavant, a group of *gourdiecs* threatened to burn down a house rather than cede the property to Acadians. Officials toyed with expelling them but eventually promised to "treat them favorably" if they demonstrated "total submission" to Belle-Ile's new order.[91]

That "submission" was a pipe dream, especially in Parlavant. Laurent Babin, a twenty-six-year-old Acadian who had married Le Palais native Marie-Françoise Carrière upon reaching Belle-Ile, discovered as much while trying to plant crops on a condemned footpath just outside the village. The path was unquestionably on Babin's land, and both le Loutre and Warren had encouraged his efforts. But the *bellilois* persisted in using it, trampling Babin's seedlings and threatening him with "total ruin." Babin appealed to Warren, who took the unusual step of sending a lone soldier from the king's regiment in Le Palais to "arrest anyone who attempted to pass through his land." At seven in the evening on March 15, 1767, six peasants from Bangor did just that as they returned home from work at the nearby farm of the sieur le Luc. "Seeing so many of them armed with pickaxes," the soldier admitted to Babin that "if they wanted to avenge themselves, he could not stop them." As the *bellilois* unsheathed daggers and "raised their pickaxes to strike," Babin brandished a sword and held them off long enough for the soldier, now feeling confident, to disarm and arrest them. The pair took the six assailants to prison in Le Palais, but by the next morning they had been released. Babin soon found himself harassed by a drunken le Luc, an angry le Sergent, and a host of *bellilois* leaders, "all of them brothers-in-law or kin to one another, and all banding together" against him.[92] Warren practically begged the besieged Acadian not to "abandon your concession, ... a fine resource that may one day be useful to your children."[93]

By late 1768, only two years into France's experiment in internal colonization, le Loutre wondered aloud to Warren what he or anyone else could do to "reestablish peace in your empire."[94] The process of rendering the island populous and fertile seemed to have stalled, and the mixture of *bellilois, gourdiec,* and Acadian into a single community of French patriots had never even begun. Emulation had been the project's aim: pliable, virtuous Acadians were to receive instruction from the elites who ruled the island, after which the *bellilois* and *gourdiecs* would follow their example. But as the colony grew, emulation seemed to flow in the opposite direction, with Acadians drinking in the vices of the allegedly "lazy" and contentious old settlers. Elizabeth Vincent, for example, gave herself over to "the most infamous debauchery," eventually forcing Warren to expel her from the island.[95] In 1769, with the *solde* expiring and expectations high for Acadian agriculture, the new colonists faltered. "The continual rain of the fall and winter, coupled with a great drought in the spring and summer," explained Charles Leblanc and Joseph-Simon Granger in August, "occasioned such a bad harvest that more than three hundred of us did not reap enough grain to pay the rent on our land."[96] Marguerite Granger, a "more than septuagenarian widow," wrote that she had arrived at Belle-Ile in 1765 with many "children, nephews, nieces, and other kin whom I had . . . served as a mother." By 1770, however, the "misery of the weather and the cost of wheat" had left her "poor children unable to support me." Driven "to the edge of the grave," Granger subsisted on charity.[97]

Bad fortune became the island's great equalizer. Conflicts between the Acadians and their *bellilois* and *gourdiec* enemies subsided as the expiration of the *solde*, poor harvests, and impoverishment leveled the playing field. By the early 1770s Belle-Ile became again what it once had been—a struggling island of fishermen and petty farmers who, according to one account, "were unable to plant the lands they had prepared . . . in spite of all of their goodwill."[98] The ambitions of France's internal colonizers were, for now, deferred. The vast majority of the 383 Acadians who came to Belle-Ile in 1765 stayed on for a generation—even Laurent Babin, whose residence in Parlavant had nearly ended in a killing spree. Others, however, left. Marie, Geneviève, and Henriette Haché, daughters of the late Jacques Haché and his widow, Aimé Boudrot, took Easter communion in Bangor in 1773, receiving written confirmation from a conciliatory le Sergent that they "lived well and had good manners." A few days later, they sailed for Morlaix with a passport from Warren, who declared the sisters "unable to live here due to the miserable weather."[99]

From imperial aspirations to clan violence to agricultural capitulation, the Belle-Ile experiment appeared to have been a waste of time. It had changed nothing: not for the French state, still saddled with a exposed, unprofitable island just off the Breton coast; not for the *bellilois* or the *gourdiecs*, whose many character flaws abided in the eyes of mainlanders; and not for the Acadians, whose situation remained as precarious as ever.

And perhaps that was true—except for one thing.

Who was who? In the years after the Treaty of Paris, this simple question became an obsession throughout the French Empire. To be sure, as the historian Sarah Maza has noted, slotting people into categories is a quintessentially French practice: social classification, she writes, "has long been a national predilection."[100] But with France's wounds in the Seven Years' War still stinging, the proper ordering of society took on special importance. In the French Caribbean, this process centered on race. Elites focused on building barriers between whites and mixed-race *gens de couleur* and on constructing ever more baroque schemes for categorizing slaves according to African origins. In France itself, the abbé Coyer, the chevalier d'Arcq, and dozens of lesser authors wrangled over what made someone noble and what that person's function ought to be. At the same time, physiocrats adapted Europe's traditional "three orders" by identifying a class of landowners, a class of those who worked the land, and a catchall "sterile" class that produced no real wealth. The great surge in postwar French nationalism situated the scheming British ("a barbarous people . . . prepared to fill the universe with horrors," wrote François-Antoine de Chevrier in 1758) beyond the pale of European civilization; but such attempts to crowbar Frenchmen into a "single family of brothers and equals" were in large part prompted by the jumble of regional identities and linguistic traditions that made the kingdom less a whole than a collection of parts.[101]

Belle-Ile's Acadians felt the weight of these developments. The French desire to categorize them was a distillation of broader trends. But their case was also shaped by some very particular fiscal realities. The *solde* alone represented a big investment, to which was added, in the case of Belle-Ile, the cost of houses, farm implements, livestock, and seed, for a total estimated cost to the crown of 56,000 livres. Acadians were thought to be worth the expense precisely because they were Acadians, not *bellilois* or *gourdiecs*. These last groups, of course, were singled out for contempt and derided as "lazy." "It is truly surprising," wrote a particularly haughty representative of the Estates of Brittany in June 1766, "that no one has yet been able to convince these [*bellilois*] settlers that they have no property on the island, that they are nothing more than tenants that the owner may move at his will."[102] But Acadians could, through hard work, piety, and virtuous love of country, transform the island's culture by example.

All of this was predicated, however, on Acadians actually being Acadians. In light of what the refugees had been through during the 1750s and 1760s, making that determination was more difficult than it might seem. Early on, Belle-Ile's boosters had sought help from the Seminary for Foreign Missions, the Parisian headquarters for most of the missionaries who had ministered to Acadians in Nova Scotia and on Ile Saint-Jean. The priests offered little good information. The abbé Pierre Cassiet, for example, told investigators that in 1758, as word spread that the British navy was on its way to Ile Saint-Jean, his fearful parishioners at Saint-Louis de la Rivière du Nord had gone into the woods and buried "all of the effects" from their little chapel, including the precious register of births, baptisms, and burials. So quickly were these Acadians expelled that the registers remained, decomposing in their own shallow grave. The abbé Jean-Baptiste de Gay Desenclaves likewise declared that "it was not possible for me to save or retain the registers" during his harried last months at Cap Sable in Nova Scotia. The abbé Jacques Girard related his departure from Ile Saint-Jean aboard the *Duke William* with 366 Acadians, most of them originally from Cobequid in Nova Scotia. The ship sank "40 leagues from the coast of England," and Girard— in a moment that would torture him for the rest of his days—managed to get on a lifeboat, but "without taking anything." He watched as his parishioners drowned, taking their registers down with them.[103]

Not all of the Acadians' old records perished, but for French officials in the 1760s they were certainly hard to come by.[104] So as the recolonization of Belle-Ile began to take shape, the French determined to reconstitute the Acadians' family histories from scratch. Already in 1765, planners from the Estates of Brittany reminded Warren to set aside some money for "the honorarium of the scribe employed to write and put in order the genealogies of the [Acadian] families."[105] As arguments arose over the proper allocation of the *solde* and other funds, Belle-Ile's leaders began to take lineages seriously. They soon learned of a 1746 case in which the inept parish priest of Sougeal, a village to the southeast of Saint-Malo, kept records on "loose sheets" that were eventually lost, leaving parishioners without vital information. In January 1767, the Estates of Brittany instituted a solution for Belle-Ile that had worked well in Sougeal. Each Acadian head of family was required to make a declaration "that will contain all the details relative to the condition of the declarer, that of his wife and children, with the most exact and clear genealogy possible of the father and mother, of the place of their births and marriages, and the place of the births of their children." Le Loutre was to be present, adding his own knowledge of "facts . . . which may be unknown to the deponent." The goal, then, was to establish a full matrix of "ascending, descending, and lateral lines, with places and dates insofar as [the Acadians] can recall."[106]

Beginning in February 1767, Acadians began trudging across Belle-Ile's cheerless winter landscape to the island's four parish churches in Le Palais, Bangor, Sauzon, and Locmaria. Honoré Leblanc, Joseph Leblanc *dit* le Maigre, Joseph-Simon Granger, and Jean-Baptiste Granger were among the first to make their declarations, converging on Le Palais from their respective villages on the parish's outskirts. They arrived together and spoke in quick succession, likely relying on one another to fill in the forgotten links among their interconnected clans. They remembered well. Joseph-Simon and Jean-Baptiste both began their stories with Laurent Granger, their seventeenth-century Acadian ancestor, who migrated from Plymouth, England, and "after his abjuration" of Protestantism married Port Royal native Marie Landry. The Leblancs traced their ancestry to the French migrant Daniel Leblanc, who arrived at "Port Royal, the chief settlement of Acadia, after the Treaty of Breda of July 31, 1661." The statement was a near miss—the Treaty of Breda had been signed on July 31, 1667. Still, at exactly a century's remove, these and dozens of similar Acadian declarations reveal a powerful sense of the familial past.[107]

Recounting the present was more painful. So many Acadians were simply gone. Brothers Joseph and Mathurin Granger of Kergoyet, for example, had grown up near Grand Pré, tending a farm on the *rivière* aux Canards with their five siblings. They were deported early in the 1755 British campaign, first to Virginia and then to England. A dozen years later, Joseph and Mathurin's brothers, both teenagers, lived in Brest and Nantes. Eldest sister Marie-Josèphe and her husband had been deported to Boston, and their whereabouts remained unknown. Middle sister Marie-Magdalene, now twenty-nine, had married a Frenchman while both were held in Falmouth, England; they had gone to Martinique together after 1763. Known only as Marie, the youngest Granger sister had married as well—in Morlaix, to Jacques-Hypolite Constant, a Frenchman who took her to Cayenne as soon as the match was made.[108] The South American settlement loomed large in the Acadians' declarations. Brothers Jean, Allain, and Pascal Hébert had taken their families there in 1764. By February 11, 1767, when their sixty-eight-year-old father made his declaration in Locmaria, Allain, Allain's wife, and Pascal had all died on the Kourou River, while Jean and his wife had simply vanished. That left only Pascal's shattered widow, Marguerite Trahan, who had escaped from Guiana and now lived near Bangor.[109] If, as one commentator has argued, the Acadians' declarations represented "a particularly generous, social, humane idea" that allowed the refugees to "find in the bosom of French society roots that events had severed," to speak aloud of such things was nonetheless gut-wrenching.[110]

Whatever the French state's intentions had been (and cost cutting, not kindness, was likely the key motivation), the Belle-Ile genealogies set in motion a chain of events that few could have foreseen. True, the island's Acadian families were supposed to set a new example for a French nation obsessed with issues of reproduction and domestic life—for, as Mably wrote in his 1763 best seller *Entretiens de Phocion*, in "the bosom of their families" the French learned "the first model" of public virtue.[111] But Acadians were also to be adopted into the metaphorical family of old-régime political society. The king, of course, played the father. Below him were millions of his children, many of whom were organized into a mind-boggling collection of *corps*, or bodies. According to one Parisian jurist, the system looked like this:

> The clergy, the nobility, the sovereign courts, the subaltern courts, the officers attached to these courts, the universities, the academies, the finance bodies, the trade companies, all present, in all parts of the state, existing bodies that may be regarded as links in a great chain, the first link of which is in the hands of Your Majesty, as head and sovereign administrator of everything that composes the body of the nation.[112]

From the nobility down to the guilds, these *corps* were distinguished by possession of privileges—literally, "private laws"—that regulated their relations with the monarchy and society at large. With wide-ranging exemptions from taxes, militia duties, and the corvée, noblemen profited most from privilege. But, to a lesser degree, others did too. Walloons were liberated from the state's salt and tobacco monopolies; Bordeaux's inhabitants eluded the *taille*, the Bourbons' much-hated land tax, while urban manufacturers and artisanal confraternities held up crown-granted privileges as a shield against taxation and regulation.

Even the peasants of Brittany would rally to the defense of their "exemptions and privileges" when, in 1789, the National Assembly maneuvered to abolish them.[113]

All privileges, then, were good. But hereditary privileges such as those belonging to the nobility were the best. And in their zeal to distinguish reliable, fertile, and patriotic Acadians from the shiftless *bellilois* and to weed out interlopers, the combined authority of the crown and the Estates of Brittany had given such privileges to the island's new settlers. They had tax exemptions, promises of free land, and general promises of "special protection," all of which marked Acadians, in the words of a provincial newspaper, as "one among the many *corps*" attached to the French king.[114]

The crown viewed the granting of Acadian privileges primarily as a way to save money. As the early expectations for Belle-Ile faded into a more mundane reality, royal officials began to repeat the tedious process of genealogical declarations elsewhere. In 1772, they charged Antoine-Philippe Lemoyne, a naval commissioner in Nantes who had served in Cayenne at the time of the Kourou disaster, with creating a "general roll" of Acadians throughout the kingdom. Plowing through mountains of data collected in northern ports, Lemoyne began making cuts. First to go were families from Ile Royale with no Acadian ancestors. Lemoyne placed them in a "separate class" from those whom "the king wishes to establish . . . in the kingdom, making them proprietors of lands."[115] Next came the impostors. There were 354 of them, Lemoyne discovered, lurking among the 2,700 "true Acadians" in the kingdom.[116] Deemed "European" and not Acadian, couples such as Louis Gressin and Angelique Gaillet found themselves pulled from the lists.[117] Likewise for one François Philibert, his wife, and "Jean Gussman, native of Seville," each of whom lived with the Acadians and drew the *solde* in the northern city of Le Havre.[118]

Lemoyne was pleased. The right people, he believed, had received "the decided protection of the Government."[119] "Truly Acadian families," he explained to former minister Henri Bertin, "are those alone which, by privilege, must enjoy the usage of the king's freely given graces, in order to put them in a state to provide, by their own work, for their own subsistence."[120]

The Acadians learned that privilege had its benefits. One group living near Saint-Malo did so in 1773, when Pierre Landry and Marie-Jeanne Hébert both died, leaving behind a three-year-old son. Soon a local notary and a financial attorney arrived to settle the couple's debts and set up a "guardianship" for the boy. Tactlessly, the Frenchmen began by discussing their fees. The Acadians would have none of it. They protested to Versailles, claiming exemption from the "costly formalities of justice." Although they had been living "in the heart of France" for fifteen years, they had been endowed with the right "to govern themselves without the constraints of local laws." As a "national body [*corps de nation*]" composed of "kinsmen who watched over one another," their situation was completely different from that of a mere "transient."[121] This was more than clannishness or tightfistedness. It was the exercise of what one French official termed "the privilege, so to speak, of an Acadian."[122]

The recolonization of Belle-Ile-en-Mer, then, had taught much to many. For the French, it revealed that imperialism was imperialism wherever it happened. Colonists and natives clashed over land, resources, and, sometimes, a stray insult or wayward look. Sneaking suspicion turned into outright antagonism. Violence, disorder, and productive paralysis followed. Perhaps Diderot, Mably, and the anti-colonial philosophes had been right after all. And yet the experiment had seemed so ingenious, so sensible. To some, internal colonization still looked like the wave of the future. In 1767, even as Belle-Ile's Acadians struggled to build homes and sow crops, the *Ephémérides du citoyen* lauded the establishment of an agricultural colony in the Sierra Morena of Andalusia. Here was imperialism come full circle: thirst for "precious metals" had made sixteenth-century Spaniards into "ferocious plunderers," shedders of "so much innocent blood," and slaves to "mad pride and detestable policies" that had impoverished the homeland. Now, however, "the king . . . has learned that it is within Spain itself that colonies must be founded." Was this not, the author exclaimed, a true "example to sovereigns"?[123]

For their part, the Acadians had gained a valuable bargaining chip—a corporate identity. And when the French crown tried one last time to colonize the *patrie*, a few among them would deploy that chip to surprising, devastating effect.

6

The Conspiracy

And thou shalt eat the fruit of thine own body, the flesh of thy sons and of thy daughters.... So that the man that is tender among you, and very delicate, his eye shall be evil toward his brother, and toward the wife of his bosom, and toward the remnant of his children which he shall leave.

—Deuteronomy 28:54

In November 1774, Anne-Robert Turgot was perhaps the busiest man in France. Louis XV had died of smallpox in May, thrusting his pudgy, insecure nineteen-year-old grandson onto the throne. Eager to court public opinion in ways that had never occurred to his callous, womanizing predecessor, the young Louis XVI made the popular Turgot his minister of the marine. In August, after a spasm of purges and resignations at Versailles, Turgot was elevated to controller general of finances, the all-important post charged with regulating the French economy.

It was a tough job, but Turgot was as qualified as anyone in the kingdom to do it. Born in 1727 and destined for the priesthood, he became something of a prodigy upon entering the Sorbonne. Before turning thirty, Turgot published a translation of the fourth book of Virgil's *Aeneid*, two Latin orations on the relationship between Christianity and human progress, and pamphlets in favor of religious tolerance. He also frequented all the best Parisian salons while developing friendships with the economist and administrator Vincent de Gournay (the man usually credited with coining the phrase *laissez-faire*) and the most prominent advocates of physiocracy.

Then, in 1761, Turgot was appointed royal intendant for the Limousin, a province in central France. Inhabited, as he put it, by "poverty-stricken peasants" who "have cultivated their farms in the same old way" for centuries, the Limousin turned Turgot into a bona fide reformer.[1] He reduced the corvée burden imposed by landowners on their tenants, reorganized local taxation, encouraged innovation in his capacity as president of the Agricultural Society of Limoges, and agitated in print for free trade on a national scale. Turgot's successes made him a celebrity among philosophes and courtiers, eventually leading young Louis XVI's mentor, the comte de Maurepas, to recommend the intendant to the new king.

Not that Turgot's appointment as controller general was uncontroversial. The abbé Galiani, an Italian wit who in 1769 had written an influential treatise on France's grain trade, wondered aloud whether "his administration of finances will resemble his brother's Cayenne"—a project bathed in good intentions that ended in tragedy and a broken reputation for the "very virtuous, very philosophical" man in charge. And within three weeks of taking office, Turgot did the very thing that Galiani prophesied would "break his neck": he deregulated France's grain trade, removing all of the old provincial privileges and corporate barriers that hampered the free flow of the kingdom's most important commodity.[2]

Channeling Gournay and the physiocrats, Turgot took the step with an eye toward the ultimate goal of "stimulating competition, from which necessarily results . . . a price the most advantageous to the buyer."[3] In the short term, he was focused on austerity measures, having been charged by Louis XVI himself with three objectives: "no national bankruptcy, no increase of taxes, no new loans." That meant slashing 20 million livres from the king's budget. Without those cuts, Turgot warned, "the first cannon ball that is fired" would force the state into total insolvency.[4] Between deregulation and drastic budget trimming, the controller general soon drew derisive criticism from almost all quarters.

Perhaps that is why, in November 1774, with his months-old administration already scrambling to defend itself, Turgot opened his handsome office at Versailles to an unlikely visitor: Jean-Jacques Leblanc, who first introduced himself as an Acadian living in the province of Poitou and then announced that he wanted to help.

They made an odd couple. Still youthful at forty-seven, Turgot had the confidence of the most powerful monarch in Europe and had basked in the approbation of the continent's greatest intellectuals for twenty-five years. Leblanc was in his early fifties and, since his deportation from Ile Saint-Jean by the British in 1758, had suffered through fifteen years of rootless poverty in Saint-Servan, a gritty dockside village near Saint-Malo. He was semiliterate but possessed a brawler's drive and a knack for smooth talk. Leblanc "lacked neither spirit nor subtlety," wrote a grudging admirer.[5]

No one knows precisely what the two men said to each other. But the dramatic events that followed their meeting at Versailles illuminate the complexities behind two seemingly straightforward stories: the demise of old-régime France's strange, ambitious attempt to colonize itself, and the end of the Acadians' *grand dérangement*.

*   *   *

Anne-Robert-Jacques Turgot, Louis XVI's controller general of finances. Courtesy of the Bibliothèque nationale de France, Paris.

Jean-Jacques Leblanc was mysterious, and probably intentionally so. But what is known is that by the early 1770s, he had grown tired of succumbing to forces beyond his control. His "cousin" Joseph Leblanc *dit* le Maigre had spent the last years of his life on Belle-Ile, pining for a voyage to Miquelon or Nova Scotia that never materialized.[6] So when Jean-Jacques was confronted with a French colonization scheme rooted, like Belle-Ile's was, in a disappointing piece of land and the disappointing people who lived there, he took action.

The piece of land in question was the province of Poitou, the ancestral home of Leblanc's family. It stretched from the borders of Brittany in the north to Saintonge and Angoumois in the south, and from the Atlantic coast inland toward the cathedral town of Bourges. Once the seat of Eleanor of Aquitaine's

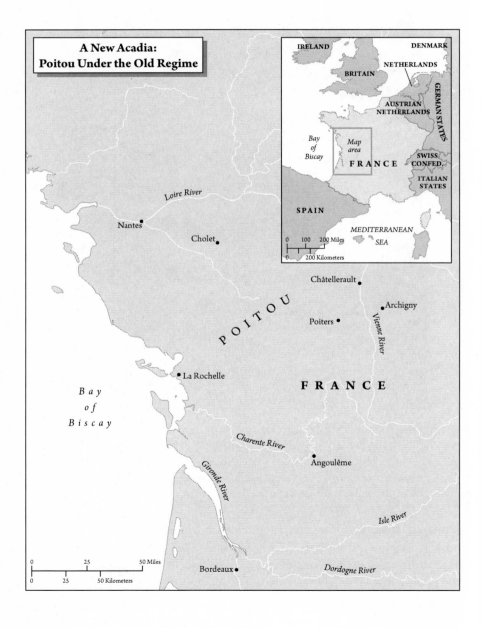

A New Acadia:
Poitou Under the Old Regime

luminous medieval court, Poitou had subsequently become best known for dirt-eating poverty. Not even locals defended it. The sixteenth-century satirist François Rabelais, a native of the Poitevin town of Chinon, claimed that when Satan tempted Christ with the kingdoms of the world, he withheld the province from view so as to make a better impression.[7]

By the 1760s, observers noted that Poitou had missed the technological changes, quickening markets, and political innovations that had of late energized agriculture in the Parisian basin.[8] The evidence abounded. In 1766, a visitor to the town of Poitiers witnessed a plowman making his ninth pass at a field of unbroken clods, working with "a kind of hook pulled by two mediocre cows."[9] Year after miserable year, such stagnation resulted in empty barns and food shortages. "We have no reason to congratulate ourselves ... on the grain harvest," wrote one contributor to a local newspaper during the early 1770s. It was an annual lament. "Poitou will never be what it could and should be," another writer claimed, "until we learn to profit from the instructions, already so widespread, on Agriculture, the principle of all wealth."[10] But according to Arthur Young, a British agronomist who rambled through Poitou on the eve of the French Revolution, those vital lessons were wasted on the province's population. In 1787, he described Poitou as an "unimproved, poor, and ugly country," wanting in "communication, demand, and activity of all kinds" and yielding "half of what it might." Young singled out the rural hinterland outside the town of Châtellerault: it was, he wrote, "thinly peopled," with estates littered across a "white chalky country" almost devoid of improvements.[11]

Others linked Poitou's sluggish agriculture to a decline in its population. Poitou's forward-thinking elites, like those elsewhere in France, feared that peasants were leaving rural areas for the "unbridled luxury" of urban life.[12] The province's problems, though, seemed particularly severe. In 1763, for example, the chevalier d'Eon, France's ambassador in London, fired off a series of harried letters detailing a British plan to lure Protestants from Poitou, Vivarais, and Languedoc. A minister named Gilbert, he claimed, had already taken families to London, promising prosperity in a silk-producing colony in Florida or South Carolina.[13] The British plan came to nothing, but the panicked French reaction revealed a widely held sense that any more population losses might send Poitou over the edge. Moreover, many at Versailles were inclined to see heartland regions such as Poitou as barometers of the health of the kingdom at large. Army men agreed that peasants made the best soldiers, while quartermasters and royal accountants knew that rural populations yielded the provisions and tax revenue that decided wars.[14] As a result, crown officials such as Henri Bertin, controller general of finances during the early 1760s, saw Poitou's "drought of inhabitants" as a domestic issue with international ramifications.[15]

As in Guiana, Saint-Domingue, *terra australis incognita*, and Belle-Ile, postwar Poitou gave rise to striving patriots who barraged Versailles with petitions, schemes, and requests for funding. In Poitou, the great exemplar of the species was Louis-Nicolas, marquis de Pérusse des Cars. Born into a family of Limousin nobles in 1724, he found an outlet for his substantial ambition in the army. At ten years of age, he carried Louis XV's standard at the Battle of Parma; at twenty, he fell wounded at the Battle of Coni in Italy; three years later he took command of his own regiment. Somewhere amid the campaigns and promotions, Pérusse married well. His wife's father blessed the union with a dowry that included a château near Châtellerault, a great deal of land in Poitou, two houses in Paris, and a sum of money. Pérusse reached the rank of brigadier general during the Seven Years' War and in 1760 helped defeat Frederick the Great at the Battle of Kloster Kamp. Dragged from the field unconscious and bloodied, he went to Châtellerault to heal in a home he had scarcely seen.[16] What he saw disgusted him. His wife's vast inheritance consisted not of handsome fields tilled by plump peasants but of "15,000 arpents . . . uncultivated, vacant, and held in common," a scene of "devastation . . . caused by the want of inhabitants." For a man still in his thirties, broken in body but alive in spirit, the conditions were appalling. Pérusse therefore vowed to foster better farming and "repeople his land."[17]

How? One way of approaching problems such as Pérusse's ran through agronomy. At root, agronomists simply argued that agriculture ought to be treated as a science, and that farming practices were susceptible to improvement through innovation, experiment, and the reasoned application of new technologies.[18] A vogue for agricultural techniques ("agromania," as boosters called it) had begun in the 1750s with the publication of Henri-Louis Duhamel du Monceau's *Traité de la culture des terres*, which introduced French readers to the British agronomist Jethro Tull, whose fertilizers and sturdy plows promised personal profits and plentiful tax income. In an age of emulation, agronomy also made cultural sense. In 1762, members of the Agricultural Society of La Rochelle declared their intention to "encourage farmers by their example, to clear uncultivated lands, to acquire new kinds of crops, and to perfect different methods of farming lands currently under cultivation."[19] The power of emulation, of course, extended beyond the furrows. Agriculture produced rustic, virtuous individuals, meaning that the adoption of proper farming by the elite would, perhaps, induce patriotic behavior in subjects up and down France's social hierarchy. Mostly, though, agronomists preferred fieldwork to grand pronouncements. Sarcey de Sutières, founder of France's first agricultural school, touted his "twenty years of experience" against those who "prescribe, from the depths of their chambers, new laws for the plowman, and sometimes even for nature."[20]

Pérusse knew plenty about agronomists and their recipe for rural renewal. He was no less familiar with a group he called their "sworn enemies"—the physiocrats.[21]

By the early 1770s, physiocracy had evolved from an esoteric theory of political economy to a true phenomenon in French political culture.[22] Physiocrats had become more and more insistent that their program of social reorientation held the sole key to the revival of a French countryside in crisis. Many spoke of this reorientation in mystical rather than practical terms, but the particulars involved the unification of scattered peasant farms into great estates managed by "agricultural entrepreneurs."[23] Landed peasants would become wage earners, their rudimentary subsistence farming discarded in favor of *la grande culture*, or large-scale commercial agriculture.[24] Privileges held by estates, towns, ecclesiastical orders, and guilds would be abolished, freeing markets and allowing goods to flow unfettered. These steps taken, the all-important *produit net*, or the surplus wealth generated by all economic activity, would rise. Demographic growth would ease the tax burden on agrarian families, allowing for earlier marriages and more children. "In the midst of a vast population," landowners would soon become "illustrious instructors" of their fellow men, spreading knowledge of "that science on which depends the happiness of the world."[25]

Agronomists and physiocrats sparred throughout the 1760s but found common ground on one subject: their distaste for French peasants of the kind that tilled Pérusse's lands so unproductively. Where the men behind the Acadian colonization of Belle-Ile had reserved their venom for *bellilois* farmers in particular, these thinkers unleashed theirs on the kingdom's entire rural population. The abbé Nicolas Baudeau, for example, glossed all peasants as "bad patriots," blaming their "miserable self-interest" for allowing "uncultivated lands to languish in sterility."[26] In economic terms, Mirabeau imagined North American Indians and French peasants to be equally backward. "Among the savages," he wrote, "the vilest hunter may consume the product of fifty arpents of land," a horrifying inefficiency replicated, almost, in places such as the wastelands of Poitou.[27] Emulation was all well and good, but in the face of such peasant stubbornness, harsher measures received a hearing. "In Sweden," snarled one rough-and-ready seigneur, "they used violence to force the people to clear lands."[28] Likewise, Baudeau touted the "salutary violence" of closing the "moors and bad woods" in which peasants (including Mirabeau's Indians) hunted, making the "spade, the hatchet, and the rake" their only recourse for food.[29]

Faced with this state of affairs, Quesnay's disciples had become boosters of the booming business of internal colonization. In part, the physiocrats and their friends at court simply wanted to compete, as a contributor to the *Journal d'agriculture, du commerce, et des finances* explained in January 1767:

> Our neighbors the English have cleared new lands. By their clearing they have augmented their riches and their population. And who knows to what degree the taste for agriculture, which has made so much progress there, influenced the successes of which they boast today? This art

makes men brave and robust, and attaches them more particularly to the homeland, of which the honor and interest are dear to them.[30]

Concrete plans soon emerged from the physiocrats' jealousy. Baudeau, for example, laid claim to "all foreign colonists whom we may settle in the kingdom." Their presence in France, he predicted, would be "one of the surest ways to remedy the depopulation of our countryside." To that end, Baudeau proposed the creation of a "General Company of Land Clearance," an enterprise headquartered at Versailles and modeled on the colonial joint-stock companies of an earlier era. Both "foreigners and French subjects enrolled in this new agricultural militia," he wrote, "will work for the state in general, for themselves, and for the company," enjoying a *solde* as they carved new "agricultural provinces" from the kingdom's wastelands.[31]

The Acadians' mixed results on Belle-Ile notwithstanding, the French bought into such arguments during the late 1760s. Some revived old schemes aimed at drying and settling marshes near Bordeaux or Rochefort, while Louis XV himself looked favorably on a proposed colony in the Fôret de Brix near Cherbourg.[32] In 1768, officials contacted the abbé le Loutre about placing Acadians on the newly acquired island of Corsica. Busy locking horns with Belle-Ile's clergy and mediating (some said causing) disputes between Acadians and *bellilois*, the priest looked over the proposal and dismissed it. Family plots were too small, tithing rates too steep, and worse, in Corsica's climate "one can even see grass burned to the root from the sun's ardor."[33] In 1769, a noble named Châteaubriand offered land near his home in Saint-Malo to migrants, while a mysterious "M. de la Pierre" hoped to settle newcomers in the Fôret de la Rocquette in lower Brittany.[34] The comte de Closnard wanted one hundred families (Acadians, if possible) for a settlement near the Loire River. In spite of early failures, internal colonization had arrived.[35]

The marquis de Pérusse stood at the cutting edge of these developments. In 1762, he began corresponding with the agronomist Louis-François-Henri Menon, marquis de Turbilly. Like Pérusse, Turbilly had served in the army; after retirement, he wrote a book on the clearing of wastelands and advised Louis XV on the founding of agricultural societies.[36] The two men hatched a plan. From his time in Germany, Pérusse recalled Bavarians with "well-cultivated farms . . . good reputations, and integrity of manners." With Turbilly's help, Pérusse sent agents across the border to make an offer. Late in 1762, four families arrived in Châtellerault from the German frontier.[37] Giving twenty-five arpents to each, Pérusse exempted them from seigneurial dues and the corvée. He predicted rapid progress. As the Germans worked, investments and migrants would follow. Local tenants would experiment with new methods. No more would men be forced into cities; with livings to be made and girls to marry, they would remain in Poitou to increase the output of grain and children. It was a great plan, and

Pérusse was breathlessly excited about it. As in other colonies, however, indige-nous people made their presence felt in Poitou. Pérusse was forced to hire "a number of valets ... as much to protect [the Bavarians] from the peasants of the canton as to aid them in their work." Turbilly noted that the colony "went mar-velously" thereafter.[38]

The little settlement became a lodestar for a French government eager to cul-tivate innovation.[39] In letters to Versailles, Pérusse delighted in his successes. "The paternal bounties of the Sovereign ... and the wise views of an Enlightened and patriotic Ministry," he wrote, demanded "encouragement" for the "relent-less" work of clearing uncultivated land.[40] He asked for a massive subvention of 450,000 livres, which would allow him to "lead [agriculture] to its perfection."[41] Pérusse planned to import more Germans, tempting the persecuted Catholics with promises of free land and the right to "exercise whatever profession seems best to them" after working for three years on his estate.[42] France's war debt, however, spoiled the plan. Although the proposal received "the most flattering praise," it did not pass. Crucially, however, Henri Bertin retained a positive image of the Poitou settlement. In 1766, he lauded the Germans (by then 130 strong) and their leader, who "fill[ed] the dual goals essential to the good of the state, providing for its population and the culture of its soil."[43] Pérusse's experiment was too striking to forget, and Bertin did not.

As Poitou continued its decline and Pérusse accelerated his scheming, the var-ious communities of Acadian refugees across northern France were disintegrat-ing at the edges. Belle-Ile, whose Acadians were trickling back to the mainland, was only one example. In Cherbourg, once a center of recruitment for the Kourou settlement, some succumbed to poor conditions and an inconsistent *solde*. As one observer reported in 1767, the weakest "languished on straw beds in their rooms," unable to jolt themselves into activity.[44] What energy the town's refugees could muster seemed to go toward fighting old battles over social prom-inence. Cherbourg's officials reported that Acadians who styled themselves "no-bles" were angling for pensions from the king instead of the daily *solde*. Their main motive, as the exasperated Frenchmen complained, was avoiding "the hu-miliation of seeing themselves mixed in with all the others who were once their vassals or servants."[45] Although most Acadians married other Acadians, unions with the French were becoming more common, embedding refugees in new families and launching them on new, complicated trajectories.[46] Elizabeth Bourg, for example, had arrived in Cherbourg from Ile Saint-Jean in January 1758 with her older sister. Courted by a soldier named Désiré, the sister married and moved to Niort in central France, taking Elizabeth with her. When the newlyweds sud-denly died, Elizabeth, by then twenty-five years old, slipped into poverty, leading Niort's mayor to request money for her support.[47] The uncertainty of breakaway

Acadian lives worried many. When a Cherbourg Acadian named Marguerite Bazer tried to enter an Ursuline convent in nearby Valognes, Choiseul himself denied her request, proposing "that she should instead marry an Acadian man."[48]

Bazer's dashed hopes hint at powerful forces arrayed along the Acadians' social boundaries, pressing inward to keep the refugees together. True, Acadians surely found comfort and security in familiar faces. But external conditions also fostered cohesion. First among these was the Acadians' identity as a privileged *corps* within French society. Rooted in genealogical memory and sweetened by promises of money and land, status as a "true Acadian" was worth fighting for. Félix Leblanc did so after being left off the "general roll" compiled by Lemoyne in 1772. Writing to Turgot's predecessor as controller general of finances, Leblanc was unable to reconstruct his family history through documents such as parish registers. So he painstakingly recounted his birth in the parish of Saint-Charles des Mines near Grand Pré, his service in the Acadian militia at Pointe Beausé-jour, and his 1755 deportation to South Carolina. He managed to escape from Charleston and eventually made his way north to the Saint John River, where he suffered "troubles and miseries" in the wilderness with Charles des Champs de Boishébert and his Acadian guerillas. Given the position of royal "mail carrier," Leblanc then hauled letters between Louisbourg and Québec before being captured on Ile Saint-Jean and sent to Boulogne-sur-Mer aboard the *Neptune*. He included the names of several Acadians who might "serve as witnesses" to his story.[49] Life inside the *corps*, Leblanc knew, offered benefits too substantial to ignore.

Beyond France's corporate political culture, transformations in the imperial world also conspired to push Acadians together. These were the same changes that had, ten years earlier, compelled the French to settle Germans and Acadians on the Kourou. Mostly they had to do with the dangers and costs of an empire powered by African slavery. On an international scale, new thinking produced a new kind of labor market, one that threatened to crush atomized individuals but favored large, cohesive groups of free white settlers. British entrepreneurs, for example, tried to move entire Greek and Corsican villages to New Smyrna in Florida, while the Spanish attempted to lure whole Swiss villages to their internal colony in the Sierra Morena.[50] Etienne-François Turgot worked hard to transport large groups of Maltese settlers to Guiana but could not sway them. And Catherine the Great hoped to plant "whole Colony's" of German or French settlers (emphatically not "fugitives and passportless people") into the borderlands of the Russian Empire.[51]

Already popular among French colonizers ranging from long-range voyagers such as Bougainville to stay-at-home types such as Pérusse, who described the refugees as "highly superior to the mass of our peasants," the Acadians' renown spread across Europe.[52] "New solicitations," wrote one nervous French administrator in 1772, came the refugees' way almost weekly.[53] The British, of course, had been active in trying to draw Acadians to the island of Jersey or even Nova Scotia since 1763.[54] In the late 1760s, the Spanish joined the fray, making overtures to refugees in Saint-Malo about opportunities in their Sierra Morena colony or Louisiana.[55]

An expanding smorgasbord of choices made for "excitement" among the once trammeled refugees. In 1772, for example, the marquis de Saint-Victour offered land near Ussel, a rocky hamlet in the Limousin, to more than a hundred Acadian families. Each would receive two hundred arpents, one hundred of which had been cleared, plus all of the usual exemptions and their royal allowance. Saint-Victour would dig a ditch down the center of the land, and after twenty years would choose one half to keep for his own.[56] In April, Acadians in Saint-Malo heard about the plan and rejected it.[57] Annoyed, Saint-Victour agreed to see Prosper Giroire and Marin Daigle, two brothers-in-law representing refugees in the Breton seaport. The pair arrived in Ussel on December 9, 1772. The meeting did not go well, and Saint-Victour withdrew his offer. Lemoyne blamed Daigle, who allegedly said that he would migrate "nowhere unless . . . assured of a thousand écus of revenue." "The Acadians' heads are absolutely spinning," Lemoyne seethed, wondering aloud if "these people imagine we will make lords of them."[58] A "part of the [Acadian] nation," one French observer declared, had managed to scuttle a promising settlement.[59] While many were "persuaded that they will find what they have long been looking for in the Limousin," some agitated for migration to Corsica or Ile-de-France (now Mauritius), "others for the Mississippi, others to return to Canada . . . and still others will not leave the coast of France."[60]

By the early 1770s, then, the three thousand Acadians scattered throughout France faced a difficult decision. To escape the fate of the landless poor, they could embrace one of two visions for the future of their community. On one hand, Acadians could risk entering the Atlantic market for colonists, betting that demand for large groups would ensure a settlement on good terms. On the other, they could cling to their status as a *corps* within the old régime, banking on the king's promise of land and hereditary rights. Whether they remained in France or tested the waters, however, the refugees were bound to move and act as a single body. Both the government's grant of corporate privileges and the nature of the imperial labor market demanded as much; as individuals, families, or small groups, Acadians faced penury in France and uncertainty beyond its shores.

In 1772, Jean-Jacques Leblanc began a long struggle to foist his vision for the Acadian future on his compatriots. Early that year, he sent a memorial to Pierre-Étienne Bourgeois de Boynes, Louis XV's minister of the marine. Claiming to speak for "113 heads of family," he reminded de Boynes that the king had promised French lands to his Acadian subjects. It had not happened. As a result, reports from Acadians in Spanish Louisiana had proven tempting. Reading a letter from "our brothers . . . who have escaped from Halifax, Maryland, and Philadelphia," Leblanc noted that his friends were "happy" in Louisiana. Knowing "how much we cost France," he asked that his group be allowed to sail for New Orleans.[61] In July, a second delegation from Saint-Malo visited Louis XV's summer retreat in Compiègne. Claiming to represent six hundred families across Brittany, they told the king that Carlos III of Spain had offered to settle them in the Sierra Morena, a scenario they preferred to more time wasted in France.[62]

The king's response stunned Leblanc. Instead of allowing the expensive guests to leave, Louis XV ordered his ministers to devise a French colony for the Acadians that would both satisfy justice and "discharge the state of the cost" of their upkeep.[63] Royal generosity, however, had limits. "Truly Acadian families" alone would merit the king's "kindnesses."[64] Leblanc's initial bid to coax the Acadian community onto the imperial market had, in effect, been hijacked. The promise of internal colonization, coupled with guarantees of the Acadians' corporate privileges, seemed certain to attach them solidly to metropolitan France.

Henri Bertin, then serving as the king's adviser on agricultural affairs, approached Pérusse about the Acadians. The marquis leapt at the chance to receive them. He hired the agronomist Sutières to examine the soil of his estates in preparation for the refugees' arrival. When only one of his own domains received Sutières's mark of "first quality," Pérusse cajoled the bishop of Poitiers and the nuns of a local convent into donating some of theirs.[65] Plans for the new colony combined rationality and elegance. Pérusse desired the 1,347 Acadians who had self-identified as "farmers" on Lemoyne's census, along with "153 others . . . whose type of industry is most analogous to agriculture." The colonists were to be divided into five villages of thirty households apiece. Ten Acadians would live in each of the colony's 150 stone houses, which included "two rooms, one of which has a chimney, a cellar, a tool closet, and a barn." Each household would receive four oxen, two cows, two plows, a cart, and animal feed for the first year. In addition to 6 sols per day until at least 1776, perks included full ownership of their cleared lands, tithes "reduced to the fortieth" for fifteen years, total exemption from royal taxes and the corvée for at least a decade, free salt, and tobacco "at the prices given to the troops."[66] Between 1774 and 1776, the king would defray these expenses with 600,000 livres in eight payments, after which the colony would sustain itself.[67] Pérusse predicted a "useful enterprise . . . which will not fail to be imitated by many."[68]

Recruitment, however, went nowhere. Officials contacted Acadians in Saint-Malo in October 1772 and arranged for a group to visit Poitou. After a tour of the region, two of the refugees said something brash. "This is not worth Acadia," they told Pérusse, "or the settlements proposed . . . by the Spanish." The confused marquis wrote that the men then headed back "to convince their brethren . . . that the lands they had seen were a kind of marsh . . . and that there was not a tree within twenty leagues."[69]

In the summer of 1773, crown officials sent Antoine-Philippe Lemoyne, the colonial administrator who had earlier assembled the "general roll" of Acadians in the kingdom, to pitch Pérusse's project to refugees in northern seaports. In Le Havre, most liked the idea.[70] In Cherbourg, Eustache Perot, Jacques L'Anglois, and dozens more signed on.[71] In July, Lemoyne met with Acadians in Saint-Malo, including Jean-Jacques Leblanc, whom he cast as "their confidence man, their orator." After Lemoyne addressed an Acadian "delegation," the refugees left and forced him to wait as they pored over the plans for Pérusse's settlement. They then returned, and one (probably Leblanc) rose to speak: "You have, sir, remitted to the heads of the nation—"

Lemoyne interrupted, flush with anger. He claimed to know the "Acadians only as French, as subjects of the king committed to obey him . . . not as a foreign nation." It was a rash statement, and it elicited a harsh response. A lone man named Martin Porcheron agreed to go to Poitou. Fifteen hundred others said no.[72]

Lemoyne held more meetings in and around Saint-Malo, but each produced the same result; a few Acadians accepted, while hundreds refused. "Tormented" by the "perfect harmony" of Saint-Malo's refugees, Lemoyne started to ask hard questions.[73] Beneath the veneer of Acadian consensus, he detected "serious intrigues," propaganda, and arm-twisting meant to "force the government's hand" and drive the refugees toward "the Mississippi."[74] So Lemoyne decided to fight chicanery with chicanery.

Launching his own campaign to "catechize" the truculent Acadians, Lemoyne sent a second Acadian deputation from Saint-Malo to view Pérusse's lands.[75] Curiously, it included the mutinous Leblanc, Simon Aucoin ("even more ill-disposed than Jean-Jacques," noted Lemoyne), and the "honest" Augustin Doucet. Lemoyne pulled out all the stops to make the tour a success. A secretary to the comte de Blossac, the province's royal intendant, guided the Acadians around Pérusse's estate in a fine carriage, while two locals, Sébastien Dupont and Louis Dansac, were paid to testify to the Acadians of the land's fertility. At various points along the way, the group descended from the carriage to probe the dirt with sticks and grind clods into powder, discussing the soil's composition, color, and depth in meticulous detail. At the end of the day, the Acadians and their hosts drafted and signed a long document at Pérusse's château. It confirmed that the land they had seen featured "six or seven thumbs of topsoil, dewy and light, and underneath a grayish-yellow soil . . . that seems to have both salts and substance; cold, but liable to be reheated by work and running water."[76] Then the royal official returned to his offices in Poitiers, Dupont and Dansac trudged off to their own farms, and the Acadians began the long trek north to Saint-Malo.

Within days of the deputation's return, an "official report" praising Poitou's soil began circulating in Saint-Malo with the Acadians' names prominently affixed to it. Lemoyne then distributed a letter from the abbé de l'Isle-Dieu, vicar general of Canada and the Acadian missions, in which the priest berated Acadians in nearby Morlaix and said that he would pray to "our Divine mediator to remove your ideas and destroy your prejudices . . . of which I am sure you will repent."[77] Parish priests in Saint-Malo received another letter imploring them to push Acadians to Poitou. A few refugees, Lemoyne told the clerics, had "refused the king's graces" for "reprehensible, even criminal motives," weaving a "veil of seduction that covers the eyes of far too many."[78] He warned that all those unwilling to go to Poitou would lose the prized allowance. Setting a tough example, he revoked the privileges of a "restless, conspiring Acadian" named Alexis Trahan.[79]

Jean-Jacques Leblanc held his ground, but it was eroding fast. With Aucoin, he claimed that the assessment of Poitou's soil had been forged, and that the government's warnings about the allowance were "only threats." "When I ask these two men if they will go," noted Lemoyne, "they respond, 'Oh my God, no!'" Two weeks after Leblanc and Aucoin's return from Poitou, however, 150 Acadians had signed on, with more responding daily.[80]

Within a month of Lemoyne's visit, most of Saint-Malo's Acadians had agreed to settle on Pérusse's lands. For most, it was a difficult choice. After his visit to Poitou in July 1773, Augustin Doucet confided that "the lands are excellent and he would not have come back [to Saint-Malo] had his wife and children been with him."[81] He did not, however, talk much with others about "the richness of the soil and the favors granted by the king," fearful that Leblanc and his allies would brand him a "bought man."[82] Only when Lemoyne's tactics undercut the consensus enforced by Leblanc and his like-minded compatriots did Doucet openly cast his lot for the internal colony of Poitou. Sensing a shift toward Pérusse's colony, Leblanc signed on. His fate and the community's, as he knew, were one and the same. However, he would have more to say about the direction that community took.

In great, disorderly caravans, the Acadians rolled into Châtellerault in October and November 1773. Pérusse and his cohort were surprised by the Acadians' sudden appearance. "The arrival of these people has embarrassed us a bit," fretted one friend, wondering aloud why Lemoyne had chosen to rush the operation.[83] Few of the projected 150 houses had been constructed, leaving the refugees in a familiar state: homelessness. Pérusse scrambled to make arrangements. He turned to friends such as M. Delauzon of Chauvigny, who agreed to quarter eight families in the outbuildings of his farm.[84] By December, fourteen hundred new colonists had arrived. Pérusse judged them "big, robust, hardworking, and very fecund," exulting that "almost all the women arrived pregnant."[85]

Pérusse did, however, notice subtle differences among the refugees. First, a few people who were not Acadians at all had sneaked into the mix. He labeled them "very different" from the rest and thanked his stars their numbers were few.[86] Second, Pérusse noted a difference in the "suppleness of character" corresponding to the "province [the Acadians] had inhabited." Those who had come from Le Havre and Cherbourg proved "docile, confident in the king's bounties, having no other desire than to be settled." Those who had previously lived in Brittany formed two classes. The Acadians who had been placed in the "countryside" or on Belle-Ile, Pérusse wrote, "want only to work and do so well," their good desires leading them to "forget Acadia." In ports such as Saint-Malo, however, the Acadians had developed a taste for oppositional politics. "They wish," he wrote, "that a deliberation be made, as in the Estates [of Brittany], on the settlement of individuals and nations."[87]

Still, the colony seemed destined for success. Construction moved forward in the spring and summer, and while local peasants grew envious of the benefits lavished on the newcomers, others elsewhere grew enamored of the colony. For his part, Sutières abandoned his other concerns and stayed on Pérusse's payroll, outfitting a farm called Champfleury, where he held forth on the latest techniques. The proud agronomist wrote essays in the local newspaper inviting local farmers (especially the "naysayers and jokers") to see the improved plows and pungent fertilizers that allowed "his grain, even when sowed in poor soil that has always produced mediocre crops," to become "the best in all the canton."[88] Slowly Acadians moved from Châtellerault out into the countryside, taking up residence in the six angular villages laid out by Pérusse the previous year.

But the death of Louis XV changed everything. Although his reputation as an agrarian-minded reformer could not have been stronger, Turgot had hated Pérusse's project from the start. "As far as I can tell, the man seems disinclined to favor this project," wrote one of Pérusse's correspondents at court.[89] Indeed, the new controller general was equal parts improver and cost cutter; in Limoges in 1762, he had shut down an experimental farm sponsored by the provincial agricultural society, castigating members for wasting its annual budget of 10,000 livres.[90] From Versailles, the Acadian colony of Poitou—a 600,000-livre holdover from a previous, poorly run administration—looked like a bad investment for a kingdom on the fiscal brink.

Beyond such practical matters, Turgot despised privilege. Like many of the physiocrats, he sought to liberate the French economy from the "particular *corps*" whose time-honored rights bred stagnation. The Acadian colony, however, depended on what Turgot called "privileges and exemptions" granted by

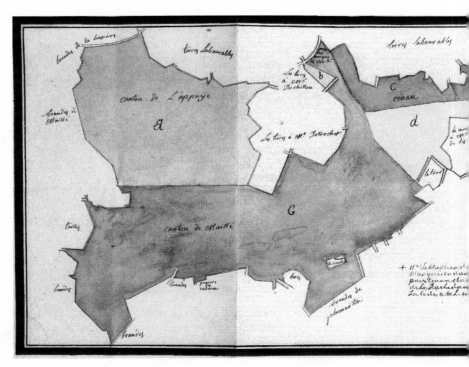

A map of the Acadian colony near Archigny, 1773. Courtesy of the
Archives départementales de la Vienne, Poitiers, France.

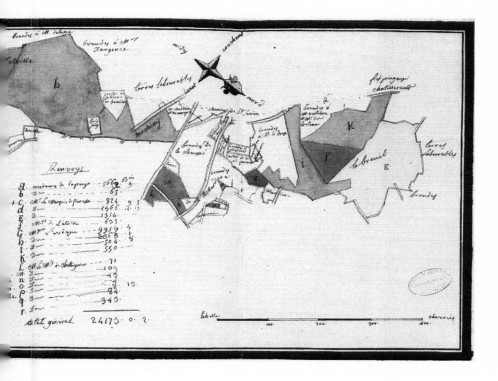

Renvoys

a. _mordanes de lapanye_ — 566 ...
b. 3m ... — 65
+ C. _M le marquis de forcerie_ — 824
d. 2m ... — 1666
e. _M de l'etoille_ — 603
f. _M de Sauvigne_ — 9959
G. 2m ... — 3858
h. 3m ... — 504
i. 3m ... — 550
K. _M le M de Chatigivre_ — 71
m. 2m ... — 109
n. 3m ... — 43
o. 4m ... — 4
p. 5m ... — 84
q. 6m ... — 349
r. 7m ... —

total général   24173 0 2

Louis XV to this "*corps* . . . in the heart of the French nation."[91] The existence of such privileges was bad enough, but worse was the ingratitude displayed by their beneficiaries. Weeks after ascending to the ministry, he complained to Pérusse that a few Acadians, "whether by indolence, idleness, or . . . ill-will," not only had refused to clear lands but had slowed the colony's progress by "communicat[ing] their way of thinking" to others.[92] Turgot, then, saw the Poitou project less as a colonial innovation than as a costly eyesore populated by serial whiners.

Turgot spent his first weeks at Versailles overhauling the Acadian settlement to ensure either its transformation or its demise. The king, he assured Pérusse, "proposed to grant this colony all the privileges that may lead to its prosperity." But to be certain "that the idle may not enjoy the same advantages that good cultivators merit," Turgot threatened the colonists with banishment and the loss of their hereditary privileges if they refused their appointed tasks. Figuring that clearing the land given to each house (roughly thirty arpents) would take three years, Turgot offered an additional 72 sols per year to those who kept pace. If twenty arpents were not cleared after two years, the new money would be forfeited and the offenders driven from their homes. More "condemnable conduct," he warned, would cause the Acadians "to lose [the king's] kindnesses" altogether.[93]

Acadian reaction to Turgot's assault was swift. With Pérusse's help, one group tried to appeal to higher powers, presenting a united front against the controller general's reforms. In a letter to one court grandee, refugees recounted hardships during the years between 1758 and the colony's foundation. "We were forgotten, and . . . endured the most awful indigence," they wrote, recalling the "state of misery that cost the lives of many of our children." Writing under Pérusse's care, the Acadians blamed these trials on "the withdrawal of a portion . . . of the six sols per day that His Majesty granted us," blaming ministers and inept local officials for failing to deliver the money. Fearful of "the return of cuts in our allowance," they requested not only this powerful person's intercession with Louis XVI, but a particular grace certain to attract "all the blessings of Heaven." They asked that one of the villages bear "your august name . . . a name so dear to France that we will be assured of success." After receiving a positive response, more than three hundred Acadians cheered the christening of the "Village de Marie-Antoinette."[94] In light of later events, this was probably a bad omen. In 1774, however, all parties in Poitou were likely pleased with their new patron. Their claim to speak for the Acadian nation (they prayed the queen to grant "the satisfaction of seeing our reunion with those of our brethren, cousins, and nephews who . . . wish to share [the colony] with us"), along with the young Austrian's help, it seemed, ensured a solid political footing.

Not all of the refugees agreed. In November 1774, Pérusse discovered that Jean-Jacques Leblanc had gone to Versailles. The intendant at Poitiers assured

Pérusse that he had issued no passports for such a voyage, but revealed that several local notables had signed a petition against the Acadian colony, which he assumed Leblanc would deposit on Turgot's desk.[95] Pérusse mulled over the possibility of the ill-disposed minister making common cause with the Acadian renegade. "I know not what success [the Acadians] will have with the controller general," he snarled to a local cleric, "but I do not doubt that they will be highly favored of the man."[96] Writing to Turgot, Pérusse described Leblanc's visit as a plot against reform. The signatures on the Acadian's petition, he claimed, came from petty landowners who resented his successes and hoped to keep Poitou's common lands uncultivated.[97] Leblanc, Pérusse claimed, had paid for the voyage to Versailles by extorting "five sols per individual, great and small," from his Acadian tenants. He asked Turgot to clap Leblanc in prison "for a few days only" upon his return to Poitou.[98] The order never came.

A record of what Turgot and Leblanc said to each other in November 1774 has not survived. In the absence of a smoking gun, however, the circumstantial evidence suggests that the two men found effective ways to work together against the success of Pérusse's colony. After Leblanc left Versailles, Turgot sacked Sutières, punctuating the firing with a recommendation that the agronomist be shipped off to Spain to direct farming in the Sierra Morena colonies. An enraged Pérusse wrote directly to Louis XVI in protest, arguing that "the state cannot be deprived of such a precious citizen" and that "the poor gentleman would perish in a climate so different from the one in which he has always lived."[99] Then Turgot suddenly ordered the colony reduced from fifteen hundred inhabitants to six hundred "satisfied with their lot." For the rest, a difficult choice awaited. "His Majesty is disposed to establish the others either on Corsica or on Ile de France," Turgot declared, demanding that Acadians decide promptly between the Mediterranean and Indian Ocean islands. Those who waited until January 1, 1776, would, in Turgot's words, "cease to enjoy the allowance that has been granted them . . . and will not be able to aspire to any of the government's graces."[100]

It was a brilliant ploy. Turgot knew that no Acadian would take his offer. Saint-Malo's Acadians, after all, had already rejected a settlement in Corsica proposed to them in 1772. Many of the colonists in Poitou had also survived the Kourou disaster, leaving them with a marked "prejudice" against tropical locales such as Ile de France.[101] Forcing Acadians to choose between two frightening destinations or the loss of their privileges, Turgot looked to trim his budget and encourage free markets. For Leblanc, the scheme promised to destroy the Acadians' status as a *corps*, leaving them no choice but to follow him toward the Atlantic.

In Poitou, Leblanc set to work. During the winter of 1774–75, Pérusse noticed ominous changes in his tenants. Few performed the routine duties of a rural household. Wood went unchopped, cattle remained untended, and land clearance ground to a halt. Pérusse blamed Leblanc and a few others who "have set up a council among themselves to decide . . . if they will or will not execute any orders given to them." The rest, leaders reported, "dare not say or do anything without their consent."[102] By spring, the clique had succeeded in "preventing their well-established comrades from laboring." Those caught working in the fields endured "mistreatment" from gangs of Acadians and local peasants.[103] Turgot chimed in, delaying the Acadians' *solde* for nine weeks in the spring, complaining that illnesses had "overburdened his offices."[104] Officials in Châtellerault placated Acadians with loans, but impoverishment bred dissatisfaction.

The conspiracy came to fruition the next summer. In July 1775, a mysterious visitor appeared in Châtellerault. Avoiding Pérusse with care, he spent several hours in an apartment with Leblanc and some other Acadians, who then escorted the stranger on a tour of their settlements. Faced with curious colonists, the man, who called himself Dubuisson, claimed powerful protectors, including the physiocrat Dupont de Nemours and Turgot himself.[105] His message was simple. This land, he told the Acadians, "would never produce a harvest." Dubuisson assured the refugees that were he in their position, he would not "give one push to the plow or one swing with the pickaxe" in fields of such quality.[106] Censure of Pérusse's administration followed, in which Dubuisson argued that the marquis had falsified reports about his soil. As one official in Châtellerault noted, any hope of "witnessing the reign of peace among the Acadians" seemed to evaporate as he spoke.[107]

Convinced of Turgot's ill will and Leblanc's perfidy, Pérusse attempted to save the colony by dismissing refugees who gave him trouble and keeping those he liked.[108] Since all had rejected Corsica and Ile de France, Turgot planned to transport nine hundred Acadians to Nantes. Off the dole, they would scrape up enough money to go elsewhere—likely Louisiana, although Pérusse remarked with disdain that a few "flatter[ed] themselves that the Americans rebelling against England would receive them gladly."[109] He demanded that Leblanc be the first to go, along with those who had "without authority . . . established themselves as heads or deputies of their Nation." Next came the lazy, and last the non-farmers. When Turgot proposed to give departing Acadians three months' pay as a gift, Pérusse shot back. He recommended that the minister subtract from this ill-considered reward the value of "tools . . . and wood taken to make furniture, as well as firewood . . . for the king's profit."[110]

With Acadians refusing to migrate to Corsica or Ile de France and the situation in Poitou growing ever more chaotic, Turgot offered to pay their way to the port at Nantes, even hinting at a continuation of the allowance for the departed. As Pérusse put it, Acadians who wished to remain a *"corps de nation"* in order to "more easily obtain the king's graces" became targets.[111] Pierre Boudrot and four friends approached Pérusse in August 1775, seeking protection from "the threats made to them by many of their neighbors." Leblanc and his allies were pressuring the five men to sign a list of families who wished to renounce their privileges and leave for Nantes. Pérusse offered semantic cover. He told the official charged with registering the signatures to allow Boudrot and company to sign a loose sheet of paper, so that if "others ask you if they have signed, you may say yes."[112]

Ruses, however, could not protect everyone. On August 27 and 28, vandals threw rocks into the houses of Acadian fence-sitters, smashed holes in their slate roofs, and choked off their wells with logs.[113] In November, Jean-Baptiste Hébert, Marin Daigle, Joseph Doucet, and his brother Jean reported a disturbing altercation at the door of a local church. As the group walked in, Simon Aucoin vowed to "knock them senseless" before his own departure for Nantes if they did not leave Poitou.[114] Leblanc's campaign had succeeded. By late fall, Pérusse admitted that "only nine families dared work the soil."[115]

The colony disintegrated that winter. Between October and December, more than nine hundred Acadians left for Nantes.[116] Pérusse was left with three hundred tenants and no promise of funds to support them. He put on a brave face, corresponding about fig trees for Acadian farms, intervening on behalf of a refugee whose cow ate the peas of a high-strung local named Jacques Velvé, and trying to prevent Marguerite Hébert, the colony's midwife, from leaving her remaining charges.[117] Others cursed the Acadians. "Too bad for them," one Châtellerault man crowed; "if they find better elsewhere, I will rejoice."[118] Privately, Pérusse plotted revenge even as his last Acadian tenants began to disappear. "One day," he resolved, those who had ruined his attempt to cultivate imperial perfection in old France "would finally fall silent."[119]

The participants moved on, but the conspiracy that decimated the Acadian colony of Poitou reverberated through their lives for years to come.

After liquidating the Acadians' homes, the marquis de Pérusse turned to politics, representing the nobility of Poitou at the Estates General in 1789 and, ultimately, in the National Assembly. But by 1791, liberal aristocrats such as Pérusse had gone hopelessly out of style. Badmouthed by name on the floor of the legislature for his sponsorship of the "atrocious" Acadian settlement in Poitou, the marquis fled France for the German border late that year. He served in the counterrevolutionary Armée des Princes until his death at Paderborn in Westphalia in 1796.[120]

Anne-Robert Turgot's love of free markets and hatred of privilege helped spark the conspiracy in Poitou. Those same qualities soon led others to conspire against him. In September 1774, Turgot deregulated France's grain trade. The next year, he tried to abolish all privileged guilds. Bread prices rose, riots ensued, and opponents derided Turgot as a threat to all corporate rights and to liberty itself. Louis XVI fired him in May 1776. The next finance minister of any significance, Jacques Necker, followed Turgot's lead when it came to Acadians. "Their pretensions," Necker wrote in response to one of Pérusse's requests to rebuild the Acadians' colony, "are hereditary only to a certain degree."[121] Like Turgot, he envisioned "dividing them up and melting them . . . into society so that each may become a sailor, soldier, artisan, merchant, or plowman according to his faculties."[122] Occupied with American affairs and the king's rapidly deteriorating finances, Necker toyed with a few Acadian colonization schemes but soon lost interest altogether. "It has been a long time," a courtier told Pérusse in 1778, "since I have heard M. Necker speak of the Acadians."[123]

When Jean-Jacques Leblanc died near Nantes in November 1781, his quest to tailor France's Acadian community for the Atlantic labor market was nearly complete. It had not come easy. Back in 1777, a group of refugees in Nantes had informed ministers at Versailles that 2,366 Acadians would settle in Corsica if their privileges remained intact. Soon after, Necker was visited by two Acadian "delegates," also from Nantes, who set him straight. The refugees advocating Corsica, the two men explained, did so "out of fear of being deprived of their allowance" and did not represent the Acadians' true wishes.[124] The men then finished the work begun in Poitou. They repudiated the Corsican colony, absolved the monarchy of responsibility for the Acadians' back pay and personal debts, and agreed to slash their own allowance from 6 to 3 sols per day.[125] Dismantling the corporate identity that had attached them to the kingdom, the maneuver effectively eliminated the Acadians' financial incentive to remain in France. Their route to security and opportunity would run not through privileges born of the old régime's internal colonies but through engagement with the entire spectrum of Atlantic empires.

In 1783, word of an impending Acadian exodus from France to Spanish Louisiana spread throughout the kingdom. The author of this new scheme was Henri Peyroux de la Coudrenière, a onetime apothecary in Nantes who had established a thriving plantation near New Orleans during the 1770s. On a return visit to Nantes, he heard the story of Pérusse's failed colony and met up with an ambitious Acadian cobbler named Olivier Terriot. Together, the two convinced Spain's ambassador in Paris, the comte de Aranda, to forward to the king in Madrid a plan to settle all of France's Acadians on the fertile but vulnerable borderlands of Louisiana. Peyroux, an amateur natural historian who admired both physiocrats and agronomists, touted the Acadians' expertise at clearing, building, and farming. The Spanish must not forget, he declared, "that the ancient inhabitants of Acadia, who today are scattered throughout Canada, Louisiana, France, and the United States, individually possessed all those talents."[126] Early in 1784, Carlos III, who had invited Acadians to the Sierra Morena fifteen years earlier, signed off, offering to pay the refugees' way across the Atlantic and provide them with good land, new houses, and free farm implements in Louisiana. The king demanded, however, that Peyroux and Terriot gather at least sixteen hundred Acadians for the journey. Otherwise, he warned, the deal was off.[127]

The terms were good, but the migration was never a foregone conclusion. Told of Peyroux's invitation, a group of Acadians in Saint-Malo wrote to Versailles expressing a strong preference for Boston, where they might live happily in the new, anti-British republic and perhaps recover their kin "raised and instructed according to the rites of the English sect" since 1755.[128] As Peyroux's primary recruiter, Terriot bore the brunt of Acadian discontent in Nantes and throughout Brittany. One evening at a tavern, while Terriot held forth on the virtues of Louisiana, an angry refugee suddenly attacked the cobbler "like a desperado, struck me several times, and would undoubtedly have killed me if some friendly Acadians, who took his knife away, had not intervened."[129] "I am sorry, but what do you expect?" exclaimed one Spanish official upon hearing Terriot's complaints. Rooted in widely circulated horror stories about Louisiana and their own harsh experience, Acadian reluctance was understandable. "The life we must live in France is hard enough," wrote Acadians in Saint-Malo, "without taking a blind chance on that in Louisiana."[130] Eventually, though, a combination of arm-twisting and benefits offered by the Spanish held sway. In 1785, sixteen hundred Acadians, or 70 percent of France's refugees, sailed from Nantes to Louisiana.

The Acadian flight from Pérusse's colony, which in turn led to their migration en masse to Louisiana, is usually portrayed as a function of ethnic consensus, shared values, and communal bonds forged during decades of ungoverned isolation in Nova Scotia. Yet there was no such straightforward expression of solidarity. Indeed, Pérusse's experiment ended in a struggle between Acadian factions desperate to construct a community suited to thrive in the Atlantic world. Some wanted to remain in Poitou, enjoying the corporate rights associated with France's internal colonization boom. Others hoped to enter a labor market dominated by states seeking settlers in bulk. With Turgot's help, Jean-Jacques Leblanc prevailed. Like his opponents, Leblanc saw the peculiar empires of the 1760s and 1770s as arbiters of land, rights, and redress, and used coercion to guarantee what he believed to be the best outcome for all of his compatriots.

For these Acadians, the world consisted of empires whose principal weakness—a chronic lack of proper colonists—made them powerful enough to dictate the nature of their most intimate relationships. True, British settlements on the Channel Islands, Spain's colonies in Louisiana and the Sierra Morena, and experiments such as Pérusse's never generated much military or economic power for governments in London, Madrid, and Paris. But for thousands of poor, mobile workers such as the Acadians, such colonial projects

structured their perceptions of the world around them, which in turn compelled them to restructure themselves.

No one knew these realities like Augustin Doucet. He was among the first
Acadians to see Pérusse's lands in 1773, but his efforts to prop up the colony
came to nothing. By the summer of 1776, Jean-Jacques Leblanc and hundreds of
settlers were gone, Turgot had stanched the flow of money, and Doucet's crops
were failing. On behalf of the "small number of Acadian families" holding on
near Archigny, Doucet appealed to Versailles. Determined to "work with all our
strength to clear the land," he asked Louis XVI's ministers for a renewal of "the
graces the king has granted us."[131] No less than Leblanc, whose will pushed the
Acadians toward Louisiana, Doucet and his friends fashioned themselves to fill
a niche in an Atlantic of empires. They merely did so in an empire that would
become an evolutionary dead end.

The Ends of the Acadian Diaspora

I call heaven and earth to record this day against you, that I have set
before you life and death, blessing and cursing: therefore, choose life,
that both thou and thy seed may live.

—Deuteronomy *30:19*

In 1817, seventy-five-year-old Marie-Josèphe Dupuis welcomed a group of
lawyers into her modest home in Assumption Parish, Louisiana. They had tracked
her down for information related to a probate dispute involving an Acadian who,
like her, had been exiled to Philadelphia from a village near Grand Pré in Nova
Scotia. Having been only thirteen years old in 1755, Marie-Josèphe confessed to
recalling little "relative to the circumstances of their removal from said province."
Her memory, however, quickened when it came to the diaspora. "To the best of
her recollection," wrote one of the deposing attorneys, the British had displaced
"about 19,000 or 20,000 souls" in all:

> The Migration was in general to Philadelphia, some settling there, some
> in Boston, some in Baltimore, Norfolk & many in Maryland. After
> remaining in these places from 5 to 20 years, they scattered into different
> countries; to England, to France, to St. Domingo, & from these last men-
> tioned countries & also from Maryland, a great many came at different
> periods to Louisiana, where they or their descendants now reside.[1]

From her vantage point, Marie-Josèphe's description of the *grand dérangement*
rang true. Most of the Acadians from Grand Pré and its hinterland had indeed
been shipped to ports between Massachusetts and Virginia in 1755, with Georgia

and South Carolina taking the partisan inhabitants of Chignecto. The "scattering" accelerated thereafter, with thousands of exiles sailing east to Europe and south to the Caribbean in multiple waves. Dupuis did not mention the date of her own arrival in Louisiana, but she recalled well that bands of Acadians set foot in the then Spanish colony "at different periods."

The first such group, consisting of four interrelated families initially exiled to Georgia, reached the lower Mississippi in 1764 by way of New York and Mobile; they were followed by Joseph Broussard *dit* Beausoleil, the Chignecto renegade who guided 192 Acadians from Halifax first to Cap Français and then New Orleans in 1765. Dozens of survivors from Môle Saint-Nicolas in Saint-Domingue came next, straggling into Louisiana later that year. By 1767, several hundred Acadians, probably including Marie-Josèphe, had arrived from Pennsylvania and Maryland. In 1785, the 1,596 Acadians recruited by the Spanish made the journey from Nantes. Totaling just over 2,500 people, migrants from all of these groups took lands upriver from New Orleans or on the prairies and bayous west of the Atchafalaya River. Home to former residents of the British Empire's great cities, Louis XV's France, the Caribbean and South American tropics, and the farms of Belle-Ile-en-Mer and Poitou, Louisiana's backwater Acadian settlements were, by certain measures, among the most cosmopolitan places in North America.[2]

They were also home to people who had, in the words of one historian, resisted the "insidious death of assimilation."[3] In other words, the Acadians of Louisiana had retained their idiosyncratic culture while tending to the reunification of their families, refusing to adopt the beliefs, practices, or identities of the societies they encountered in the diaspora. The same might be said of the several thousand who, by the mid-1770s, had ended up in Canada. At the invitation of James Murray, the postwar governor of the new British province of Québec, hundreds of Acadians migrated from New England to the Saint Lawrence Valley in 1766 and 1767, linking up with former compatriots who had escaped from Nova Scotia and Ile Saint-Jean during the dark days of the 1750s. They settled in villages and rural *seigneuries*, or proprietary domains, from Montréal to Trois Rivières.[4] Still others filtered into the expulsion-era refugee camps in Miramichi, the Baie des Chaleurs, and the Gaspé Peninsula, farming and fishing along the western shores of the Gulf of Saint Lawrence.[5] Some even went back to Nova Scotia. Seizing on conciliatory policies during the late 1760s, they formed a string of communities that began just southwest of Annapolis Royal and dotted the Atlantic coastline all the way up to Cape Breton Island.[6] Québécois and Anglo-Canadian neighbors noted that Acadians kept to themselves, nursing wounds from an injustice that, according to a Nova Scotia physician in the 1790s, had no equal "in cruelty and atrociousness" except, perhaps, the "Massacre of St. Bartholemew."[7]

No doubt, the *grand dérangement* had not turned the Acadians of Louisiana and Canada into Bostonians, Philadelphians, Charlestonians, Englishmen, Caribbean planters, African slaves, or French peasants. But the diaspora had left its mark. The communities that emerged in its aftermath owed much to the fast-moving demand for good colonists that had swept across the imperial world during the 1750s, 1760s, and 1770s. The bulk of the Acadians who settled in Louisiana in 1785, for example, had endured the violence that overwhelmed Pérusse's colony. Moreover, everyone who crossed the Atlantic in the Spanish flotilla had been thrust together in no small part by the efforts of men such as Jean-Jacques Leblanc, who conspired to forge a single Acadian body from a disjointed mass of refugees. Perhaps less dramatically, the same processes shaped the Acadian presence in Canada. Murray's desire to place Acadians in Québec, after all, reflected a reorientation of British imperial thinking that mirrored events in the French Empire. Faced with the prospect of governing a land populated almost entirely by "popish recusants," Britons such as Murray rethought decades of anti-Catholic policy, focusing less on orthodoxy than on the creation of communities to meet the province's most pressing need: the rebuilding of Canada's war-torn agrarian economy.

Acadians fit the bill. In 1766, Murray wrote to Francis Bernard, governor of Massachusetts, who knew the exiles well. On January 1, 1765, he had received a letter from Jean Trahan and several other Acadians in Boston, wishing him a "happy new Year" and begging for help in migrating to Saint-Domingue. Unwilling to let British subjects change sovereigns and reasoning that "it is improbable that they will survive the effects of the climate," Bernard had refused to let the Acadians go—but upon hearing from Murray, he changed his mind.[8] Rather than boosting French power in Saint-Domingue, hardworking Acadians could now "become a fresh accession of wealth and strength to the British Empire in America."[9] Out of imperial competition, then, began an Acadian exodus from New England to the Saint Lawrence Valley, where the exiles' distinctive villages and parishes soon dotted the landscape.

The desire to reunite families and renew friendships, of course, helped inspire the Acadians to do what they did. Antonio de Ulloa, the governor of Spanish Louisiana in the 1760s, complained that Acadian migrants declined to settle on the colony's northern borderlands, instead moving only to lands "contiguous to those of the other Acadians."[10] Seen from an ethnic or national perspective, the key storyline of the *grand dérangement* may indeed be the Acadians' dogged refusal to assimilate. But seen from another angle, one that takes in the pan-Atlantic moment of experimentation triggered by the Seven Years' War, the Acadians *did* assimilate, bending to the demands and soaking in the characteristics of the imperial world around them. The creative, brutal commodification of laboring

people that defined that world was etched into the communities inhabited by
onetime exiles such as Marie-Josèphe Dupuis in the years after 1755.

But as Marie-Josèphe could sense only dimly in 1817, neither the Acadians
turned Cajuns of southwestern Louisiana nor the Acadians of Canada represented the cut-and-dried end of the diaspora. Her estimate that "19,000 or
20,000 souls" had endured the *grand dérangement* only slightly exceeds those of
modern historians, who put the pre-expulsion Acadian population at somewhere between 15,000 and 18,500. About 2,500 Acadians made it to Louisiana,
while several thousand eventually put down roots in Québec, New Brunswick,
Nova Scotia, or Prince Edward Island in Canada; these figures include many
children born in exile. In short, it appears that perhaps half of those captured or
driven off in the 1750s managed to reach the major Acadian settlements of
North America. What happened to the rest?

A horrifying number, of course, had died. Shipwreck, disease, and malnutrition claimed thousands of lives during the British campaign in Nova Scotia, and
conditions in exile were hardly conducive to good health. But thousands more
Acadians did survive and made choices—albeit constrained ones—that landed
them elsewhere. For all their terrors, Saint-Domingue and Guiana retained hundreds of refugees even after the 1760s: hundreds of Acadians remained in
France after the great migration to Louisiana in 1785; a similar number lingered
on in the British colonies (later American states) after 1763; hardy folk such as
the Cyr family might have stayed in Port Saint-Louis on East Falkland had the
affairs of Europe not intervened.

Contemporaries confronted the scope of the diaspora often. Judges in the
admiralty court of Halifax did so in 1777, when British sailors towed the crippled
French brig *Copinambou* into the town's harbor, accusing its captain, Jean-
Jacques Pichot, of smuggling supplies to the rebelling American colonists. As
Pichot protested that his cargo, ruined by leaks sustained near the Azores, consisted only of salt bound for Cap Français in Saint-Domingue, the judges discovered that the *Copinambou*'s crew was composed almost entirely of Acadians from
Nantes. With the French monarchy barring sailors with naval experience from
leaving the country on nonmilitary voyages, Acadians (who, Pichot remarked,
"enjoyed the privilege of foreigners in France") had become an indispensable
resource.[11]

Stories such as that of the *Copinambou*'s nameless Acadian crew are important. On the ragged edges of the *grand dérangement*, they reveal with even
greater force the link between the inner workings of the Acadian diaspora and
the complexities of the outside world.

By the late 1770s, the site of the Acadian colony near Châtellerault had become
an eerie, half-dead place. Some of the original settlers were there, but native

squatters and weeds had claimed many of the Acadians' stone houses. To Pérusse and various royal officials, "the unfortunate inhabitants of the New Acadia" painted "a portrait of the greatest misery," detailing suspended allowances, bad harvests, and evaporating credit.[12] Locals continued to hold grudges. In 1780, Ambroise Guillot protested to Louis XVI's intendant in Poitiers that after selling and delivering several oxen to a landowner named Pertier for 156 livres, the buyer had refused payment, claiming that "he was owed more than 400 livres for provisions sold during the first settlement of the Acadians."[13] Most pathetically of all, Martin Porcheron—the first and only Acadian to declare his eagerness to migrate to Poitou from Saint-Malo when Lemoyne first pitched the settlement in 1773—kept insisting on his special rights as an Acadian, badgering anyone who would listen for free firewood and other benefits.[14]

For those controlling the purse strings, it was a little hard to stomach. "After all of the care taken and expenses made by the government in this affair," wrote controller general Necker from Versailles in 1779, "I would have expected at least a community of sixty households capable of subsisting by itself."[15] But thanks to Jean-Jacques Leblanc, Anne-Robert Turgot, and the allure of settlements across the sea, it was not there. While Necker lauded the Acadians' "rare attachment and loyalty, which produced all sorts of sacrifices," he eyed the economic bottom line: "I believe that those in condition to work cannot ask for assistance that we do not give to ordinary subjects of the king."[16] Pérusse's dream slowly disintegrated, sending its Acadian settlers trickling back toward the seaports from which they had come.

Those who had weighed Louisiana in the balance and found the Spanish colony wanting had, it seemed, made an exceptionally poor choice. Acadian patriarch Michel Quessy, for example, turned up on the census lists of Saint-Malo in the summer of 1787. Unemployed and starving, he strained to care for three of his seven children, including a thirty-year-old son who had gone mad. Quessy's fellow Acadians had it no better. Pierre Broussard and Madeleine Henry struggled with a deaf and mute twenty-year-old son, while Anne Haché, who had fled Belle-Ile-en-Mer as a young woman many years earlier, was now an unemployed widow watching over six young children. In nearby Morlaix, fourteen-year-old Jean-Baptiste Hébert had lived off charity since his father, doubtless a sailor aboard a slave ship, died off the coast of "Guinea." Once robust, Guillaume Gallet was a shell of himself in Lorient, "worn out" by sickness and work.[17]

In February 1791, however, an unusually harmonious discussion on the subject of Acadians like Gallet took place on the floor of the National Constituent Assembly. Less than two years earlier, many members of the Constituent Assembly had been deputies at the Estates General, the ancient deliberative body called by Louis XVI to deal with the kingdom's heightening financial crisis.

Combining with some forward-thinking clerics and nobles (including the marquis de Pérusse) on June 20, 1789, the deputies of the Third Estate took refuge
in an outdoor tennis court near the palace at Versailles after being locked out of
their usual quarters. Declaring themselves representatives of the entire French
nation, the crowd of rebels swore an oath not to disband until they had produced a written constitution. Since that day, the men of the Constituent
Assembly had staked out an uneasy peace with the monarchy of Louis XVI.
Pushing against the reluctant king, they had abolished serfdom and engineered
the most far-reaching political revolution in Europe's history. By February
1791, however, plodding drafters had yet to finish the constitution, and the
mixture of Parisian radicalism, foreign military threats, and wild rhetoric that
would produce the Terror was beginning to boil.

With such challenges in the air, Louis-Marie de la Réveillière-Lepeaux, head
of the Constituent Assembly's committee on pensions, rose to give a report. His
topic, he bellowed, was the tragic plight of certain "citizens that the old régime
repaid for their tender attachment to the mother country by treating them with
the utmost barbarity." However well argued Réveillière-Lepeaux's case was, the
financial strains and ideological currents confronting the Constituent Assembly
seemed to preclude giving anyone much help. With its economy still reeling
from political upheaval and bad harvests, France was on the cusp of an expensive
war with Austria and Great Britain. Moreover, the revolutionaries had taken up
Turgot's war on privilege with abandon, rolling back the tax exemptions and
cherished rights of the nobility while abolishing tariffs and trade barriers in the
provinces; in June 1791 they would go on to outlaw guilds and other privileged
labor associations. A new era of equality and patriotic productivity had dawned.
"Each man," wrote the revolutionary jurist Guy-Jean Target, "must . . . renounce
all corporative spirit, belong only to the greater society and be a child of the
fatherland."[18]

But Acadians, Réveillière-Lepeaux claimed, constituted an exception. Their
history showed as much. A "people worthy of praise for the simplicity of their
manners," the refugees were, like the revolutionaries themselves, "victims of
quarrels among kings." Convinced that "even if the French government abandoned them, it still had no right to give up their country and their lives like a
mere tenant farm and its herds," Acadians had fought in Nova Scotia to remain
good subjects of Louis XV. After refusing to "submit themselves to the laws of a
foreign nation," they had endured the hardships of the expulsion in 1755. Many
then had come to France, Réveillière-Lepeaux reported, where they received the
solde in recognition of their poverty and faithfulness. Then, in 1773, the marquis
de Pérusse, who may or may not have been present for this particular speech,
had schemed to settle hundreds of Acadians on "the most unforgiving, sterile
lands" of Poitou. Pérusse's "barbarous enterprise," Réveillière-Lepeaux claimed,

caused most of the colonists to "perish of hunger and exhaustion." In the wake of the disaster, the Acadians' *solde* had been slashed by the odious Necker, leaving survivors in dire straits. They now had nothing, save for their treasury of "all of the domestic virtues, the unique basis of all public morality and the happiness of nations."

To deal with the "bothersome" refugees who remained, Réveillière-Lepeaux continued, the old régime had taken "the easy way out." "The Acadians who did not die in Poitou were transported to Louisiana," he roared, "and there, at last, almost all reached the end of their misery: death!" After 1785, Acadians in France were left to fend for themselves, save for some royal assistance "of excessive modesty" during the frigid winter of 1789. Even then, "only those who called themselves nobles" received help, while "the people got nothing." The whole affair had whipped Réveillière-Lepeaux into an anti-monarchical frenzy. "Can one look upon this unparalleled plunderer without the saddest indignation?" he wondered of Louis XVI, amazed at the king's capacity to "turn away wretches whose only crime was to have loved their country too much, even as he lavished the blood of the people upon whom? You know the answer—perverse men, fallen women!"[19]

Réveillière-Lepeaux's rant produced results. The Constituent Assembly passed a decree reviving the *solde* (8 sols per day for Acadians sixty years of age and older, 6 sols for parents, widows, and widowers, and 4 sols for children and orphans "until the age of 20") and promising to make payments retroactive to January 1, 1790. Having received letters from Acadians in Cherbourg and Le Havre, the legislators immediately set aside money for refugees in those towns. Nastazie-Rose Gaudet, who in 1764 was hunted through Cherbourg's streets by local officials for reneging on her promise to migrate to Guiana, received 54 livres.[20] But the specter of the undeserving impostor taking the Acadians' *solde* haunted the revolutionaries. The Constituent Assembly ordered a new census, requiring those who "claim to have rights to this relief" to present themselves to their town leaders, who would in turn prepare a report for officials at the *département* level, who would "verify the facts" and send still another report to Paris. Once again, it paid to be an Acadian.

Word spread, and Acadians emerged all over northern France. Not fast enough, however, for the Constituent Assembly. In November 1791, one member of Réveillière-Lepeaux's committee lamented delays in the payment of the *solde*. How, he asked, could the nation abandon a people that "loves us in spite of our forgetfulness and ingratitude, when we have paid Frenchmen who hate us for so long?" Another demanded to know if "the negligence of the executive power" was to blame for the foot-dragging, castigating his fellow legislators for leaving important business up to a corrupt king. A final speaker then took the podium. "I am myself an Acadian," he said, "and although I receive no *solde*, I am concerned with the fate of my compatriots." Having helped many refugees with the "formalities" of the new census, the speaker (whose identity remains a mystery) knew that few had received any help. He proposed that the Constituent Assembly demand an accounting from the minister of the interior within twenty-four hours.[21] To press for answers in one day struck even the toughest members of the Constituent Assembly as aggressive. Still, they passed a motion pressing for quick action on behalf of "this precious class of individuals turned Frenchmen."[22]

The culprit, however, was the complexity of Acadian genealogy, not the king or his ministers. Officials in Nantes, for example, counted 91 "true Acadians who had not intermarried with the French," but they also found 137 people "only linked to the Acadians by marriage." Among them were French people who, under the old régime, had "received the *solde* as if they had been Acadians."[23] In the push to marry humane rule and revolutionary justice, the burden of proof fell on the refugees. Ruffin Pot de Vin (whose family name translates to "Wine Jug," a slang term for a bribe) produced his baptismal certificate from Ile Saint-Jean, a document signed by officials in Rochefort confirming that he had received the *solde* up until 1768, and records of his marriage to a French woman in Nantes and the births of his two children. Pot de Vin made it onto the list of "true Acadians," but his children, officials ruled, could not "enjoy the assistance of the nation."[24] In Rouen, Marie-Joseph Baron convinced census takers to include her by presenting "papers and information" demonstrating her Acadian ancestry.[25] Gervais Gautreau, the grandfather of Achille Gotrot, whose suicide off the coast of New Zealand opened this book, did likewise in Boulogne-sur-Mer. Together with his friend and fellow Acadian mariner Firmin Aucoin, Gervais regaled authorities with tales of Guiana and the Poitou colony, obtaining his 6 sols per day without incident.[26]

Just as they had during the 1760s and 1770s, Acadians did not resist power, but rather sought connection to it. In the month of Frimaire, year II of the French Republic (late 1793, well after Louis XVI and Marie-Antoinette had been guillotined), Acadians wrote to revolutionary leaders in Nantes, then engaged in a vicious war against royalist insurgents, describing themselves as fellow "victims of despotism and tyranny."[27] The radicalism of the Terror proved temporary, but the allure of privileges and rights granted to "true Acadians" endured. On June 30, 1814, just under three months after Napoleon Bonaparte abdicated the imperial throne, a group of Acadians wrote to representatives of the restored Bourbon monarchy. Mainly from La Rochelle and Rochefort, they wanted the *solde* promised them by Louis XV in 1762. The Constituent Assembly, they claimed, had indeed paid them for a short time. But when the *assignat*, the paper money of the revolutionary government, had suddenly plunged in value, they had "no bread, and that for many years."[28] As late as 1822, the mayor of La

Rochelle received petitions from dozens of Acadians, some of whom had been in France for years, some of whom were more recent arrivals from Saint-Pierre and Miquelon off the coast of Newfoundland.[29]

The Acadians who clung to the underside of the rapidly sinking old régime, and who later begged for mercy at the feet of Jacobins, Corsican despots, and reinstated kings, might be dismissed as weaklings. Given the choice between a new start alongside old compatriots in Louisiana and continued servility in France, they had chosen the latter. But in many ways, these refugees demonstrated real strength. Resisting the coercive pressure applied by men such as Jean-Jacques Leblanc while rejecting the uncertainty of fresh settlements (which they knew well from Guiana, Saint-Domingue, the Falklands, Belle-Ile, and Poitou), they took a course of action that appeared most likely to ensure their survival.

If the Acadian community of late eighteenth- and early nineteenth-century France retained any sense of coherence, it did so in pursuit of privileges and benefits rooted in the old régime's involvement in the world of Atlantic empires. Given the story behind the 1785 Acadian migration back to the New World, however, the same might be said of those who planted themselves in Louisiana. True, the prospect of togetherness mattered. But that togetherness could exist only within a framework forged by the political realities of an imperial age. That, as much as resilience during trials or unity among compatriots, may well be the hard, central truth of the Acadian diaspora.

This book opened with the story of a lone man dying. Geographically, culturally, and emotionally, Achille Gotrot was far removed from the main currents of the *grand dérangement*, having followed the course of empire to New Zealand and to his suicide in the hull of the *Jean Bart*. It seems fitting to end on a similar note.

The backdrop for this final act is hardly so exotic as the Bay of Islands, with its Maori headhunters and drunken whalers. The cause of the protagonist's death is far less dramatic than a pistol shot. Unlike Achille Gotrot, the doomed Acadian in this story was not implicated in the more interesting destinations of the *grand dérangement*. Neither he nor his immediate family had been sent to the Kourou River, Môle Saint-Nicolas, Port Saint-Louis, Belle-Ile-en-Mer, or Poitou. With one important exception, his adult life seems to have been spent in the narrow corridor joining southeastern Pennsylvania and Maryland. But by August 1816, when sixty-eight-year-old Charles White died of lung failure in the spare bedroom of Benjamin and Elizabeth Cross, noise from the bustling corner of Fifth and Spruce in Philadelphia ringing in his ears, he knew as well as anyone that the sinews of empire and the bonds of Acadian community were often one and the same.

As some of Philadelphia's most prominent lawyers and judges would discover, White was a tough man to figure out. In October 1755, seven-year-old
Charles and his family had been captured near their homes in Pisiquid, Nova
Scotia, "stowed in bulk" below the deck of the sloop *Three Friends*, and shipped
south toward Pennsylvania.[30] A few weeks later, as the refugees huddled on Province Island in the Delaware River awaiting permission to disembark at Philadelphia, the boy's mother, Marguerite Vincent, died of smallpox. By late 1756,
Charles was living with his older brother, François, and his father, also named
Charles, in a rented room near Saint Joseph's Chapel in Philadelphia, one of
the only Catholic churches in all of British North America. The chapel's Jesuits
ministered to dozens of Acadians who managed to stay in the city, avoiding the
province's push to transport all of the new arrivals to outlying towns. Charles,
however, spent much of his time at the "French Houses," the tenement near
Sixth and Pine that became an informal religious school for the city's Acadian
children.[31]

School at the French Houses was a welcome distraction, for Charles's father,
a brash former "deputy" to the British government in Nova Scotia, was soon in
trouble. With his Pisiquid neighbor Jean-Baptiste Galerne and the Quaker
Anthony Benezet, the elder Charles Leblanc presented several increasingly shrill
petitions to the Pennsylvania Assembly, finally demanding that the Acadians be
"Transported to our own Country."[32] In response, John Campbell, fourth Earl of
Loudoun, then serving as commander in chief of Britain's military in North
America, declared the Acadians "entirely French subjects." Having "found
among these neutrals one who has been a spy," Loudoun gleaned the names of
"five principal leading men" bent on fostering Acadian collusion with French-
allied Indians and hampering all efforts to "put their children . . . out to work."
Charles Leblanc's father was among them. Loudoun clapped the five men in the
Walnut Street Jail early in 1757; a few weeks later, he transferred the shackled
Leblanc aboard the *Sutherland*, flagship of the upcoming British expedition
against Louisbourg. After the ship sailed, one witness later recalled, Leblanc was
"never heard from again."[33]

Not yet ten, Charles had become an orphan. For the next several years, he
and François were raised in Philadelphia by their aunt. For his part, young
Charles spent much of his time near the wharf on Walnut Street, where he
worked as a "shoe boy at a Quaker gentleman's store." He stayed on the payroll,
reported an Acadian who knew him, "until he was a good big boy."[34] François,
however, was pulled from the orbit of Quaker commerce toward the resurgent
French Empire. After the Seven Years' War ended, he took his rudimentary
training in carpentry and headed for Saint-Domingue. Bypassing Môle Saint-
Nicolas, François went instead to the administrative center of Port-au-Prince "to
follow his trade." The town had been destroyed by an earthquake in 1751, and

with Louis XV's postwar ambitions fueling a boom in construction, François soon "collected some property" in Saint-Domingue. But after only a few years, François "died at Port-au-Prince unmarried and without issue." Although his experience as an adult traveler consisted of "attending a traveling gentleman as his waiter" in Annapolis, Charles boarded a ship sometime in the late 1760s or early 1770s, sailing to the Caribbean "to receive the property his brother had left." After "succeeding in this object," remembered one contemporary, "he returned to the United States."[35]

Honed during long hours on the Philadelphia docks, Charles's commercial sense ensured that François's money paid dividends. Sometime before 1777, Charles opened a store "in Water-Street, two doors below Market-Street." He had by now taken to calling himself Charles White, the simplest Anglicization of his French family name. On September 2, 1777, only weeks before the British army occupied Philadelphia, White advertised "French RUM in hogsheads and tierces, claret in hogsheads, brandy in pipes or quarter casks, geneva, whisky, pepper, loaf sugar, indigo of the best quality, &c. &c."[36] By 1790, White had begun a second career as a landlord, offering "the House the Post-Office is now kept in" and urging interested parties to "apply to Charles White, in Water-Street, below the said house."[37] His French connections also proved valuable. Tapping into Philadelphia's prodigious demand for coffee, White imported beans from Saint-Domingue beginning in February 1793, when the Constituent Assembly in Paris opened ports in the French Caribbean to American merchants.[38] By December 1794, the *Philadelphia Gazette and Daily Universal Advertiser* bellowed that "50,000 wt. of Green COFFEE, of the first quality, just arrived in the schooner *Neptune*, from Jeremie, will be landed on Monday at Market Street wharf" and sold by Charles White.[39]

By 1816, White was rich. His holdings in cash, stock, and real estate, including his own brick house at Fourth and Spruce, totaled $20,000.[40] He never married, but Philadelphians often saw White about town with three women. The oldest was his cousin Margaret Montgomery (née Marguerite Blanchard), a child exile who had sailed from Nova Scotia aboard the *Three Friends*. The others were Montgomery's two married daughters, Elizabeth Cross (from Margaret's first marriage to an Irish migrant named Thomas Betagh) and Elizabeth Baker (from Margaret's second, current marriage to Philadelphia businessman Charles Montgomery). Of the two Elizabeths, White was especially fond of Cross. Her husband, Benjamin, directed the choir at Saint Augustine's Catholic Church, where White attended mass but never took communion.[41] Early in 1816, the Cross family moved into White's neighborhood, possibly renting his "brick house and land" on Fifth and Spruce.[42] Neighbors later reported that White made a habit of peering "into the house of said Mrs. Cross," calling on her "almost every day."[43]

Charles White's neighborhood. William Birch, *View in Third Street, from Spruce Street*. Courtesy of the Library of Congress.

Those neighbors had no love for White. Banker Benjamin Norris disparaged him as "very miserly and saving of money," while Thomas Bradford called him a "dumpy round faced man."[44] White was apparently a bad landlord to boot: Ursula LaZèle, who rented a room in White's house at 6 South Water Street, complained that he "would not keep it in repairs."[45] His tightfistedness seemed to spring from a desire to leave plenty of money to his relatives. Peter Stephen du Ponceau, a French polymath who became the early republic's foremost expert in international law, rented part of White's house on Front Street. Upon learning of White's final illness in the summer of 1816, du Ponceau went to his landlord's bedside and blurted out a proposition. "I asked him," du Ponceau explained, "to give me the house in which I lived as he had no relations to leave it to." Once "portly" but now gaunt and "panting for want of breath," White refused: "He said he had plenty of relations and they were all poor."[46] Others angling for White's fortune met with similar results. Reverend Michael Hurley from Saint Augustine's tried with no success to talk him into funding an "orphan house," while former tenant Elizabeth Biddle hinted that she wanted a valuable piece of property. "O that will be more than your share," White replied, reminding her that "Mrs. Betagh [Margaret Montgomery] and her children . . . must have some."[47]

And yet for all his concern over the financial well-being of his "relations," White refused to make out a will. His stubbornness on this score struck everyone who knew him as strange. A few days before his death, the ever-persistent Elizabeth Biddle asked White "if he did not think of making a will." He changed the subject in a huff.[48] William McDonough, who lived on the corner of Fourth and Spruce opposite White's home, saw him that same week: "Said I, Mr White, you seem to be very bad, asked him if he would make a will; he said no; he would make no will."[49] Now resigned to White's unwillingness to pay for an orphanage, Reverend Hurley admonished him to make a will. White, however, "paid no attention to it, asked what [Hurley] meant, said there was no need of it."[50] For a man with $20,000 to his name, who rented a house to Philadelphia's most prominent lawyer, who had himself once benefited from an inheritance, and whose relations with nearby family members seemed healthy, this was odd behavior.

And then, in the early fall of 1816, Charles White died at Fifth and Spruce in the care of Elizabeth Cross. Margaret Montgomery and her daughters quickly laid claim to his entire fortune, having "never heard nor understood that the Said Chas. White . . . had any other relations." As word of White's death made its way along the Atlantic coast, however, an unexpected challenge emerged. Catherine Boudreau, one of the "nuns" who had catechized White at Sixth and Pine back in the 1760s, had since moved to Baltimore. Upon hearing the details of Montgomery's case, she hired an attorney to pursue her claim, as White's first cousin, to at least some of his money. Others soon joined her. They included Hypolite Boudreau of Louisiana; Elizabeth Huet de Lachelle, "a subject of his most Christian Majesty the king of France"; Alexandre de Valcourt, "a gentleman coming from Baltimore"; and several Acadians from Philadelphia. Together they filed a suit accusing Montgomery and her daughters of "combining and confederating with each other . . . to sell and waste" White's estate before all of his heirs could get to it.[51]

Eventually the dispute went to the courts. Perhaps looking to make up via legal fees for his failure to acquire White's Front Street house, Peter Stephen du Ponceau took the case. He and his associates conducted a small-scale tour of the *grand dérangement*, ranging from Pennsylvania to Louisiana to Canada to interview Acadians and others who had known either Charles White or Charles Leblanc. There were many of them. "I came to this country in the same vessel with [Charles White] and his parents," testified seventy-seven-year-old Anne-Joseph Landry, recalling their "forty days' passage" from Grand Pré to Philadelphia in November 1755.[52] Others recalled White's father as a "strong handsome good looking man," while Catherine Baugis testified that she "used to go to church" with White and his brother in Nova Scotia. But on his relationship to the parties in the suit there was no consensus.[53] Reverend

Hurley, who knew Catherine Boudreau from her time in Philadelphia, "never understood from her or from any one that she was related to C.W."[54] Marie Trépagnier, on the other hand, had attended catechism at Sixth and Pine with White, and reported that he and Boudreau "used to behave to one another as if they were cousins."[55]

Finally, du Ponceau found Marie-Josèphe Dupuis in Assumption Parish. After regaling the visiting attorneys with her take on the *grand dérangement*, Dupuis made an oracular pronouncement. She revealed that the parish registers of Saint-Charles des Mines, the church nearest Charles White's boyhood home in Pisiquid, "were all brought away" during the expulsion: "They are at present deposited in the Church of St. Gabriel in Iberville [Louisiana]."[56] The lawyers hurried to Iberville and determined, finally, that Catherine Boudreau had been right all along. Margaret Montgomery and Elizabeth Cross tried to bog the case down in legal technicalities, but they could do little more than delay the inevitable.[57] In 1828, the U.S. Circuit Court for the Third District ordered the liquidation of White's estate, which had appreciated to over $35,000, and its distribution to more than one hundred members of the Leblanc family.[58] A few, including the disappointed Montgomery, got more than $2,000. Most, like White's distant cousin Betsy Jenkins, received something like "1/4 of 1/4 of 1/16" of the total estate. Factoring in du Ponceau's fees, she collected just under $140.[59]

But why had Charles White not simply made out a will? Was he just a greedy, avaricious old man? Perhaps we can never really know. But the most reasonable answer to that question suggests that the exiles themselves appreciated how much the strands of Acadian family and community had become entangled in the coarse fabric of imperial history.

White had always known that he had uncles, aunts, and cousins who survived the *grand dérangement*'s darkest hours. He cared for them, too, as his doting attention to Margaret Montgomery and the two Elizabeths demonstrates. But he had no idea how many such relatives there were, or where they might be. The French, after all, had begun to instigate Acadian migrations from villages near Pisiquid early in the 1750s. Members of the extended Leblanc family had doubtless been drawn west of the Missaguash River or to Ile Saint-Jean, and from there to the southern colonies, England, or France by the close of the decade. White knew that after 1763, Acadians such as his brother François had washed across the French Caribbean, the South Atlantic, and finally Louisiana. Given the scale of the diaspora, the reconstitution of his family beyond Margaret Montgomery and her daughters was a thorny problem. White seems to have devised a counterintuitive solution: dying intestate. With so many Acadians simply lost and others hidden in plain sight like himself, consigning his fortune to the Acadian grapevine and the American courts may well have been the only way to ensure that his "poor relations" received any money. In effect, White hoped that his family would transcend the disorder of the *grand dérangement*—but he counted on greed to energize those old relationships.

What would Henry Wadsworth Longfellow have thought? Centered on the corner of Fourth and Spruce, Charles White's world and the Philadelphia of *Evangeline*'s last days ("Where the streets still re-echo the names of the trees of the forest") were awfully similar. But there was one significant difference. For Evangeline, time had stopped in 1755. Indeed, within Longfellow's fictional *grand dérangement*, time "was not." Like the unbroken Acadian community he represented, Gabriel Lajeunesse existed "within [Evangeline's] heart . . . / . . . Clothed in the beauty of love and youth, as last she beheld him / Only more beautiful made by his deathlike silence and absence."[60]

But the real Acadian diaspora had thrust Charles White and thousands like him into time's most treacherous crosscurrents. Acadian exiles had been pulled toward the classical past by Bougainville's obsession with *terra australis incognita* and the old régime's demographic insecurity. They had been pushed forward into an ultramodern future of free white labor in the Caribbean and productive colonies dotting the French countryside. Acadians witnessed the rise and fall of a new imperial era, all as their own lives flowed inexorably away. Their response was not an uncomplicated turn inward to the memory of their Bay of Fundy villages dismantled in 1755. When refugees such as White did look to the past, it was a garbled mess. So they rebuilt in the ever-changing present, using the materials at hand. The results, like their destinations, were nothing if not diverse.

Now to a final image, drawn from Peter Stephen du Ponceau's voluminous notes on the case of Charles White's estate. A few years before his death, White's neighbor William McDonough gave him a mysterious message from a Baltimore woman named Anne Fisher. The daughter of White's uncle Jean Leblanc, Fisher had struck up a chance conversation with McDonough in Maryland. After learning of the woman's unusual background, McDonough described the peculiar Acadian who lived at Fourth and Spruce. Suspecting that Charles White was in fact her cousin Charles Leblanc, Fisher asked McDonough to arrange a meeting during her next visit to Philadelphia. He did so, and recorded what happened next:

> I told Mr. White his cousin Mrs. Fisher was in Town & wanted to see him very bad; He asked me to go to the house with him; I went, he took her by the hand, & asked Cousin, Cousin, how do you do? Happy to see her. It was cousin here and cousin there between them. They began to talk about old times; how happy they had been together in their young days, & I left them together.

Speaking in French, White asked Fisher "what circumstances she was in," eager to know if she "did not want for anything." Whenever he saw McDonough thereafter, White "enquired after his cousin."[61]

The expulsion that drove these two Acadian cousins apart was indeed a tragedy. The imperial experiments that scattered men and women like them across the Atlantic world were indeed outlandish and often cruel. That many Acadians reversed the effects of the *grand dérangement* and lived together again was indeed a triumph—although one tinged with coercion and pain. But the reunion of two Acadians named Charles White and Anne Fisher, clutching each other and prattling cheerfully amid the bustle of early national Philadelphia, speaks to the many constraints imposed and possibilities created by the Acadian diaspora. Although the powers of heaven and earth had, it seemed, recorded the days against them, White and Fisher had endeavored, as the scripture says, to "choose life, that both thou and thy seed may live."

ABBREVIATIONS

AAS	American Antiquarian Society, Worcester, Massachusetts
AMWP	Acadian Museum, West Pubnico, Nova Scotia
ADIV	Archives départementales de l'Ille-et-Villaine, Rennes, France
ADV	Archives départementales de la Vienne, Poitiers, France
AMAE	Archives du ministère des affaires étrangères, Paris, France
AMPC	Archives de la Marine, Port de Cherbourg, Cherbourg, France
AN	Archives nationales, Paris, France
ANOM	Archives nationales d'outre-mer, Aix-en-Provence, France
BMB MSS 1480	Mss. 1480, "Recueil des pièces concernants les acadiens," Bibliothèque municipale de Bordeaux, Bordeaux, France
CCIM	Chambre de commerce et d'industrie de Marseille, Marseille, France
CEA	Centre d'études acadiennes, Université de Moncton, Moncton, New Brunswick
CRSG	Allen D. Candler, Kenneth Coleman, and Milton Ready, eds., *The Colonial Records of the State of Georgia* (Atlanta: Franklin, 1904–16; Athens: University of Georgia Press, 1976–89), 32 vols.
DRCHNY	E. B. O'Callaghan, ed., *Documents Relative to the Colonial History of the State of New York* (Albany, 1861), vol. X
DRIA	William L. McDowell, ed., *Colonial Records of South Carolina: Documents Relating to Indian Affairs* (Columbia: University of South Carolina Press, 1958–70), 2 vols.
HL	Houghton Library, Harvard University, Cambridge, Massachusetts

HSP   Historical Society of Pennsylvania

JCHA   J. H. Easterby, Terry W. Lipscomb, and R. Nicholas Olsberg, eds., *The Journal of the Commons House of Assembly* (Columbia: University of South Carolina Press, 1951–89), 14 vols.

LAC   Library and Archives of Canada, Ottawa, Ontario

LCP   Library Company of Philadelphia

MHS   Massachusetts Historical Society, Boston

MSA   Massachusetts State Archives, Boston

NAMAP   National Archives Mid-Atlantic Branch, Philadelphia

NSA II   Archibald MacMechan, ed., *Nova Scotia Archives II: A Calendar of Two Letter-Books and One Commission Book in the Possession of the Government of Nova Scotia, 1713–41* (Halifax, NS: 1900)

NSA III   Archibald N. MacMechan, ed., *Nova Scotia Archives III: Original Minutes of His Majesty's Council at Annapolis Royal, 1720–1739* (Halifax, NS: PANS, 1908)

NSA IV   Charles Bruce Fergusson, ed., *Nova Scotia Archives IV: Minutes of His Majesty's Council at Annapolis Royal, 1736–1749* (Halifax: PANS, 1967)

PA   *Pennsylvania Archives* (Harrisburg, 1838–1935), 138 vols.

PRO   Public Record Office, Kew, England

SPD   Thomas Beamish Akins, ed., *Selections from the Public Documents of the Province of Nova Scotia* (Ottawa, 1869)

NOTES

Introduction

1. David R. Slavitt, ed. and trans., *Ovid's Poetry of Exile* (Baltimore: Johns Hopkins University Press, 1990), 122.

2. Susan L. Einbinder, *No Place of Rest: Jewish Literature, Expulsion, and the Memory of Medieval France* (Philadelphia: University of Pennsylvania Press, 2009), 54.

3. On population removals from antiquity through the present, see Andrew Bell-Fialkoff, *Ethnic Cleansing* (New York: St. Martin's, 1996).

4. Historians and social scientists have engaged in a lively debate over the definition of diaspora. Some favor breadth, envisioning diaspora as a category that encompasses multiple models of dispersal, while others seek more rigor, classifying subsequent diasporas in relation to the original Jewish case or, alternatively, insisting on diaspora as a modern "stance" or "idiom" rather than a category of analysis good for all times and places. On this controversy, see Rogers Brubaker, "The 'Diaspora' Diaspora," *Ethnic and Racial Studies* 28, no. 1 (January 2005): 1–19. Like the historian Maya Jasanoff, who has written eloquently of the "loyalist diaspora" in the wake of the American Revolution, I envision diaspora as a general notion flexible enough to accommodate diverse instances of dispossession and migration. See Jasanoff, *Liberty's Exiles: American Loyalists in the Revolutionary World* (New York: Knopf, 2011), 8.

5. On the Acadian population during the eighteenth century, see especially Stephen A. White, "The True Number of the Acadians," in Ronnie-Gilles LeBlanc, ed., *Du Grand Dérangement à la Déportation: Nouvelles perspectives historiques* (Moncton, NB: Chaire d'études acadiennes, Université de Moncton, 2005), 21–56.

6. On Acadian neutrality in comparative perspective, see Jon Parmenter and Mark Power Robison, "The Perils and Possibilities of Wartime Neutrality on the Edges of Empire: Iroquois and Acadians Between the French and British in North America, 1744–1760," *Diplomatic History* 31 (April 2007): 167–206.

7. "Journal of Abijah Willard of Lancaster, Mass., An Officer in the Expedition Which Captured Fort Beauséjour in 1755," ed. J. C. Webster, *Collections of the New Brunswick Historical Society* 13 (1930): 41–42.

8. Thomas Hutchinson, *The History of the Colony and Province of Massachusetts-Bay* (Cambridge, MA: Harvard University Press, 1936), 30. The best recent accounts of the 1755 expulsion are John Mack Faragher, *A Great and Noble Scheme: The Tragic Story of the Expulsion of the French Acadians from Their American Homeland* (New York: W. W. Norton, 2005), and Geoffrey Plank, *An Unsettled Conquest: The British Campaign Against the Peoples of Acadia* (Philadelphia: University of Pennsylvania Press, 2001).

9. Scholarly treatments of the Acadian diaspora include Emile Lauvrière, *La tragédie d'un peuple: Histoire du peuple acadien de ses origines à nos jours*, 2 vols. (Paris: Editions Bossard,

1923); Oscar William Winzerling, *Acadian Odyssey* (Baton Rouge: Louisiana State University Press, 1955); Carl A. Brasseaux, *The Founding of New Acadia: The Beginnings of Acadian Life in Louisiana, 1764–1803* (Baton Rouge: Louisiana State University Press, 1987); Carl A. Brasseaux, *Scattered to the Wind: Dispersal and Wanderings of the Acadians, 1755–1809* (Lafayette, LA: Center for Louisiana Studies, 1991).

10. Yves-Joseph de Kerguelen-Trémarec, "Réflexions sur les avantages que peut procurer la France Australe," in Kerguelen-Trémarec, *Rélation de deux voyages dans les mers australes et des Indes, faits en 1771, 1772, 1773, et 1774* (Paris: Serpent de Mer, 2000), 95.

11. Acadians to Pierre-Etienne Bourgeois de Boynes, n.d., ANOM, AC, série F2A 14, 221–22.

12. Faragher, *A Great and Noble Scheme*, 434–35.

13. On Acadians in Louisiana, see Brasseaux, *Founding of New Acadia*; Carl A. Brasseaux, *Acadian to Cajun: Transformation of a People, 1803–1877* (Jackson: University of Mississippi Press, 1992). On Acadians in the late eighteenth- and early nineteenth-century Maritime Provinces, see especially Mason Wade, "After the Grand Dérangement: The Acadians' Return to the Gulf of St. Lawrence and to Nova Scotia," *American Review of Canadian Studies* 5 (1975): 42–65.

14. The most prominent histories of the Acadians and the *grand dérangement* have followed this line of thinking. Naomi E. S. Griffiths frames her interpretation by arguing that before 1755, Acadians "considered themselves to be first and foremost Acadians rather than members of any other group," and that after the expulsion they "once more asserted their identity as a separate and distinct people." See Griffiths, *From Migrant to Acadian: A North American Border People, 1604–1755* (Montreal: McGill-Queen's University Press, 2005), xv–xvi. John Mack Faragher, whose work focuses more on the origins and execution of the 1755 expulsion, describes the "transplantation of a way of life from the meadows of l'Acadie to the prairies of Louisiana," and argues that "the reunification of their extended families was foremost in the minds of the Acadian exiles." See Faragher, *A Great and Noble Scheme*, 429, 388.

15. For quote, see David A. Bell, *The Cult of the Nation in France: Inventing Nationalism, 1680–1800* (Cambridge, MA: Harvard University Press, 2001), 84. On French imperialism after the Seven Years' War, see, for example, Kenneth Banks, *Chasing Empire Across the Seas: Communication and the State in the French Atlantic* (Montreal: McGill-Queen's University Press, 2002), 7, for the argument that empire was, after 1763, "defined universally and overwhelmingly in negative terms." Gilles Havard and Cécile Vidal, two of the most accomplished historians of the early modern French Atlantic, conclude that "the French Empire ended in 1763." See Havard and Vidal, "Making New France New Again," *Common-Place* 7 (July 2007), www.common-place.org/vol-07/no-04/harvard. In his fine survey of eighteenth-century France, Gwynne Lewis argues that in the wake of the Treaty of Paris, French politicians and thinkers "concentrate[d] more on the countryside than on the colonies." See Lewis, *France, 1715–1804: Power and the People* (New York: Longman, 2004), 184. On the historiography of French imperialism in this period and more generally, see Christopher Hodson and Brett Rushforth, "Absolutely Atlantic: Colonialism and the Early Modern French State in Recent Historiography," *History Compass* 7 (2009): 1–17.

16. The best single-volume history of the Seven Years' War remains Fred Anderson, *Crucible of War: The Seven Years' War and the Fate of Empire in British North America* (New York: Knopf, 2000). Anderson eloquently advocates resistance to "the subtler tyranny of a hindsight that suggests that the creation of the American republic was somehow foreordained" by the events of the 1750s and 1760s (xxv). For a sweeping, transnational account of the war's origins, see Paul A. Mapp, *The Elusive West and the Contest for Empire, 1713–1763* (Chapel Hill: University of North Carolina Press, 2010).

17. See Robert Darnton, *The Literary Underground of the Old Regime* (Cambridge, MA: Harvard University Press, 1982), 78, for some of eighteenth-century France's other *hommes à projets.*

18. See Christopher L. Brown, *Moral Capital: Foundations of British Abolitionism* (Chapel Hill: University of North Carolina Press, 2006).

19. See Michael Craton, *Testing the Chains: Resistance to Slavery in the British West Indies* (Ithaca: Cornell University Press, 1982), 125–39; Vincent Brown, *The Reapers' Garden: Death and*

Power in the World of Atlantic Slavery (Cambridge, MA: Harvard University Press, 2008), 148–49.

20. [Sébastien-Jacques] Courtin, "Mémoire sommaire sur les prétendues pratiques magiques et empoisonnements," 1758, ANOM, AC, série F3, vol. 88, 209. On Makandal, see Pierre Pluchon, *Vaudou, sorciers, empoisonneurs de Saint Domingue à Haiti* (Paris: Karthala, 1987); Karol Weaver, *Medical Revolutionaries: The Enslaved Healers of Eighteenth-Century Saint-Domingue* (Urbana: University of Illinois Press, 2006); John Garrigus, "The Cultural Construction of Resistance: The Legend of Makandal the Poisoner," paper presented to the Rocky Mountain Seminar in Early American History, February 27, 2010.

21. Craton, *Testing the Chains*, 138; *Relation d'une conspiration tramée par les nègres dans l'Isle de St.-Domingue* (Paris, 1758), 8.

22. Abbé Raynal, cited in John D. Garrigus, *Before Haiti: Race and Citizenship in French Saint-Domingue* (New York: Palgrave Macmillan, 2006), 112.

23. Louis-Antoine de Bougainville, "Mémoire sur différents objets relatifs à l'expédition des Navires l'Aigle et le Sphinx, actuellement en armement à St. Mâlo," n.d., ANOM, AC, série F2A, vol. 14, 1.

24. This account of *Evangeline*'s origins is culled primarily from Manning Hawthorne and Henry Wadsworth Longfellow Dana, *The Origin and Development of Longfellow's "Evangeline"* (Portland, ME: Anthoensen Press, 1947), 12–13; see also Naomi E. S. Griffiths, "Longfellow's Evangeline: The Birth and Acceptance of a Legend," *Acadiensis* 11 (1982): 28–41.

25. Henry Wadsworth Longfellow, *Evangeline: A Tale of Acadie* (London: David Bogue, 1854), 48.

26. On Longfellow's *Evangeline* and its varied receptions, see also Patricia Lockhart Fleming and Yvan Lamonde, eds., *The History of the Book in Canada*, vol. 2: *1840–1918* (Toronto: University of Toronto Press, 2004), 60–61; M. Brook Taylor, "The Poetry and Prose of History: *Evangeline* and the Historians of Nova Scotia," *Journal of Canadian Studies/Révue d'études canadiennes* 23 (Spring/Summer 1988): 54.

27. On this point, see Plank, *Unsettled Conquest*, 165–67.

28. This précis of Achille Gotrot's final voyage is drawn from Yves Boyer-Vidal, *Le retour des Acadiens: Errances terrestres et maritimes, 1750–1850* (Paris: Editions du Gerfaut, 2005), 173–93. My deepest thanks to Mr. Boyer-Vidal for sharing his insights on this subject with me. For the circulation of the *Jean Bart*'s story in Conolly and Longfellow's Boston, see *New Bedford Mercury*, March 29, 1839, August 2, 1839, and June 12, 1840.

29. See Stephen A. White, *Dictionnaire généalogique des familles acadiennes* (Moncton, New Brunswick, 1999), 2:698.

30. Marquis de Pérusse to l'Evêque de Tagaste, May 18, 1774, Montoiron, ADV, série J, dépôt 22, liasse 98.

31. See Bruno Haffreingue, "Mon ancêtre d'Acadie, Firmin Aucoin (1754–1802)," *Cahiers de la société historique acadienne* 33 (2002): 88–105.

32. Boyer-Vidal, *Le retour des acadiens*, 149–50.

33. On de Thierry, see J. D. Raeside, *Sovereign Chief: A Biography of the Baron de Thierry* (Christchurch, NZ: Caxton Press, 1977); Muriel Proust de la Gironière, *La France en Nouvelle Zélande, 1840–1846: Un vaudeville coloniale* (Paris: Editions de Gerfaut, 2002).

Chapter 1: The Expulsion

1. Chevalier de la Hossaye to Surlaville, August 2, 1753, Fort Gaspereaux, in J. C. Webster, *The Forts of Chignecto* (Shediac, NB, 1930), 132.

2. The entire story of the death of André Boudin *dit* Blondain is recounted by Pichon in Fonds Thomas Pichon, MG 18, vol. F-12, vol. 1, 116–17, LAC.

3. Pichon to Mme. [de Beaumont], Fonds Thomas Pichon, 11, LAC.

4. John Mack Faragher, *A Great and Noble Scheme: The Tragic Story of the Expulsion of the French Acadians from Their American Homeland* (New York: W. W. Norton, 2005), 310.

5. On Pichon, see especially Lawrence Henry Gipson, *The Great War for Empire: The Years of Defeat, 1754–1757*, vol. 6 of *The British Empire Before the American Revolution* (New York: Knopf, 1942), 212–42.

6. Philipps to the Secretary of State, undated letter, in *SPD*, 55.

7. On the history of population removals worldwide, see Andrew Bell-Fialkoff, *Ethnic Cleansing* (New York: St. Martin's, 1996). On Ireland, see especially Nicholas Canny, *Making Ireland British, 1580–1650* (New York: Oxford University Press, 2001); on Native Americans, see, for example, Colin Calloway, *New Worlds for All: Indians, Europeans, and the Remaking of Early America* (Baltimore: Johns Hopkins University Press, 1998); on the Highland Scots, see Geoffrey Plank, *Rebellion and Savagery: The Jacobite Rising of 1745 and the British Empire* (Philadelphia: University of Pennsylvania Press, 2006) and Colin Calloway, *White People, Indians, and Highlanders: Tribal Peoples and Colonial Encounters in Scotland and America* (New York: Oxford University Press, 2008).

8. On the *reducciones*, see Steve J. Stern, *Peru's Indian Peoples and the Challenge of Spanish Conquest: Huamanga to 1640* (Madison: University of Wisconsin Press, 1982), 76–77.

9. On the Huguenots, see Bertrand van Ruymbeke and Randy Sparks, eds., *Memory and Identity: The Huguenots in France and the Atlantic Diaspora* (Columbia: University of South Carolina Press, 2003).

10. See, for example, Herbert S. Klein, *The Atlantic Slave Trade* (New York: Cambridge University Press, 1999) or, more evocatively, Marcus Rediker, *The Slave Ship: A Human History* (New York: Viking, 2007).

11. William Shirley to the Duke of Newcastle, Boston, July 28, 1746, in Charles Henry Lincoln, ed., *The Correspondence of William Shirley* (New York: Macmillan, 1912), 1:335.

12. On forts and imperial competition in the midcentury backcountry, see Eric Hinderaker, *Elusive Empires: Constructing Colonialism in the Ohio Valley, 1673–1800* (New York: Cambridge University Press, 1997); for a more general narrative, see Fred Anderson, *Crucible of War: The Seven Years' War and the Fate of Empire in British North America* (New York: Knopf, 2000).

13. John Clarence Webster, *Sir Brook Watson, Friend of the Loyalists, First Agent of New Brunswick in London* (Sackville, NB: Reprinted from the Argosy, Mount Allison University, 1924), 7.

14. On the 1750s, see John G. Reid, *Six Crucial Decades: Times of Change in the History of the Maritimes* (Halifax: Nimbus, 1987).

15. Jacau de Fiedmont, *The Siege of Fort Beauséjour in 1755: A Journal of the Attack on Beauséjour written by Jacau de Fiedmont*, ed. J. C. Webster (Sackville, NB: Tribune Press, 1936), 11.

16. J. C. Webster, *The Life of Thomas Pichon, "The Spy of Beauséjour"* (Halifax: PANS, 1937), 32.

17. De la Houssaye to Surlaville, May 12, 1753, and M. de Saint-Ours de Chaillon to M. des Herbiers and M. de Raymond, July 30, 1751 in Webster, *The Forts of Chignecto*, 130, 123.

18. Augustin Doucet to Madame Languedoc, August 5, 1750, Port-la-Joie, Colonial Office 42, vol. 23, 1, PRO, microfilm copy at LAC.

19. Pichon to Mme. [de Beaumont], n.d., Fonds Thomas Pichon, 12, LAC.

20. Mi'kmaq subsistence patterns prior to European contact are a source of debate among ethnohistorians and anthropologists. For a good overview, see David V. Burley, "Proto-Historic Ecological Effects of the Fur Trade on Micmac Culture in Northeastern New Brunswick," *Ethnohistory* 28 (Summer 1981), 203–16.

21. Patricia Nietfeld, "Determinants of Aboriginal Micmac Political Structure," PhD. diss., University of New Mexico, 1981, 252–53.

22. D. B. Quinn, "The Voyage of Etienne Bellenger to the Maritimes in 1583: A New Document," *Canadian Historical Review* 43 (1962): 340–41.

23. On disease among the Mi'kmaq, see William Wicken, "Encounters with Tall Sails and Tall Tales: Mi'kmaq Society, 1500–1760," Ph.D. Diss., McGill University, 1994), 190–203.

24. Pierre Biard, "Relation of 1616," in Reuben Gold Thwaites, ed., *Jesuit Relations and Allied Documents* (Cleveland: Burrows, 1896–1901), 3:89. On the Holy Gathering, see Wicken, "Encounters with Tall Sails," 134–38.

25. Saint-Ovide to Minister of the Marine, November 3, 1728, ANOM, AC, série C11B, vol. 10, f. 67.

26. Andrew Hill Clark, *Acadia: The Geography of Early Nova Scotia to 1760* (Madison: University of Wisconsin Press, 1968), 58. On the Mi'kmaq generally, see L. F. S. Upton, *Micmacs and Colonists: Indian-White Relations in the Maritimes, 1713–1867* (Vancouver: University of British Columbia Press, 1979).

27. Naomi E. S. Griffiths, *From Migrant to Acadian: A North American Border People, 1604–1755* (Montreal: McGill-Queen's University Press, 2005), 4.

28. On the Parisian hatters and the Canadian/Acadian fur trade, see Michael Sonenscher, *The Hatters of Eighteenth-Century France* (Berkeley: University of Calofirnia Press, 1987)

29. Clark, *Acadia*, 86; Griffiths, *From Migrant to Acadian*, 17.

30. See Naomi E. S. Griffiths and John G. Reid, "New Evidence from New Scotland, 1629," *William and Mary Quarterly* 49 (July 1992): 492–508.

31. "Convention avec le Sr. de Razilly pour aller recevoir la restitution du Port Royal de l'Acadie des mains des Anglais, et en mettre en possession la Compagnie de la Nouvelle France," March 27, 1632, ANOM, AC, série C11A, vol. 1, 47.

32. Griffiths, *From Migrant to Acadian*, 48.

33. "Lettre du Rev. Père Ignace, Capucin, Senlis, ce 6e Aoust 1653," in *Collection de manuscrits contenant lettres, mémoires, et autres documents historiques relatifs à la Nouvelle-France* (Québec: A. Coté, 1888), 1:137.

34. Faragher, *A Great and Noble Scheme*, 57.

35. Griffiths, *From Migrant to Acadian*, 61–63.

36. François de la Noue, *Discours politiques et militaires* (Geneva: Droz, 1967), 190; noble cahier from the diocese of Castres, cited in Davis Bitton, *The French Nobility in Crisis, 1560–1640* (Stanford, CA: Stanford University Press, 1969), 64. Generally, see Mack Holt, *The French Wars of Religion, 1562–1629* (New York: Cambridge University Press, 2005).

37. *Lettre du roy à Monseigneur d'Halincourt, avec le veritable discours de ce qui s'est passé au voyage de sa Majesté, & de la deffaicte des Rebelles de Poictou* (Lyon: Nicolas Jullieron & Claude Largot, 1622), 5.

38. J. Russell Major, *From Renaissance Monarchy to Absolute Monarchy: French Kings, Nobles, and Estates* (Baltimore: Johns Hopkins University Press, 1994), 125–26.

39. See Geneviève Massignon, "La seigneurie de Charles de Menou d'Aulnay, gouverneur de l'Acadie, 1635–1650," *Revue d'histoire de l'amérique française* 16 (1963): 469–501.

40. Sherman Bleakney, *Sods, Soil, and Spades: The Acadians at Grand Pré and Their Dykeland Legacy* (Montreal: McGill-Queen's University Press, 2004), 5.

41. Marc Lescarbot, *Histoire de la Nouvelle France* (Paris, 1611), 577.

42. "Account of the Voyage of Monsieur de Meulles to Acadie, 1685–1686," in William Inglis Morse, ed., *Acadiensia Nova (1598–1779)* (London: Bernard Quatrich, 1935), 1:107.

43. Clark, *Acadia*, 52.

44. William Lawson Grant, ed., *Voyages of Samuel de Champlain, 1604–1616* (New York, 1907), 79.

45. See Karl L. Butzer, "French Wetland Agriculture in Atlantic Canada and Its European Roots: Different Avenues to Historical Diffusion," *Annals of the Association of American Geographers* 92 (September 2002): 454.

46. Ibid., 459.

47. Ibid., 461.

48. Cited in Clark, *Acadia*, 103.

49. "Lettre du Rev. Père Ignace, Capucin, Senlis, ce 6e Aoust 1653," in *Collection de manuscrits*, 138.

50. Bleakney, *Sods, Soil, and Spades*, 46.

51. Ibid., 50–51.

52. Dièreville, cited in Butzer, "French Wetland Agriculture," 456.

53. Marc Lescarbot, *Histoire de la Nouvelle-France* (Paris, 1866), 2:530; Bleakney, *Sods, Soil, and Spades*, 24–25.

54. Bleakney, *Sods, Soil, and Spades*, 25.

55. Ibid., 25–32.

56. Butzer, "French Wetland Agriculture," 459.

57. Jean-Baptiste de le Croix Chevrières de Saint-Vallier, *Estat present de l'eglise et de la colonie françoise dans la Nouvelle-France* (Paris, 1688), 94.
58. "Sojourn of Gargas in Acadie, 1687–1688," in Morse, ed., *Acadiensia Nova*, 1:181.
59. See Con Desplanque and David Mossman, "Storm Tides of the Fundy," *Geographical Review* 98 (January 1999): 23–33.
60. Bleakney, *Sods, Soil, and Spades*, 130.
61. "Sojourn of Gargas in Acadie, 1687–1688," in Morse, ed., *Acadiensia Nova*, 1:179–80.
62. John Clarence Webster, ed., *Acadia at the End of the Seventeenth Century: Letters, Journals and Memoirs of Joseph Robineau de Villebon* (Saint John, NB: New Brunswick Museum, 1934), 132–33.
63. The geographer Matthew Hatvany explains that "tidal salt marshes have one of the highest productivity rates of any ecosystem in the world. On average, southern and northern salt marshes illustrate production rates of up to 10 tons of organic matter annually per acre, in contrast to the best hay lands in North America, which produce about 4 tons per acre." See Hatvany, "The Origins of the Acadian Aboiteau: An Environmental-Historical Geography of the Northeast," *Historical Geography* 30 (2002): 128–29.
64. These population statistics, based on a French census of Acadia taken in 1701, hint at the rapid growth of Minas relative to Port Royal, Beaubassin, and the other Acadian settlements. In 1686, Port Royal's inhabitants numbered 583, Minas's 57, and Beaubassin's 127; in 1707, the last census undertaken by the French régime listed Minas's population as 570, Beaubassin's as 270, and Minas's as 585. See Clark, *Acadia*, 123–29.
65. Sieur de Dierevile, *Relation du voyage du Port Royal de l'Acadie ou de la Nouvelle France* (Rouen, 1708), 71.
66. "Exposition de l'état ou j'ay trouvé l'Eglise du Canada," ANOM, AC, série F5A, vol. 3, 24.
67. Saint-Vallier, *Estat present de l'eglise et de la colonie françoise dans la Nouvelle-France*, 96–97.
68. George Rawlyk, *Nova Scotia's Massachusetts: A Study of Massachusetts–Nova Scotia Relations, 1630 to 1784* (Montreal: McGill-Queen's University Press, 1973), 23–24.
69. Griffiths, *From Migrant to Acadian*, 82.
70. Ibid., 83.
71. Joshua Scottow, *Old Men's Tears, for Their Own Declensions* (Boston, 1691), 44–45; *A Narrative of the Planting of the Massachusetts Bay Colony Anno 1628* (Boston, 1694), 39.
72. [Jacques de Meulles], "Mémoire concernant Beaubassin ou Chignitou et la Baye Verte," 1686, ANOM, AC, série C11D, vol. 8, f. 49.
73. Nelson himself kept a warehouse at Port Royal into the 1690s. See Richard Johnson, *John Nelson: Merchant Adventurer* (New York: Oxford University Press, 1991), 25–26; Griffiths, *From Migrant to Acadian*, 120–21; Donald F. Chard, "John Nelson," *Dictionary of Canadian Biography*, http://www.biographi.ca/index-e.html; Clément Cormier, "Jacques Bourgeois," *Dictionary of Canadian Biography*, http://www.biographi.ca/index-e.html.
74. "Mémoire concernant l'Acadie par le chevalier de Grandfontaine," 1671, ANOM, AC, série C11D, vol. 2, f. 139.
75. On this *noyau dur*, or "hard core," of Port Royal society, see Jacques Vanderlinden, *Se marier en Acadie française XVIIe et XVIIIe siècles* (Moncton, NB: Université de Moncton, 1997), 92–111.
76. Wicken, "Encounters with Tall Sails," 389.
77. Jacques Vanderlinden, *Le lieutenant civil et criminal: Mathieu de Goutin en Acadie française, 1688–1710* (Moncton, NB: Chaire d'études acadiennes, 2004), 187>; "Mémoire sur le Port Royal," 1686, ANOM, AC, série C11D, vol. 8, f. 54.
78. Pierre Chiron to Monsieur don Miguel Henry, September 8, 1713, ANOM, AC, série G3, notariat de Terre-Neuve, f. 56A.
79. Clarence J. d'Entremont, "Claude Petitpas," *Dictionary of Canadian Biography*, http://www.biographi.ca/index-e.html.
80. "Arret du conseil sur une lettre de monsieur de Saint-Ovide," November 21, 1719, ANOM, AC, série C11B. vol. 4, 64.
81. Ibid., 64v, 65.
82. D'Entremont, "Claude Petitpas."

83. Vaudreuil and Bégon to the Minister of the Marine, October 17, 1722, ANOM, AC, série F2C, vol. 3, 556v; Petitpas dossier, ANOM, AC, série E, vol. 335, 1.
84. Vaudreuil and Bégon to the Minister of the Marine, October 17, 1722, ANOM, AC, série F2C, vol. 3, 557–58.
85. Ibid., 556–556v.
86. Petitpas dossier, ANOM, AC, série E, vol. 335, 2–3.
87. Saint-Ovide to Minister of the Marine, November 3, 1728, ANOM, AC, série C11B, vol. 10, f. 68–68v.
88. On the Phips expedition, see Griffiths, *From Migrant to Acadian*, 150–60.
89. For Benjamin Church's raids in 1696 and 1704, see Geoffrey Plank, *An Unsettled Conquest: The British Campaign Against the Peoples of Acadia* (Philadelphia: University of Pennsylvania Press, 2001), 33–38.
90. Fred L. Israel, ed., *Major Peace Treaties of Modern History, 1648–1967* (New York: Chelsea House, 1967–80), 1:210.
91. Richard Philipps to Secretary Craggs, September 27, 1720, Annapolis Royal, in *SPD*, 52.
92. Rales à Vaudreuil, September 9, 1713, in *Bulletin des recherches historiques* 37 (1931): 290, cited in Wicken, "Tall Tales and Tall Sails," 389.
93. Habitans de Port Royal to Vaudreuil, November 13, 1710, ANOM, AC, série C11D, vol. 7, 98–99.
94. Griffiths, *From Migrant to Acadian*, 263.
95. *NSA III*, 63.
96. Barry Moody, "Making a British Nova Scotia," in John G. Reid et al., *The "Conquest" of Acadia, 1710: Imperial, Colonial, and Aboriginal Constructions* (Toronto: University of Toronto Press, 2004), 129.
97. Acadians of Port Royal, Mines, Beaubassin to Saint-Ovide, 1718, in Henri-Raymond Casgrain, ed., *Collection de documents inédits sur le Canada et l'Amérique publiés par le Canada-Français* (Québec: L. J. Demers & Frère, 1888–90), 1:128.
98. *NSA III*, 130.
99. Ibid., 47, 100–101. On Robichaud, see Plank, *An Unsettled Conquest*, 94–96.
100. Paul Mascarene, "Description of Nova Scotia," in *SPD*, 46.
101. [William Douglass], *A Discourse Concerning the Currencies of the British Plantations in America* (Boston, 1740), 55; cited in T. H. Breen, *The Marketplace of Revolution: How Consumer Politics Shaped American Independence* (New York: Oxford University Press, 2004), 75.
102. *NSA II*, 24–25.
103. [Thomas Pichon], "Réprésentations des habitants de l'Acadie, 40 ans après le traité d'Utrecht soit 1753," in Fonds Thomas Pichon, 240, LAC.
104. *NSA III*, 2.
105. Ibid., 239–40.
106. *NSA II*, 205–6.
107. Ibid., 208.
108. Ibid., 214–15.
109. Ibid., 55–56.
110. Paul Mascarene, "Description of Nova Scotia," *SPD*, 46.
111. Thomas Garden Barnes, "'The Dayly Cry for Justice': The Juridical Failure of the Annapolis Royal Regime, 1713–1749," in Philip Girard and Jim Phillips, eds., *Essays in the History of Canadian Law*, vol. III: *Nova Scotia* (Toronto: University of Toronto Press, 1990), 18; *NSA II*, 177–78.
112. *NSA III*, 303–4.
113. Council Minutes, September 19, 1734, in ibid., 305. Spelling modernized.
114. *NSA III*, 173.
115. *The Trials of Five Persons for Piracy, Felony and Robbery* (Boston, 1726), 5.
116. Charles Bruce Fergusson, ed., *Nova Scotia Archives IV: Minutes of His Majesty's Council at Annapolis Royal, 1736–1749* (Halifax: PANS, 1967), 14–17.
117. Sieur l'Hermitte to M. de la Ronde, July 12, 1714, Louisbourg, ANOM, AC, série C11B, vol. 1, 114.

118. "Mémoire sur les habitans de Plaisance et de l'Acadie," n.d., AMAE, Correspondance Poli- tique, Angleterre, v. 284, 235; on this episode, see especially Plank, *Unsettled Conquest*, 62.
119. D. C. Harvey, *The French Régime in Prince Edward Island* (New Haven: Yale University Press, 1926), 35.
120. Gotteville de Belile, "Description de l'île Saint-Jean," January 28 1721, ANOM, AC, série C11A, vol. 43, 134–36.
121. Saint-Ovide to Minister, December 18, 1725, Ile Royale, ANOM, AC, série, C11B, vol. 7, 201v.
122. Saint-Ovide to Minister, November 10, 1727, Ile Royale, ANOM, AC, série C11B, vol. 9, 52v.
123. Saint-Ovide to Minister, November 3, 1728, Ile Royale, ANOM, AC, série C11B, vol. 10, 80.
124. Duquesne to Machault, October 13, 1754, in *DRCHNY*, 264.
125. Habitans de Mines to de Gannes, October 13, 1744, ANOM, AC, série C11D, vol. 8, 114.
126. Mascarene to M. de St. Poncy, April 22, 1739, Annapolis Royal, Papers of Paul Mascarene of Nova Scotia, 1728–1745, in Sparks Manuscripts, MS Am 813F, HL.
127. [Paul Mascarene], "Representation of the State of His Majesties Province of Nova Scotia and Fort and Garrison of Annapolis Royal," November 8, 1745, in *NSA IV*, 84; Mascarene to Ladeveze, November 1752, in Gay Papers, vol. 1, 88, MHS.
128. *NSA IV*, 80–84.
129. Ibid., 84.
130. *A copy of a letter from Quebeck in Canada, to a Pr——e M——e in France, dated October 11, 1747* (Boston, 1747), 1.
131. Ibid., 1.
132. *The preliminaries productive of a premunire [sic]: or, Old England caught in a trap* (London, 1748), 18.
133. Mascarene to Ladeveze, November 1752, Gay Papers, vol. 1, 88, MHS; on Cornwallis, the Scots uprising, and Nova Scotia, see Plank, *Rebellion and Savagery*.
134. Otis Little, *The State of Trade in the Northern Colonies Considered; with an Account of their Produce, and a particular Description of Nova Scotia* (Boston, 1749), 33; Clark, *Acadia*, 357.
135. *Boston Gazette*, January 16, 1750, August 22, 1749; "Satire on Halifax in Nova Scotia," Du Simitière Papers 1411.Q.15.a, LCP. Many thanks to Yvie Fabella for leading me to this source.
136. "Lettre lue au roi," August 29, 1749, ANOM, AC, série C11A, vol. 94, 77.
137. Beauharnois and Hocquart to Maurepas, in *DRCHNY*, 3.
138. "Lettre lue au roi," August 29, 1749, ANOM, AC, série C11A, vol. 94, 77.
139. Fonds Thomas Pichon, 194–96, LAC.
140. Mascarene to Davidson, in Gay Papers, vol. 5, 122, MHS.
141. Fonds Thomas Pichon, 194, LAC.
142. Webster, *Forts of Chignecto*, 104–5.
143. Earl of Albemarle to M. Puysieulx, July 7, 1750, Compiègne, in *DRCHNY*, 216; Puysieulx to Earl of Albemarle, July 15, 1750, in ibid., 218.
144. On this boundary dispute, see especially *The Memorials of the English and French Commis- saries Concerning the Limits of Nova Scotia or Acadia* (London, 1755).
145. Harvey, *French Regime*, 139, 166.
146. Le Loutre, "Autobiography," 46–47.
147. Ibid., 46.
148. Genesis 41:46–57.
149. Rousseau de Villejoin, "Projet d'un établissement dans LaBrador," July 1751, Fonds Thomas Pichon, 211, LAC.
150. Pichon to [Governor-General], February 1, 1754, in Fonds Thomas Pichon, 293–95, LAC.
151. Pichon to Rouillé, n.d., Fonds Thomas Pichon, 179–93, LAC.
152. Faragher, *A Great and Noble Scheme*, 472.
153. Ibid., 288, 290, 328.
154. *Correspondence of William Shirley*, 1:137, 220.
155. Lawrence to Monckton, July 31, 1755, in *SPD*, 267–69.

156. *The Journal of Abijah Willard, 1755–1758*, ed. J. C. Webster (St. John, NB, 1930), 28, 34–35, 41–42.

157. J. C. Webster, *Journals of Beauséjour* (Sackville, NB: Tribune Press, 1937), 25.

158. Lotbinière to Minister, November 2, 1756, in *DRCHNY*, 496.

159. Gorham to Boscawen, December 6, 1758, Halifax, Chatham Papers, vol. 6, 144–50, LAC.

160. "Deuxième suite de l'extrait de la lettre de M. l'évêque de Québec à l'abbé de l'Isle-Dieu," October 30, 1757, ANOM, AC, série C11A, vol. 102, 303.

Chapter 2: The Pariahs

1. Connecticut Archives, War, 1675–1774, series 1, vol. 6, document 179, Connecticut State Library, Hartford CT. I am very grateful to the staff of the Acadian History Museum in West Pubnico, Nova Scotia, for leading me to this document.

2. For the Acadians' removal from Woodbury to New Milford and Litchfield, see Connecticut Archives, War, 1675–1774, series 1, vol. 6, document 180; for Paul Landry's petition to the Connecticut General Assembly, see Connecticut Archives, War, 1675–1774, series 1, vol. 6, document 236.

3. John Williams, *The Redeemed Captive Returning to Zion* (Boston, 1707), title page, 35.

4. On Eunice Williams in Massachusetts and Connecticut, see John Demos, *The Unredeemed Captive: A Family Story from Early America* (New York: Vintage, 1995), 201–2.

5. On Edwards's influence on the transatlantic revivals of the 1730s and 1740s, see Avihu Zakai, "Jonathan Edwards, the Enlightenment, and the Formation of Protestant Tradition in America," in Elizabeth Mancke and Carole Shammas, *The Creation of the British Atlantic World* (Baltimore: Johns Hopkins University Press, 2005), 186–87.

6. Jonathan Edwards, *The Justice of God in the Damnation of Sinners* (Boston, 1773), 23.

7. Lawrence to Provincial Governors, August 11, 1755, in *Collections of the Nova Scotia Historical Society* 3 (1883): 82.

8. Corinne LaPlante, "Bastarache, dit Basque, Michel," *Dictionary of Canadian Biography*, http://www.biographi.ca/index-e.html; John Mack Faragher, *A Great and Noble Scheme: The Tragic Story of the Expulsion of the French Acadians from Their American Homeland* (New York: W. W. Norton, 2005), 388.

9. *Boston Gazette*, March 1, 1756.

10. Joseph Leblanc to Charles Leblanc, September 21, 1757, Liverpool, Admiralty 97/122, Medical Department In-Letters (Miscellaneous), PRO, copy at LAC.

11. Geoffrey Plank, *An Unsettled Conquest: The British Campaign Against the Peoples of Acadia* (Philadelphia: University of Pennsylvania Press, 2001), 141; Carl A. Brasseaux, *The Founding of New Acadia: The Beginnings of Acadian Life in Louisiana, 1764–1803* (Baton Rouge: Louisiana State University Press, 1987), 47.

12. Naomi E. S. Griffiths, *From Migrant to Acadian: A North American Border People, 1604–1755* (Montreal: McGill-Queen's University Press, 2005), 464.

13. *Considerations on the exchange of seamen, prisoners of war* (London, 1758), 13–15.

14. *Proceedings of the Committee appointed to manage the contributions begun at London . . . for cloathing French prisoners of war* (London, 1760); George Whitefield, *A Short Address, to Persons of all Denominations, Occasioned by the Alarm of an Intended Invasion* (Boston, 1756), 12.

15. George Whitefield, *A Short Address*, 11. For rising anti-French sentiment in mid-century New England, see Ann M. Little, *Abraham in Arms: War and Gender in Colonial New England* (Philadelphia: University of Pennsylvania Press, 2006), 166–204.

16. *Boston Evening-Post*, October 13, 1755.

17. *Boston Gazette*, August 23, 1756.

18. Charles Carroll, *Dear Papa, Dear Charlie: The Papers of Charles Carroll of Carrollton, 1748–1782*, ed. Ronald Hoffman and Sally Mason (Chapel Hill, NC: University of North Carolina Press, 2001), 1:30, 104, 143.

19. *The Papers of Henry Laurens*, vol. 2: *November 1, 1755—December 31, 1758*, ed. Philip M. Hamer and George C. Rogers (Columbia: University of South Carolina Press, 1970), 61, 76. Rice prices had fallen to thirty shillings per hundredweight by January 1756, down from

eighty shillings per hundredweight two years earlier. See David R. Chestnutt, *South Carolina's Expansion into Colonial Georgia, 1720–1765* (New York: Garland, 1989), 232.

20. *Papers of Henry Laurens*, 2:77.
21. Ibid., 2:105.
22. Ibid., 2:112.
23. Ibid., 2:157.
24. Ibid., 2:143.
25. Glen to Commons House, January 15, 1756, *JCHA* vol. 14, 31.
26. For population figures, see Peter Coclanis, *The Shadow of a Dream: Economic Life and Death in the South Carolina Low Country, 1670–1920* (New York: Oxford University Press, 1989), 171–72. I estimate Charleston's midcentury population at five thousand based on Coclanis's data from the 1730s and the 1770s. Coclanis writes, "The black population in Charleston was roughly equal to the permanent white population of the town through much of the eighteenth century."
27. John Reynolds to Board of Trade, April 17, 1758, *CRSG*, vol. 28, pt. 1, 138. On Savannah's proportions, see Edward J. Cashin, *Governor Henry Ellis and the Transformation of British North America* (Athens: University of Georgia Press, 1994), 88.
28. Walter L. Robbins and John Tobler, "John Tobler's Description of South Carolina (1753)," *South Carolina Historical Magazine* 71 (July 1970): 161.
29. Reynolds to Board of Trade, April 17, 1758, *CRSG*, vol. 28, pt. 1, 143.
30. Faragher, *A Great and Noble Scheme*, 383–84.
31. See Gregory E. Dowd, "The Panic of 1751: The Significance of Rumor on the South Carolina-Cherokee Frontier," *William and Mary Quarterly* 53 (July 1996): 547.
32. *South Carolina Gazette*, June 24, 1751.
33. *South Carolina Gazette*, April 29 and June 24, 1751.
34. See *South Carolina Gazette*, October 23, 1751, for Indians using Acadian dikes as cover. Silvanus Conant, *The Art of War, the Gift of GOD* (Boston, 1759), 5; cited in Little, *Abraham in Arms*, 184.
35. See *JCHA*, vol. 14, 18–20.
36. Chapman J. Milling, *Exile Without an End* (Columbia, SC: Bostick and Thornley, 1943), 25; see also Clarence J. d'Entremont, "Brossard (Broussard), *dit* Beausoleil, Joseph," *Dictionary of Canadian Biography*, http://www.biographi.ca/index-e.html.
37. James H. Merrell, "'Their Very Bones Shall Fight': The Catawba-Iroquois Wars," in James H. Merrell and Daniel K. Richter, eds., *Beyond the Covenant Chain: The Iroquois and their Neighbors in Indian North America, 1600–1800* (Syracuse, NY: Syracuse University Press, 1987), 115.
38. Tom Hatley, *The Dividing Paths: Cherokees and South Carolinians Through the Era of Revolutions* (New York: Oxford University Press, 1993), 72.
39. Merrell, "Their Very Bones Shall Fight," 125.
40. Ibid., 130.
41. See Daniel K. Richter, *Facing East from Indian Country: A Native History of North America* (Cambridge, MA: Harvard University Press, 2001), 169.
42. *CRSG*, vol. 7, 173.
43. David H. Corkran, *The Creek Frontier, 1540–1783* (Norman: University of Oklahoma Press, 1967), 167.
44. Julie Ann Sweet, *Negotiating for Georgia: British-Creek Relations in the Trustee Era, 1733–1752* (Athens: University of Georgia Press, 2005), 162–63.
45. *DRIA*, vol. II, 85.
46. Ibid., vol. I, 211. For a remarkable interpretation of the Acorn Whistler affair, see Joshua Piker, "Lying Together: The Imperial Implications of Cross-Cultural Untruths," *American Historical Review* 116 (October 2011): 964–86.
47. Ibid., vol. I, 453.
48. Hatley, *The Dividing Paths*, 98.
49. *DRIA*, vol. I, 525.
50. Hatley, *The Dividing Paths*, 72.
51. *DRIA*, vol. II, 68.

52. Ibid., vol. II, 79.

53. *JCHA*, vol. 14, 11.

54. *JCHA*, vol. 14, 22, 33.

55. *JCHA*, vol. 14, 10.

56. Ruth Allison Hudnut and Hayes Baker-Crothers, "Acadian Transients in South Carolina," *American Historical Review* 43 (April 1938): 502.

57. *South Carolina Gazette*, February 12, 1756.

58. *JCHA*, vol. 14, 82.

59. Ibid, vol. 14, 16–17.

60. *New York Mercury*, April 26, 1756.

61. *JCHA.*, vol. 14, 39.

62. Ibid,. vol. 14, 42, 40.

63. Ibid,. vol. 14, 57–60. Deriding the interpreter, identified only as "Monsieur St. Martin," as a "little man [who] thinks it criminal in [the Acadians] to breathe a sigh," Glen declared himself "apt to think that if Monsieur St. Martin had been in that Person's place, his Groans wou'd have been a little louder."

64. Ibid., vol. 14, 55–56.

65. CRSG, vol. 7, 136–42.

66. Plank, *Unsettled Conquest*, 113.

67. Jonquière to Minister, May 1, 1751, ANOM, AC, série F3, vol. 50, 467.

68. Plank, *Unsettled Conquest*, 143; J. C. Webster, *Journals of Beauséjour* (Sackville, NB: Tribune Press, 1937), 19.

69. CRSG, vol. 28, pt. 1, 143.

70. On Vigneau, see especially Plank, *Unsettled Conquest*, 152–57.

71. CRSG, vol. 18, 188–91.

72. Letter to the Rev. Dr. Hales, F.R.S., from Captain Henry Ellis, F.R.S., dated January 7, 1750–51 at Cape Monte, Africa, Ship Earl of Halifax," *Philosophical Transactions* 47 (1752): 213. My thanks to Michael Guenther for this source on Ellis.

73. Henry Ellis, *Considerations on the Great Advantages which would arise from the Discovery of the North West Passage* (London: 1750, 3; Ellis, *A voyage to Hudson's-Bay, by the Dobbs Galley and California, in the years 1746 and 1747, for discovering a north-west passage* (Dublin, 1749), vi.

74. Harold E. Davis, *The Fledgling Province: Social and Cultural Life in Colonial Georgia, 1733–1776* (Chapel Hill: University of North Carolina Press, 1976), 98.

75. Arthur Dobbs, *An Essay on the Trade and Improvement of Ireland* (Dublin, 1729), 1:16.

76. CRSG, vol. 28, pt. 1, 7.

77. CRSG, vol. 7, 506.

78. Edward J. Cashin, *Governor Henry Ellis and the Transformation of British North America* (Athens: University of Georgia Press, 1994), 99.

79. CRSG, vol. 13, 492–93.

80. Dinwiddie to the Earl of Halifax, November 15, 1755, in R. A. Brock, ed., *The Official Records of Robert Dinwiddie* (Richmond: Virginia Historical Society, 1884), 2:273. I have modernized Dinwiddie's spelling.

81. Dinwiddie to the Earl of Granville, November 15, 1755, in ibid., 275.

82. Dinwiddie to Sir Thomas Robinson, November 24, 1755, in ibid., 283.

83. Dinwiddie to Sir Thomas Robinson, December 24, 1755, in ibid., 306.

84. Dinwiddie to Henry Fox, May 10, 1756, in ibid., 408.

85. Dinwiddie to the Lords of Trade, November 15, 1755, in ibid., 268.

86. See Dinwiddie to Charles Lawrence, August 17, 1756, in ibid, 479.

87. Dinwiddie to Henry Fox, November 9, 1756, in ibid., 537–38.

88. Honoré LeBlanc to Commissioner of Sick and Hurt Board, September 20, 1757, in Admiralty 97:122, PRO, copy at LAC.

89. Claude Pitré to Commissioner of Sick and Hurt Board, May 27, 1757, in Admiralty Papers 97:121, PRO, copy at LAC. Pitré's affection for the British government does not seem to have been a passing fancy of 1755. In 1744, with Nova Scotia in the throes of King George's War, Pitré informed the garrison government at Annapolis Royal of the illegal movement of

black cattle and sheep from the village of Mines to Louisbourg by French partisans Joseph Leblanc *dit* le Maigre and Joseph Dugas; see Charles Bruce Ferguson, ed., *Nova Scotia Archives IV, Minutes of His Majesty's Council at Annapolis Royal, 1736–1749* (Halifax: Public Archives of Nova Scotia, 1967), 52.

90. Edward Lloyd to James Hollyday, December 9, 1755, cited in William D. Hoyt Jr., "A Contemporary View of the Acadian Arrival in Maryland, 1755," *William and Mary Quarterly* 5, no. 4 (October 1948): 575.

91. J. Thomas Scharf, *A History of Maryland from the Earliest Period to the Present Day* (Hatboro, PA: Tradition Press, 1967), 476.

92. Belcher to Morris, November 25, 1755, Elizabethtown, NJ, *PA*, series I, vol. 2, 513–14.

93. Morris to Jonathan Belcher, November 22, 1755, Philadelphia, *PA*, series I, vol. 2, 509.

94. Otis Little, *The State of Trade in the Northern Colonies Considered; with an Account of their Produce, and a particular Description of Nova Scotia* (Boston, 1749), 25s.

95. Morris to Governor Sharpe, January 5, 1756, in *Minutes of the Provincial Council of Pennsylvania, from the Organization to the Termination of the Proprietary Government* (Harrisburg, PA, 1852), 7:14–15.

96. Jean-Baptiste Galerne, *The relation of the French Neutrals* (Philadelphia, 1756), 1; see also *PA*, series 1, vol. 3, 565–68.

97. Acadians of Pennsylvania to George II, cited in Robert Walsh, *An Appeal from the Judgments of Great Britain respecting the United States of America* (New York: Negro Universities Press, 1969), 437–42.

98. *The lawfulness of defensive war* (Philadelphia, 1756), 3.

99. Ibid., 16.

100. *An Address to those Quakers, who perversely refused to pay any regard to the late provincial fast* (Philadelphia, 1756), 1.

101. For a brief summary, see Fred Anderson, *Crucible of War: The Seven Years' War and the Fate of Empire in British North America* (New York: Knopf, 2000), 160–62.

102. Anthony Benezet, *Observations on the inslaving, importing, and purchasing of Negroes* (Germantown, PA, 1759), 1, 10.

103. Anthony Benezet, *Thoughts on the nature of war, and its repugnancy to the Christian life* (Philadelphia, 1766), 9. This was the published version of a sermon given by Benezet in 1759. On Benezet, see especially Maurice Jackson, *Let This Voice Be Heard: Anthony Benezet, Father of Atlantic Abolitionism* (Philadelphia: University of Pennsylvania Press, 2009).

104. Petition of Alexis Tibaudeau et al., August 27, 1756, in *PA*, series 8, vol. 5, 4293–95.

105. See petition of Pierre Doucet et al., September 2, 1756, in *PA*, vol. 7, 239–40; for Denny's response, see 240–41.

106. *JCHA*, vol. 14, 17.

107. Petition of Oliver Tibaudat et al. to the Assembly of Pennsylvania, February 8, 1757, in *PA*, series 8, vol. 6, 4509–10.

108. Ibid., 4510–12.

109. Cited in Anderson, *Crucible of War*, 210.

110. Loudon to William Pitt, April 25, 1757, Loudon Papers, LO 3467, Huntington Library, San Marino, CA.

111. *Minutes of the Provincial Council of Pennsylvania*, 7:446.

112. See Christopher Hodson, "Exile on Spruce Street: An Acadian History," *William and Mary Quarterly* 67, no. 2 (April 2010): 249–78.

113. William Griffitts to Richard Peters, January 22, 1757, in *PA*, series 1, vol. 3, 92–93. The provincial government decided that "that the Governor, since the late Law has passed requiring the Overseers of the Poor to take care and maintain these Neutrals, cannot concern himself in this Matter, or give any Directions therein." See Minutes of the Provincial Council, January 24, 1757, in *PA*, vol. 7, 393.

114. Hodson, "Exile on Spruce Street," 269.

115. "Extracts From the Diplomatic Correspondence of Conrad Alexander Gérard, First Minister Plenipotentiary to the United States, July, 1778 to October, 1779," *Records of the American Catholic Historical Society* 31 (1920): 228.

116. Paul Loiron, Joseph Bourg, Bruneau Trahan, Pierre Landry to Nivernais, June 20, 1763, Philadelphia, AMAE, Correspondence Politique, Angleterre, vol. 450, 415.

117. *Boston Gazette,* April 12, 1756.

118. *A Specimen of the Unrelenting Cruelty of Papists in France* (Boston, 1756), 3, 10.

119. Massachusetts House of Representatives, April 20, 1756, in Placide Gaudet, ed., *Rapport concernant les archives canadiennes pour l'année 1905* (Ottawa: National Archives of Canada, 1906), 145; see also Massachusetts Archives, Number 25, French Neutrals, vol. 23, 1755–1758, n.p., MSA.

120. See Lawrence Henry Gipson, *The Great War for Empire: The Years of Defeat, 1754–1757,* vol. 6 of *The British Empire Before the American Revolution* (New York: Knopf, 1942), 327.

121. Petition of Amot Fuller et al., December 20, 1757, in Gaudet, *Rapport,* 174–75.

122. Massachusetts Archives, Number 25, French Neutrals, vol. 23, 1755–1758, n.p., MSA.

123. "An account of the charge the Town of Newton," May 31, 1756, Massachusetts Archives, Number 25, French Neutrals, vol. 23, 1755–1758, n.p., MSA.

124. Daniel Vickers, *Farmers and Fishermen: Two Centuries of Work in Essex County, Massachusetts, 1630–1850* (Chapel Hill: University of North Carolina Press, 1994), 219.

125. *An Address to Farmers,* Salem, Massachusetts, 1796, cited in Vickers, *Farmers and Fishermen,* p. 238.

126. *A Protestant's Resolution: shewing his reasons why he will not be a papist* (Boston, 1746), 27–28, 26.

127. Petition of Claude Bourgeois, in Gaudet, *Rapport,* 161.

128. Petition of Charles and Nicholas Breau, in ibid., 160–61.

129. Petition of Lawrence Mieuse, January 1757, in ibid., 173–74.

130. Petition of Augustin Hebert, October 7, 1756, in ibid., 64.

131. Petition of Francis Miuse, November 18, 1757, in ibid., 172.>

132. Petition of John Labardor, December 26, 1757, in ibid., 175.

133. Petition of Jacques LeBlanc, n.d., in ibid., 177.

134. Petition of Jacques Mireau and Joseph D'Entremont, n.d., in ibid., 162.

135. Petition of Joseph Mitchell, March 30, 1756, in ibid., 158–59.

136. Petition of Belloni Melançon, February, 1757, in ibid., 166–67.

137. Selectmen of Marblehead to Spencer Phips, October 6, 1756, Massachusetts Archives, Number 25, French Neutrals, vol. 23, 1755–1758, n.p., MSA.

138. Council Minutes, February 24, 1757, in Gaudet, *Rapport,* 167.

139. Ebenezer Parkman, *Reformers and Intercessors sought by GOD: Who grieves, when they are hard to be found* (Boston: S. Kneeland, 1757), 15.

140. Entry for October 16, 1756, Diary of Ebenezer Parkman, AAS. I have modernized some of Parkman's spelling and punctuation.

141. Ibid., entry for October 19, 1756. Other sources from Westborough describe the family as follows: "Simon Le Blank his Wife and two sons and two daughters the old man sixty eight and his wife sixty nine. Both very infirm and not able to support them selfs." See Massachusetts Archives, number 26, French Neutrals, vol. 24, 1758–1769.

142. Parkman was pleased, and perhaps a bit taken aback, that Leblanc's wife managed to prepare tea "properly." See Parkman Journal, entry for December 22, 1756.

143. Ibid., entry for November 27, 1756.

144. Ibid., entry for December 10, 1756.

145. Ibid., entry for December 22, 1756.

146. Ibid., entry for January 6, 1757.

147. Ibid., entry for January 26, 1757.

148. Ibid., entry for December 22, 1757.

149. Ibid., entry for January 26, 1757.

150. See Gaudet, *Rapport,* 172.

151. Parkman Journal, entries for December 27, 1757, and April 27, 1758.

152. Ibid., entry for January 21, 1757; Joel 2:1, 6, 20.

153. Parkman Journal, entries for January 26, April 18, April 19, May 18, June 8, June 15, July 22, and August 29, 1757.

154. Ibid., entries for November 16 and December 1, 1757.

155. Ibid., entries for September 4, 1758, and March 1, 1759.
156. Parkman, *Reformers and Intercessors*, 42.
157. Francis Parkman, *A Half-Century of Conflict: France and England in North America* (Boston: Little, Brown, 1933), 173–74,.
158. Parkman Journal, entry for January 12, 1757.
159. Ibid., entries for May 18 and May 31, 1757.

Chapter 3: The Tropics

1. Colin Jones, *The Great Nation: France from Louis XV to Napoleon* (New York: Penguin, 2003), 236.
2. Edmond-Jean-François Barbier, *Journal historique et anecdotique du règne de Louis XV* (Paris, 1856), 4:447; Jones, *Great Nation*, 236.
3. Jean-Baptiste-Christophe Fusée Aublet, *Histoire des plantes de la Guiane françoise, rangees suivant la méthode sexuelle* (Paris, 1775), 1:i–v.
4. Ibid., vi, x–xi; on Malagasy slaves on Ile de France, see Megan Vaughan, *Creating the Creole Island: Slavery in Eighteenth-Century Mauritius* (Durham, NC: Duke University Press, 2005), 46, 104–5. The Malagasy had a double-edged reputation as the most "advanced" Africans and as those most likely to rebel against masters, become maroons, and commit infanticide.
5. On this episode, in which Aublet argued that Poivre had misled authorities by misidentifying "true nutmeg," see E. D. Spary, "Of Nutmegs and Botanists: The Colonial Cultivation of Botanical Identity," in Londa Schiebinger and Claudia Swan, eds., *Colonial Botany: Science, Commerce, and Politics* (Philadelphia: University of Pennsylvania Press, 2004), 187–203.
6. This colony was known by multiple names. Strictly speaking, Cayenne referred to an small, fortified island just off the South American mainland, but seventeenth- and eighteenth-century Frenchmen often used that name to refer to the entire colony, which (theoretically) stretched from the Brazilian border in the south to Dutch Surinam in the north, reaching deep into the South American interior. The colony was also called *la France équinoxiale* or Guiana, and is now the *département* known as French Guiana.
7. For Aublet's role, see Marion F. Godfroy-Tayart de Borms, "La guerre de sept ans et ses conséquences atlantiques: Kourou ou l'apparition d'un nouveau système colonial," *French Historical Studies* 32 (April 2009): 180.
8. Aublet, *Histoire des plantes*, 1:xvii.
9. On bioprospecting and empire, see Londa Schiebinger, *Plants and Empire: Colonial Bioprospecting in the Atlantic World* (Cambridge, MA: Harvard University Press, 2004), 10–11. For Aublet's plan, see "Réponse à la lettre du Sr. Aublet dattée de Cayenne du 16 Mars 1763," n.d., ANOM, AC, série C14, régistre 26, 349.
10. Henry Pouillard, "Sommaire," 1761, ANOM, AC, série F3 21, f. 260.
11. Charles Becker and Victor Martin, "Mémoires d'Adanson sur le Sénégal et l'île de Gorée," *Bulletin d'IFAN* 42 (1980): 727, 760.
12. Aublet, *Histoire des plantes*, 2:111, 117, 119–20.
13. Schiebinger, *Plants and Empire*, 55, 139.
14. "Voyage fait par le Sieur Aublet de Cayenne à la crique Galibi," ANOM, AC, série C14, régistre 27, 213.
15. Aublet to Accaron, July 18, 1763, ANOM, AC, série C14, carton 88, no. 7.
16. D'Orvilliers and Morisse to Accaron, March 27, 1763, ANOM, AC, série C14, régistre 26, 149.
17. "Réponse à la lettre du Sr. Aublet dattée de Cayenne du 16 Mars 1763," n.d., ANOM, AC, série C14, régistre 26, 349.
18. For recent scholarship on the Kourou colony, see Emma Rothschild, "A Horrible Tragedy in the French Atlantic," *Past and Present* 192 (Spring 2006): 67–108; Christopher Hodson, "'A Bondage So Harsh': Acadian Labor in the French Caribbean, 1763–1766," *Early American Studies* 5 (Spring 2007): 95–131; Godfroy-Tayart de Borms, "La guerre de Sept ans et ses consequences atlantiques," 167–92. See also David M. Epstein, "The Kourou Expedition to Guiana: The Genesis of a Black Legend," *Boletin de Estudios Latonoamericanos y del*

Caribe 37 (December 1984): 85–97; Jacques Michel, *La Guyane sous l'Ancien Régime: Le désastre Kourou et ses scandaleuses suites judiciaries* (Paris: Harmattan, 1989).

19. Henry Pouillard, "Sommaire," 1761, ANOM, AC, série F3, vol. 21, f. 260.
20. See E. P. Panagopoulos, *New Smyrna: An Eighteenth-Century Greek Odyssey* (Gainesville: University of Florida Press, 1966).
21. On Russia, see Roger Bartlett, *Human Capital: The Settlement of Foreigners in Russia, 1762–1804* (New York: Cambridge University Press, 1979); on the Banat, see Dominic G. Kosary, *A History of Hungary* (New York: Arno Press, 1971), 150–55.
22. Naomi E. S. Griffiths, "Acadians in Exile: The Experiences of the Acadians in British Seaports," *Acadiensis* 4 (1974): 74.
23. [Duc de Nivernais], "Mémoire sur les Acadiens," AMAE, Correspondance Politique, Angleterre, vol. 449, 71–72, 75.
24. "Porté au Roy," January 15, 1757, ANOM, AC, série C11A, vol. 102, 229.
25. Vaudreuil to Minister, April 19, 1757, Montréal, ANOM, AC, série C11A, vol. 102, 46.
26. Amherst to Belcher, April 28, 1761, New York, Colonial Office 5, 61, 138, PRO, copy at LAC.
27. Abbé Maillard to Sieur Leblanc, December 31, 1759, ANOM, AC, série C11A, vol. 105, 140.
28. Jacques Girard to the marquis de Pérusse, December 13, 1774, ADV, série J, dépôt 22, liasse 124.
29. Vaudreuil to Minister, April 18, 175, ANOM, AC, série C11A, vol. 102, 10.
30. Andrew Rollo to Boscawen, October 10, 1758, Fort Amherst, Chatham Papers, vol. 6, 95, LAC.
31. On the 1758 deportation from Ile Saint-Jean, see especially Earle Lockerby, "The Deportation of the Acadians from Ile St.-Jean, 1758," *Acadiensis* 27 (Spring 1998): 45–94.
32. Ibid., 62–63.
33. Tobias Smollett, *Travels Through France and Italy*, ed. Frank Felsenstein (New York: Oxford University Press, 1979), 40.
34. See La Rochette to Nivernois, May 18, 1763, Southampton, in Fonds Monseigneur de la Rochette, vol. 1, 388, LAC.
35. The essential source on Acadians in France is Jean-François Mouhot, *Les réfugiés Acadiens en France, 1758–1785: L'impossible réintégration?* (Montréal: Septentrion, 2009).
36. *Plan for the Abolition of Slavery in the West Indies* (London, 1772), 4; Choiseul to Nivernais, Versailles, March 11, 1763, ANOM, AC, série B, vol. 117, 183.
37. "Mémoire touchant la religion et les moeurs de la colonie de Cayenne," 1687, ANOM, AC, série F3, vol. 21, 65–65v.
38. Régis Burrone[t?] to Minister, "Cayenne de 6 mars 1739," ANOM, AC, série F3, vol. 21, 186–88.
39. Pierre Barrère, *Nouvelle relation de la France équinoxiale* (Paris, 1743), 7, 39, 46, 70.
40. D'Orvilliers to Minister, February 2, 1750, ANOM, AC, F3, vol. 21, n.p.
41. Antoine-Philippe Lemoyne to Minister, January 19, 1756, Cayenne, ANOM, AC, série C14, régistre 24, 122.
42. Henry Pouillard, "Sommaire," 1761, ANOM, AC, série F3, vol. 21, f. 263v.
43. Copy of anonymous correspondence, 1726, ANOM, AC, F3, vol. 22, 130.
44. Régis Burrone[t?] to Minister, May 14, 1740, ANOM, AC, F3, vol. 22, 147–147v.
45. Henry Pouillard, "Sommaire," 1761, ANOM, AC, série F3, vol. 21, f. 263v.
46. Cited in Gérard Prost and Jacqueline Zonzon, eds., *Histoire de la Guyane* (Cayenne, 1990), 2:n.p.
47. D'Orvilliers to Minister, March 28, 1753, ANOM, AC, série F3, vol. 95, n.p.
48. D'Orvilliers to Minister, Jaunary 29, 1756, ANOM, AC, série F3, vol. 95, n.p.
49. Lemoyne to Minister, March 20, 1759, ANOM, AC, série C14, régistre 24, 170v–171.
50. Marie Polderman, *La Guyane Française, 1676–1763: Mise en place et evolution de la société coloniale, tensions et métissage* (Petit-Bourg: Ibis Rouge, 2004), 154.
51. Lemoyne to Minister, March 20, 1759, ANOM, AC, série C14, régistre 24, 171.
52. Elizabeth Fox-Genovese, *The Origins of Physiocracy: Economic Revolution and Social Order in Eighteenth-Century France* (Ithaca: Cornell University Press, 1976), 9.

53. Pierre-Samuel Dupont de Nemours, *La Physiocratie; ou constitution naturelle du gouvernement le plus avantageux au genre humain* (Leyde, 1768), 107.

54. Dupont de Nemours, *De l'origine et progrès d'une science nouvelle*, 7; *Ephémérides du Citoyen, ou chronique de l'esprit nationale* (Paris), tome VI (1768), 207.

55. Gail Bossenga, "Status, Corps, and Monarchy: Roots of Modern Citizenship in the Old Regime," in Robert M. Schwartz and Robert A. Schneider, eds., *Tocqueville and Beyond: Essays on the Old Regime in Honor of David D. Bien* (Newark: University of Delaware Press, 2003), 141.

56. *Ephémérides du Citoyen*, tome V (1766), 146.

57. Victor Riqueti, Marquis de Mirabeau, *L'ami des hommes, ou traité de la population* (Paris, 1883), 551.

58. Charles-Louis de Secondat, Comte de Montesquieu, *Lettres Persanes* (Paris, 1721); see also Carol Blum, *Strength in Numbers: Population, Reproduction, and Power in Eighteenth-Century France* (Baltimore: Johns Hopkins University Press, 2002).

59. Mirabeau, *L'ami des hommes*, 552–53, 551.

60. Gabriel Bonnot de Mably, *Le droit public de l'Europe, fondé sur les traités* (Geneva, 1764), quoted in Carl Lokke, *France and the Colonial Question: A Study of Contemporary French Opinion, 1763–1801* (New York, 1932), 37.

61. *Ephémérides du Citoyen*, tome II (1766), 35.

62. Victor Riqueti, Marquis de Mirabeau, *La philosophie rurale, ou économie générale et politique de l'Agriculture, reduite à l'ordre immuable des Loix physiques & morales, qui assurent la prospérité des Empires* (Amsterdam, 1764), 239.

63. Mirabeau, *L'ami des hommes*, 178, 180.

64. Dupont de Nemours, *La physiocratie*, xlix; Mirabeau, *L'ami des hommes*, 554.

65. See D'Orvilliers to Minister, Jaunary 29, 1756, ANOM, AC, série F3, vol. 95, n.p.

66. See Jean-Antoine de Préfontaine, *La Maison Rustique, à l'usage des habitans de la partie de la France équinoxiale, connue sous le nom de Cayenne* (Paris, 1763). Later published and given to the colonists of "La Nouvelle Colonie," Préfontaine's original manuscript contained his vision for the project as of 1762.

67. See Godfroy-Tayart de Borms, "La guerre de sept ans," 170–75.

68. Michel, *La Guyane*, 26.

69. See "Texte officiel énumérant les conditions de recrutement des futures colons," in Jacques-François Artur, *Histoire des colonies françoises de la Guianne*, ed. Marie Polderman (Paris: Ibis Rouge, 2002), 713–14.

70. Bruletout de Préfontaine, *La Maison Rustique*, 105.

71. See "Lettre de mission addressée par le roi aux responsables de la future colonie, Etienne François Turgot et Thibault de Chanvalon," in Artur, *Histoire des colonies françoises de la Guianne*, 716.

72. Ibid., 716.

73. See Pierre-Samuel Dupont de Nemours, *La Physiocratie, ou constitution naturelle du gouvernement le plus avantageux au genre humain* (Leyden, 1768), xciii, 111–14. For an attempt by the Marquis de Mirabeau to undertake similarly physiocratic social reforms in France, see Peter Jones, *Liberty and Locality in Revolutionary France: Six Villages Compared, 1760–1820* (New York: Cambridge University Press, 2003), 231–245.

74. Michel, *La Guyane*, 19.

75. Ibid., 20.

76. [Duc de Nivernais], "Mémoire sur les Acadiens," February 17, 1763, London, AMAE, Correspondance Politique, Angleterre, vol. 449, 78.

77. "Mémoire sur les Acadiens," 78.

78. Ibid., 80–82; on Nivernais, see Ernest Martin, *Les exilés acadiens en France au XVIIIe siècle* (Paris, 1936), 58–59.

79. M. de la Rue DeFrancy to Choiseul, March 3, 1763, Cherbourg, AMPC, 4P1-A, fol. 2, 3, copy at CEA.

80. Choiseul to M. le Controlleur-General, April 4, 1763, Versailles, ANOM, AC, série B, vol. 117, 218.

81. Choiseul to Nivernais, March 11, 1763, Versailles, ANOM, AC, série B, vol. 117, 183; Choiseul to M. Ribot, September 12, 1763, Versailles, ANOM, AC, série B, vol. 117, 507.

82. Griffiths, "Acadians in Exile," 70.

83. De Francy to Glien, May 24, 1765, AMPC, 4P1-B, fol. 54v; De Francy to Choiseul, September 13, 1765, AMPC, 4P1-B, fol. 64.

84. "Projet de lettre à M. le Controlleur Général," May 9, 1772, BMB MS 1480, 78.

85. Choiseul to M. les Maire et Echevins de Cherbourg, September 28, 1761, ANOM, AC, série B, vol. 117, n.p.

86. Choiseul, "Circulaire," November 14, 1761, ANOM, AC, série B, vol. 117, 312.

87. De Francy to Mistral and Choiseul, December 30, 1763 to February 27, 1764, AMPC, 4P1-A, fol. 79v–93.

88. De Francy to Choiseul, March 16, 1764, AMPC, 4P1-B, fol. 3v; De Francy to Mistral, April 13, 1764, AMPC, 4P1-B, fol. 11v.

89. De Francy to Mistral, March 29, 1764, AMPC, 4P1-B, folio 7, 7v.

90. De Francy to Choiseul, March 16, 1764, AMPC, 4P1-B, fol. 4.

91. Bernard Cherubini, "Les acadiens en Guyane française: des colons exemplaires pour une colonisation en dilettantes (1762–1772)," *Bulletin du centre d'histoire des éspaces Atlantiques* 5 (1990): 163.

92. Chanvalon to Minister, February 18, 1764, ANOM, AC, série F3, vol. 22, 264–264v.

93. Cited in *Précis Historique de l'éxpédition du Kourou (Guyana Française) 1763–1765* (Paris: Imprimerie Royale, 1842), 48.

94. Artur, *Histoire des colonies françaises de la Guianne*, 691.

95. Ibid., 693.

96. See "Texte officiel énumérant les conditions de recrutement des futures colons," in Artur, *Histoire des colonies françoises de la Guianne*, 713.

97. Michel, *La Guyane*, 47.

98. Choiseul to M. Hocquart, June 18, 1764, ANOM, AC, série B, vol. 120, 273.

99. Michel, *La Guyane*, 51.

100. "Engagement du tambourineur," March 17, 1763, ANOM, AC, série F3, vol. 22, 216.

101. Michel, *La Guyane*, 53.

102. Ibid., 54.

103. Ibid., 54.

104. Migrants were to be given three sols per day per league traveled between the German border and their point of departure; see "Notte des avantages qui serot fait aux familles qui voudront aller s'établir aux colonies françoises de l'Amérique," ANOM, AC, série F3, vol. 22, 209. In practice, however, the Germans were often simply passed from one royal administrator to the next as they made their way across the kingdom; see Rothschild, "A Horrible Tragedy," 76, for an account of destitute Germans begging in front of the Comédie Italienne in Paris.

105. Choiseul to the Bishops of France, October 25, 1763, ANOM, AC, série B, vol. 117, 570.

106. See Rothschild, "A Horrible Tragedy," 77.

107. "Voyage du Duc de Praslin à Cayenne," série LXVII, article 1, Fonds Georges Roux de Corse, CCIM.

108. Ibid.

109. Ibid.

110. Chanvalon to Minister, April 7, 1764, ANOM, AC, série F3, vol. 22, 260.

111. [Pierre Campet] to E. F. Turgot, June 14, 1764, ANOM, AC, série F3, vol. 22, n.p.

112. Ibid.; Michel, *La Guyane*, 65.

113. Chanvalon to Minister, July 17, 1764, ANOM, AC, série F3, vol. 22, n.p.

114. Rothschild, "A Horrible Tragedy," 80–82.

115. Jean-Louis Carra, *Mémoires historiques et authentiques sur la Bastille* (Paris, 1789), 150.

116. Cherubini, "Acadiens en Guyane française," 174–78.

117. Ibid., 180.

118. Fiedmont to Minister, April 22, 1768, ANOM, AC, série C14, régistre 22, f. 109.

119. François de Barbé-Marbois, *The History of Louisiana* (Baton Rouge: Louisiana State University Press, 1977), 127.

120. Rothschild, "A Horrible Tragedy," 75; Godfroy-Tayart de Borms, "La guerre de sept ans et ses conséquences atlantiques," 173.

121. Choiseul to Nivernais, March 11, 1763, ANOM, AC, série B, vol. 117, 183; Antoine-Philippe Lemoyne to intendant of Montpelier, August 15, 1772, BMB MS 1480, 136.
122. Artur, *Histoire des colonies françoises de la Guianne*, 711.
123. Jacques-Nicolas Bellin, *Description des débouquemens qui sont au nord de l'isle de Saint-Domingue* (Versailles: Imprimerie du Département de la Marine, 1773), 7–9.
124. Cited in John Garrigus, *Before Haiti: Race and Citizenship in French Saint-Domingue* (New York: Routledge, 111)
125. Garrigus, *Before Haiti*, remains the essential source on postwar reform in Saint Domingue.
126. "Observations de M. le Chevalier de Montreuil sur la deffense de l'Isle de St. Domingue," n.d., ANOM, AC, série C9A, vol. 118, n.p.
127. D'Estaing to Choiseul, September 21, 1765, ANOM, AC, série C9A, vol. 124, n.p.
128. See Garrigus, *Before Haiti*, 26, 96, 118.
129. Vaucresson to Minister, October 7, 1712, ANOM, AC, série F3, vol. 88, n.p.
130. Pierre Pluchon, *Vaudou, Sorciers, Empoisonneurs de Saint Domingue à Haiti* (Paris: Karthala, 1987), 152.
131. "Extrait des déclarations de Médor," May 26, 1757, ANOM, AC, série F3, vol. 88, 214v.
132. On Makandal, see Karol K. Weaver, *Medical Revolutionaries: The Enslaved Healers of Eighteenth-Century Saint-Domingue* (Urbana, IL: University of Illinois Press, 2006), 76–97.
133. "Mémoire pour servir á l'information des Procès contre les nègres," 1758, ANOM, AC, série F3, vol. 88, 235v.
134. One source estimated that 6,000 people, both white and black, had been killed during the poisoning spree. See Pluchon, *Vaudou*, 165.
135. Ibid.; L'Huillier de Marigny, "Mémoire sur les poisons que régnent á St. Domingue," 1762, ANOM, AC, série F3, vol. 88, 280.
136. L'Huillier de Marigny, "Mémoire sur les poisons que régnent á St. Domingue," 1762, ANOM, AC, série F3, vol. 88, 280.
137. Ibid.
138. Borthon, "Mémoire," 1764, ANOM, AC, série C9A, vol. 120, n.p.
139. "Representations qui present au Roi l'assemblé des deux conseils superieurs à St. Domingue," April 1, 1764, ANOM, AC, série C9A, vol. 118, n.p.
140. L'Huillier de Marigny, "Mémoire sur les poisons que régnent á St. Domingue," 1762, ANOM, AC, série F3, vol. 88, 280.
141. D'Estaing to Minister, January 2, 1764, ANOM, AC, série C9A, vol. 120, n.p.
142. L'Huillier de Marigny, "Mémoire sur les poisons que régnent á St. Domingue," 1762, ANOM, AC, série F3, vol. 88, 280v.
143. D'Estaing and Magon to Choiseul, April 29, 1764, ANOM, AC, série C9A, vol. 120, n.p.
144. Clugny to Accaron, January 25, 1764, ANOM, AC, série C9A, vol. 119, n.p.
145. Acadians of Maryland to the Duc de Nivernais, July 7, 1763, AMAE, Correspondance Politique, Angleterre, vol. 450, 438.
146. Balthazzard Corne, Marain Leblanc, Jacque Hugond to Nivernais, August 12, 1763, Charleston, AMAE, Correspondance Politique, Angleterre, vol. 451, 62.
147. D'Estaing to Acadians, June 26, 1764, Cap François, in Placide Gaudet, ed., *Rapport concernant les archives canadiennes pour l'année 1905* (Ottawa: National Archives of Canada, 1906), 148.
148. "Mémoire de Messrs. Le Chevalier de Montreuil et de Clugny pour l'Etablissement du Môle St. Nicolas," January 27, 1764, ANOM, AC, série C9A, vol. 122, n.p. "Mémoire de M. le Chevalier de Montreuil sur l'Etablissement du Môle St. Nicolas," January 24, 1764, Cap Français, ANOM, AC, série C9A, vol. 122, n.p. A *carreau* contained between 2.79 and 3.00 English acres. McClellan, *Colonialism and Science*, xvii.
149. "Etat des ouvriers blancs & des nègres du Roy, employés aux travaux du Mole, présents aux ateliers le 6 fevrier 1766," Fonds d'Estaing, 562 AP, box 15, AN.
150. Saltoris to Clugny, February 2, 1764, ANOM, AC, série C9A, vol. 123, n.p.
151. Saltoris to Clugny, February 8, 1764, ANOM, AC, série C9A, vol. 123, n.p.
152. Saltoris to Clugny, February 11, 1764, ANOM, AC, série C9A, vol. 123, n.p.
153. Ibid.
154. Saltoris to Clugny, March 12, 1764, ANOM, AC, série C9A, vol. 123, n.p.

155. Saltoris to Clugny, February 15, 1764, ANOM, AC, série C9A, vol. 123, n.p.
156. Saltoris to Clugny, February 19, 1764, ANOM, AC, série C9A, vol. 123, n.p.
157. Entry for April 27, 1764, Journal of René Magon, intendant at Port-au-Prince, ANOM, AC, série C9A, vol. 121, n.p.
158. Ibid. See Saltoris's dossier, cited in Gabriel Debien, "The Acadians in Santo Domingo: 1764–1789," in Glenn Conrad, ed., *The Cajuns: Essays on Their History and Culture* (Lafayette: Center for Louisiana Studies, University of Southwestern Louisiana, 1978), 93, note 34.
159. Saltoris to Montreuil, February 22, 1764, ANOM, AC, série C9A, vol. 123, n.p.
160. Saltoris to Clugny, April 2, 1764, ANOM, AC, série C9A, vol. 123, n.p.
161. Saltoris to Clugny, April 2, 1764, ANOM, AC, série C9A, vol. 123, n.p.
162. Saltoris to Clugny, March 31, 1764, ANOM, AC, série C9A, vol. 123, n.p.
163. Saltoris to d'Estaing, April 12, 1764, ANOM, AC, série C9A, vol. 123, n.p.
164. D'Estaing to Choiseul, September 21, 1765, ANOM, AC, série C9A, vol. 124, n.p.
165. Entry for July 7, 1764, Journal of René Magon, intendant at Port-au-Prince, ANOM, AC, série C9A, vol. 121, n.p.
166. Saltoris to D'Estaing, November 1, 1764, ANOM, AC, série C9A, vol. 123, n.p.
167. D'Estaing to Choiseul, September 21, 1765, ANOM, AC, série C9A, vol. 124, n.p.
168. Entry for July 7, 1764, Journal of René Magon, intendant at Port-au-Prince, ANOM, AC, série C9A, vol. 121, n.p.
169. D'Estaing to Choiseul, September 21, 1765, ANOM, AC, série C9A, vol. 124, n.p.
170. D'Estaing to Choiseul, September 21, 1765, ANOM, AC, série C9A, vol. 124, n.p.
171. D'Estaing to Minister, September 22, 1765, ANOM, AC, série C9A, vol. 124, n.p.; d'Estaing to Minister, September 21, 1765, ANOM, AC, série C9A, vol. 124, n.p.; Aublet to Choiseul, September 11, 1764, ANOM, AC, série C9A, vol. 125, n.p.
172. D'Estaing to Minister, September 21, 1765, ANOM, AC, série C9A, vol. 124, n.p.
173. D'Estaing to Minister, February 28, 1765, ANOM, AC, série C9A, vol. 124, n.p.
174. Lescallier to d'Estaing, March 26, 1765, Fonds d'Estaing, 562 AP, box 15, AN.
175. On the Broussard brothers, see Warren A. Perrin, *Acadian Redemption: From Beausoleil Broussard to the Queen's Royal Proclamation* (Opelousas, LA: Andrepont, 2004)s.
176. "Etat des ouvriers blancs et des négres du Roy employés aux travaux du Môle aux ateliers, le 6 fevrier 1766," Fonds d'Estaing, 562 AP, box 15, AN.
177. "Extrait du role des officiers, employés, ouvriers Acadiens, Allemands, Soldats, Négres du Roy, & autres personnes composantes l'établissement du Môle & autres lieux de sa dépendance, fait le 1er juin 1766," Fonds d'Estaing, 562 AP, box 15, AN.
178. Debien, "The Acadians in Santo Domingo: 1764–1789," 60–71.

Chapter 4: The Unknown

1. François Veron de Forbonnais, *Elémens de commerce* (Leyde, 1766), 5.
2. [Denis Diderot], *Histoire philosophique et politique des établissements et du commerce des Européens dans les deux Indes*, cited in Sankar Muthu, *Enlightenment Against Empire* (Princeton: Princeton University Press, 2003), 74.
3. *Ephémérides du Citoyen, ou chronique de l'esprit nationale* (Paris), tome VI (1766), 139, 186.
4. *Ephémérides du citoyen*, tome I (1765), 228.
5. Charles de Brosses, *Histoire des navigations aux terres Australes* (Paris, 1756), 22.
6. Ibid., iv.
7. Ibid., 6.
8. Ibid., 4.
9. Ibid., 16, 18.
10. Bernard le Bovier de Fontenelle, *Conversations on the Plurality of Worlds* (Dublin, 1761), 62.
11. Charles-François Tiphaigne de la Roche, *Giphantia: or, a view of what has passed, or what is now passing, and during the present century, what will pass, in the world* (Dublin, 1761), 41.
12. David A. Bell, *The Cult of the Nation in France: Inventing Nationalism, 1680–1800* (Cambridge, MA: Harvard University Press, 2003), 96; R. A. Leigh, "Jean-Jacques Rousseau and the Myth of Antiquity in the Eighteenth Century," in R. R. Bolgar, ed., *Classical*

Influences on Western Thought, a.d. 1650–1870 (New York: Cambridge University Press, 1979), 157, 159.

13. Elizabeth Rawson, *The Spartan Tradition in European Thought* (New York: Oxford University Press, 1969), 227.

14. Leigh, "Rousseau and the Myth of Antiquity," 158; for the "spirit of community," see the article "Législateur" in Denis Diderot and Jean le Ronde d'Alembert, *Encyclopédie, ou Dictionnaire raisonné des sciences, des arts et des métiers, par une société des gens de letters* (Paris: 1751–80).

15. Cited in Rawson, *The Spartan Tradition*, 234.

16. Johnson Kent Wright, *A Classical Republican in Eighteenth-Century France: The Political Thought of Mably* (Stanford, CA: Stanford University Press, 1997), 49, 46.

17. De Brosses, *Histoire des navigations*, 19.

18. Alexander Dalrymple, *An Historical Collection of the Several Voyages and Discoveries in the South Pacific Ocean* (New York: Da Capo Press, 1967), xxviii; Yves-Joseph de Kerguelen-Trémarec, "Réflexions sur les avantages que peut procurer la France Australe," in Kerguelen-Trémarec, *Rélation de deux voyages dans les mers australes et des Indes, faits en 1771, 1772, 1773, et 1774* (Paris: Serpent de Mer, 2000), 95–110.

19. De Brosses, *Histoire des navigations*, 41–42.

20. Louis-Antoine de Bougainville, *A Voyage Round the World* (London, 1772), 38.

21. "Journal of a Voyage to Nova Scotia made in 1731 by Robert Hale of Beverly," in *Essex Institute Historical Collections* (Salem, 1906), 42:232–33.

22. Barry Gough, *The Falkland Islands/Malvinas: The Contest for Empire in the South Atlantic* (Atlantic Highlands, NJ: Athlone, 1992), 15–16.

23. Stephen A. White, "Les acadiens aux Iles Malouines en 1764," *Les cahiers de la société historique acadienne* 15 (June and September 1984): 100–105.

24. Bernard Penrose, *An Account of the Last Expedition to Port Egmont, in Falkland's Islands, in the year 1772* (London, 1775), 19.

25. Alan Gurney, *Below the Convergence: Voyages Toward Antarctica, 1699–1839* (New York: W. W. Norton, 1997), 55–56.

26. Glyndwr Williams and Alan Frost, "*Terra Australis*: Theory and Speculation," in Glyndwr Williams and Alan Frost, eds., *Terra Australis to Australia* (Melbourne: Oxford University Press, 1988), 1. See also Alfred Hiatt, *Terra Incognita: Mapping the Antipodes Before 1600* (Chicago: University of Chicago Press, 2008); Gurney, *Below the Convergence*, 3–5; William Eisler, *The Furthest Shore: Images of Terra Australis from the Middle Ages to Captain Cook* (New York: Cambridge University Press, 1995), 9; Paul Simpson-Housley, *Antarctica: Exploration, Perception, and Metaphor* (New York: Routledge, 1992), 3.

27. Gurney, *Below the Convergence*, 5.

28. See John Carey, "Ireland and the Antipodes: The Heterodoxy of Virgil of Salzburg," *Speculum* 64 (January 1989): 1, 4.

29. Eisler, *The Furthest Shore*, 11; for more on the unknown southern continent in medieval cartography, see Marcia Kupfer, "The Lost Mappamundi at Chalivoy-Milon," *Speculum* 66 (July 1991): 540–71.

30. Eisler, *The Furthest Shore*, 11.

31. Ibid., 26.

32. Williams and Frost, "*Terra Australis*: Theory and Speculation," 9.

33. Pedro Fernandes de Quieros [sic], *Terra australis incognita: or, a new southern discovery* (London, 1720), 7–8.

34. Gracie Delépine, *Histoires extraordinaires et inconnues dans les mers australes: Kerguelen, Crozet, Amsterdam et Saint-Paul* (Rennes: Editions Ouest-France, 2002), 19–21.

35. For Paulmier's early career, see Abbé Jean Paulmier, *Mémoires touchant l'établissement d'une mission chréstienne dans le troisième monde, autrement appelé, la terra australe, méridionale, antarctique, & inconnue*, ed. Margaret Sankey (Paris: Honoré Champion, 2006), 18.

36. Ibid., 78.

37. Ibid., 19.

38. Ibid., 258.

39. Ibid., 257, 259, 260.

40. Ibid., 177, 195.
41. De Brosses, *Histoire des Navigations aux Terres Australes*, 103.
42. "Projet d'armement pour former un établissement de commerce aux Isles Cabaldes," May 5, 1714, ANOM, AC, série F2A 14, vol. 1, 1–2.
43. Delépine, *Histoires extraordinaires*, 27–32.
44. Paulmier, *Mémoires*, 95.
45. De Brosses, *Histoire des navigations*, 1:62–63.
46. Woodes Rogers, *A cruising voyage round the world: first to the South-Sea, thence to the East-Indies, and homewards by the Cape of Good Hope* (London, 1726), 325.
47. See Mary Terrall, *The Man Who Flattened the Earth: Maupertuis and the Sciences in the Enlightenment* (Chicago: University of Chicago Press, 2002), 118.
48. Alexander Dalrymple, *An Historical Collection of the Several Voyages and Discoveries in the South Pacific Ocean* (London, 1770), 12.
49. De Brosses, *Histoire des navigations*, 13.
50. Dalrymple, *An Historical Collection*, 19.
51. Henry Home Kames, *Sketches on the History of Man* (Dublin, 1774–75), 46.
52. Claude Gros de Boze, *Éloge de M. le Cardinal de Polignac* (Paris, 1749), 13.
53. Cardinal de Polignac, *L'Anti-Lucrèce, poème sur la religion naturelle* (Paris, 1749), vi, xv; on Polignac's philosophical position, see Ernest J. Ament, "The Anti-Lucretius of Cardinal Polignac," *Transactions and Proceedings of the American Philological Association* 101 (1970): 29–49.
54. Ament, "The Anti-Lucretius of Cardinal Polignac," 47.
55. Victor Suthren, *The Sea Has No End: The Life of Louis-Antoine de Bougainville* (Toronto: Dundurn, 2004), 17.
56. Lucretius, *On the Nature of Things*, ed. and trans. Martin Ferguson Smith (Indianapolis: Hackett, 2001), 31.
57. Jean-Pierre de Bougainville, *Dissertation qui a remporté le prix de l'Académie Royale des Inscriptions et Belles Lettres, en l'année 1745* (Paris, 1745), 17, 73.
58. Many now argue that Pytheas's Ultima Thule was either Iceland or an island off the Norwegian coast. For the Icelandic hypothesis, see Barry Cunliffe, *The Extraordinary Voyage of Pytheas the Greek* (New York: Penguin, 2001).
59. Jean-Etienne Martin-Allanic, *Bougainville: navigateur et les découvertes de son temps* (Paris: Presses Universitaires de France, 1964), 1:21.
60. Cunliffe, *Voyage of Pytheas*, 15, 17.
61. Ibid., 129.
62. Martin-Allanic, *Bougainville*, 1:18–19.
63. Ibid., 31–32; see Terrall, *The Man Who Flattened the Earth*, 240–43.
64. Jean-Pierre de Bougainville, *Mémoire sur les découvertes & les établissemens faits le long des cotes d'Afrique par Hannon, amiral de Carthage* (Paris, 1754), 10, 14. This work is often mistakenly attributed to Louis-Antoine de Bougainville.
65. Ibid., 13.
66. Ibid., 21.
67. Ibid., 260.
68. Ibid., 24. See also J. D. Fage and Roland Anthony Oliver, *The Cambridge History of Africa*, vol. 2: *c. 500 b.c. – c.1050 a.d.* (New York: Cambridge University Press, 1986), 137–38.
69. Bougainville, *Mémoire sur les découvertes*, 291, 290.
70. Ibid., 26.
71. Ibid., 28.
72. Ibid., 299.
73. Ibid., 14.
74. Martin-Allanic, *Bougainville*, 1:29.
75. "Mémoire," July 4, 1764, AC, série F2A 14, 40.
76. Mary Kimbrough, *Louis-Antoine de Bougainville, 1729–1811: A Study in French Naval History and Politics* (Lewiston, ME: Edwin Mellen, 1990), 7.
77. Louis-Antoine's most recent biographer assesses Jean-Pierre's influence in these terms: "Jean-Pierre's interest in the science of cartography may have planted in the young

Louis-Antoine an interest in the wider world beyond Europe . . . and may have been the burr under the young man's career saddle that made him restless rather than comforted by the security of a Parisian lawyer's life; certainly Jean-Pierre did all he could to encourage the skills and abilities he saw emerging in his stocky, robust younger brother, having the youth at his elbow as he edited and published Freret's hand-drawn collection of more than a thousand maps and charts." Suthren, *The Sea Has No End*, 19–20. See also Martin-Allanic, *Bougainville*, 1:34.

78. Edward Hamilton, ed., *Adventure in the Wilderness: The American Journals of Louis-Antoine de Bougainville, 1756–1760* (Norman: University of Oklahoma Press, 1964), 65, 284, 175.
79. Louis-Antoine de Bougainville, "Réflexions sur la campagne prochaine," *Rapport de l'Archiviste de Québec pour 1923–1924* (Québec, 1924), 17.
80. De Brosses, *Histoire des navigations aux terres australes*, 4, 45, 372, 375.
81. John Dunmore, ed., *The Pacific Journal of Louis-Antoine de Bougainville, 1767–1768* (London: Hakluyt Society, 2002), xx.
82. Gough, *The Falkland Islands/Malvinas*, xi; *Ephémérides du citoyen*, tome III (1766), 49.
83. This sketch is drawn from Gough, *The Falkland Islands/Malvinas*, 3.
84. Martin-Allanic, *Bougainville*, 1:85.
85. Ibid., 7–8.
86. Glyndwr Williams, *The Prize of All the Oceans: The Triumph and Tragedy of Anson's Voyage Round the World* (New York: Harper Collins, 1999), 167.
87. George Anson [Richard Walter and Benjamin Robins], *A Voyage Round the World in the Years MDCCXL, I, II, III, IV* (New York: Oxford University Press, 1974), 97–98.
88. Ministre to the comte de Vaulgrenant, January 9, 1750, ANOM, AC, série F2A, vol. 14, 4.
89. Martin-Allanic, *Bougainville*, 1:87.
90. Bougainville, *Adventure in the Wilderness*, 116, 192.
91. De Brosses, *Histoire des navigations*, 1:41.
92. Mémoire sur differents objets relatifs à l'expedition des Navires l'Aigle et le Sphinx, actuellement en armement à St. Mâlo," n.d., ANOM, AC, série F2A, vol. 14, 3v.
93. White, "Les acadiens aux Iles Malouines en 1764," 100–105. The Boucher family is described in "Liste de l'Etat major, matelots, ouvriers et habitants restés aux Isles Malouines," September 5, 1764, ANOM, AC, série F2A, vol. 14, 63bis.
94. Mémoire sur differents objets relatifs à l'expedition des Navires l'Aigle et le Sphinx, actuellement en armement à St. Mâlo," n.d., ANOM, AC, série F2A, vol. 14, 3v.
95. Antoine-Dom [Joseph] Pernéty, *Journal Historique d'un Voyage fait aux Iles Malouïnes en 1763 & 1764* (Berlin, 1769), 32, 39–40.
96. Ibid., 52.
97. "Journal de Pierre St. Marc, 1er pilote de la frigate l'Aigle," ANOM, AC, série F2A, vol. 14, n.p.
98. Ibid., 109.
99. Ibid., 157; "Journal de Pierre St. Marc, 1er pilote de la frigate l'Aigle," ANOM, AC, série F2A, vol. 14, n.p.
100. Pernèty, *Journal Historique*, 215–16.
101. Gough, *The Falkland Islands/Malvinas*, 15–16.
102. "Copie de l'acte de prise de possession au nom de sa majesté des Isles Malouines par M. de Bougainville," April 5, 1763, ANOM, AC, série F2A, vol. 14, 51.
103. Thomas Falkner, S.J., *A Description of Patagonia and the Adjoining Parts of South America* (Chicago: Armann & Armann, 1935; orig. pub. London, 1774), 93.
104. Antoine-Joseph Pernéty, *The history of a voyage to the Malouine (or Falkland) Islands, made in 1763 and 1764, under the command of M. de Bouganville* (London; 1773), 203.
105. Kimbrough, *Louis-Antoine de Bougainville*, 41.
106. Martin-Allanic, *Bougainville*, 1:206.
107. White, Les Acadiens aux Iles Malouines," 101; Martin-Allanic, *Bougainville*, 215.
108. Martin-Allanic, *Bougainville*, 1:206.
109. White, Les Acadiens aux Iles Malouines," 103–4.

110. "Mémoire," August 29, 1764, ANOM, AC, série F2A, vol. 14, 44;."Mémoire," July 4, 1764, ANOM, AC, série F2A, vol. 14, 40.

111. "Mémoire," August 29, 1764, ANOM, AC, série F2A, vol. 14, 44.

112. Martin-Allanic, *Bougainville*, 1:534.

113. Gough, *Falkland Islands/Malvinas*, 13.

114. [Bougainville de Nerville], "Détails sur le séjour aux Isles Malouines de la frégate angloise le Jason, Capitaine Jean Macbride," n.d., ANOM, AC, série F2A, vol. 14, 166.

115. Gough, *Falkland Islands/Malvinas*, 10.

116. Ibid., 247.

117. "Copie de la lettre du Roy écritte á M. de Bougainville de Nerville, commandant aux Isles Malouines," August 30, 1766, ANOM, AC, série F2A, vol. 14, 110–11.

118. Bougainville de Nerville to Dubuq, September 2, 1767, ANOM, AC, F2A, vol. 14, n.p.

119. "Rolle des noms et surnoms des cy-devant habitants des Isles Malouines," 1767, ANOM, AC, série F2A, vol. 14, 157–59.

120. Martin-Allanic, *Bougainville*, 1:544.

121. Falkner, *Description of Patagonia*, 95.

122. Martin-Allanic, *Bougainville*, 1:544.

123. Bougainville, *Voyage Round the World*, 219, 251, xxv–xxvi.

124. [Praslin] to Guillot, July 10, 1769, ANOM, AC, série B, vol. 134, 239.

125. Acadians to de Boynes, n.d., ANOM, AC, série F2A, vol. 14, 221–22.

126. Dalrymple, *Historical Collection*, 1:xxvii.

127. Samuel Johnson, "Thoughts on the Late Transactions Respecting Falkland's Islands," in J. P. Hardy, ed., *The Political Writings of Dr. Johnson: A Selection* (London: Routledge and Kegan Paul, 1968), 78.

128. "Mémoire sur differents objets relatifs à l'expedition des Navires l'Aigle et le Sphinx, actuellement en armement à St. Mâlo," n.d., ANOM, AC, série F2A, vol. 14, 1.

129. Gracie Delépine, *Les Iles Australes Françaises: Kerguelen, Crozet, Amsterdam, Saint-Paul* (Rennes: Éditions Ouest-France, 1995), 11.

130. Yves-Joseph de Kerguelen-Trémarec, "Réflexions sur les avantages que peut procurer la France Australe," "Mémoire sur l'établissement d'une colonie dans la France Australe," Kerguelen-Trémarec, *Rélation de deux voyages*, 95–110.

Chapter 5: The Homeland

1. "Mémoire à presenter à Monseigneur le Duc de Praslin . . . en faveur du nommé Joseph Le Blanc dit Le Maigre agé de 70 ans Acadien d'origine," August 1, 1767, ANOM, AC, série C11A, vol. 105, 577v.

2. "Bordereau des services que le nommé Joseph Leblanc dit Le Maigre a rendus dans la colonie de l'Acadie et les différents postes où il s'est trouvé suivant qu'il lui est aisé de le constater et de le justifier par les ordres et certificats qu'il joint ici," n.d., ANOM, AC, série C11A, vol. 105, 580.

3. Council Minutes, January 25, 1744/5, in *NSA IV*; September 24, 1745, in ibid., 78.

4. William Shirley, Circular Letter, October 20, 1747, Boston, in Placide Gaudet, ed., *Rapport concernant les archives canadiennes pour l'année 1905* (Ottawa: National Archives of Canada, 1906), 105.

5. "Mémoire à presenter à Monseigneur le Duc de Praslin . . . en faveur du nommé Joseph Le Blanc dit Le Maigre agé de 70 ans Acadien d'origine," August 1, 1767, ANOM, AC, série C11A, vol. 105, 578–79.

6. Prévost to Ministère, December 1, 1750, Louisbourg, ANOM, AC, série C11B, vol. 29, 182.

7. "Mémoire à presenter à Monseigneur le Duc de Praslin . . . en faveur du nommé Joseph Le Blanc dit Le Maigre agé de 70 ans Acadien d'origine," August 1, 1767, ANOM, AC, série C11A, vol. 105, 578v–579v.

8. J. C. Piquet, "Arrest de la Cour, rendu sur les Remontrance & Conclusions de Monsieur le Procureur Général du Roi, concernant les Acadiens actuellement établis à Belle-Isle," January 12, 1767, AMAE, Memoires et documents, Angleterre, vol. 47, 10–13.

9. Henri-Raymond Casgrain, ed., *Collection de documents inédits sur le Canada et l'Amérique publiés par le Canada-Français* (Québec: L. J. Demers & Frère, 1888–90), 2:175–76.

10. Abbé Le Loutre to Séminaire des Missions Étrangères, February 1, 1771, ANOM, AC, série E, E275, 11.

11. Abbé de l'Isle-Dieu to the Comte de Warren, April 23, 1773, Paris, Archives Départementales du Morbihan, copy in série E, A9-2-7, CEA.

12. *The annual register, or a view of the history, politics, and literature, for the year 1771* (London, 1772), 2.

13. Charles-Louis Secondat, baron de Montesquieu, *Persian Letters*, ed and trans. C. J. Betts (New York: Penguin, 1993), 205.

14. Ibid., 202.

15. "Population," in Jean le Rond d'Alembert and Denis Dicerot, eds., *Encyclopédie, ou Dictionnaire raisonné des sciences, des arts, et des métiers, par une société de gens de lettres* (Paris: 1751–66), 13:89–90.

16. Ibid., 13:100.

17. Jean-Baptiste Gaultier, *Les lettres persanes convancues d'impiété* (n.p., 1751), 82–84, cited in Carol Blum, *Strength in Numbers: Population, Reproduction, and Power in Eighteenth-Century France* (Baltimore: Johns Hopkins University Press, 2002), 55.

18. Mylo Freeman, *A word in season to all true lovers of their liberty and their country* (Boston, 1748), 5.

19. *Gentlemen's Magazine*, November 1753, 499–502.

20. See D. V. Glass, *Numbering the People: The Eighteenth-Century Population Controversy and the Development of Census and Vital Statistics in Britain* (London: Gordon and Cremonesi, 1978), 24.

21. Joseph Massie, *A plan for the establishment of charity-houses for exposed or deserted women and girls, and for penitent prostitutes* (London, 1758), 102, 146, 88.

22. Philippe-Auguste de Sainte-Foix, chevalier d'Arcq, *La noblesse militaire, ou le patriote français* (Paris, 1756), 70.

23. See Philippe-Laurent Withof, *Dissertation sur les eunuques* (Duisbourg, 1756), cited in Blum, *Strength in Numbers*, 50.

24. "Habillement, équipement, et armament des troupes," in *Encyclopédie*, 8:9.

25. *Journal d'Agriculture, du Commerce, et des Finances*, October 1766, 66.

26. "Luxe," in *Encyclopédie*, 9:764.

27. A. Rebelliau, *Vauban* (Paris, 1962), 293–96, cited in Blum, *Strength in Numbers*, 8.

28. "Invalides," *Encyclopédie*, 17:802; for Mirabeau, see Blum, *Strength in Numbers*, 49.

29. See, for example, John Shovlin, "Emulation in Eighteenth-Century Economic Thought," *Eighteenth-Century Studies* 36 (Winter 2003): 224–30, and Thomas Crow, *Emulation: Making Artists for Revolutionary France* (New Haven: Yale University Press, 1995).

30. Sieur de Diéreville, *Relation du voyage de Port Royal de l'Acadie ou de la Nouvelle France* (Rouen, 1708), 74–76.

31. Naomi E. S. Griffiths, Griffiths, *From Migrant to Acadian: A North American Border People, 1604–1755* (Montreal: McGill-Queen's University Press, 2005), 305; Shirley and Warren to Greene, October 14, 1746, in *The Correspondence of William Shirley*, ed. Henry Lincoln (New York: Macmillan, 1910), 1:359.

32. [Louis-Nicolas, marquis de Pérusse des Cars], "Mémoire sur les Acadiens présenté au roy," ADV, série J, dépôt 22, liasse 98.

33. Abbé Gabriel-François Coyer, *Oeuvres de M. l'Abbé Coyer* (London, 1765), 2:84.

34. D'Arcq, *La noblesse militaire*, 81, 128.

35. Ange Goudar, *Les interets de la France mal entendus* (Amsterdam, 1757), 1:11.

36. Ibid., 11.

37. Victor de Ricqueti, marquis de Mirabeau, *La philosophie rurale, ou économie genérale et politique de l'agriculture, reduite à l'ordre immuable des loix physiques &morales, qui assurent la prospérité des empires* (Amsterdam, 1764), 238.

38. "Mémoire des avances . . . pour etablir en France les Acadiens," n.d., AMAE, Correspondance Politique, Angleterre, vol. 450, 86–87.

39. Choiseul to Ribot, September 12, 1763, ANOM, AC, série B, vol. 117, 507.

40. Choiseul to Controller-General, June 10, 1764, ANOM, AC, série B, v. 120, 264; for "miracle," see Saint-Victour to Lemoyne, November 3, 1772, BMB MS 1480, 187.

41. See "Mémoire pour établir les Acadiens," n.d., ANOM, AC, série C11D, vol. 8, 303–12; "Extrait des régistres des Etats tenues à Nantes en l'an 1764," March 5, 1765, BMB MS 1480, 13.

42. Comte de Tressan, "Projet pour établir un Certain nombre de Canadiens dans le comté de Bitche," July 20, 1763, Bitche, ANOM, AC, série C11D, vol. 8, 235–240v. At this stage of the *grand dérangement*, Acadians, Canadians, and former residents of Ile Royale were often conflated.

43. "Colonies," April 6, 1763, ANOM, AC, série C11D, vol. 8, 252v.

44. Ministre to Duval, October 8, 1755, ADIV, C1949.

45. Choiseul to Juge de Landivisiau, September 4, 1764, ANOM, AC, série B, vol. 120, 362.

46. See Jean-Marie Fonteneau, *Les Acadiens: citoyens de l'Atlantique* (Rennes: Editions Ouest-France, 1996), 221.

47. "Mémoire addressée á M. l'indendant de Bretagne," ADIV, C1949.

48. See Léandre le Gallen, *Belle-Ile, histoire politique, religieuse, et militaire* (Vannes, 1906).

49. Le Sergent to Intendant of Brittany, January 6, 1742, ADIV, C1949.

50. Le Sergent to Intendant of Brittany, January 20, 1742, ADIV, C1949.

51. Trudaine to subdelegate at Belle-Ile, October 31, 1749, ADIV, C1949; Trudaine to subdelegate at Belle-Ile, March 23, 1749, ADIV, C1949; "Etat des pauvres mendians des Villes, Bourgs, et Campagnes de l'isle de Belle-Ile-en-Mer," n.d., ADIV, C1949; "Marché de grain pour les pauvres de Belle-Ile," May 13, 1753, ADIV, C1949.

52. Pierre d'Isambert to Estates of Brittany, July 4, 1763, ADIV, C5128.

53. "Mémoire," n.d., ADIV, C5127.

54. Pierre d'Isambert to Estates of Brittany, July 4, 1763, ADIV, C5128.

55. Estates of Brittany to Minister, July 18, 1763, ADIV, C5127.

56. La Bourdonnaye to Estates of Brittany, July 4, 1763, ADIV, C5127.

57. Daumesnil to Raudot, July 20, 1763, Morlaix, ADIV, C5156.

58. Cited in Jean-François Mouhot, *Les réfugiés Acadiens en France, 1758–1785: L'impossible réintégration?* (Montréal: Septentrion, 2009), 89. See also "Mémoire," n.d., ADIV, C5128, in which the anonymous author argues that a key "motive" for settling the Acadians was "to provide an object of emulation for the old settlers of Belle-Ile, who have the reputation of being lazy."

59. "Réponses au mémoire de Nosseigneurs les Commissaires portant les conditions pour l'établissement de soixante dix sept familles acadiennes á Belleisle en Mer," February 17, 1764, ADIV, C5156.

60. Daumesnil to Raudot, July 20, 1763, Morlaix, ADIV, C5156; Coetancour to Estates of Brittany, November 20, 1763, ADIV, C5156.

61. Abbé de Cargouet et al. to M.M. les Commissaires des Domaines et Controles, July 5, 1763, ADIV, C5156.

62. Coetancour to Estates of Brittany, November 20, 1763, ADIV, C5156.

63. "Réponse au Mémoire de Nosseigneurs les Commissaires des États de Bretagne," October 30, 1763, ADIV, C5156.

64. [Choiseul] to M. les Commissaires des Provinces . . . de la Bretagne, December 3, 1763, Versailles, ANOM, AC, série B, vol. 117, 627.

65. George Collingwood to William Walmesley, August 4, 1756, State Papers, SP 42, vol. 64, n.p., PRO, microfilm copy at LAC.

66. Choiseul to le Loutre, December 3, 1763, ADIV, C5156.

67. Fonteneau, *Les Acadiens*, 279.

68. "Réponse au mémoire de Nosseigneurs les commissaries portant les conditions pour l'établissement de soixante dix sept familles accadiennes á Belleisle en Mer," February 3, 1764, ADIV, C5156.

69. Alexis Trahan et al. to d'Aiguillon, n.d., ADIV, C5156.

70. Estates of Brittany to Choiseul, n.d., ADIV, C5156.

71. Alexis Trahan et al. to d'Aiguillon, n.d., ADIV, C5156; Gosselin to Estates of Brittany, April 23, 1766, ADIV, C5156.

72. Estates of Brittany to Choiseul, November 4, 1763, ADIV, C5156.
73. Ibid., 279.
74. Fonteneau, *Les Acadiens*, 276–77; Marguerite Daligault, "L'installation belliloise en 1766," *Association pour l'histoire de Belle-Ile-en-Mer, Bulletin Trimestriél*, 1977, 21–22.
75. "Etat des colons qui doivent déguerpir des villages destines a l'établissement des acadiens," n.d., ADIV, C5158.
76. [Pierre d'Isambert], "Observations sur l'établissement des colons de l'Isle et des Accadiens," April 1764, ADIV, C5158.
77. "L'état des terres destinées aux acadiens," n.d., ADIV, C5156.
78. Ibid., 287–88.
79. "Etat général de l'établissement des acadiens á Belle-Ile-en-Mer," n.d., ADIV, C5157; Fonteneau, *Les Acadians*, 234–35.
80. Le Loutre and Isambert to Estates of Brittany, March 24, 1766, ADIV, C5142.
81. Estates of Brittany to Isambert, April 9, 1766, ADIV, C5142.
82. Le Sergent to Warren, March 26, 1765, ADIV, C5158.
83. "Remboursement de la somme de 28065 payée par les Etats aux anciens fermiers de Belle-Ile-en-Mer," n.d., ADIV, C5127.
84. Fonteneau, *Les Acadiens*, 288, 299.
85. Le Loutre to Estates of Brittany, June 14, 1766, ADIV, C5157.
86. Choblet to Warren, September 18, 1766, ADIV, C5143.
87. Le Sergent to Estates of Brittany, June 24, 1766, ADIV, C5143.
88. Recteurs de Belle-Ile to Estates of Brittany, October 29, 1766, ADIV, C5143.
89. Isambert to Estates of Brittany, January 24, 1766, ADIV, C5142.
90. Fonteneau, *Les Acadiens*, 355.
91. Isambert to Estates General, April 9, 1766, ADIV, C5142.
92. Babin to Estates of Brittany, April 4, 1768, ADIV, C5158.
93. Le Loutre to Warren, November 26, 1768, A9-2-7, CEA.
94. Ibid.
95. Le Loutre to Warren, July 10, 1771, A9-2-7, CEA.
96. Charles Leblanc, Jean Melançon, Pierre Doucet, Joseph-Simon Granger to Estates of Brittany, August 27, 1769, ADIV, C5157.
97. Marguerite Granger to M. Ruis-Embito, July 21, 1771, A9-2-7, CEA.
98. Warren to Estates of Brittany, n.d. [but likely 1770 or 1771], A9-2-7, CEA.
99. Sergent, Certificat Haché, May 26, 1773; Warren, Passport, May 26, 1773, ANOM, AC, série E, carton E1, dossier Haché.
100. Sarah Maza, *The Myth of the French Bourgeoisie: An Essay on the Social Imaginary, 1750–1850* (Cambridge, MA: Harvard University Press, 2003), 1.
101. [François-Antoine de] Chevrier, *L'Acadiade, ou prouesses angloises en Acadie, Canada, etc.* (Cassel, 1758), 11–12 (copy at LAC); David Bell, *The Cult of the Nation in France: Inventing Nationalism, 1680–1800* (Cambridge, MA: Harvard University Press, 2001), 19.
102. Estates of Brittany to Isambert, June 20, 1766, ADIV, C5142.
103. Statements from Cassiet, Desenclaves, and Girard, 1764, ADIV, C5158.
104. See Christopher Hodson, "Exile on Spruce Street: An Acadian History," *William and Mary Quarterly* 67, no. 2 (April 2010): 249–78, for a case in which a copy of the parish registers from Saint-Charles des Mines in Grand Pré were eventually deposited in Iberville, Louisiana.
105. "Tableau général de l'établissement . . ." 1765, BMB MS 1480, 23.
106. J. C. Picquet, "Arrest de la Cour, rendu sur les Remonstrances et Conclusions de Monsieur le Procureur Général dur Roy concernant les Accadiens actuellement établis à Belleisle," January 12, 1767, AMAE, Memoires et documents, Angleterre, vol. 47, 10–13.
107. Casgrain, *Documents Inédits*, 2:170, 180.
108. Ibid., 2:189.
109. Ibid., 3:11–12.
110. Fonteneau, *Les Acadiens*, 357.
111. Cited in Maza, *Myth of the French Bourgeoisie*, 59.
112. Cited in Colin Jones, "The Great Chain of Buying: Medical Advertisement, the Bourgeois Public Sphere, and the Origins of the French Revolution," *American Historical Review* 101 (February 1996): 14.

113. See P. M. Jones, *Reform and Revolution in France: The Politics of Transition, 1774–1791* (New York: Cambridge University Press, 1995), 58–59; Michael Sonenscher, *Work and Wages: Natural Law, Politics, and the Eighteenth-Century French Trades* (New York: Cambridge University Press, 1989), 216–18.

114. *Affiches du Poitou*, July 7 and 21, 1774.

115. Lemoyne to de Boynes, June 1, 1772, BMB MS 1480, 86.

116. Lemoyne to de Boynes, December 1772, BMB MS 1480, 257.

117. Lemoyne to Guillot, June 20, 1773, Le Havre, BMB MS 1480, 321.

118. Mistral to Lemoyne, October 18, 1773, Le Havre, BMB MS 1480, 389.

119. LeMoyne to Bertin, September 14, 1772, BMB MS 1480, 129.

120. "Mémoire [LeMoyne to Bertin]," September 3, 1772, BMB MS 1480, 132.

121. "Mémoire pour les Acadiens," n.d., St Servan, BMB MS 1480, 299–301.

122. Lemoyne to de Boynes, June 1, 1772, BMB MS 1480, 86.

123. *Ephémérides du Citoyen, ou chronique de l'esprit nationale* (Paris), tome X (1767), 222–24.

Chapter 6: The Conspiracy

1. Douglas Dakin, *Turgot and the Ancien Regime in France* (London, 1939), 40.

2. *Correspondance de l'abbé Galiani*, ed. Lucien Perry and Gaston Maugras (Paris, 1881), 2:345–46.

3. Dakin, *Turgot and the Ancien Regime*, 304.

4. Jean-Antoine-Nicolas de Caritat, marquis de Condorcet, *The life of M. Turgot, Comptroller General of the Finances of France, in the years 1774, 1775, and 1776* (London, 1787), 85.

5. [Marquis de Pérusse], "Noms des deputes accadiens et notes les concernants," n.d., ADV, série J, dépôt 22, liasse 97.

6. Jean-Jacques Leblanc to Rimano, April 23, 1773, CEA, A9-2-7.

7. Louis-Antoine de Caraccioli, *The Travels of Reason in Europe* (London, 1778), 253.

8. On the unevenness of French agricultural development during the eighteenth century, see Peter M. Jones, *Reform and Revolution in France: The Politics of Transition, 1774–1791* (New York: Cambridge University Press, 1995), 83–88.

9. *Ephémérides du Citoyen, ou chronique de l'esprit nationale* (Paris), tome II (1767), 80.

10. *Les Affiches du Poitou*, October 20 and December 1, 1774.

11. Arthur Young, *Travels in France During the Years 1787, 1788, 1789*, ed. Miss Betham-Edwards (London: George Bell and Sons, 1900), 72–73.

12. *Ephémérides du Citoyen*, tome I (1765), 228.

13. Chevalier d'Eon to duc de Praslin, September 6, 1763, London, AMAE, Correspondance Politique, Angleterre, vol. 451, 118; see also Praslin to comte de Guerchy, November 11, 1763, AMAE, Correspondance Politique, Angleterre, vol. 452, 48, D'Eon to Praslin, August 30, 1763, London, AMAE, Correspondance Politique, Angleterre, vol. 451, 105.

14. On peasant-soldiers, see Joseph Spengler, *French Predecessors of Malthus: A Study in Eighteenth-Century Wage and Population Theory* (Durham, NC: Duke University Press, 1942), 73; on population as a source of tax revenue, see ibid., 39.

15. Henri Bertin, "Arrêt du Conseil d'État du Roi qui autorise le Sieur Marquis de Pérusse ...," June 14, 1763, ADV, série J, dépôt 22, liasse 98. On the imperial ramifications of domestic agriculture, see Peter M. Jones, *Liberty and Locality in Revolutionary France: Six Villages Compared, 1760–1820* (New York: Cambridge University Press, 2003), 231.

16. This sketch of Pérusse's life is based on Ernest Martin, *Les exilés acadiens en France au XVIIIe siècle* (Paris, 1936), 124–25.

17. "Mémoire," 1771, ADV, série J, dépôt 22, liasse 7. Although local variants existed throughout France, Pérusse likely estimated the area of his land in *arpents de Paris*, of which one equals about 0.84 acres.

18. See especially André J. Bourde, *Agronomie et agronomes en France au XVIII siècle*, (Paris, 1967), 3:1594–603.

19. *Arrest du conseil d'État du roi, qui ordonne l'établissement d'une société d'Agriculture dans la généralité de la Rochelle* (Paris, 1762), 1.

20. Sarcey de Sutières, *Agriculture expérimentale, à l'usage des agriculteurs, fermiers, & laboureurs* (Yverdon, 1765), 13–15.

21. Pérusse to M. de Simon, July 28, 1775, Targé, ADV, série J, dépôt 22, liasse 124.

22. *Ephémérides du citoyen,* tome VI (1767), 22.

23. Ibid., 79.

24. On *la grande culture,* see Pierre-Samuel Dupont de Nemours, *La physiocratie, ou constitution naturelle du gouvernement le plus avantageux au genre humain* (Leyden, 1768), 112–14.

25. Ibid., xciii.

26. *Ephémérides du Citoyen,* tome III (Paris, 1766), 193–94.

27. Victor de Riquetti, Marquis de Mirabeau, *L'ami des hommes, ou traité de la population* (Paris, 1883), 13, 29.

28. *Journal d'Agriculture, du Commerce, et des Finances,* January 1767, 89.

29. *Ephémérides du Citoyen,* tome III (1766), 194.

30. *Journal d'agriculture, du commerce, et des finances,* January 1767, 89.

31. *Ephémérides du Citoyen,* tome III (1766), 189–94.

32. "Mémoire pour établir les Acadiens," AC, C11D, vol. 8, 308–10; De Francy to Moreau, directeur général des pépinières, August 1, 1767, AMPC, 4P1-C, f. 125; Deboynes to LeMoyne, October 8, 1772, BMB MS 1480, 150.

33. Le Loutre to Praslin, n.d, BMB MS 1480, 29–33.

34. Ministre to Le Loutre, July 3, 1769, Versailles, ANOM, AC, B, vol. 134, 229; Ministre to Mistral, December 27, 1771, ANOM, AC, B, vol. 139, 784.

35. Lemoyne to Deboynes, May 9, 1772, BMB MS 1480, 76; Saint-Victour to Lemoyne, November 3, 1772, BMB MS 1480, 187; Le Loutre to Praslin, n.d., BMB MS 1480, 29; "Extrait des régistres des Etats tenues à Nantes en l'an 1764," March 5, 1765, BMB MS 1480, 13; Praslin to Controller-General, August 26, 1768, BMB MS 1480, 27.

36. Louis-François-Henri de Turbilly, *Mémoire sur les Défrichemens* (Paris, 1762). On Turbilly, see John Shovlin, *The Political Economy of Virtue: Luxury, Commerce, and the Origins of the French Revolution* (Ithaca: Cornell University Press, 2006), 78, 86–87.

37. "Mémoire pour le défrichement des terreins incultes qui se trouvent dependant de la Terre de Montoiron située dans la Généralité de Poitiers," 1764, ADV, série J, dépôt 22, liasse 124, partie 2 (temporary).

38. Turbilly to Pérusse, October 6, 1762, ADV, série J, dépôt 22, liasse 98.

39. Like Pérusse's initial German experiment, the Acadian colony of Poitou represented an agrarian version of state-sponsored, privileged improvements in manufactures and other economic activities. See Pierre Deyon and Philippe Guignet, "The Royal Manufactures and Economic and Technological Progress in France before the Industrial Revolution," *Journal of European Economic History* 9 (Winter 1980), 611–32. For a concrete example of an old régime enterprise that made use of the state's resources, see Leonard N. Rosenband, *Paper-making in Eighteenth-Century France: Management, Labor, and Revolution at the Montgolfier Mill, 1761–1805* (Baltimore: Johns Hopkins University Press, 2000). For a compelling attempt to yoke internal improvements to territorial expansion into a single conceptual frame, see Barbara Fuchs, "Imperium Studies: Theorizing Early Modern Expansion," in Patricia Clare Ingham and Michelle R. Warren, eds., *Postcolonial Moves: Medieval through Modern* (New York: Palgrave, 2003), 71–90.

40. "Mémoire sur les défrichements et sur les moyens de les Encourager et de les Etendre," n.d., ADV, série J, dépôt 22, liasse 124, partie 2.

41. "Déffrichements du Marquis de Pérusse," 1764, ADV, série J, dépôt 22, liasse 124, partie 2.

42. Henri Bertin, "Arrêt du Conseil d'Etat du Roi qui autorise le Sieur Marquis de Pérusse . . ." June 14, 1763, ADV, série J, dépôt 22, liasse 98.

43. Henri Bertin, "Extrait des régistres du conseil d'Etat," February 12, 1766, ADV, série J, dépôt 22, liasse 98.

44. De Francy to Mistral, October 10, 1767, AMPC, 4P1-C, fol. 150v.

45. De Francy to Mistral, December 19, 1766, AMPC, 4P1-C, fol. 70v.

46. On Acadian marriages in France, see especially Jean-François Mouhot, *Les réfugiés Acadiens en France, 1758–1785: L'impossible réintégration?* (Montréal: Septentrion, 2009), 260–71.

47. Rouger de [illegible] to Pérusse, May 7, 1774, Niort, ADV, série J, dépôt 22, liasse 124.

48. De Francy to Mistral, September 26, 1767, Cherbourg, AMPC, 4P1-C, fol. 145v.

49. Félix Le Blanc to [Terray], 1774, ADV, série J, dépôt 22, liasse 98.

50. On the British recruitment of Greeks for Florida, see E. P. Panagopoulos, *New Smyrna: An Eighteenth-Century Greek Odyssey* (Gainesville: University of Florida Press, 1966).

51. Roger P. Bartlett, *Human Capital: The Settlement of Foreigners in Russia, 1762–1804* (New York: Cambridge University Press, 1979), 26.

52. Pérusse to l'Évêque de Tagaste, May 18, 1774, Montoiron, ADV, série J, dépôt 22, liasse 98.

53. Choiseul to Nivernais, March 11, 1763, ANOM, AC, B, vol. 117, 183; Guillot to Lemoyne, November 17, 1772, BMB MS 1480, 219.

54. On Jersey, see Martin, *Exilés acadiens*, 97; on a possible return to Nova Scotia, see De Francy to Choiseul, March 3, 1763, AMPC, 4P1-A, fol. 2, 3.

55. On Spain's internal colony in the Sierra Morena, see Anthony H. Hall, *Charles III and the Revival of Spain* (Washington, DC, 1981), 167–68; and Paul J. Hauben, "The First Decade of an Agrarian Experiment in Bourbon Spain," *Agricultural History* 39 (1965): 34–40.

56. LeMoyne, "Etablissement des Accadiens, Mémoire," February 19, 1772, Paris, BMB MS 1480, 10–11; LeMoyne to Bertin, October 23, 1772, BMB MS 1480, 162–64.

57. Paul Dugats [*sic*] to M. l'abbé Le Loutre, April 5, 1772, BMB MS 1480, 146.

58. LeMoyne to Guillot, January 19, 1773, BMB MS 1480, 251–52.

59. Guillot to LeMoyne, October 31, 1772, BMB MS 1480, 185.

60. Guillot to Lemoyne, November 22, 1772, BMB MS 1480, 218.

61. Lemoyne to de Boynes and Le Loutre, March 26, 1772, BMB MS 1480, 89–91.

62. Carl A. Brasseaux, *The Founding of New Acadia: The Beginnings of Acadian Life in Louisiana, 1764–1803* (Baton Rouge: Louisiana State University Press, 1987), 61–62; Oscar William Winzerling, *Acadian Odyssey* (Baton Rouge: Louisiana State University Press, 1955), 66–67.

63. "Projet de lettre à M. le Controlleur Général," May 9, 1772, BMB MS 1480, 78.

64. Lemoyne to Bertin, September 3, 1772, BMB MS 1480, 132.

65. Pérusse to Turgot, November 23, 1774, ADV, série J, dépôt 22, liasse 98.

66. "Etablissement des familles acadiennes sur la Terre de Monthoiron," ADV, série J, dépôt 22, liasse 124, partie 2 (temporary); "Projet d'établissement des familles Acadiennes pour concilier les offers de M. le Marquis de Pérusse avec les intentions du ministère," in Placide Gaudet, ed., *Rapport concernant les archives canadiennes pour l'année 1905* (Ottawa: National Archives of Canada, 1906), 205–8.

67. "Mémoire sur les Acadiens ou François Neutres," 1777, AMAE, Correspondance Politique, Angleterre, vol. 47, 17.

68. Pérusse to M. Hay, "Mémoire sur les défrichements, généralité de Poitiers," n.d., ADV, série J, dépôt 22, liasse 97.

69. Pérusse to Turgot, November 23, 1774, ADV, série J, dépôt 22, liasse 98;

70. Lemoyne, "Etablissement des familles accadiennes . . ." n.d, Le Havre, BMB MS 1480, 328.

71. Lemoyne to Controller General, June 21, 1773, Le Havre, BMB MS 1480, 322.

72. LeMoyne to Controller General, July 22, 1773, St. Malo, BMB MS 1480, 340, 341v; Martin Porcheron did migrate to Pérusse's lands, remaining there even after the exodus of 1775. On May 28, 1780, he requested firewood from the intendant of Poitiers. See Blossac to Pérusse, May 28, 1780, Poitiers, ADV, série J, dépôt 22, liasse 124.

73. Lemoyne to Pérusse, July 14, 1773, St. Malo, BMB MS 1480, 333.

74. Lemoyne to Bacancour, August 16, 1773, St. Malo, BMB MS 1480, 358v, 359.

75. Lemoyne to Guillot, November 9, 1772, BMB MS 1480, 175.

76. Hérault to Pérusse, July 30, 1773, Archives Départementales de la Vienne, Poitiers, France, ADV, série J, dépôt 22, Liasse 124, part 3, n.p.

77. L'Isle-Dieu to Acadians of Morlaix, July 20, 1773, Paris, BMB MS 1480, 349.

78. "Circulaire écrite aux Recteurs, Curés des Paroisses de St. Servan," August 21, 1773, Saint-Malo, BMB MS 1480, 370.

79. Lemoyne to Terray, July 26, 1773, Saint-Malo, BMB MS 1480, 347.

80. Lemoyne to Bacancour, August 16, 1773, Saint-Malo, BMB MS 1480, 358v.

81. Lemoyne to Bacancour, August 16, 1773, Saint-Malo, BMB MS 1480, 358v.

82. Given the irregularities surrounding the report on Pérusse's soil, Doucet's later appointment as a *syndic*, or community representative, for Acadians in Archigny, and the gift of a certificate of commendation from the mayor of Chatellerault, Doucet may well have been one. See Beauregard to Pérusse, September 12, 1774, ADV, série J, dépôt 22, liasse 124.

83. Beauregard to Pérusse, September 5, 1773, Poitiers, ADV, série J, dépôt 22, liasse 124.
84. Delauzon to Beauregard, July 10, 1774, Chauvigny, ADV, série J, dépôt 22, liasse 124.
85. [Pérusse], "Mémoire sur les Acadiens présenté au Roy," ADV, série J, dépôt 22, liasse 98; Pérusse to l'Eveque de Tagaste, May 18, 1774, Montoiron, ADV, série J, dépôt 22, liasse 98.
86. Pérusse to l'Éveque de Tagaste, May 18, 1774, Montoiron, ADV, série J, dépôt 22, liasse 98.
87. Pérusse to Nivernois, July 20, 1774, Montoiron, ADV, série J, dépôt 22, liasse 98.
88. *Affiches du Poitou,* June 2, 1774.
89. Blossac to Pérusse, August 2, 1774, ADV, série J, dépôt 22, liasse 124.
90. Dakin, *Turgot and the Ancien Régime,* 80.
91. Turgot to Pérusse, July 18, 1774, Paris, ADV, série J, dépôt 22, liasse 124, partie 2; Jacques Necker to Gabriel-Antoine Sartine, April 25, 1778, Versailles, Fonds des Colonies, série F2B, carton 6, 4, AN.
92. Turgot to Pérusse, July 18, 1774, ADV, série J, dépôt 22, liasse 124, partie 2 (temporary).
93. Ibid.
94. Acadians to Marie-Antoinette, n.d., ADV, série J, dépôt 22, liasse 97.
95. Blossac to Pérusse, November 13, 1774, ADV, série J, dépôt 22, liasse 124.
96. Pérusse to l'Eveque de Cerain, November 12, 1774, Montoiron, ADV, série J, dépôt 22, liasse 98.
97. Pérusse to Turgot, November 9, 1774, Targé, ADV, série J, dépôt 22, liasse 98.
98. Pérusse to Blossac, November 29, 1774, Montoiron, ADV, série J, dépôt 22, liasse 98.
99. Pérusse to Louis XVI, August 17, 1774, Montoiron, ADV, série J, dépôt 22, liasse 98.Pérusse to Blossac, August 31, 1774, Montoiron, ADV, série J, dépôt 22, liasse 98.
100. M. le Controlleur Général [Turgot] to Blossac, n.d. ADV, série J, J64, liasse M7.
101. For Corsica, see Le Loutre to Praslin, n.d., BMB MS 1480, 29–33; for "prejudice" against the tropics, see Choiseul to Guillot, June 5, 1764, AC, série B, vol. 120, 261v.
102. Pérusse to Blossac, December 13, 1774, ADV, série J, dépôt 22, liasse 98.
103. Pérusse to M. de Simon, July 28, 1775, Targé, ADV, série J, dépôt 22, liasse 124; L'Eveque de Poitiers to Pérusse, February 8, 1775, Poitiers, ADV, série J, dépôt 22, liasse 124.
104. Blossac to Pérusse, April 21, 1775, ADV, série J, J64, liasse M7.
105. Pérusse to M. de St. Simon, July 28, 1775, Targé, ADV, série J, dépôt 22, liasse 124. Dubuisson had long occupied and managed a farm in near Soissons in eastern France; in 1765, he wrote and published an agricultural treatise called *Mémoires sur la généralité de Soissons* at the request of Dupont de Nemours. In 1768, the physiocrats' journal, *Ephémérides du Citoyen,* reported that a careless servant had set fire to Dubuission's stables, killing nineteen horses. "The creators and nomenclators of economic science," he wrote, "have spoken of me in an advantageous way; I dare to give them thanks, and to implore them to take interest in my unhappy situation." The abbé Baudeau, then editing the journal, encouraged readers to "come to his aid." See Martin, *Les exilés acadiens,* 212; *Ephémérides du Citoyen,* tome VI (1768), 262–63.
106. Blossac to Taboureau, December 29, 1776, Poitiers, ADV, série J, dépôt 22, liasse 97.
107. Beauregard to Hérault, July 31, 1775, ADV, série J, J64, liasse M7.
108. Blossac to Pérusse, August 2, 1775, ADV, dépôt 22, liasse 124.
109. Pérusse to Blossac, November 26, 1775, ADV, série J, dépôt 22, liasse 124.
110. Pérusse to [Blossac], October 7, 1775, Targé, ADV, série J, J64, liasse M7.
111. Pérusse to M. de la Croix, September 22, 1775, ADV, série J, dépôt 22, liasse 124.
112. Pérusse to Hérault, August 17, 1775, Montoiron, ADV, série J, J64, liasse M7.
113. Martin, *Les exilés acadiens,* 218.
114. Pérusse to M. de la Croix, December 1, 1775, ADV, série J, dépôt 22, liasse 124.
115. Pérusse to M. de la Croix, September 22, 1775, Montoiron, ADV, série J, dépôt 22, liasse 124.
116. Martin, *Les exilés acadiens,* 220.
117. Dubel to Pérusse, November 28, 1775, Orléans, ADV, série J, dépôt 22, liasse 124; Pérusse to Hérault, September 2, 1775, Montoiron, ADV, série J, J64, liasse M7; Blossac to Hérault, March 3, 1776, Poitiers, ADV, série J, J64, liasse M7.
118. Blossac to Pérusse, January 7, 1776, Poitiers, ADV, série J, dépôt 22, liasse 124.

119. Pérusse to Sutières, March 15, 1777, ADV, série J, dépôt 22, liasse 97.
120. Martin, *Les exilés acadiens*, 253.
121. Necker to Pérusse, 27 Mars 1777, Paris, ADV, série J, dépôt 22, liasse 124.
122. Necker to Sartine, April 25, 1778, Versailles, AC, série F2B, carton 6.
123. Blossac to Pérusse, November 18, 1778, ADV, série J, dépôt 22, liasse 124.
124. Necker to Sartine, April 25, 1778, Versailles, AC, série F2B, carton 6.
125. Winzerling, *Acadian Odyssey*, 84–86; Brasseaux, *Founding of New Acadia*, 64–65.
126. Winzerling, *Acadian Odyssey*, 96.
127. Mouhot, *Les réfugiés acadiens en France*, 287.
128. Acadians of Saint-Malo to Minister, February 19, 1784, ANOM, AC, C11D, vol. 8, 320.
129. Brasseaux, *The Founding of New Acadia*, 70.
130. Winzerling, *Acadian Odyssey*, 102, 122.
131. Pierre Melanson, Augustin Doucet, Jean Breaux, et al. to Monseigneur l'Intendant de Police [Antoine-Gabriel de Sartine], n.d., ADV, série J, dépôt 22, liasse 124.

Conclusion

1. Deposition of Marie-Josèphe Dupuis, 1817, in Peter Stephen du Ponceau Papers, box 4, folder 4, Papers Relating to Charles White Estate, HSP.
2. See especially Carl A. Brasseaux, "A New Acadia: The Acadian Migrations to South Louisiana, 1764–1803," *Acadiensis* 15 (1985): 123–32; Carl A. Brasseaux, *Acadian to Cajun: Transformation of a People, 1803–1877* (Jackson: University of Mississippi Press, 1992), 4; John Mack Faragher, *A Great and Noble Scheme: The Tragic Story of the Expulsion of the French Acadians from Their American Homeland* (New York: W. W. Norton, 2005), 428–32.
3. Carl A. Brasseaux, *The Founding of New Acadia: The Beginnings of Acadian Life in Louisiana, 1764–1803* (Baton Rouge: Louisiana State University Press, 1987), 34.
4. See Pierre-Maurice Hebert, *The Acadians of Quebec*, trans. Melvin Surette (Pawtucket, RI: Quintin Publications, 2002).
5. See Mason Wade, "After the Grand Dérangement: The Acadians' Return to the Gulf of St. Lawrence and to Nova Scotia," *American Review of Canadian Studies* 5 (1975): 42–65.
6. See Faragher, *A Great and Noble Scheme*, 439.
7. Andrew Brown, "A private Anecdote," August 18, 1791, in Reverend Andrew Brown Collection, Mss. 19073, 113, MG 21, vol. 34, LAC.
8. Bernard to House of Representatives, January 18, 1764, in Gaudet, *Rapport*, 147; Jean Trahant et al. to Governor Bernard, January 1, 1765, in ibid., 150; Bernard to House of Representatives, January 25, 1765, in ibid., 151.
9. Faragher, *A Great and Noble Scheme*, 437.
10. ibid., 432.
11. "Memoire concernant le Brigantin le Copinambou," 1777, ANOM, Archives de la Marine, série B4, vol. 130, 29.
12. Jean-Baptiste Demondion et al. to Pérusse, n.d., ADV, série J, dêpot 22, liasse 124.
13. De Blossac to Pérusse, January 25, 1780, ADV, série J, dêpot 22, liasse 124.
14. De Blossac to Pérusse, May 28, 1780, ADV, série J, dêpot 22, liasse 124.
15. Necker to Pérusse, August 22, 1779, ADV, série J, dêpot 22, liasse 124.
16. Necker to de Blossac, February 12, 1779, ADV, série J, dêpot 22, liasse 124; Necker to Pérusse, December 29, 1776, ADV, série J, dêpot 22, liasse 124.
17. "État des Acadiens . . . de St. Malo," June 12, 1787, ADIV, copy at CEA, A9-3-1, 10; "État des Acadians . . . de Morlaix, March 12, 1786, Archives de la Préfecture de l'Ille-et-Villaine, copy at CEA, A9-3-4, 3; État des Acadiens . . . de Lorient, June 27, 1785, ADIV, copy at CEA, A9-3-1, 9.
18. Cited in Colin Jones, *The Great Nation: France from Louis XV to Napoleon* (New York: Penguin, 2003), 401.
19. *Archives Parlementaires* (Paris, 1860), 23:378–79.
20. Ibid., 23:380.
21. Ibid., 25:106–7.

22. Ibid., 43:4.

23. Département de la Loire-Inférièure, June 11, 1972, F15 (Hospices et secours), vol. 3492, AN, Paris, France.

24. "Rapport," December 1792, F15 (Hospices et secours), vol. 3492, AN.

25. "Demande de Marie-Joseph Baron de jouir des secours accordés aux acadiens," July 17, 1792, F15 (Hospices et secours), vol. 3492, AN.

26. "Etat des acadiens demeurant á Boulogne, qui prétendent aux secours mentionnés en l'article 2 de la loi du 21 février 1791," F15 (Hospices et secours), vol. 3492, AN.

27. Les habitants du Canada et de l'Acadie to Conseil général de Nantes, 19 frimaire, an II, ADIV, L867, microfim F-1041 at CEA.

28. "Mémoire de plusieurs Canadiens et Acadiens . . ." 30 Juin 1814, ANOM, AC, série C11D, vol. 10, 189.

29. "Liste des réfugies," July 1, 1822, Bibliothéque municipale de la Rochelle, dossier 5Q2, copy at CEA.

30. Faragher, *A Great and Noble Scheme*, 361; for the full story of Charles White, see Christopher Hodson, "Exile on Spruce Street: An Acadian History," *William and Mary Quarterly* 67, no. 2 (April 2010): 249–78.

31. "Deposition of Mary Joseph Trepagnié," Peter Stephen du Ponceau Papers, Box 4, folder 4: Papers relating to Charles White Estate, 1811–1825, HSP.

32. *Minutes of the Provincial Council of Pennsylvania*, 7: 240.

33. Ibid., 7:446; "Interrogations to be administered to witnesses particularly Catherine Bijeo and Samuel Mangeant," March 1817, Peter Stephen du Ponceau Papers, Box 4, folder 4: Papers relating to Charles White Estate, 1811–1825, HSP; on Mangeant, see Charles Carroll, *Dear Papa, Dear Charlie: The Papers of Charles Carroll of Carrollton, 1748–1782*, ed. Ronald Hoffman and Sally Mason (Chapel Hill: University of North Carolina Press, 2001), 1:104, 143.

34. "Deposition of Mary Joseph Trepagnié," Peter Stephen du Ponceau Papers, Box 4, folder 4: Papers relating to Charles White Estate, 1811–1825, HSP.

35. "Interrogations to be administered to witnesses particularly Catherine Bijeo and Samuel Mangeant," March 1817, Peter Stephen du Ponceau Papers, Box 4, folder 4: Papers relating to Charles White Estate, 1811–1825, HSP.

36. *Pennsylvania Evening Post*, September 2, 1777.

37. *Pennsylvania Packet, and Daily Advertiser*, December 16, 1790.

38. See Michelle Craig McDonald, "The Chance of the Moment: Coffee and the New West Indians Commodities Trade," *William and Mary Quarterly* 62 (July 2005): 460.

39. *Federal Gazette, and Philadelphia Evening Post*, November 20, 1793; *Philadelphia Gazette and Universal Daily Advertiser*, December 29, 1794.

40. See "Real Estate Owned by Charles Leblanc in the City of Philadelphia at the Time of his Death August 1816," Charles Leblanc Mss., William Laimbeer Collection, HSP.

41. See Hodson, "Exile on Spruce Street," 272.

42. "Real Estate Owned by Charles Leblanc in the City of Philadelphia at the Time of his Death August 1816," Charles Leblanc Mss., William Laimbeer Collection, HSP, Philadelphia, PA.

43. "Deposition of Elizabeth Biddle," in Peter Stephen du Ponceau Papers, box 4, folder 4: Papers relating to Charles White Estate, 1811–1825, HSP.

44. "Deposition of Benjamin Norris," "Deposition of Thomas Bradford," n.d., Charles Leblanc Mss., William Laimbeer Collection, HSP, Philadelphia, PA.

45. "Deposition of Ursula LaZele," Clarence J. D'Entremont Collection, AMWP, n.p.

46. "Deposition of Peter S. du Ponceau," n.d., Clarence J. D'Entremont Collection, AMWP, NS, n.p.

47. "Deposition of the Reverend Michael Hurley," "Deposition of Elizabeth Biddle," in Peter Stephen du Ponceau Papers, box 4, folder 4: Papers relating to Charles White Estate, 1811–1825, HSP.

48. "Deposition of Elizabeth Biddle," in Peter Stephen du Ponceau Papers, box 4, folder 4: Papers relating to Charles White Estate, 1811–1825, HSP.

49. "Deposition of Wm. McDonough," Peter Stephen du Ponceau Papers, Box 4, folder 4: Papers relating to Charles White Estate, 1811–1825. HSP.

50. "Deposition of the Reverend Michael Hurley," in Peter Stephen du Ponceau Papers, box 4, folder 4: Papers relating to Charles White Estate, 1811–1825, HSP.

51. "To the Honorable the Judges of the Circuit Court of the United States in and for the District of Pennsylvania," [April 1819], in Peter Stephen du Ponceau Papers, Box 4, folder 4: Papers relating to Charles White Estate, 1811–1825. HSP; "Deposition of John Tanguy," Peter Stephen du Ponceau Papers, Box 4, folder 4: Papers relating to Charles White Estate, 1811–1825, HSP.

52. "Deposition of Anne-Joseph Landry," Charles Leblanc Mss., William Laimbeer Collection, n.p., HSP.

53. "Interrogations to be administered to witnesses particularly Catherine Bijeo and Samuel Mangeant," March 1817, Peter Stephen du Ponceau Papers, Box 4, folder 4: Papers relating to Charles White Estate, 1811–1825, HSP.

54. "Deposition of the Reverend Michael Hurley," in Peter Stephen du Ponceau Papers, box 4, folder 4: Papers relating to Charles White Estate, 1811–1825, HSP.

55. "Deposition of Mary Joseph Trepagnié," Peter Stephen du Ponceau Papers, Box 4, folder 4: Papers relating to Charles White Estate, 1811–1825, HSP.

56. Ibid.

57. The Montgomerys did so by hiring the lawyer and politician Horace Binney, who argued that some of the depositions that favored Boudreau and the other Acadian plaintiffs had been taken illegally. In 1821, Bushrod Washington ruled that although irregularities existed, even imperfect depositions could, like hearsay, be used to demonstrate pedigree. This ruling made *Boudereau* [sic] *v. Montgomery* an important precedent in nineteenth-century probate law. On Binney, see "Exception on the part of the defendants to the Report of the Master in this case," Peter Stephen du Ponceau Papers, Box 4, folder 4: Papers relating to Charles White Estate, 1811–1825, HSP. For Washington's 1821 ruling, see *Boudereau v. Montgomery*, C.C. Pa 1821, Case No. 1694, 4 Wash C.C. 186, also cited as 3 F. Cas. 993. On the subsequent use of *Boudereau v. Montgomery*, see William G. Myer, *Federal Decisions: Cases Argued and Determined in the Supreme, Circuit, and District Courts of the United States* (St. Louis, 1887), 17:348.

58. Report of James G. Smith, Master, June 19, 1828, *Boudereau v. Montgomery* Case File, NAMAP.

59. Report of James G. Smith, Master, June 19, 1828, *Boudereau v. Montgomery* Case File, NAMAP.

60. Henry Wadsworth Longfellow, *Evangeline: A Tale of Acadie* (London: David Bogue, 1854), 80–1.

61. "Deposition of Wm. McDonough," Peter Stephen du Ponceau Papers, Box 4, folder 4: Papers relating to Charles White Estate, 1811–1825. HSP.

INDEX